You Can EASILY Play HYMNS

The songbook that makes hymn playing as simple as ABC

By
Sharlene Reyes

TEACH Services, Inc.
PUBLISHING
www.TEACHServices.com

World rights reserved. This book or any portion thereof may not be copied or reproduced in any form or manner whatever, except as provided by law, without the written permission of the publisher, except by a reviewer who may quote brief passages in a review.

This book was written to provide truthful information in regard to the subject matter covered. The author assumes full responsibility for the accuracy of all facts and quotations as cited in this book. The opinions expressed in this book are the author's personal views and interpretation of the Bible, Spirit of Prophecy, and/or contemporary authors and do not necessarily reflect those of TEACH Services, Inc.

This book is sold with the understanding that the publisher is not engaged in giving spiritual, legal, medical, or other professional advice. If authoritative advice is needed, the reader should seek the counsel of a competent professional

---

Copyright © 2011 TEACH Services, Inc.
ISBN-13: 978-1-57258-681-9 (Paperback)
ISBN-13: 978-1-57258-682-6 (Spire Wire)
ISBN-13: 978-1-57258-683-3 (Ebook)
Library of Congress Control Number: 2011930611

People deserving special mention:
Bobi Escasa, whose friendship and encouragement have been invaluable—
"Iron sharpeneth iron; so a man sharpeneth the countenance of his friend" (Proverbs 27:17);
Sam Leer, Tita Rose Rada, and **Heidi Cerna** for granting permission to use their songs in Appendix C;
Lowell & Miriam Salido, and **Arman Martino** for their help with the photo illustrations in Appendix B;
Ed & Connie, Kyayen & Laura, Toto & Mannyl, Wayne & Joy, Jonalie, Aileen, and **Apollo**
for their selfless contributions;
Lolo Norbing, Uncle Johny & Auntie Blemy, Uncle Vic & Auntie Eve—whose love and untiring support have inspired me to persevere, despite numerous setbacks, in seeing this project to completion!

All Scripture quotations are from the King James Version.

Quote on page 6 is from Ellen White, *Evangelism* (Washington D.C.: Review and Herald, 1946), p. 505.

Published by
TEACH Services, Inc.
www.TEACHServices.com

Dedication

This book is lovingly dedicated to the memory of my father,

Ruel M. Reyes
October 13, 1946–April 24, 2008

A music lover from his youth, Daddy enjoyed strumming the guitar, played the euphonium in the school band during college, and sang bass in the choir. Though he could read notes and had managed to attempt playing hymns on the piano from the hymnal, he never did play as skillfully as he wished he could.

It was Daddy who prodded me to pursue a degree in Music Performance at the University of the Philippines College of Music, with Piano as my major instrument. From him I learned to develop a taste for wholesome, uplifting music. More importantly, he instilled in me a love for the Master, and devotion to His cause.

Throughout his life, yes, even through his illness, Dad kept a song in his heart. The day he fell asleep in Jesus, his voice still rang out loud and clear as we sang to close morning worship, "God Will Take Care of You." Someday soon, Daddy's voice will yet be lifted up again, blending with thousands of other voices to swell that grand, triumphant chorus of the redeemed.

I also dedicate this book—

To Mom, who even in childhood showed more potential as a secretary than as a pianist, with her youthful fingers finding pounding on the typewriter keys more thrilling than tickling the ivories;

To Sharon, my sister and practice student during my greenhorn years as a teacher, whose present limited piano-playing ability is, in all likelihood, my fault;

To Arnold, my favorite brother-in-law (and my four-hands piano duet partner in a recital three decades ago) who once bravely served as "struggling accompanist" of their kids' Junior Choir in church, so that they, too, can experience the joy of employing every talent in God's service;

To two young promising pianists, namely my niece, Faith (who is growing adept at playing the guitar, too) and my nephew, Joshua (an aspiring wind or brass instrument player besides);

And to every music enthusiast for whom hymn playing had in times past always been— pure wishful thinking.

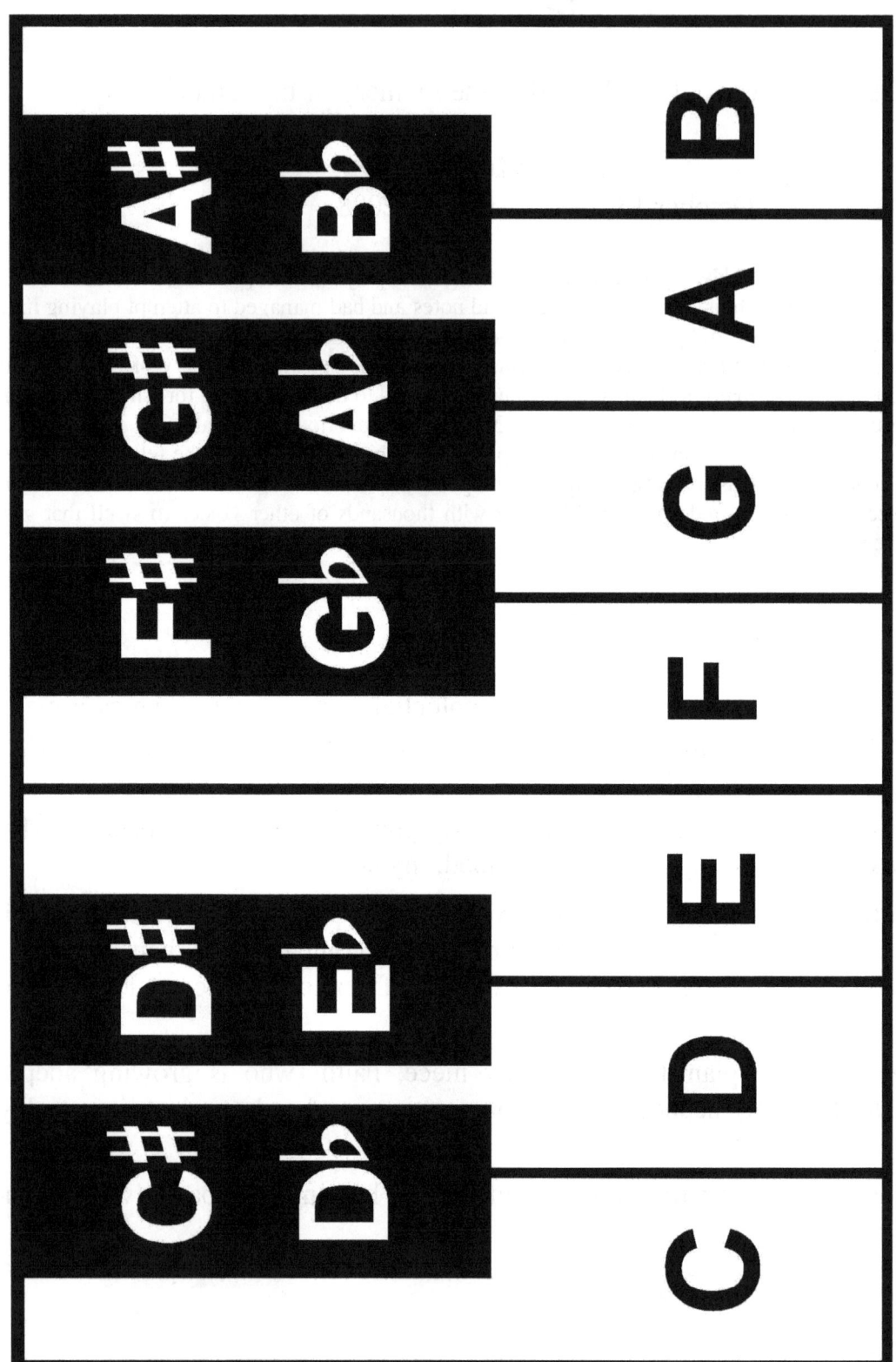

Letter–names of the White and Black Keys

Contents

Dedication iii

Letter-names of the Keys Chart iv

Table of Contents v

Definitions (and Explanations) of Some Terms vi

Foreword 1

How to Use This Book 2

Key Concepts to Note 4

Hymns 7-155

Appendix A: Exploring Some Variations in Playing Chords on the Piano 156

Appendix B: Interpreting Guitar Chord Diagrams 158

Appendix C: Special Additional Songs 159

Index of Hymns 163

A Final Word 165

"Let the word of Christ
dwell in you richly in all wisdom;
teaching and admonishing one another
in psalms and hymns and spiritual songs,
singing with grace in your hearts
to the Lord."

Colossians 3:16

Definitions (and Explanations) of Some Terms Used in This Book

Bar line - the vertical line that extends from the top line of the staff to the bottom line.

Chord diagram - a picture illustration that shows which keys on the piano make up a particular chord; or for guitar, which strings should be fingered and played. (See Chapter One, "How to Use This Book".)

Chord symbol - the abbreviated form of the name of a chord. Though it is not necessary to know the proper names of the different chords in order to be able to play from this book, just as a matter of information they are listed here.

D = D major   **Dm** = D minor   **D dim** = D diminished   **D7** = a seventh chord, but read "D seven"

Dm7 = D minor seven   **D7sus** = D seven suspended   **D Aug** = D augmented

Hymn - While 150 of the titles included in this songbook are found in *The Seventh-day Adventist Hymnal*[1], in the strictest sense, they are not all hymns. Many of them are gospel songs. It might be helpful to be aware of some differences between the two. Note that both types have their rightful place in the singing life of the church and that not all songs will easily fall under one category or the other.

A hymn tends to focus on doctrine, employs more poetic language, and rarely has a chorus or refrain. Musically, the harmonies for hymns are more complex, with chords changing almost every beat. For this reason, it is quite difficult to arrange hymns for simplified playing and sadly, much of their grandeur is inevitably lost in the process. The best effort has been exerted in this book to preserve each hymn's beauty as far as possible while making it easy to play.

Gospel songs often communicate a testimony using simpler language, and generally have a chorus or refrain. They use fewer chords, and chord changes are not as frequent as in hymns.

Measure - a section of the staff extending from one bar line to the next.

Piano - In this book, the term "piano" is used rather loosely and does not solely refer to the acoustic *pianoforte*. It includes other keyboard instruments such as digital pianos, organs, and electronic keyboards. If you are using an electronic instrument that features different "voices" or sounds, you might want to pick a sound other than piano. You will find that either a *strings* sound or a *chapel* or *church organ* sound will prove effective especially with **block chord playing** (see Chapter One, "How to Use This Book").

Staff - the five horizontal lines with four spaces in between where notes are written to indicate which keys are to be played.

---

[1] Washington D.C.: Review and Herald, 1985.

Foreword

The command to "sing unto the LORD" echoes all throughout the Scriptures. And it behooves each of us to heed it, for the very One who deserves our songs of praise Himself sings over us in gladness. Among the many verses in the Bible that I consider quite fascinating is:

"The LORD thy God in the midst of thee is mighty; He will save, He will rejoice over thee with joy; He will rest in His love, *He will joy over thee with singing*" (Zephaniah 3:17, emphasis supplied).

Yes, we are made in the image of a Creator who sings! No wonder we find such pleasure in lifting our voices in song.

However, a different level of enjoyment is achieved by playing a musical instrument—be it something you strum like a guitar, blow like a flute, bow like a violin, or strike like a xylophone. Once more, we note that we have a divine example in this matter. We read that God has an instrument—a trumpet (1 Thessalonians 4:16), and that He will blow it (Zechariah 9:14). Thus, it should be no surprise that God's children are commanded to praise Him not just with singing, but with the sound of musical instruments, as well (see, for example, Psalms 81:1-3; 98:5, 6).

Not everyone, though, is given the opportunity to take music lessons in order to become music literate and proficient in playing an instrument. Do you happen to be among the "musically illiterate" who wish you could somehow play some favorite hymns on the piano or accompany yourself on the guitar? If so, then this book is for you!

Disclaimer

Let me tell you outright that this book is NOT meant to teach you how to read music. Nor does it dream of turning you into an accomplished concert artist. Rather, its humble aim is to enable the non-reader of music to enjoy playing hymns *at the most basic level* – that is, either playing just the melody, or just the harmony (simple chord accompaniment), or possibly both if playing on a keyboard instrument like the piano or organ.

Although there are other instruments you can use this book with, it was conceptualized primarily for the piano (or electronic keyboard), and secondarily for the guitar. Hence, the hymns are set only in keys that are relatively easy to play on these instruments. This means that in many instances the key setting of a hymn will be different from what is printed in the regular hymnal. Furthermore, the complex harmonies of some hymns have been simplified for easier playing.

Since, as mentioned earlier, the book does not endeavor to make you music literate, time signatures and rhythmic values of notes are not explained. It is assumed that you are already familiar with the hymns you will choose to play and therefore will not be dependent on the notation for correct rhythm.

In spite of its limitations, it is my fervent prayer that this book affords you many blessed hours of music making previously unavailable to you. May it usher you into a new dimension of musical experience that will bring you more closely in tune with Him who is the Author of music. Remember that the heart lifted up in praise and the soul engaged in worshipful song is in harmony with heaven.

Happy hymn playing!

Sharlene Reyes
February, 2009

How to Use This Book

Playing the Melody on the Piano[1]

To play the melody of a hymn, simply play the keys indicated by the letter-names written inside the noteheads. It is best to play the melody with your right hand, and to stay in the middle register of the keyboard where the pitches match the normal vocal range. In a few hymns you will see unlabeled noteheads; these are tied notes and are not to be played.

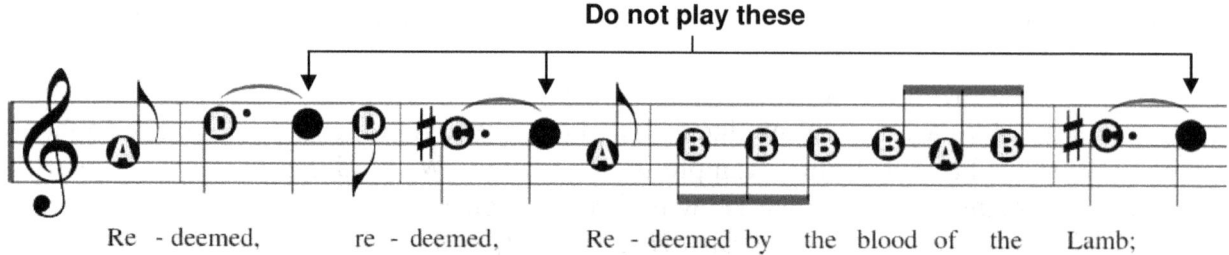

If you are unfamiliar with the names of the piano keys, the chapter "Key Concepts to Note" contains valuable instruction to help you. Also, there is a chart on page iv showing the letter-names of the white and black keys. You might want to photocopy this page so you can place the chart where it can serve as a handy guide to refer to while you play.

Playing Chord Accompaniment on the Piano

The small dotted grids that are right above the staff where the melody is notated are chord diagrams for guitar; ignore these if you are playing on the piano. Only take note of the chord symbols written on top of the guitar chord diagrams and find the matching keyboard chord diagrams printed on the lower right portion of the page.

The simplest way to play chords is to play them in *block* style, meaning just play all three (or four) notes simultaneously and hold them down for the entire measure[2]—unless there is a new chord symbol before the end of the measure, in which case, of course, you play the new chord. **IMPORTANT: If for more than one measure there is no chord change, just keep repeating the same chord at the beginning of every succeeding measure until the next chord symbol comes along.**

Since chord accompaniment generally sounds better when played in the lower middle register, it is recommended that you play your chords somewhere in the area left of center on the keyboard. In this connection, it is more practical to use your left hand to play chords.

There are other more interesting ways of playing piano chords other than the block style. A few suggestions are discussed in Appendix A.

Chord Inversions

Chords can be played on the piano in different positions called inversions. In this book, an asterisk after the chord symbol indicates that the chord is to be played in its first inversion; two asterisks mean to play the second inversion of the chord[3]. If a hymn employs a chord inversion, the chord diagram for the inversion—just as the chord diagram for each of the rest of the chords used in that particular song—is printed on the same page for easy reference. (For a more detailed explanation about chord inversions, see Appendix A.)

Playing Melody and Chord Accompaniment

Once you've mastered playing the melody alone with your right hand, as well as playing the chord accompaniment alone with your left hand, you can try playing both hands together. This may be a bit confusing at first, but the more you practice, the easier it gets. While still learning to coordinate your two hands, play at a much slower tempo and increase your speed gradually as you gain mastery of the hymn you are playing.

Playing Chord Accompaniment on the Guitar

The guitar chord diagrams written above the melody are your guide in playing guitar accompaniment. Remember to just keep playing the same chord until the next chord change. For total beginners in guitar playing, Appendix B "Interpreting Guitar Chord Diagrams" will prove helpful.

---

[1] See p. vi for an explanation of the use of the term "piano" in this book.
[2] If you do not know the meaning of this musical term, see p. vi for its definition.
[3] This method of indicating chord inversions with the use of asterisks is *not* a standard practice. It is employed in this book for convenience.

"Praise the LORD with harp: sing unto Him
with the psaltery and an instrument of ten strings.
Sing unto Him a new song;
play skillfully with a loud noise."

Psalm 33:2, 3

Key Concepts to Note

In order to use this book with ease, it is essential to get a good grasp of a few fundamentals. If you are already familiar with the piano keyboard's design and are completely acquainted with the names of the keys, you may skip this section.

Direction

First, let's talk about direction. On the piano keyboard, the high-sounding pitches are to your RIGHT, and the low-sounding ones are to your LEFT. This means the pitch goes higher as you play going towards the right; when you play towards the left, it goes lower. So if the tune of the hymn you are playing is ascending, you will play keys going rightward; if the tune is descending, then you play leftward.

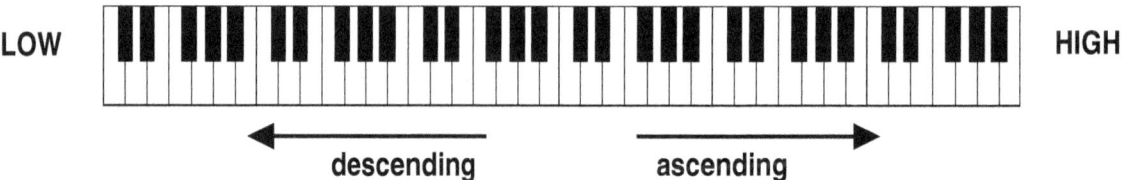

In relation to the printed music, if the direction of a succession of notes is upward on the page, you play going towards the right:

If the written notes are going down, you play going towards the left:

Arrangement of Black and White Keys

The piano keyboard has **white** keys and **black** keys. Notice how the black keys are positioned—they are in sets of TWO and THREE, placed in *alternate* fashion. You will never find consecutive sets of three black keys—they are always two, three, two, three, and so on.

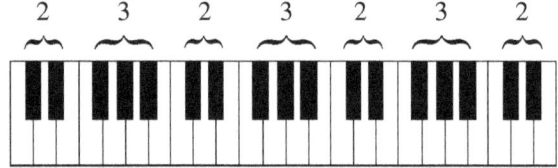 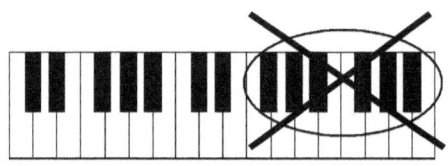

Names of the White Keys

The first seven letters of the alphabet are used for naming the white keys.

The THREE WHITE KEYS that go with the set of two black keys are C, D, and E.  And the cluster of FOUR WHITE KEYS that are together with the three black keys are F, G, A, B.

It is imperative that you master these names well before attempting to play from this book.

What About the Black Keys?

No additional letters of the alphabet are used to name the five black keys. Instead, they are referred to in relation to the white keys that are *closest* to them. If a black key is immediately to the RIGHT of (and thus, is HIGHER than) a white key, it is called the SHARP of that particular white key. For example, the black key immediately **to the right of F** is called **F sharp**—or in symbols, **F♯**. In music notation, the sharp (♯) symbol is written *before* the notehead.

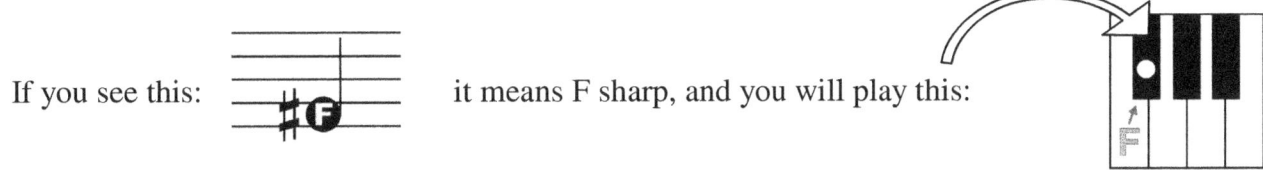

On the other hand, a black key that is immediately to the LEFT of (hence, is LOWER than) a white key takes the FLAT name of that key. For example, **B flat** (or **B♭**) is the black key adjacent to **B, on its left**. Again, on the written music score, the flat (♭) symbol is placed before the note.

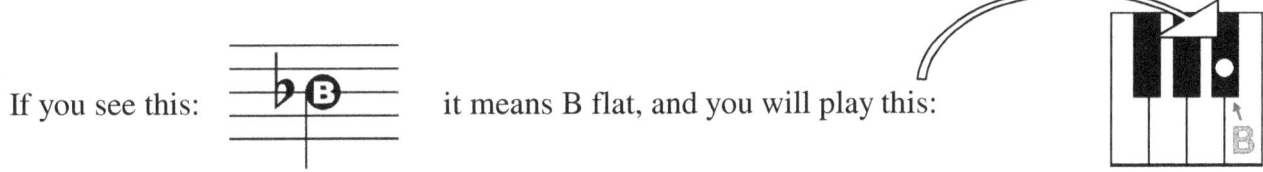

By now you must have figured that every black key can be named two ways: either as a *sharp* of a white key or as a *flat* of another. The diagram on the right shows the black keys with both their sharp and flat names.

Canceling a Sharp or Flat

One last symbol to explain is the **natural ♮**. A natural simply cancels a recent sharp or flat and indicates a note is to be played as is (unaltered). For example, if you have just played a **C♯**, then soon after you have to play a "plain" **C** (not sharp, not flat), a natural (♮) symbol is placed before the note to emphasize that what is being referred to this time is the regular white key C, and not the black key C♯.

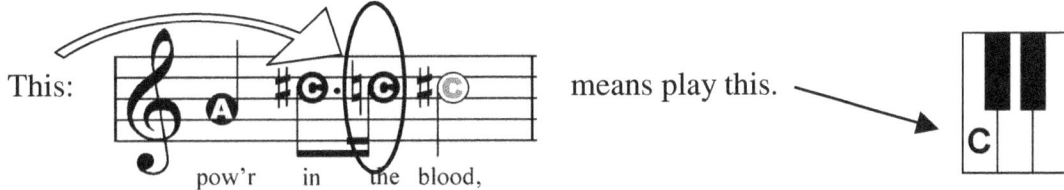

Music should have beauty, pathos, and power.
Let the voices be lifted in songs of praise and devotion.
Call to your aid, if practicable, instrumental music,
and let the glorious harmony ascend to God, an acceptable offering.

Ellen White (1827-1915)

A Mighty Fortress

English translation by Frederick Hedge

Words and music by Martin Luther

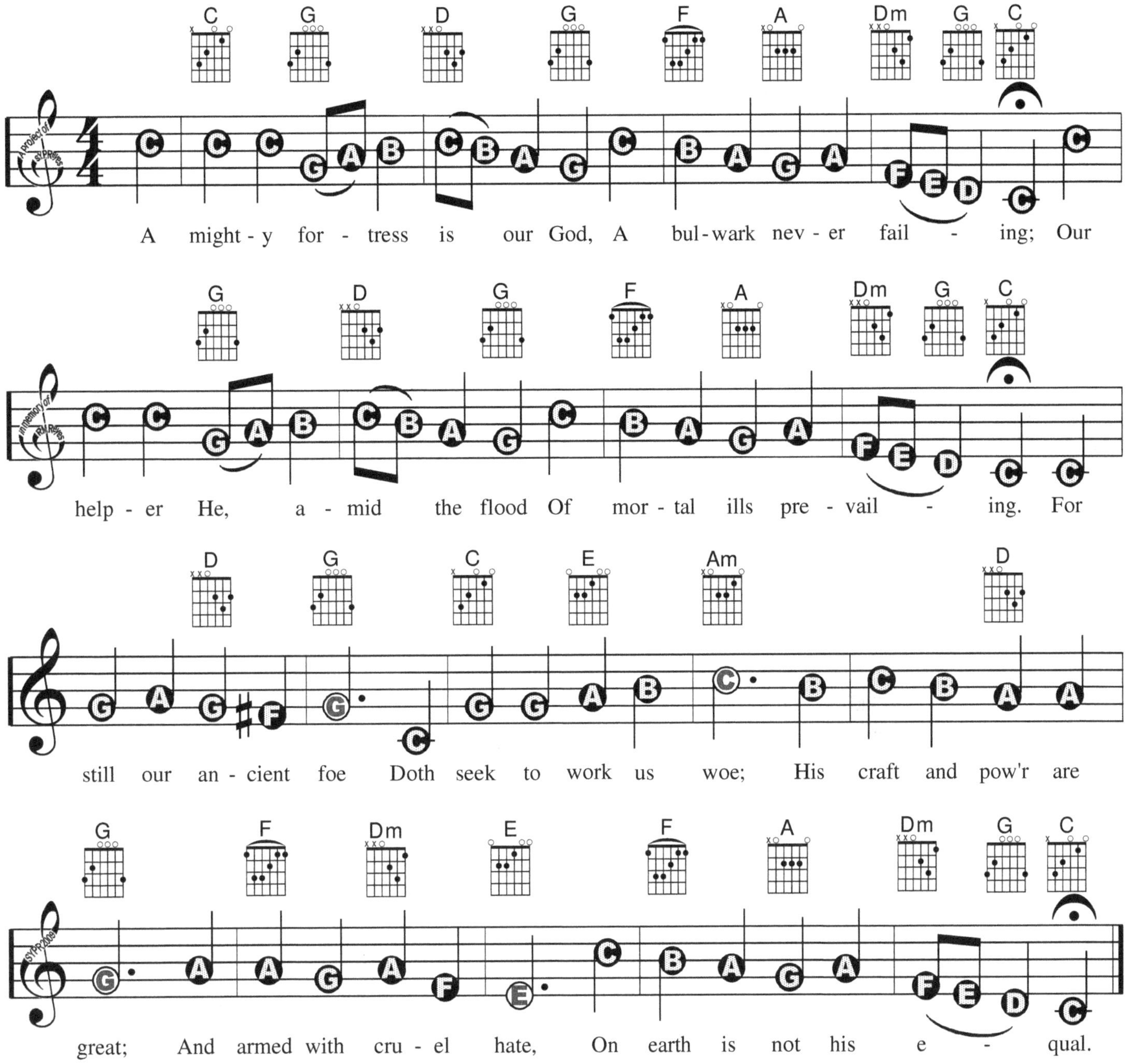

C G D G F A Dm G C
C C C G A B C B A G C B A G A F E D C C
A might - y for - tress is our God, A bul - wark nev - er fail - ing; Our
G D G F A Dm G C
C C G A B C B A G C B A G A F E D C C
help - er He, a - mid the flood Of mor - tal ills pre - vail - ing. For
D G C E Am D
G A G F G C G G A B C B C B A A
still our an - cient foe Doth seek to work us woe; His craft and pow'r are
G F Dm E F A Dm G C
G A A G A F E C B A G A F E D C
great; And armed with cru - el hate, On earth is not his e - qual.

2. Did we in our own strength confide, Our striving would be losing,
Were not the right Man on our side, The Man of God's own choosing.
Dost ask who that may be? Christ Jesus, it is He,
Lord Sabaoth His name, From age to age the same,
And He must win the battle.

3. And though this world, with devils filled, Should threaten to undo us,
We will not fear, for God hath willed His truth to triumph through us.
The prince of darkness grim, We tremble not for him;
His rage we can endure, For lo! his doom is sure,
One little word shall fell him.

4. That word above all earthly pow'rs, No thanks to them, abideth;
The Spirit and the gifts are ours Through Him who with us sideth;
Let goods and kindred go, This mortal life also;
The body they may kill; God's truth abideth still,
His kingdom is forever.

C
G
D
F
A
Dm
E
Am

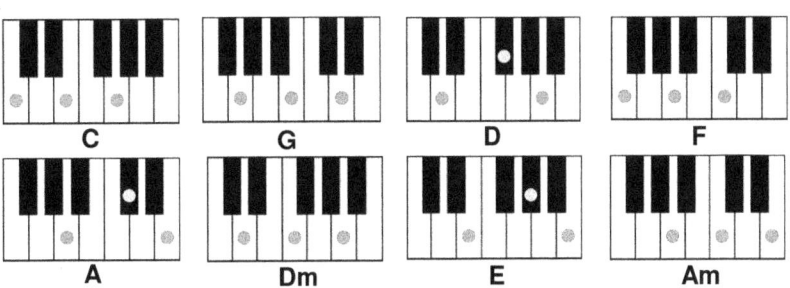

A Shelter in the Time of Storm

Words by Vernon Charlesworth
Music by F. E. Belden

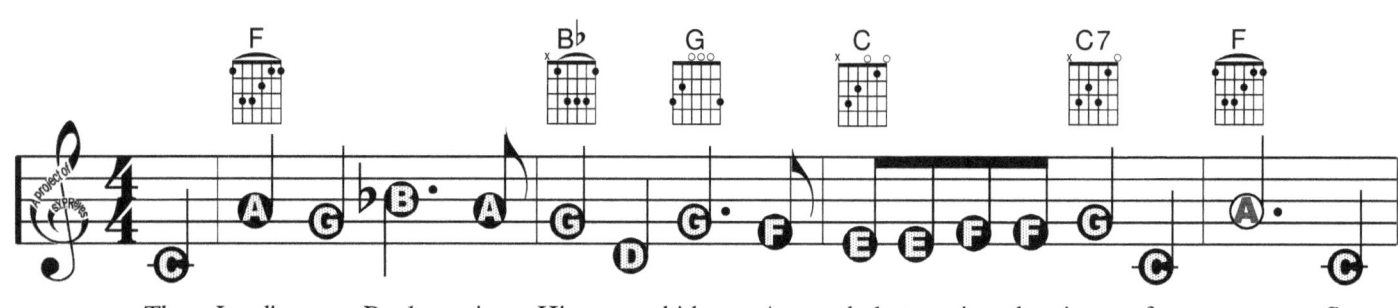

The Lord's our Rock, in Him we hide, A shel-ter in the time of storm; Se-

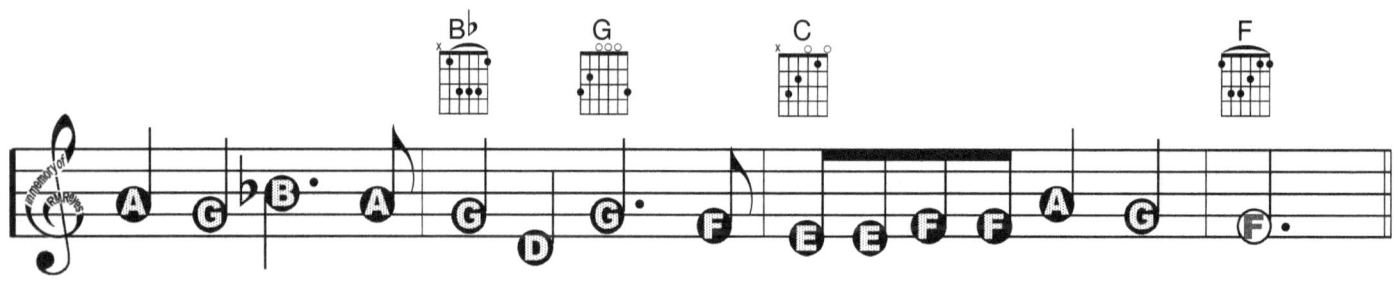

cure what-ev-er may be-tide, A shel-ter in the time of storm.

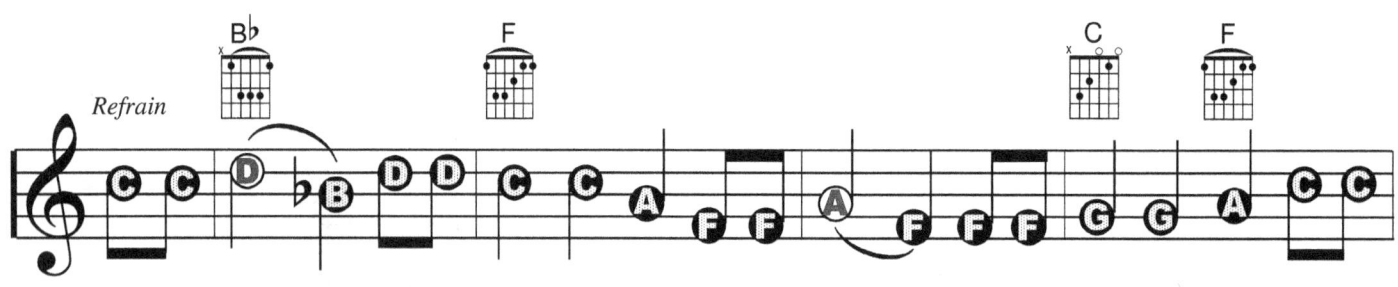

Refrain
Might-y Rock in a wea-ry land, Cool-ing shade on the burn-ing sand, Faith-ful

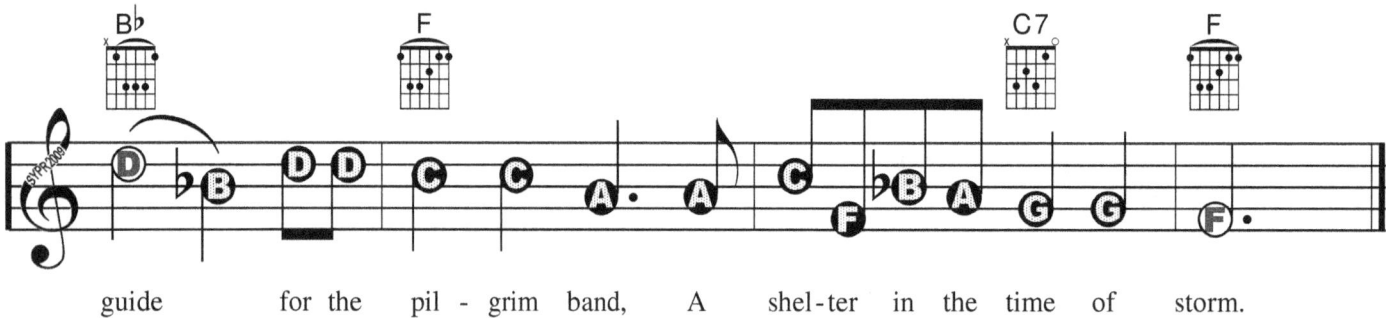

guide for the pil-grim band, A shel-ter in the time of storm.

2. A shade by day, defense by night, A shelter in the time of storm;
No fears alarm, no foes affright, A shelter in the time of storm.
(Refrain)

3. The raging floods may round us beat, A shelter in the time of storm;
We find in God a safe retreat, A shelter in the time of storm.
(Refrain)

4. O Rock divine, O Refuge dear, A shelter in the time of storm;
Be Thou our helper, ever near, A shelter in the time of storm.
(Refrain)

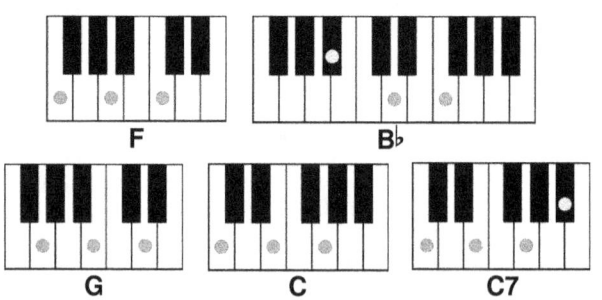

All Hail the Power of Jesus' Name

Words by Edward Perronet
Music by Oliver Holden

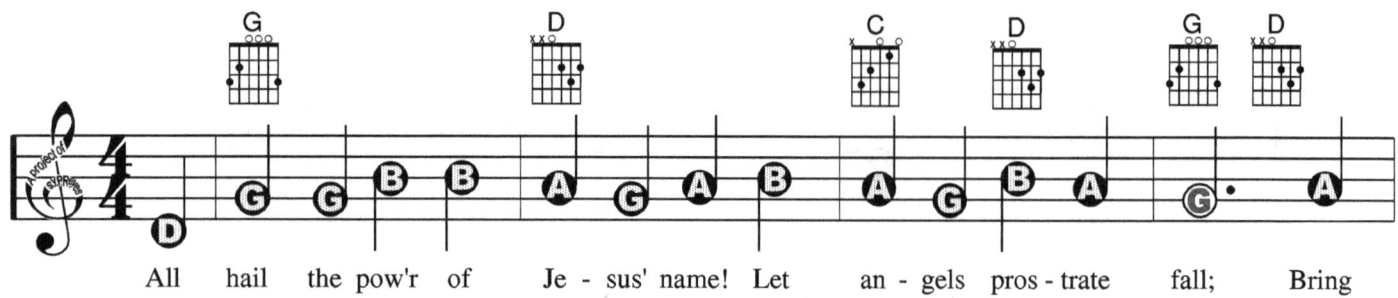

All hail the pow'r of Je-sus' name! Let an-gels pros-trate fall; Bring

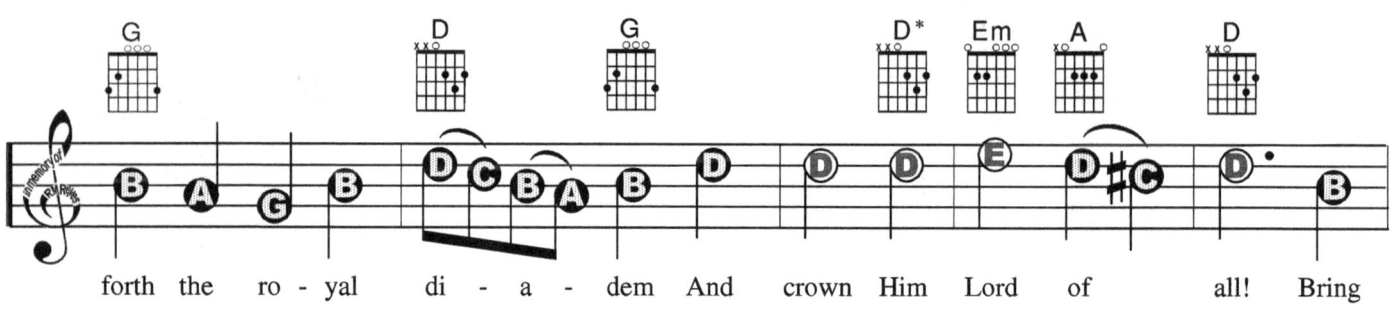

forth the ro - yal di - a - dem And crown Him Lord of all! Bring

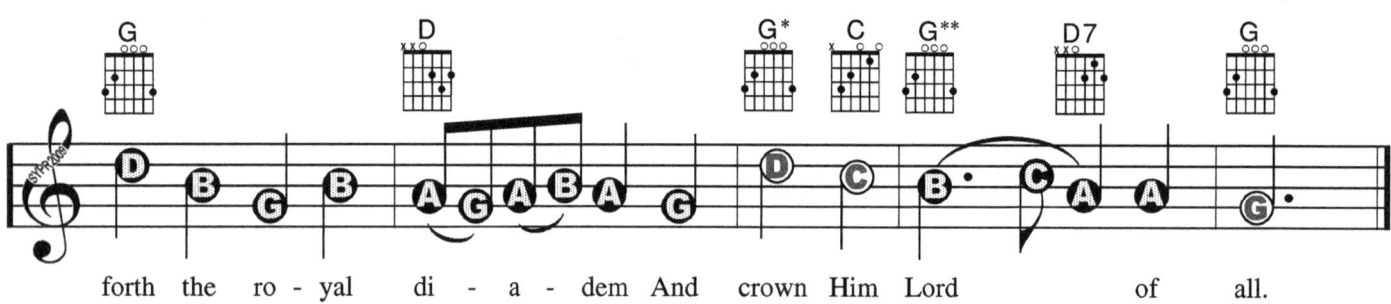

forth the ro - yal di - a - dem And crown Him Lord of all.

2. Ye seed of Israel's chosen race, Ye ransomed of the fall,
   Hail Him who saves you by His grace, And crown Him Lord of all!
   Hail Him who saves you by His grace, And crown Him Lord of all.

3. Let every kindred, every tribe, On this terrestrial ball,
   To Him all majesty ascribe, And crown Him Lord of all!
   To Him all majesty ascribe, And crown Him Lord of all.

4. Oh, that with yonder sacred throng We at His feet may fall,
   Join in the everlasting song, And crown Him Lord of all!
   Join in the everlasting song, And crown Him Lord of all.

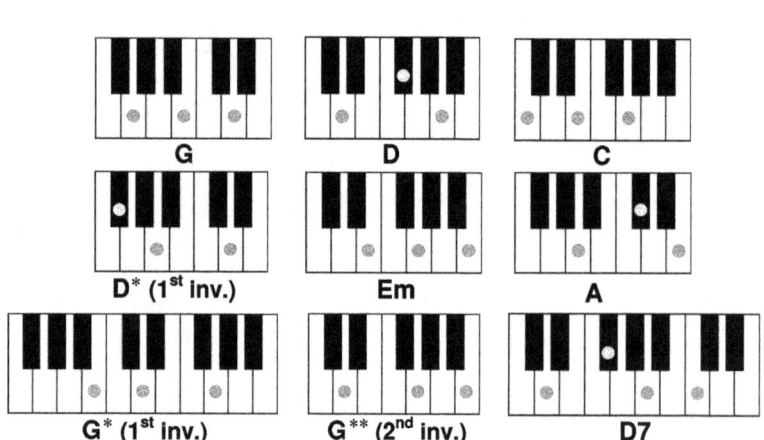

*On keyboard instrument, play first inversion
**On keyboard instrument, play second inversion

10

All the Way

Words by Fanny Crosby
Music by Robert Lowry

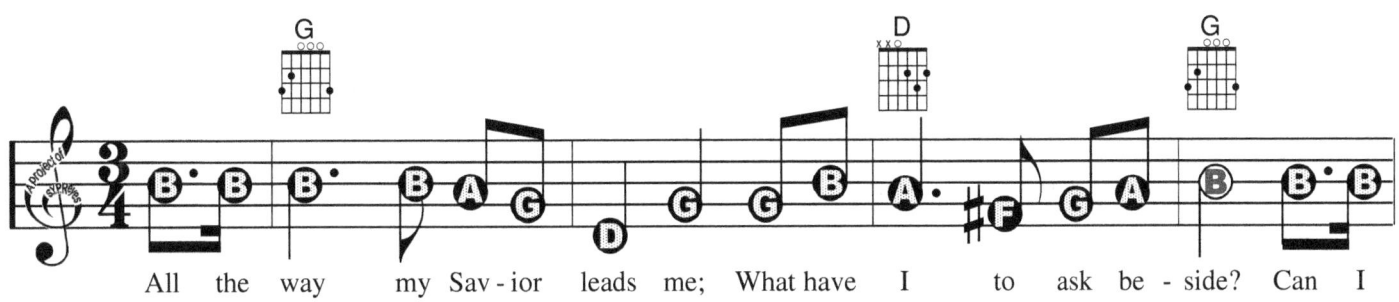
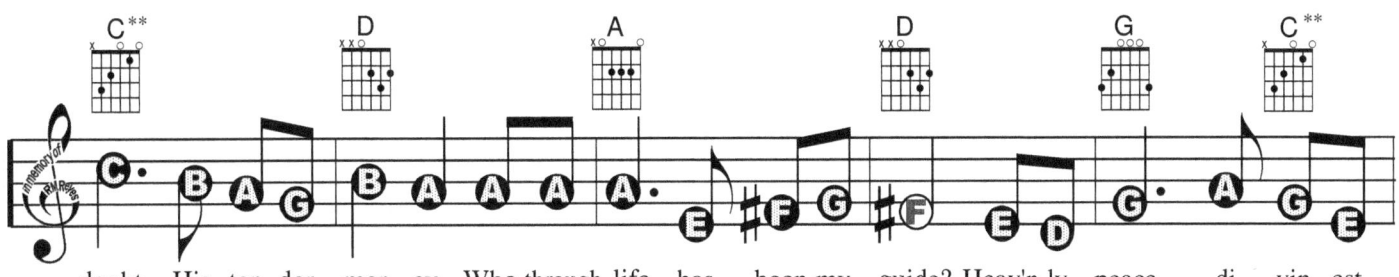
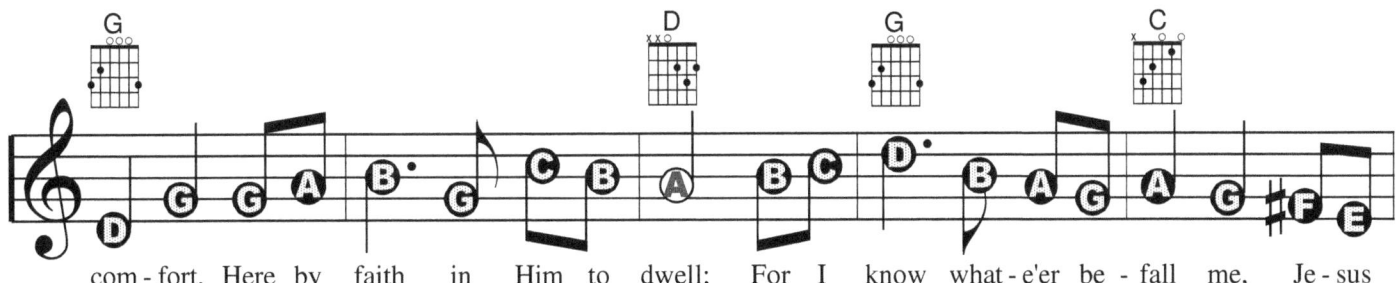
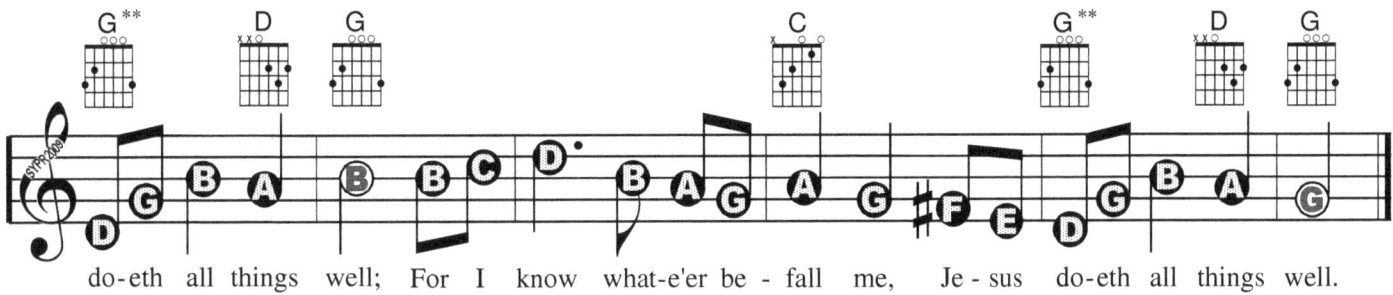

2. All the way my Savior leads me; Cheers each winding path I tread;
   Gives me grace for every trial, Feeds me with the living bread;
   Though my weary steps may falter, And my soul athirst may be,
   Gushing from the Rock before me, Lo, a spring of joy I see;
   Gushing from the Rock before me, Lo, a spring of joy I see.

3. All the way my Savior leads me; O the fullness of His love!
   Perfect rest to me is promised In my Father's house above;
   When I wake to life immortal, Wing my flight to realms of day,
   This my song through endless ages, Jesus led me all the way;
   This my song through endless ages, Jesus led me all the way.

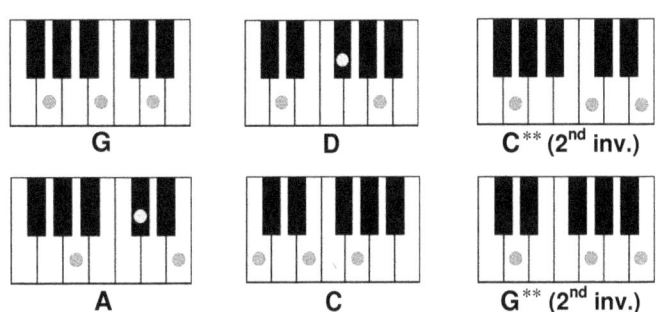

On keyboard instrument, play second inversion

Amazing Grace

Words by John Newton

Music from *Virginia Harmony*

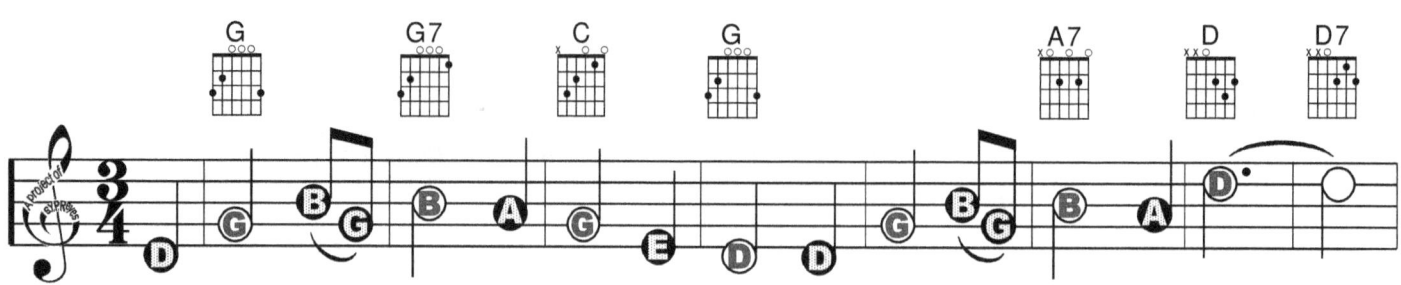

A - maz - ing grace! how sweeet the sound, That saved a wretch like me!

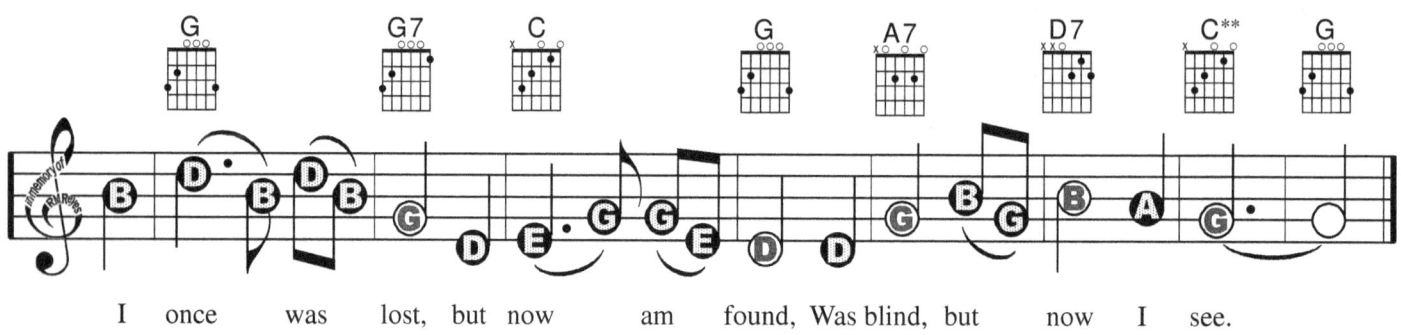

I once was lost, but now am found, Was blind, but now I see.

2. 'Twas grace that taught my heart to fear, And grace my fears relieved;
   How precious did that grace appear The hour I first believed!

3. The Lord has promised good to me, His word my hope secures;
   He will my shield and portion be As long as life endures.

4. Through many dangers, toils and snares, I have already come;
   'Tis grace hath brought me safe thus far, And grace will lead me home.

5. When we've been there ten thousand years, Bright shining as the sun,
   We've no less days to sing God's praise Than when we'd first begun.

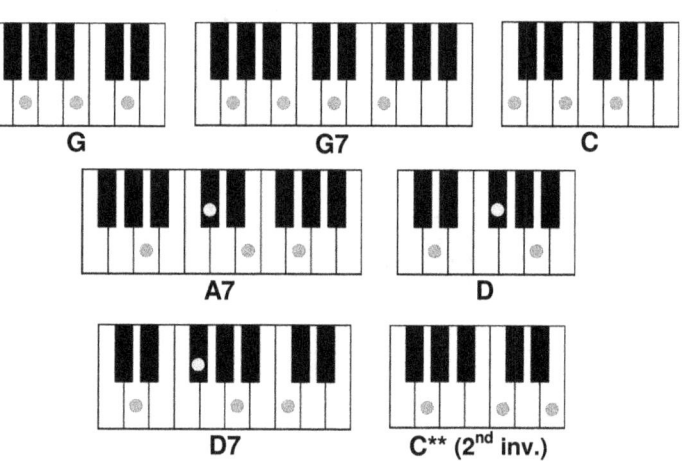

**On keyboard instrument, play second inversion

12

And Can It Be?

Words by Charles Wesley
Music by Thomas Campbell

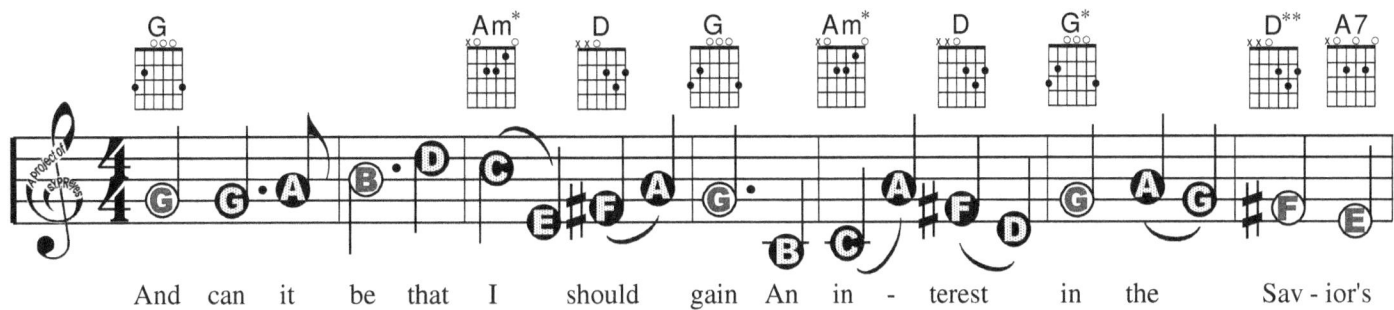
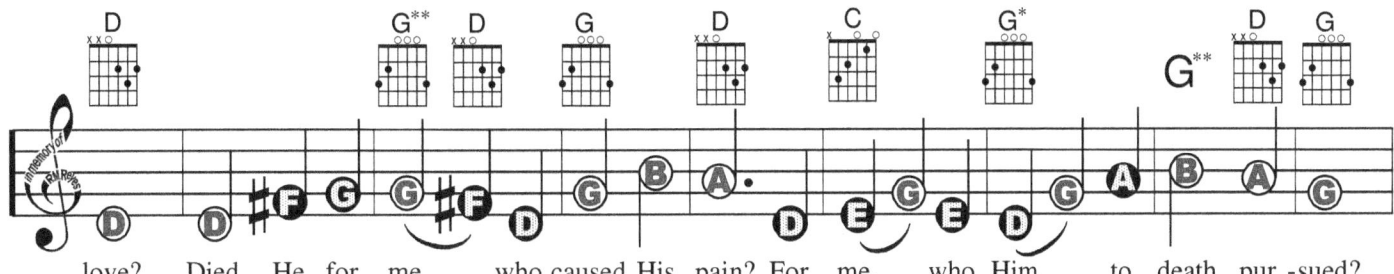
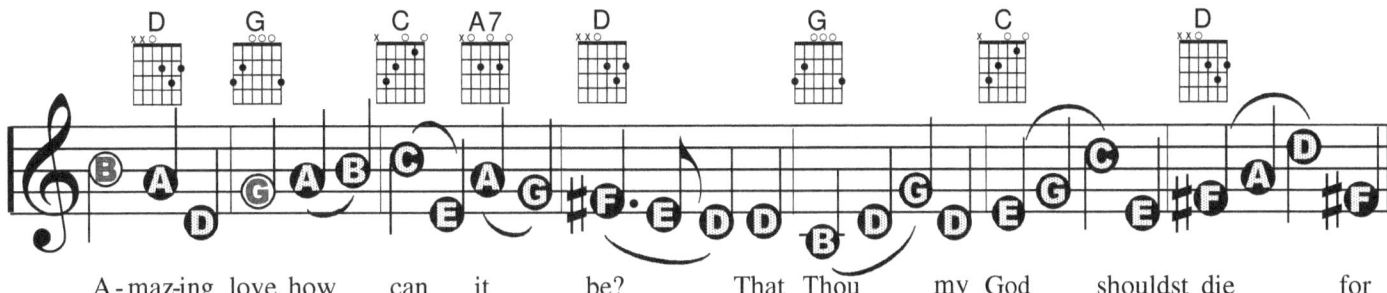
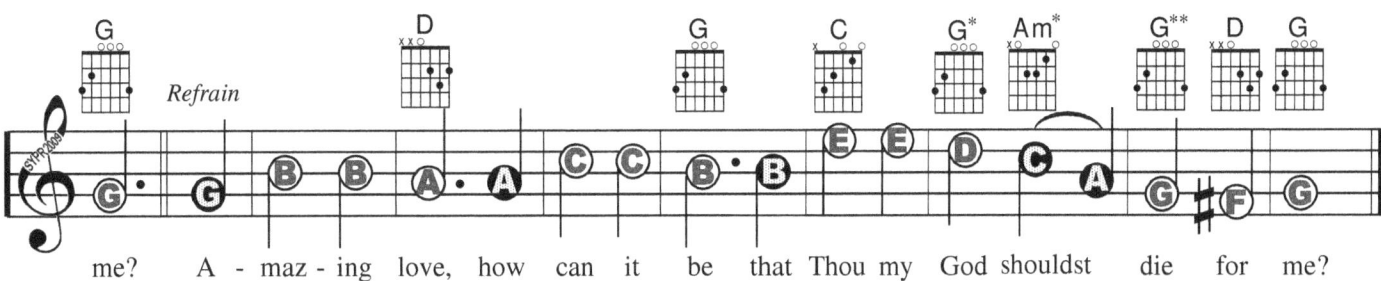

2. He left His Father's throne above, So free, so infinite His grace;
   Emptied Himself of all but love, And bled for Adam's helpless race;
   'Tis mercy all, immense and free; For, O my God, it found out me.
   (Refrain)

3. Long my imprisoned spirit lay Fast bound in sin and nature's night;
   Thine eye diffused a quick'ning ray, I woke, the dungeon flamed with light;
   My chains fell off, my heart was free; I rose, went forth and followed Thee.
   (Refrain)

4. No condemnation now I dread; Jesus and all in Him, is mine!
   Alive in Him, my living Head, And clothed in righteousness divine,
   Bold I approach th' eternal throne, And claim the crown, through Christ my own.
   (Refrain)

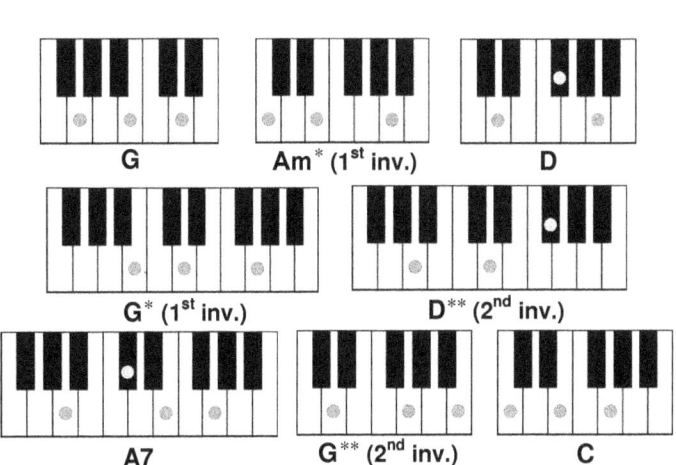

*On keyboard instrument, play first inversion
**On keyboard instrument, play second inversion

Anywhere With Jesus

Words by Jessie Brown
Music by Daniel Towner

An-y-where with Jesus, I can safe-ly go, An-y-where He leads me in this world be-low; An-y-where with-out Him, dear-est joys would fade; An-y-where with Jesus I am not a-fraid. An-y-where! an-y-where! Fear I can-not know; An-y-where with Jesus I can safe-ly go.

2. Anywhere with Jesus I am not alone;
   Other friends may fail me, He is still my own;
   Though His hand may lead me over dreary ways,
   Anywhere with Jesus is a house of praise.
   (Refrain)

3. Anywhere with Jesus I can go to sleep,
   When the gloomy shadows round about me creep,
   Knowing I shall waken nevermore to roam;
   Anywhere with Jesus will be home, sweet, home.
   (Refrain)

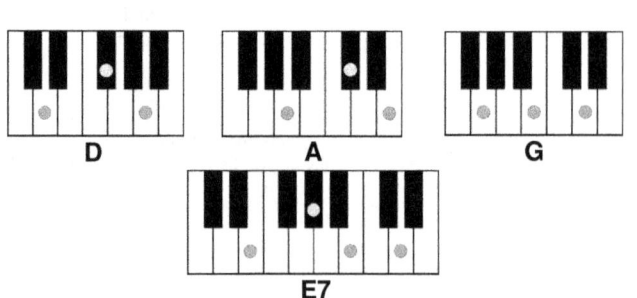

At the Cross

Words by Isaac Watts

Music by Ralph Hudson

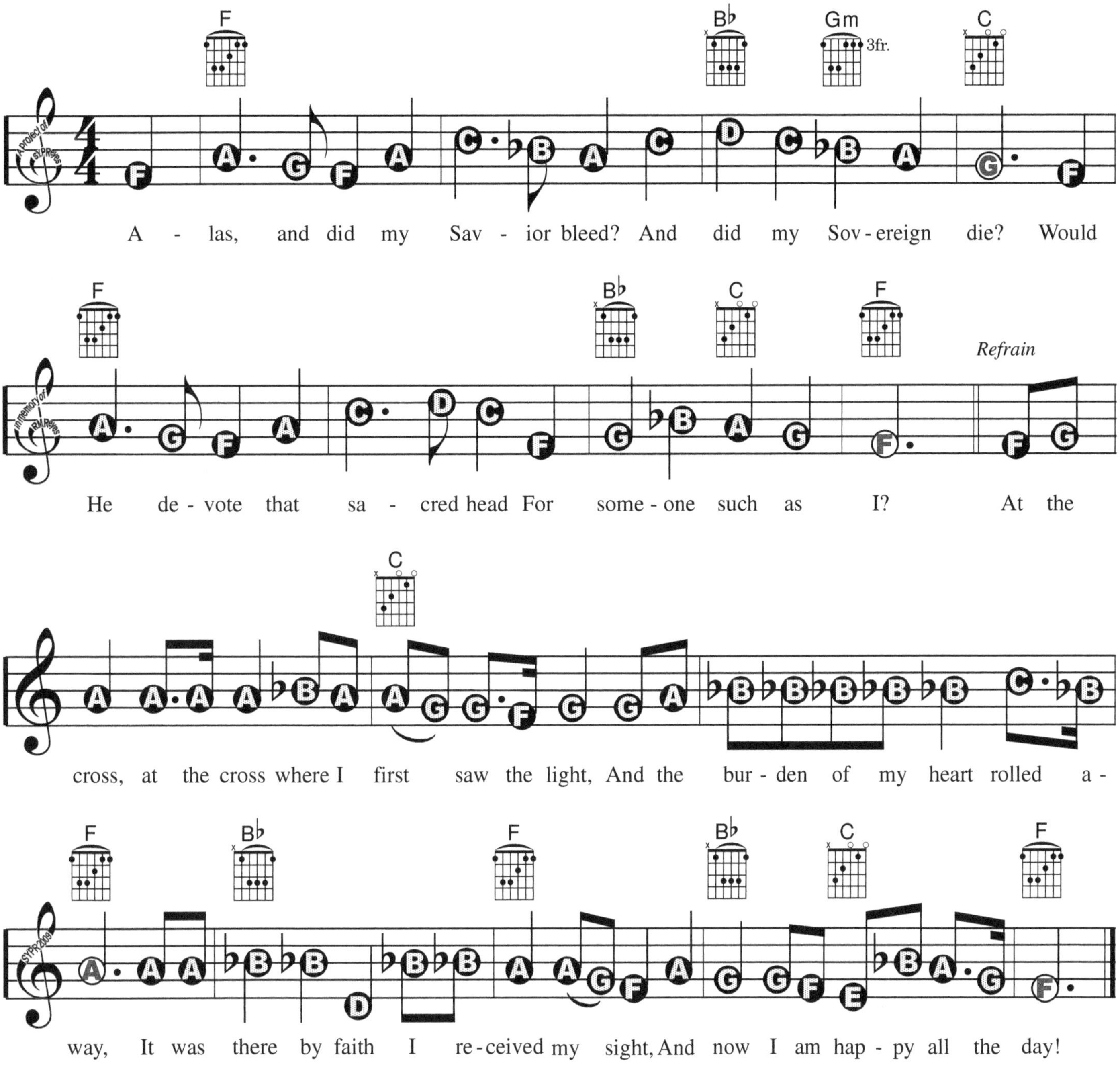

F
B♭
Gm
3fr.
C
A - las, and did my Sav - ior bleed? And did my Sov - ereign die? Would
He de - vote that sa - cred head For some - one such as I?
Refrain
At the
cross, at the cross where I first saw the light, And the bur - den of my heart rolled a -
way, It was there by faith I re - ceived my sight, And now I am hap - py all the day!

2. Was it for crimes that I have done, He suffered on the tree? Amazing pity! grace unknown! And love beyond degree! (Refrain)

3. But drops of grief can ne'er repay The debt of love I owe: Here, Lord, I give myself away, 'Tis all that I can do! (Refrain)

F
B♭
Gm
C

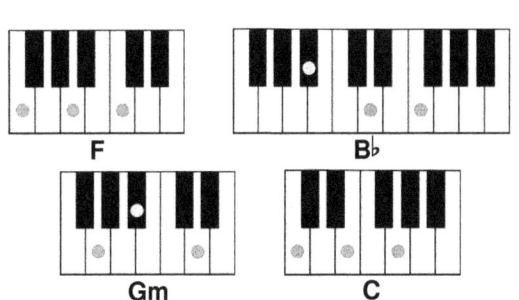

Away in a Manger

Words from *Little Children's Book*

Music by William Kirkpatrick

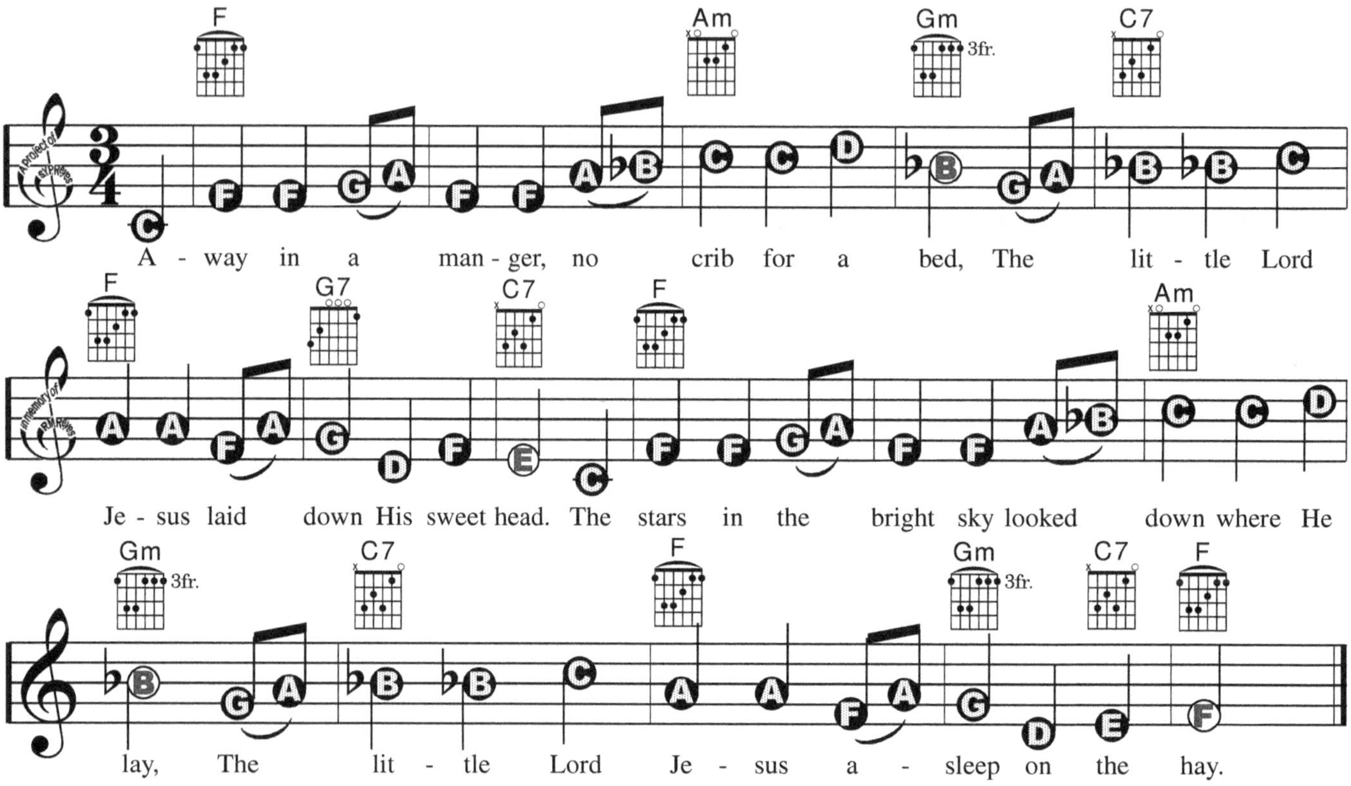
F Am Gm 3fr. C7
A - way in a man - ger, no crib for a bed, The lit - tle Lord
F G7 C7 F Am
Je - sus laid down His sweet head. The stars in the bright sky looked down where He
Gm 3fr. C7 F Gm 3fr. C7 F
lay, The lit - tle Lord Je - sus a - sleep on the hay.

Away in a Manger (Alternate tune)

Music by James Murray

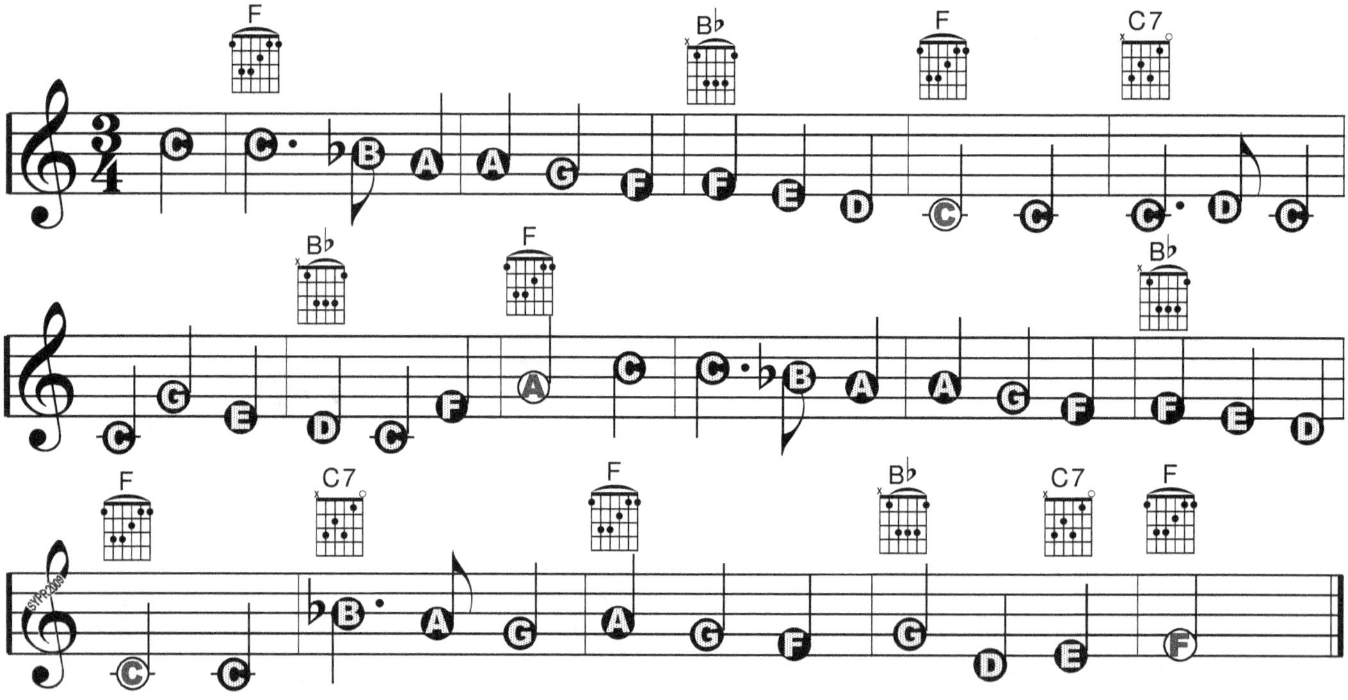
F B♭ F C7
B♭ F B♭
F C7 F B♭ C7 F

2. The cattle are lowing, the baby awakes,
   But little Lord Jesus no crying He makes.
   I love Thee, Lord Jesus! look down from the sky,
   And stay by my side till the morning is nigh.

3. Be near me, Lord Jesus; I ask Thee to stay
   Close by me forever, and love me, I pray.
   Bless all the dear children in Thy tender care,
   And fit us for heaven, to live with Thee there.

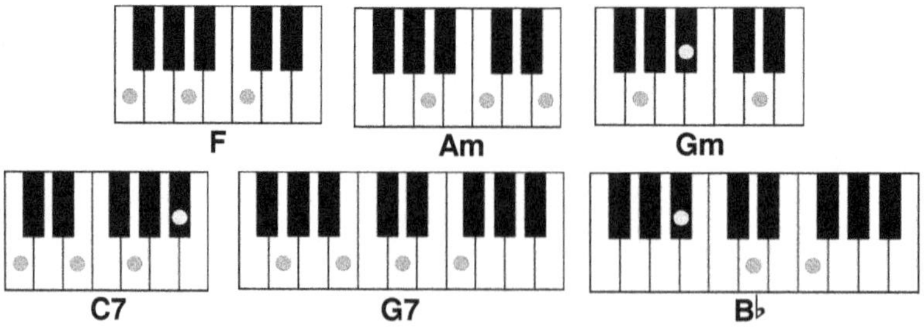
F
Am
Gm
C7
G7
B♭

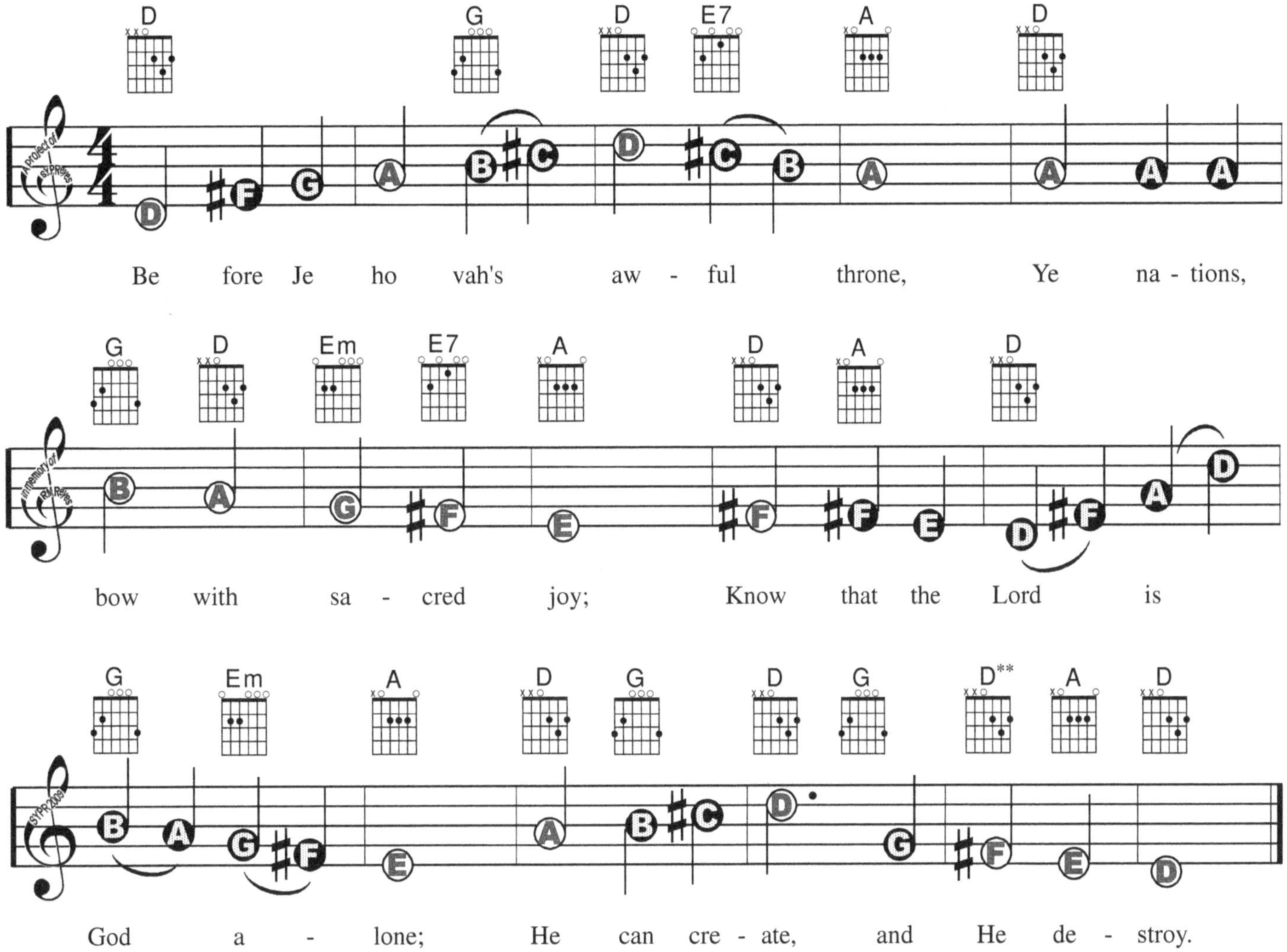

Before Jehovah's Awful Throne

Words by Isaac Watts

Music by John Hatton

D G D E7 A D
Be fore Je ho vah's aw - ful throne, Ye na - tions,
G D Em E7 A D A D
bow with sa - cred joy; Know that the Lord is
G Em A D G D G D** A D
God a - lone; He can cre - ate, and He de - stroy.

2. His sovereign power, without our aid,
   Made us of clay, and formed us men;
   And when like wandering sheep we strayed,
   He brought us to His fold again.

3. We'll crowd His gates with thankful songs,
   High as the heavens our voices raise;
   And earth, with her ten thousand tongues,
   Shall fill His courts with sounding praise.

4. Wide as the world is His command,
   Vast as eternity His love;
   Firm as a rock His truth shall stand,
   When rolling years shall cease to move.

D
G
E7
A
Em
D** (2nd inv.)

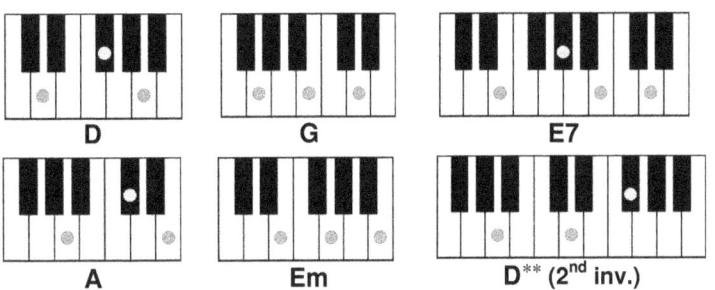

***On keyboard instrument, play second inversion*

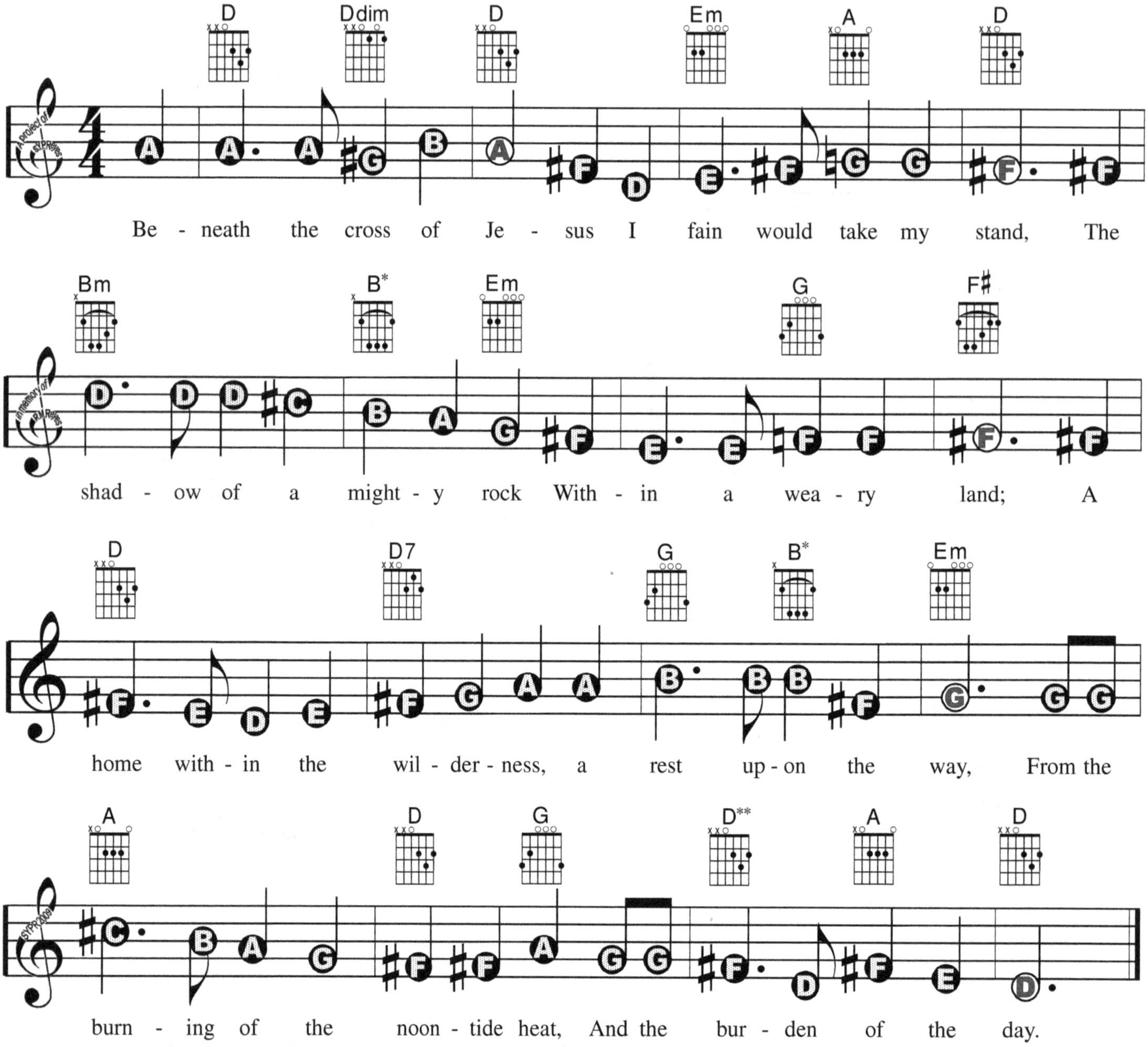

Beneath the Cross of Jesus

Words by Elizabeth Clephane

Music by Frederick Maker

D Ddim D Em A D
Be - neath the cross of Je - sus I fain would take my stand, The
Bm B* Em G F♯
shad - ow of a might - y rock With - in a wea - ry land; A
D D7 G B* Em
home with - in the wil - der - ness, a rest up - on the way, From the
A D G D** A D
burn - ing of the noon - tide heat, And the bur - den of the day.

D
D dim
Em
A
Bm
B* (1st inv.)
G
F♯
D7
D** (2nd inv.)

2. Upon that cross of Jesus Mine eye at times can see
   The very dying form of One Who suffered there for me;
   And from my smitten heart with tears Two wonders I confess:
   The wonders of redeeming love And my unworthiness.

3. I take, O cross, thy shadow For my abiding place;
   I ask no other sunshine than The sunshine of His face;
   Content to let the world go by, To know no gain nor loss,
   My sinful self my only shame, My glory all the cross.

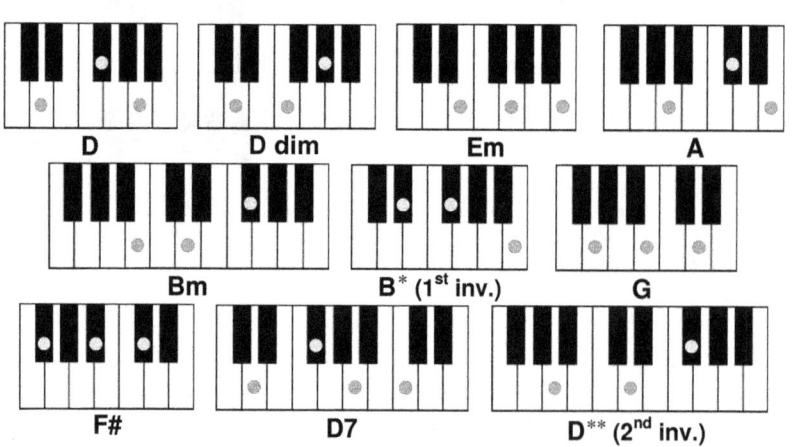

*On keyboard instrument, play first inversion
**On keyboard instrument, play second inversion

Blessed Assurance, Jesus Is Mine!

Words by Fanny Crosby   Music by Mrs. Joseph Knapp

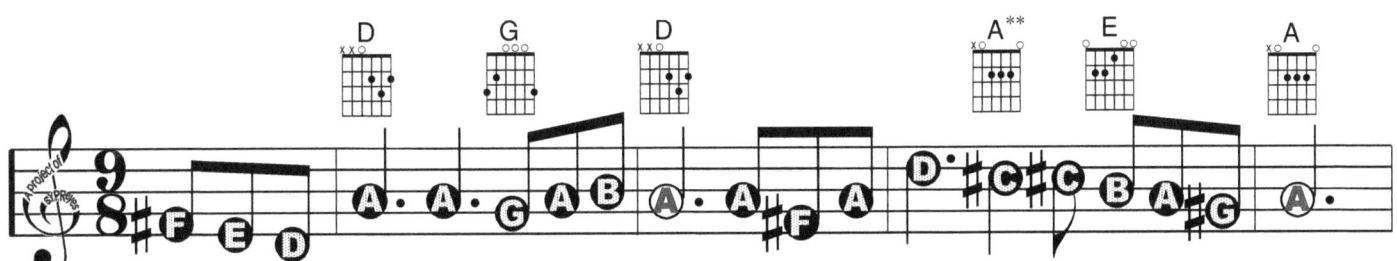

Bless-ed as - sur - ance, Je - sus is mine! O, what a fore - taste of glo - ry di - vine!

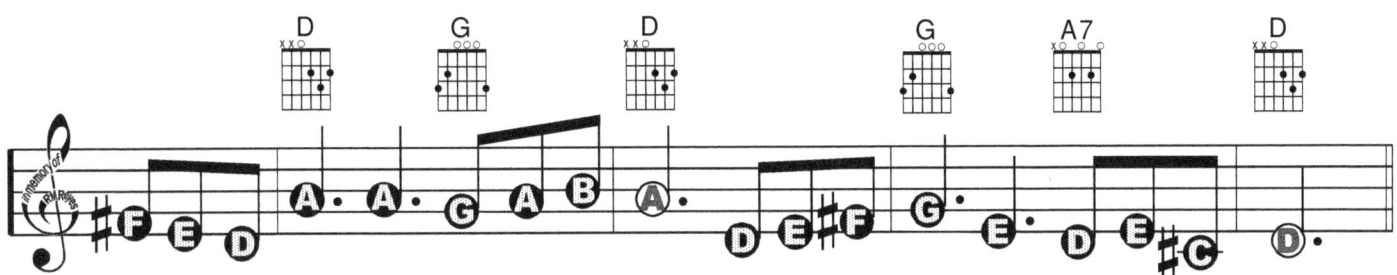

Heir of sal - va - tion, pur - chase of God, Born of His Spir - it, washed in His blood.

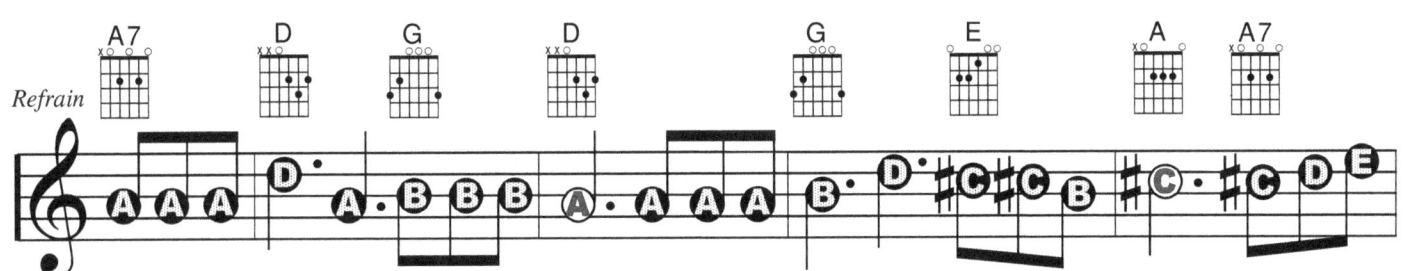

Refrain

This is my sto - ry, this is my song, Prais - ing my Sav - ior all the day long; This is my

sto - ry, this is my song, Prais - ing my Sav - ior all the day long.

2. Perfect submission, perfect delight,
   Visions of rapture now burst on my sight.
   Angels descending bring from above
   Echoes of mercy, whispers of love.
   (Refrain)

3. Perfect submission, all is at rest,
   I in my Savior am happy and blest,
   Watching and waiting, looking above,
   Filled with His goodness, lost in His love.
   (Refrain)

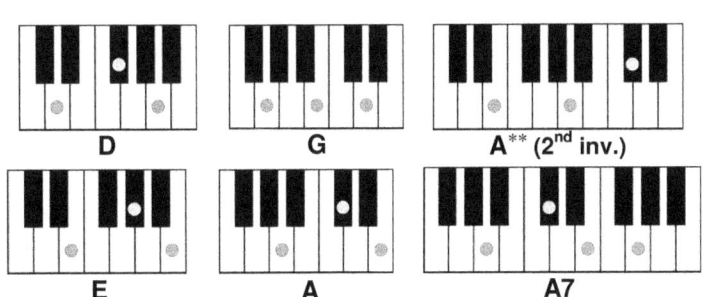

**On keyboard instrument, play second inversion*

19

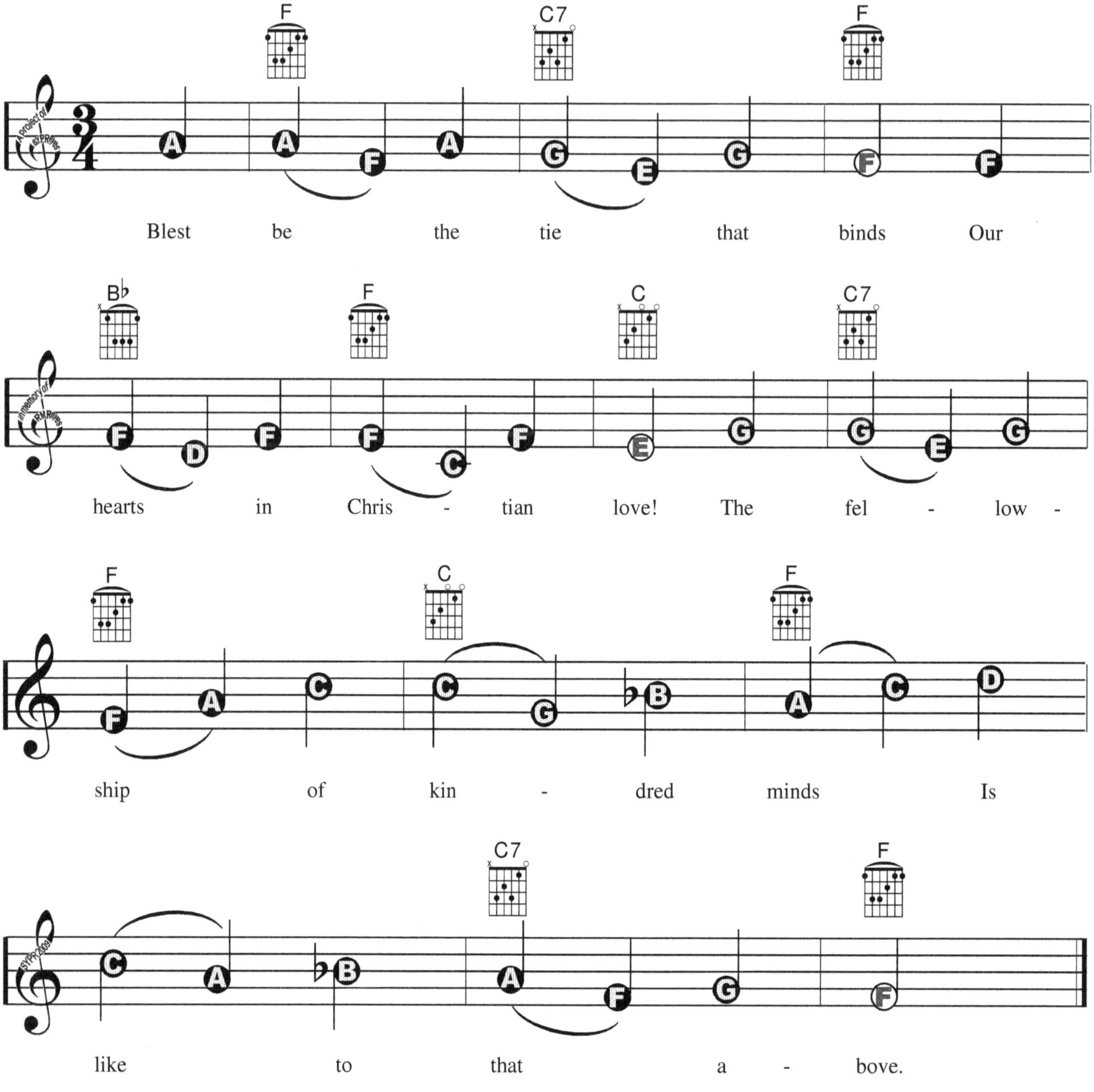

Blest Be the Tie That Binds

Words by John Fawcett

Music by Johann Naegeli

F C7 F
A A F A G E G F F
Blest be the tie that binds Our
B♭ F C C7
F D F F C F E G G E G
hearts in Chris - tian love! The fel - low -
F C F
F A C C G ♭B A C D
ship of kin - dred minds Is
C7 F
C A ♭B A F G F
like to that a - bove.

2. Before our Father's throne We pour our ardent prayers;
Our fears, our hopes, our aims are one, Our comforts and our cares.

3. We share our mutual woes, Our mutual burdens bear,
And often for each other flows The sympathizing tear.

4. When we asunder part, It gives us inward pain;
But we shall still be joined in heart, And hope to meet again.

F
C7
B♭
C

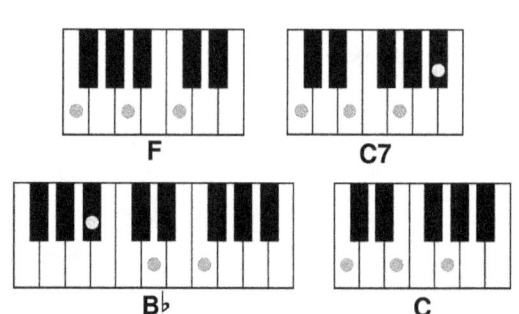

Break Thou the Bread of Life

Words by Mary Lathbury

Music by William Sherwin

2. Bless Thou the truth, dear Lord, to me, to me,
   As Thou didst bless the bread By Galilee;
   Then shall all bondage cease, All fetters fall;
   And I shall find my peace, My all in all.

3. Spirit and life are they, Words Thou dost speak;
   I hasten to obey, But I am weak;
   Thou art my only help, Thou art my life;
   Heeding Thy holy Word I win the strife.

**On keyboard instrument, play second inversion

Come, Christians, Join to Sing

Words by Christian Henry Bateman
Tune title: MADRID

Come, Christians join to sing, Alleluia! Amen!
Loud praise to Christ our King; Alleluia! Amen!
Let all, with heart and voice, Before His throne rejoice;
Praise is His gracious choice: Alleluia! Amen!

2. Come, lift your hearts on high; Alleluia! Amen!
   Let praises fill the sky; Alleluia! Amen!
   He is our Guide and Friend; To us He'll condescend;
   His love shall never end: Alleluia! Amen!

3. Praise yet our Christ again; Alleluia! Amen!
   Life shall not end the strain; Alleluia! Amen!
   On heaven's blissful shore His goodness we'll adore,
   Singing forevermore, Alleluia! Amen!

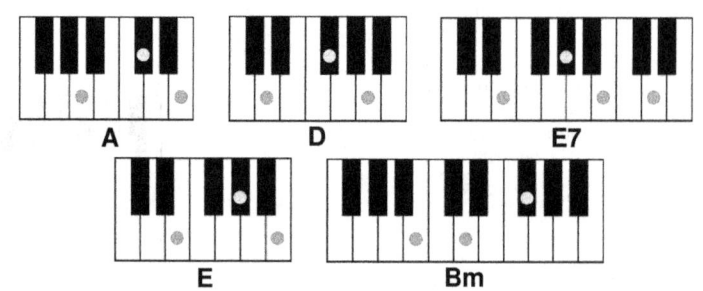

22

Come, Thou Almighty King

Author unknown

Music by Felice de Giardini

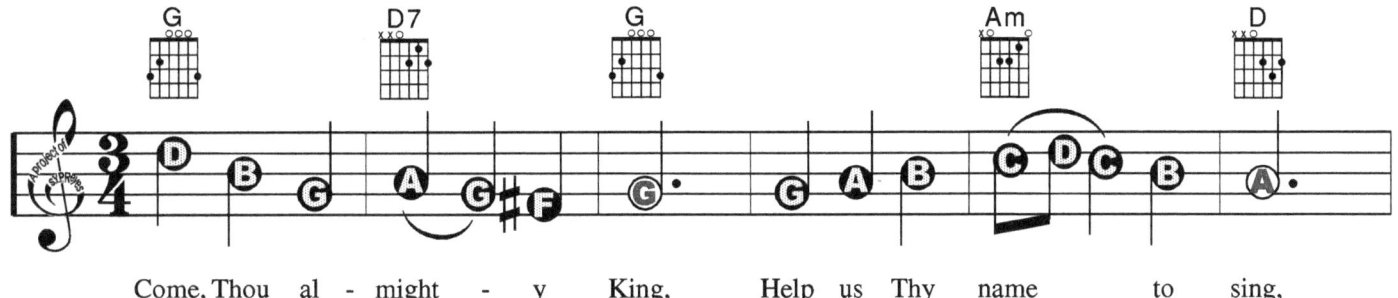

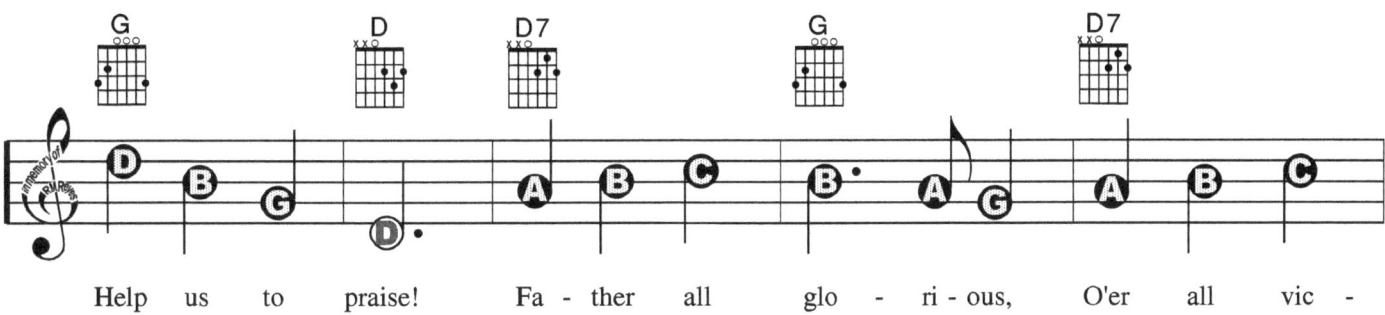

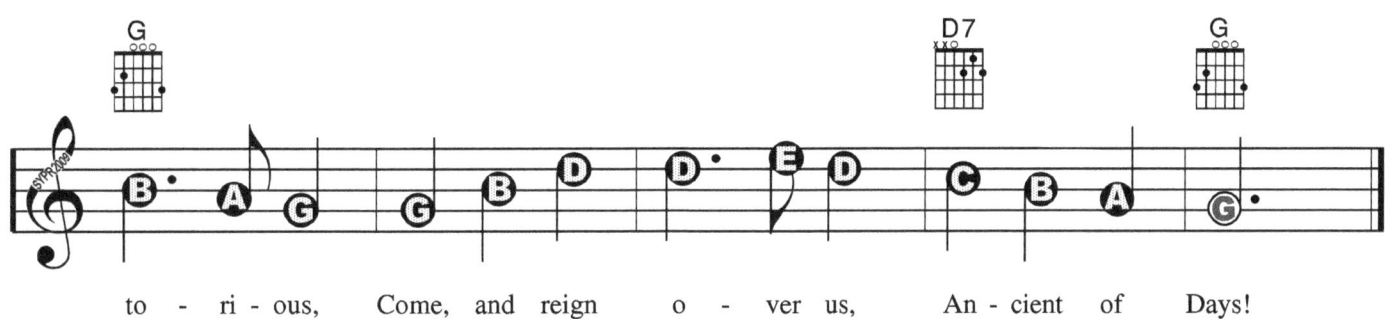

2. Come, Thou incarnate Word, Gird on Thy mighty sword,
   Our prayer attend; Come, and Thy people bless, And give Thy Word success;
   Spirit of holiness, On us descend!

3. Come, holy Comforter, Thy sacred witness bear,
   In this glad hour: Thou who almighty art, Now rule in every heart,
   And ne'er from us depart, Spirit of power!

4. To Thee, great One in three, Eternal praises be,
   Hence, evermore: Thy sovereign majesty May we in glory see,
   And to eternity Love and adore!

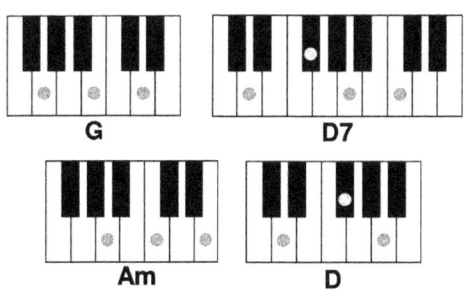

Cover With His Life

Words and music by F. E. Belden

2. Deep are the wounds transgression has made;
   Red are the stains; my soul is afraid.
   O to be covered, Jesus, with Thee,
   Safe from the law that now judgeth me!
   (Refrain)

3. Longing the joy of pardon to know;
   Jesus holds out a robe white as snow;
   "Lord, I accept it! leaving my own,
   Gladly I wear Thy pure life alone."
   (Refrain)

4. Reconciled by His death for my sin,
   Justified by His life pure and clean,
   Sanctified by obeying His word,
   Glorified when returneth my Lord.
   (Refrain)

Does Jesus Care?

Words by Frank Graeff
Music by J. Lincoln Hall

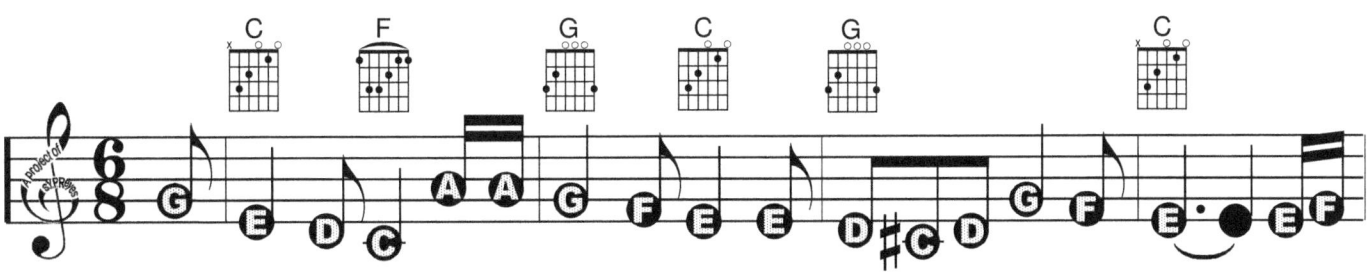

Does Je-sus care when my heart is pained Too deep-ly for mirth and song; As the

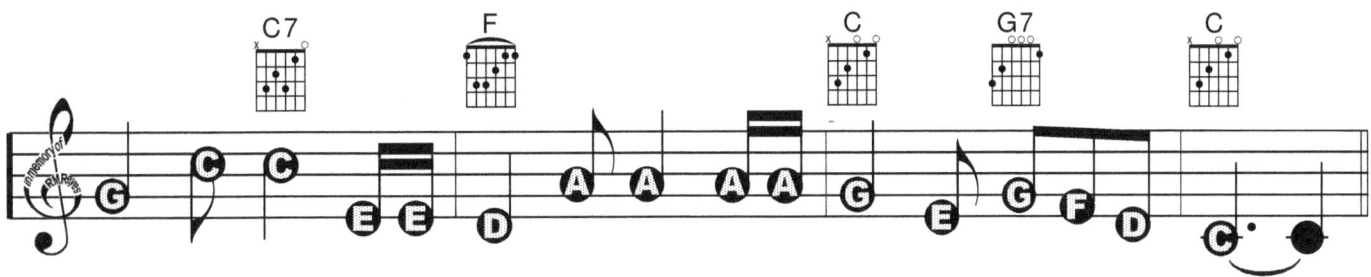

bur-dens press, and the cares dis-tress, And the way grows wea-ry and long?

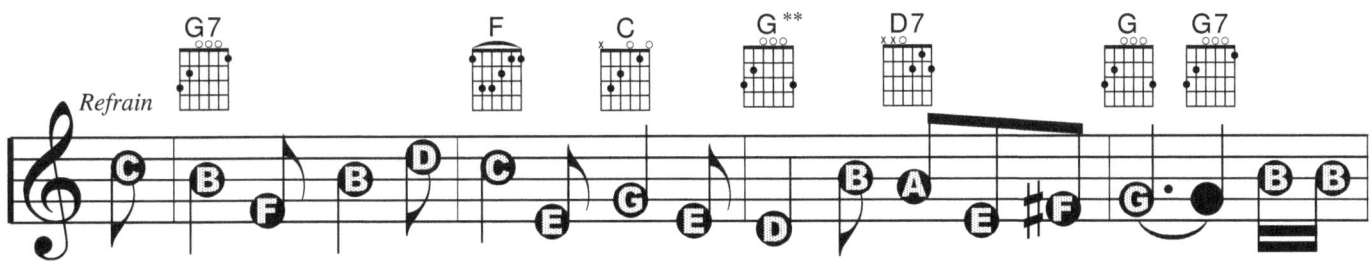

Refrain
O yes, He cares— I know He cares! His heart is touched with my grief; When the

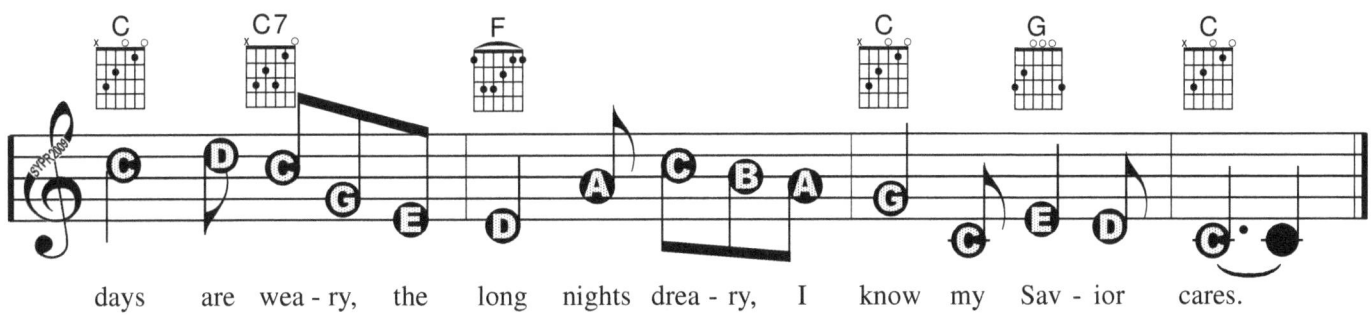

days are wea-ry, the long nights drea-ry, I know my Sav-ior cares.

2. Does Jesus care when my way is dark
   With a nameless dread and fear?
   As the daylight fades into deep night shades,
   Does He care enough to be near?
   (Refrain)

3. Does Jesus care when I've said goodbye
   To the dearest on earth to me,
   And my sad heart aches till it nearly breaks--
   Is it aught to Him? does He see?
   (Refrain)

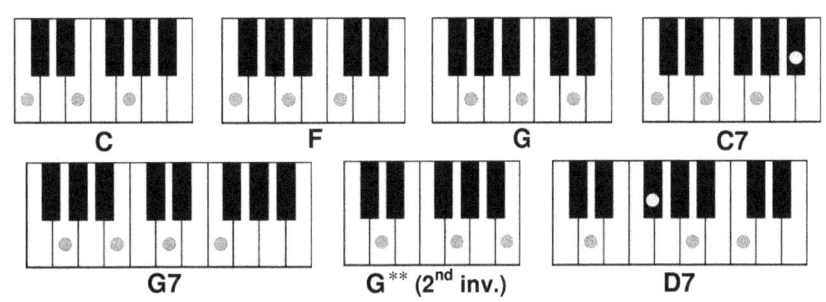

**On keyboard instrument, play second inversion

Don't Forget the Sabbath

Words by Fanny Crosby
Music by William Bradbury

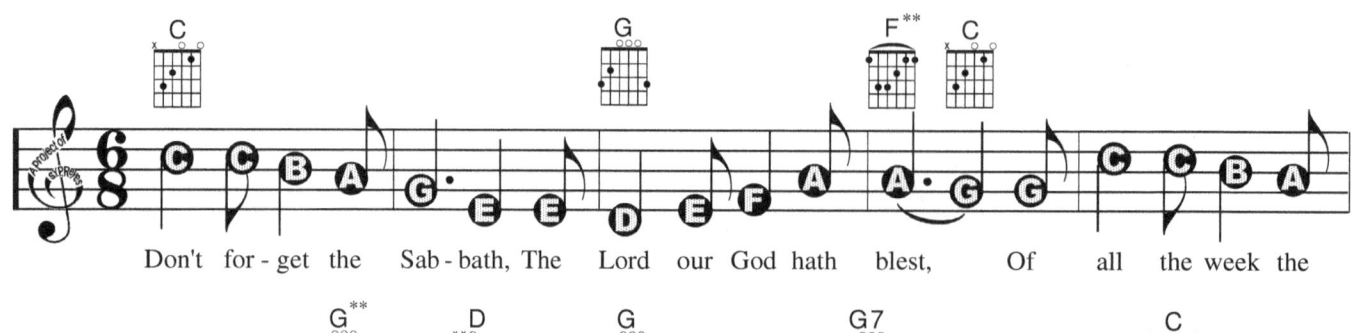
Don't for-get the Sab-bath, The Lord our God hath blest, Of all the week the

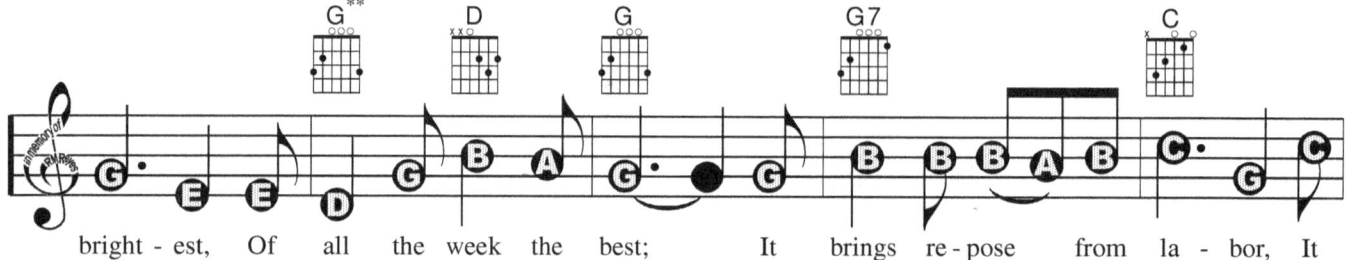
bright-est, Of all the week the best; It brings re-pose from la-bor, It

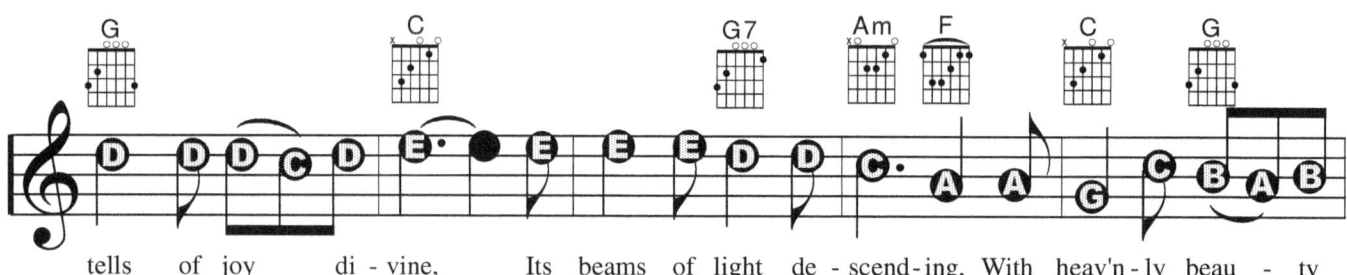
tells of joy di-vine, Its beams of light de-scend-ing, With heav'n-ly beau-ty

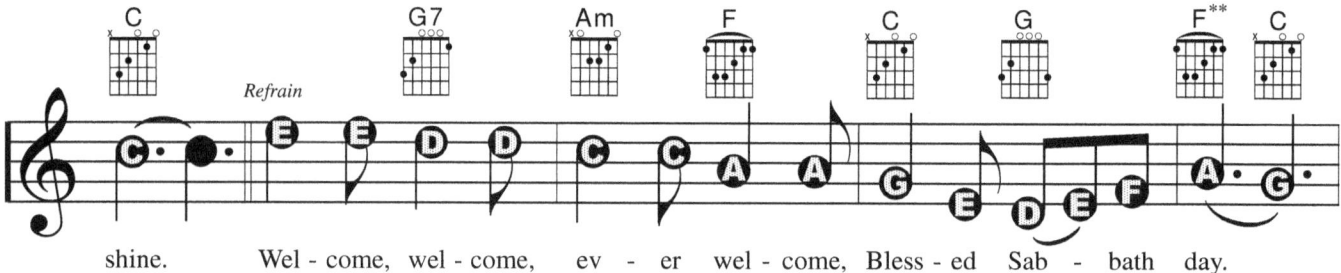
shine. *Refrain* Wel-come, wel-come, ev-er wel-come, Bless-ed Sab-bath day.

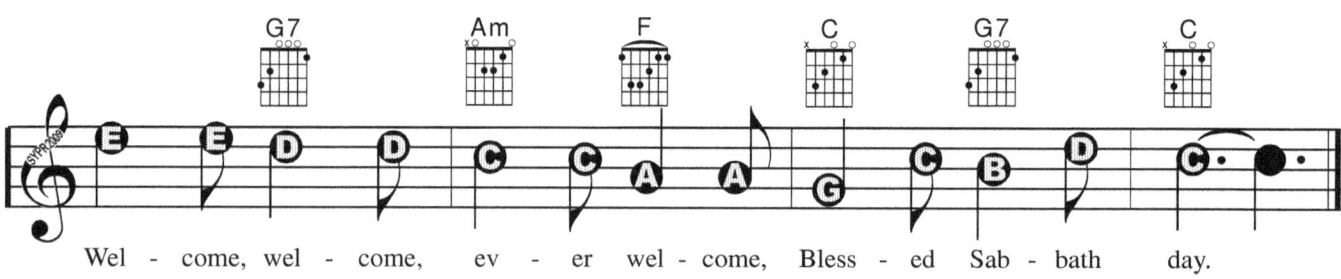
Wel-come, wel-come, ev-er wel-come, Bless-ed Sab-bath day.

2. Keep the Sabbath holy, And worship Him today,
Who said to His disciples, "I am the living way;"
And if we meekly follow Our Savior here below,
He'll give us of the fountain Whose streams eternal flow.
(Refrain)

3. Day of sacred pleasure! Its golden hours we'll spend
In thankful hymns to Jesus, The children's dearest Friend;
O gentle loving, Savior, How good and kind Thou art,
How precious is Thy promise To dwell in every heart!
(Refrain)

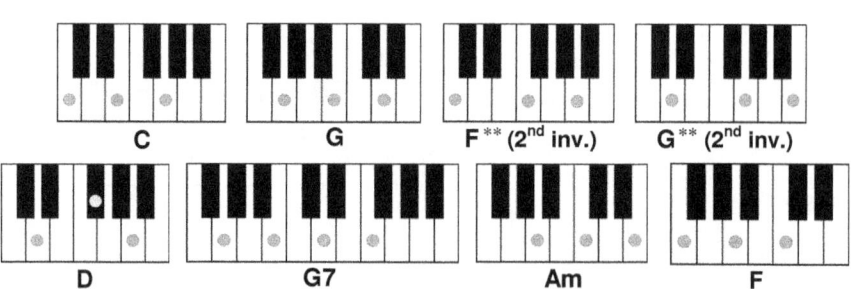

**On keyboard instrument, play second inversion*

Draw Me Nearer

Words by Fanny Crosby
Music by William Doane

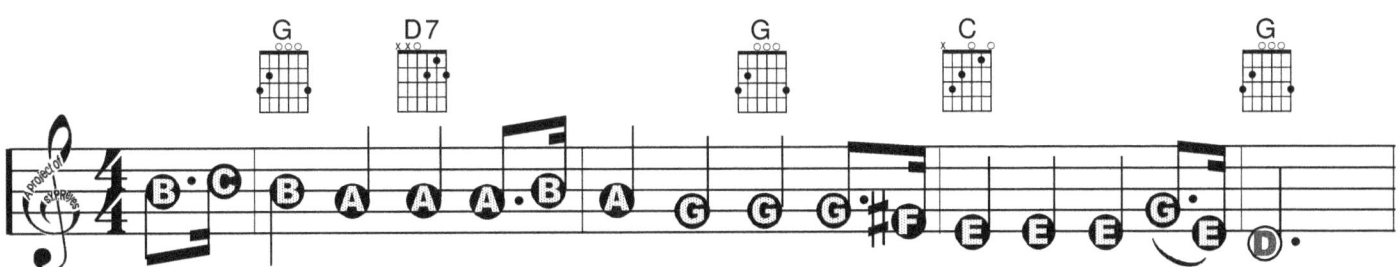
I am Thine, O Lord, I have heard Thy voice, And it told Thy love to me;

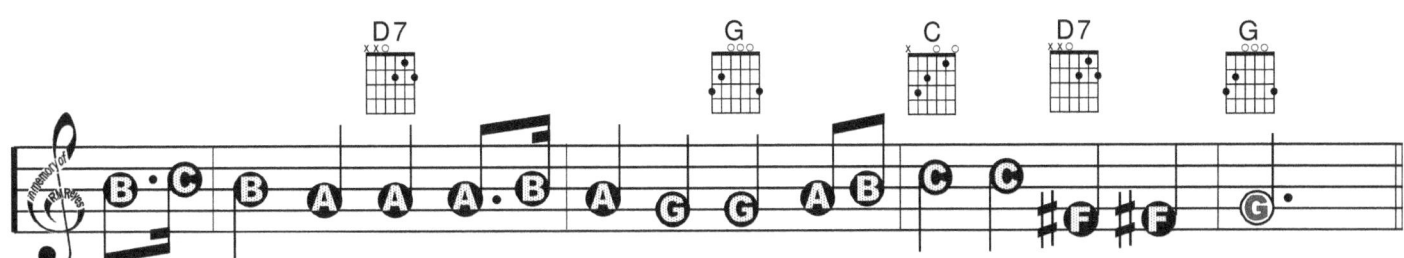
But I long to rise in the arms of faith, And be clos-er drawn to Thee.

Refrain
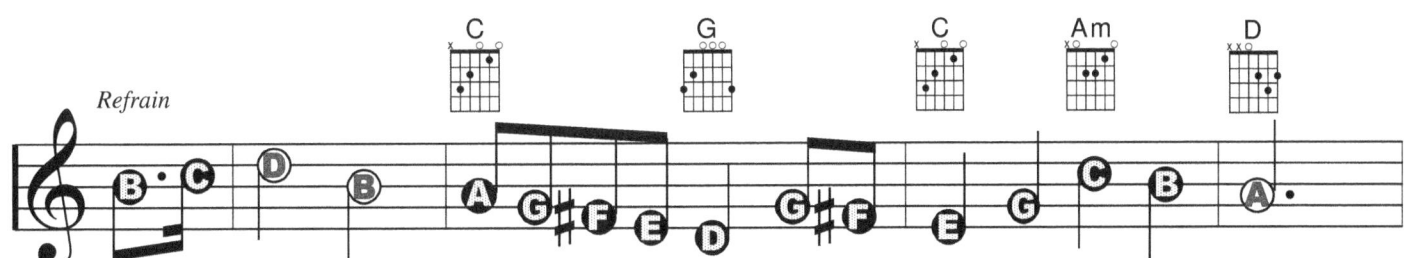
Draw me near-er, near-er, bless-ed Lord, To the cross where Thou hast died;

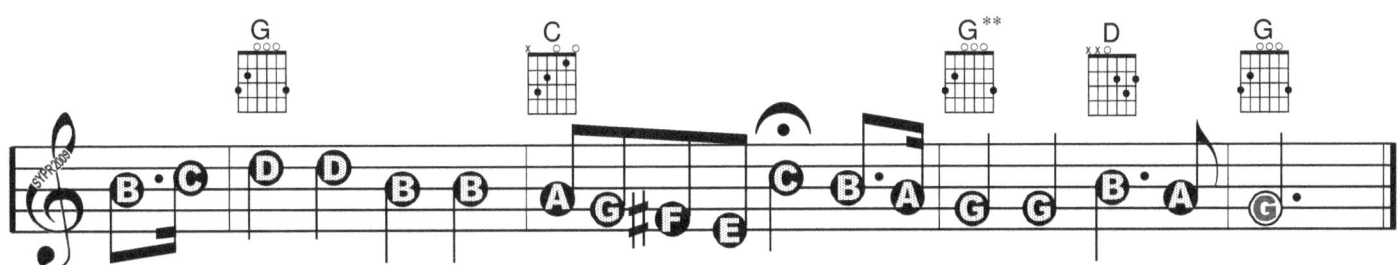
Draw me near-er, near-er, near-er bless-ed Lord, To Thy pre-cious bleed-ing side.

2. Consecrate me now to Thy service, Lord,
   By the power of grace divine;
   May my soul look up with a steadfast hope
   And my will be lost in Thine.
   (Refrain)

3. O the pure delight of a single hour
   That before Thy throne I spend,
   When I kneel in prayer, and with Thee, my God,
   I commune as friend with friend!
   (Refrain)

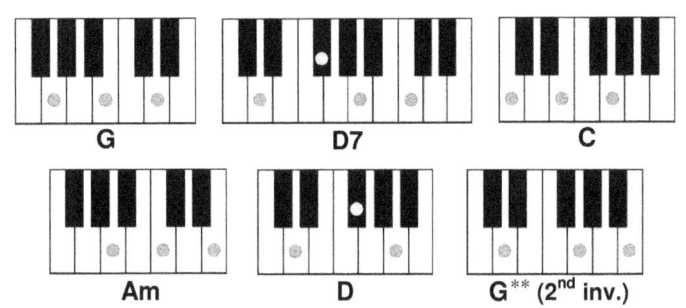

**On keyboard instrument, play second inversion

29

Face to Face

Words by Mrs. Frank Breck
Music by Grant Colfax Tullar

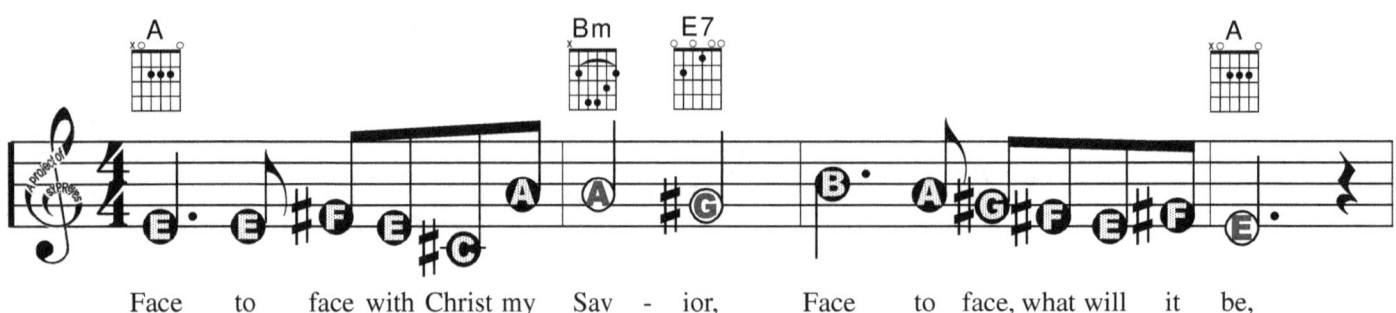

Face to face with Christ my Sav-ior, Face to face, what will it be,

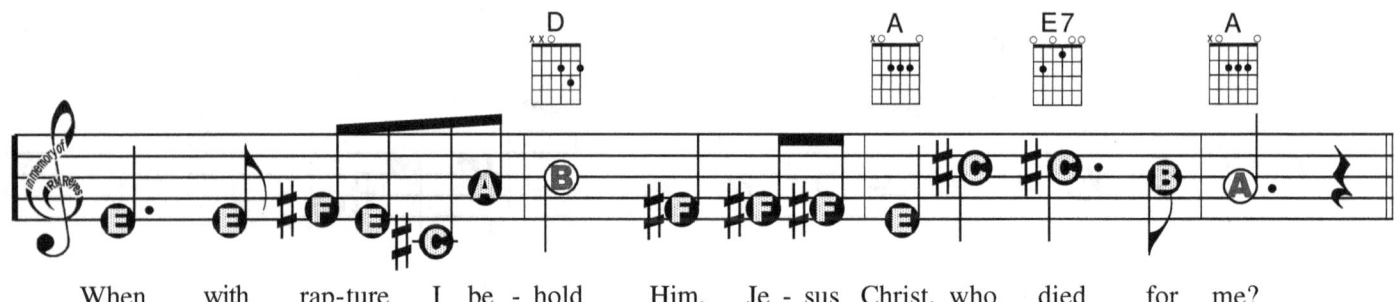

When with rap-ture I be-hold Him, Je-sus Christ, who died for me?

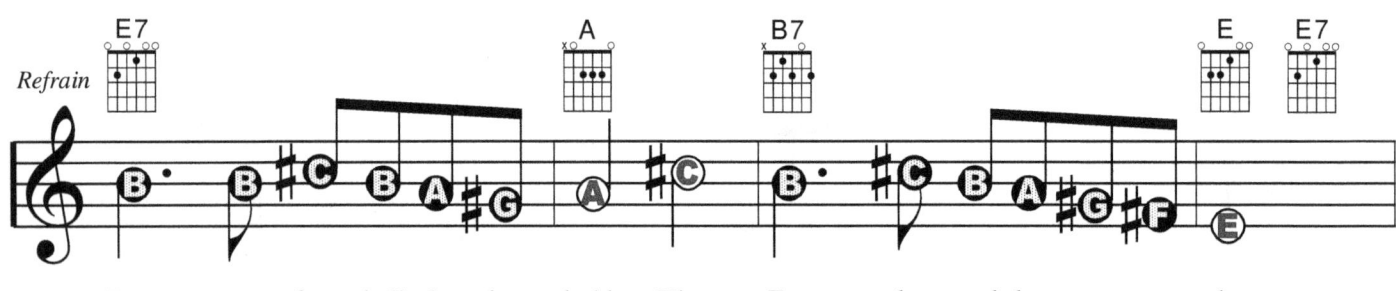

Refrain
Face to face shall I be-hold Him, Far be-yond the star-ry sky;

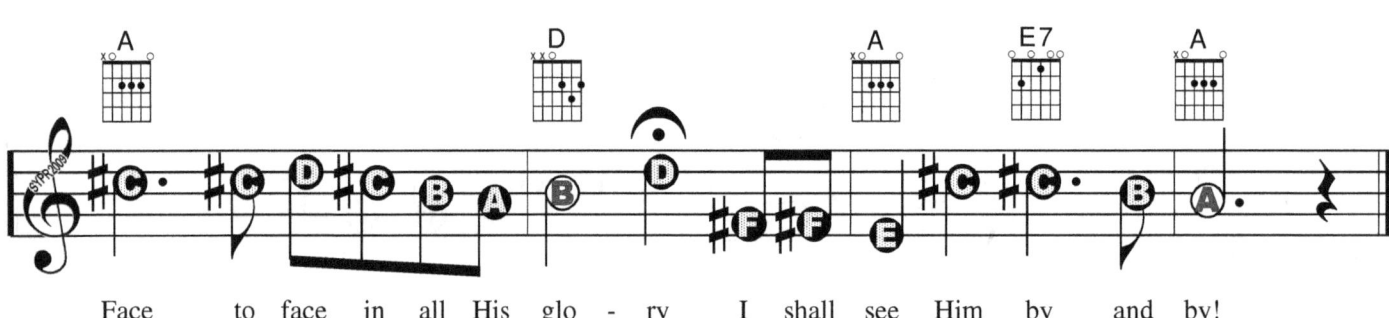

Face to face in all His glo-ry I shall see Him by and by!

2. Only faintly now I see Him, With the darkening veil between,
But a blessed day is coming, When His glory shall be seen.
(Refrain)

3. What rejoicing in His presence, When are banished grief and pain;
When the crooked ways are straightened, And the dark things shall be plain!
(Refrain)

4. Face to face! oh, blissful moment! Face to face--to see and know;
Face to face with my Redeemer, Jesus Christ, who loves me so.
(Refrain)

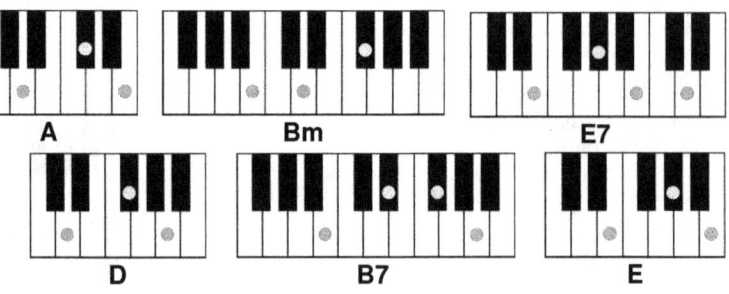

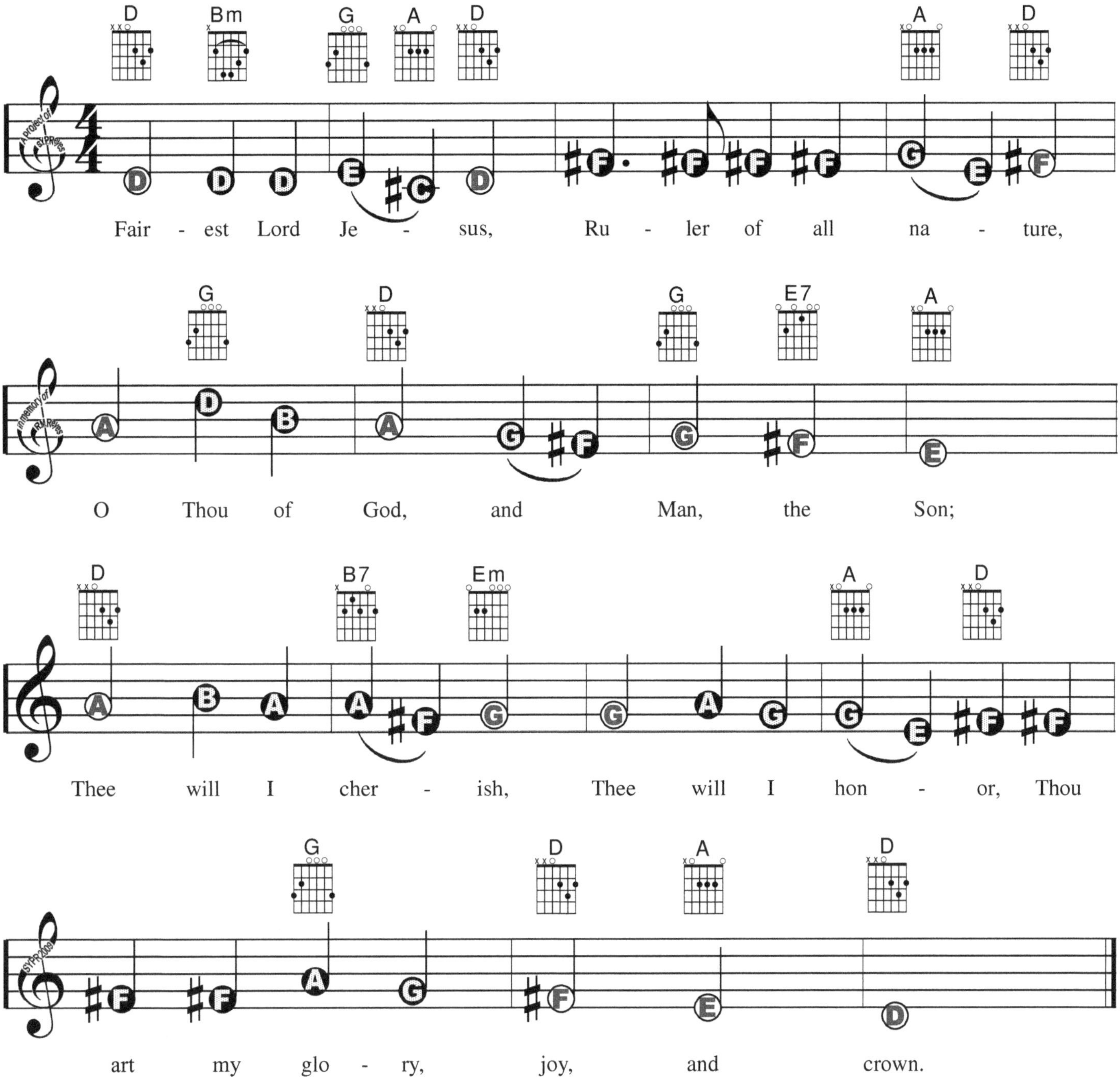

Fairest Lord Jesus

English translation by Joseph Seiss

Tune from *Schlesische Volkslieder*

D Bm G A D A D
Fair - est Lord Je - sus, Ru - ler of all na - ture,
G D G E7 A
O Thou of God, and Man, the Son;
D B7 Em A D
Thee will I cher - ish, Thee will I hon - or, Thou
G D A D
art my glo - ry, joy, and crown.

2. Fair are the meadows, Fairer still the woodlands,
Robed in the blooming garb of spring;
Jesus is fairer, Jesus is purer,
Who makes the woeful heart to sing.

3. Fair is the sunshine, Fairer still the moonlight,
And all the twinkling, starry host;
Jesus shines brighter, Jesus shines purer
Than all the angels heaven can boast.

D
Bm
G
A
E7
B7
Em

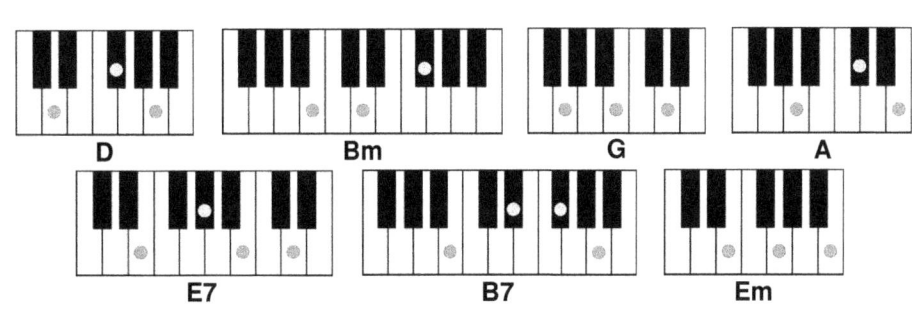

Faith Is the Victory

Words by John Yates
Music by Ira Sankey

En-camped a-long the hills of light, Ye Chris-tian sol-diers, rise, And press the bat-tle ere the night Shall veil the glow-ing skies. A-gainst the foe in vales be-low Let all our strength be hurled; Faith is the vic-to-ry, we know, That o-ver-comes the world.

Refrain

Faith is the vic-to-ry! Faith is the vic-to-ry! O, glo-ri-ous vic-to-ry, That o-ver-comes the world.

2. On every hand the foe we find Drawn up in dread array;
   Let tents of ease be left behind, And onward to the fray;
   Salvation's helmet on each head, With truth all girt about,
   The earth shall tremble 'neath our tread, And echo with our shout.
   (Refrain)

3. To him that overcomes the foe, White raiment shall be giv'n,
   Before the angels he shall know His name confessed in heav'n.
   Then onward from the hills of light, Our hearts with love aflame,
   We'll vanquish all the hosts of night, In Jesus' conquering name.
   (Refrain)

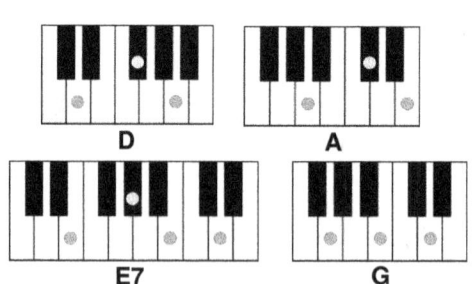

Faith of Our Fathers

Music by Frederick Faber
Music by Henri Hemy

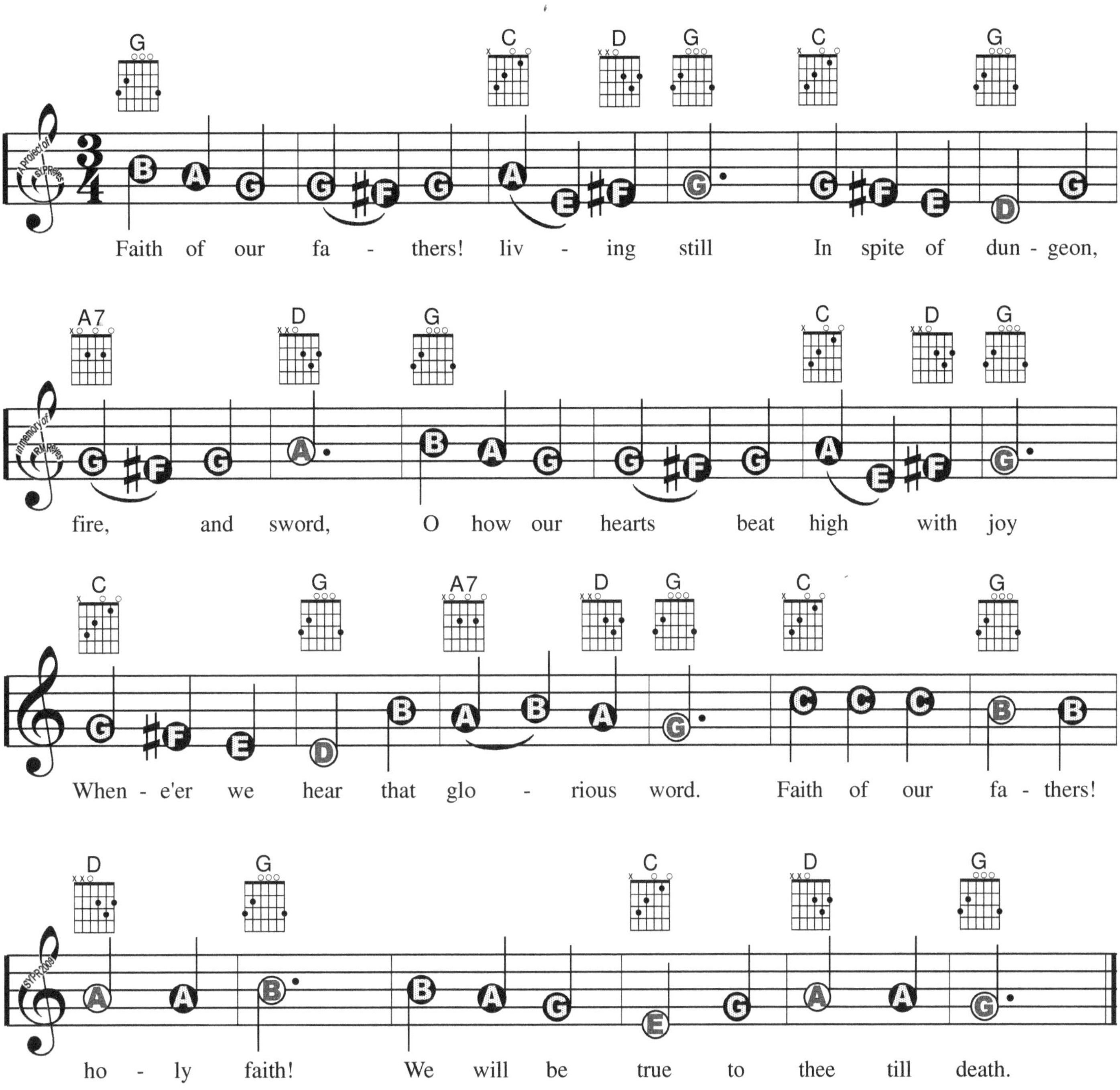

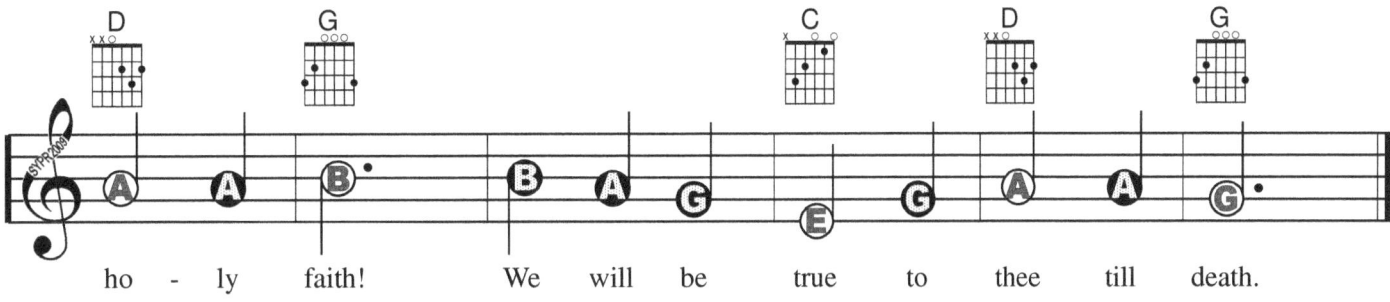

2. Our fathers, chained in prisons dark, Were still in heart and conscience free;
How sweet would be their children's fate, If they, like them, could die for thee!
Faith of our fathers! holy faith! We will be true to thee till death.

3. Fatih of our fathers! we will love Both friend and foe in all our strife,
And preach thee, too, as love knows how, By kindly words and virtuous life.
Faith of our fathers! holy faith! We will be true to thee till death.

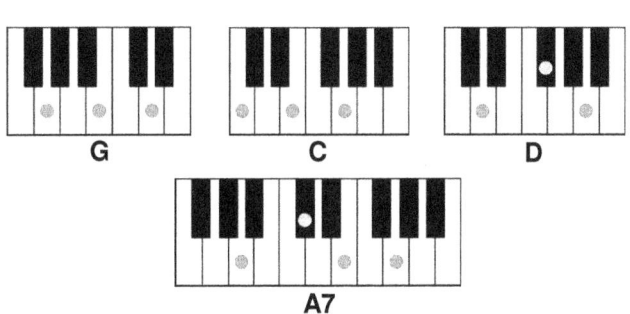

Far From All Care

Words and music by D. A. R. Aufranc

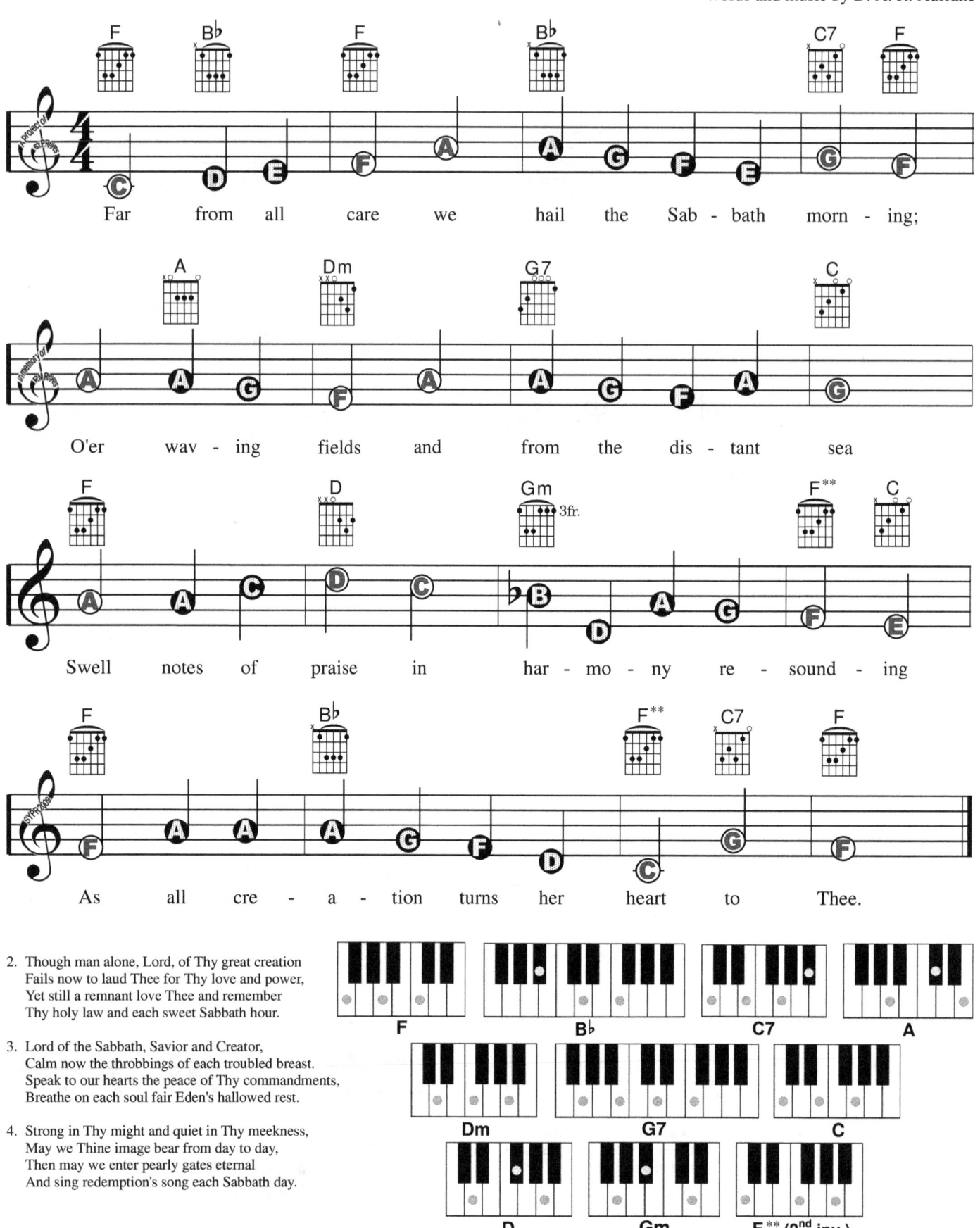

2. Though man alone, Lord, of Thy great creation
Fails now to laud Thee for Thy love and power,
Yet still a remnant love Thee and remember
Thy holy law and each sweet Sabbath hour.

3. Lord of the Sabbath, Savior and Creator,
Calm now the throbbings of each troubled breast.
Speak to our hearts the peace of Thy commandments,
Breathe on each soul fair Eden's hallowed rest.

4. Strong in Thy might and quiet in Thy meekness,
May we Thine image bear from day to day,
Then may we enter pearly gates eternal
And sing redemption's song each Sabbath day.

*On keyboard instrument, play second inversion

For the Beauty of the Earth

Words by Folliott Pierpoint

Music by Conrad Kocher

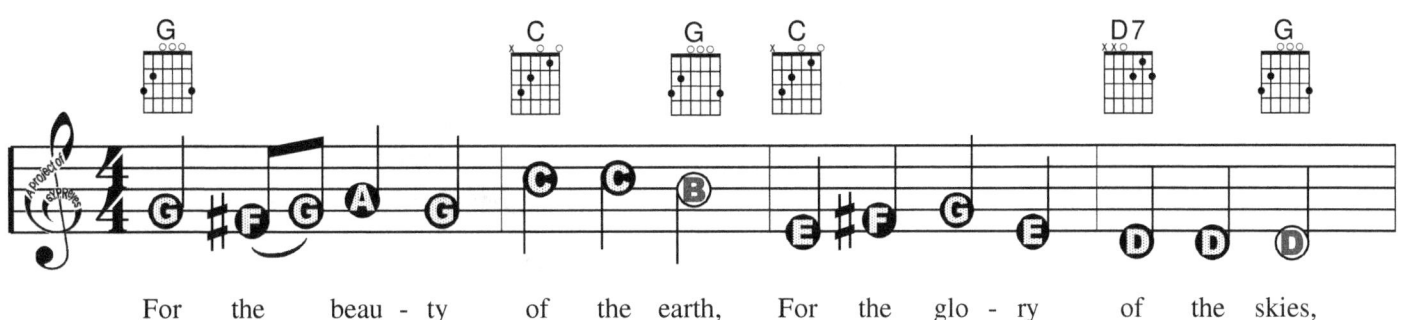

For the beau-ty of the earth, For the glo-ry of the skies,

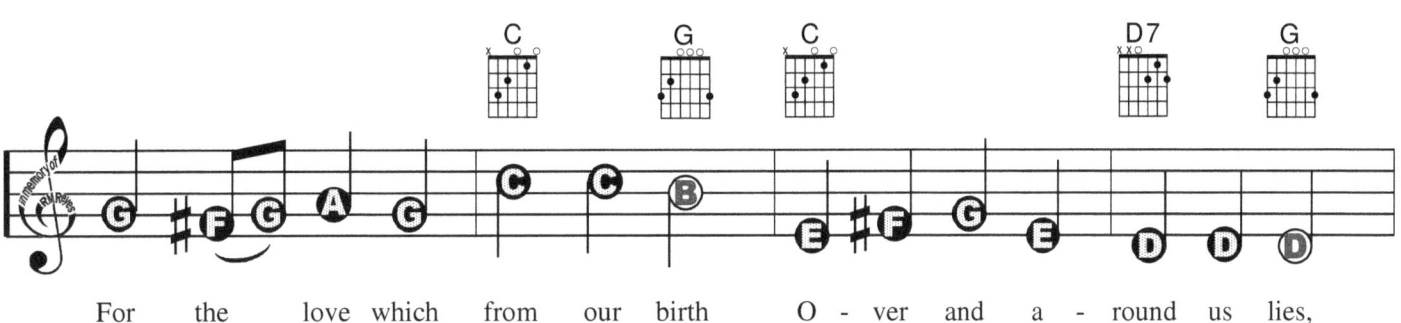

For the love which from our birth O-ver and a-round us lies,

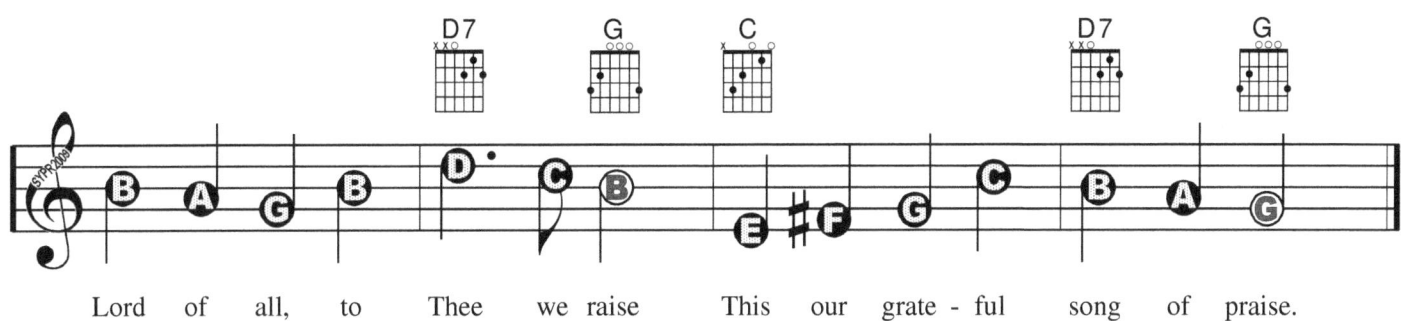

Lord of all, to Thee we raise This our grate-ful song of praise.

2. For the joy of human love, Brother, sister, parent, child,
Friends on earth and Friend above, Pleasures pure and undefiled,
Lord of all, to Thee we raise This our grateful song of praise.

3. For the gift of Thy dear Son, For the hope of heaven at last,
For the Spirit's victory won, For the crown when life is past,
Lord of all, to Thee we raise Songs of gratitude and praise.

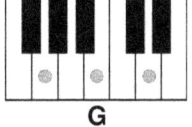
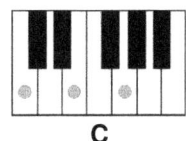
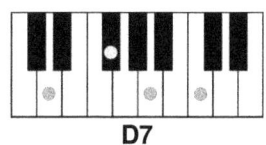

Give Me the Bible

Words by Priscilla Owens
Music by E. S. Lorenz

Give me the Bi-ble, star of glad-ness gleam-ing, To cheer the wan-derer, lone and tem-pest tossed,
No storm can hide that peace-ful ra-diance beam-ing, Since Je-sus came to seek and save the lost.

Refrain
Give me the Bi-ble, ho-ly mes-sage shin-ing, Thy light shall guide me in the nar-row way,
Pre-cept and prom-ise, law and love com-bin-ing, Till night shall van-ish in e-ter-nal day.

2. Give me the Bible when my heart is broken,
   When sin and grief have filled my soul with fear;
   Give me the precious words by Jesus spoken,
   Hold up faith's lamp to show my Savior near.
   (Refrain)

3. Give me the Bible, all my steps enlighten,
   Teach me the danger of these realms below;
   That lamp of safety, o'er the gloom shall brighten,
   That light alone the path of peace can show.
   (Refrain)

God Will Take Care of You

Words by Civilla Martin
Music by W. Stillman Martin

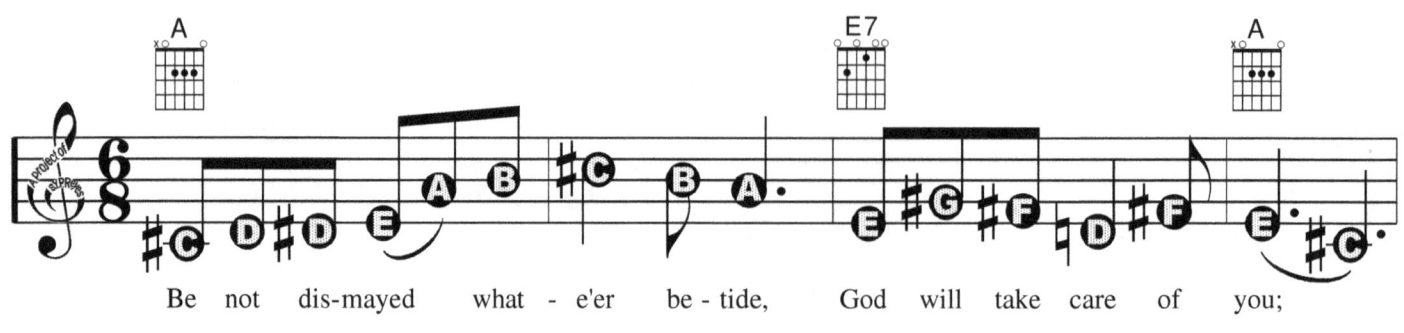

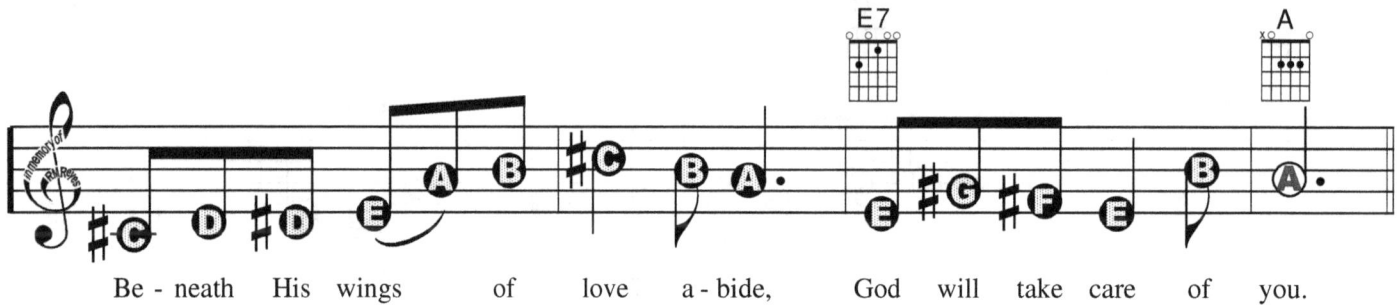

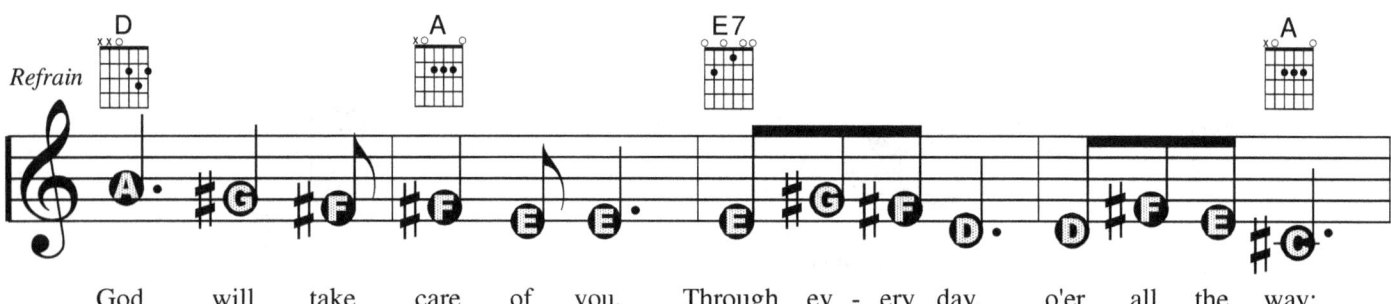

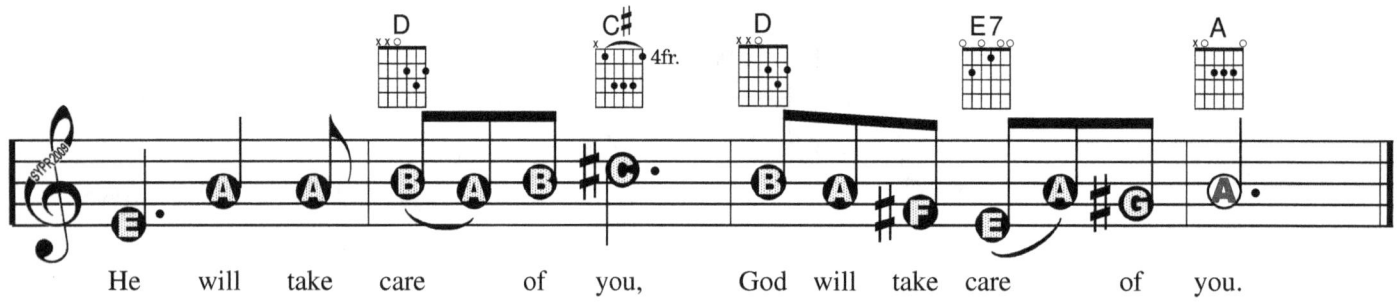

2. Through days of toil when your heart doth fail, God will take care of you;
   When dangers fierce your path assail, God will take care of you.
   (Refrain)

3. All you may need He will provide, God will take care of you;
   Nothing you ask will be denied, God will take care of you.
   (Refrain)

4. No matter what may be the test, God will take care of you;
   Lean, weary one, upon His breast, God will take care of you.
   (Refrain)

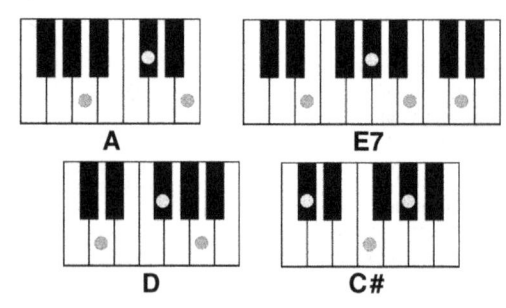

Hail Him the King of Glory

Words and music by Henry de Fluiter

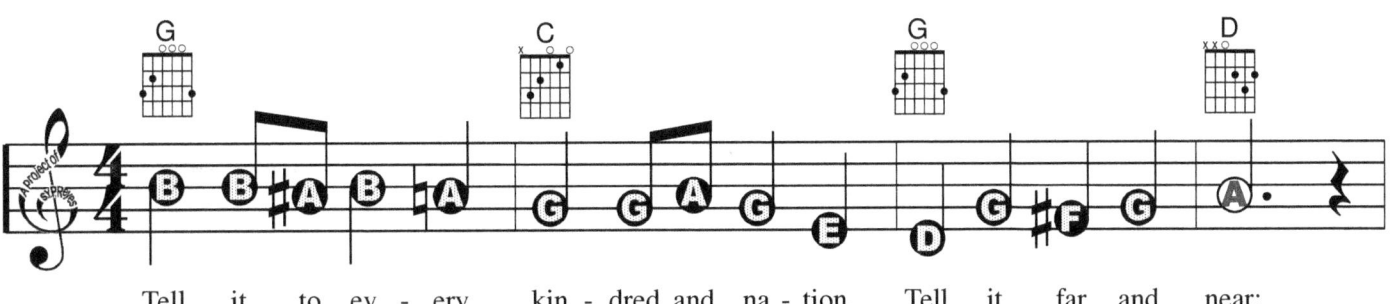

Tell it to ev - ery kin - dred and na - tion, Tell it far and near;

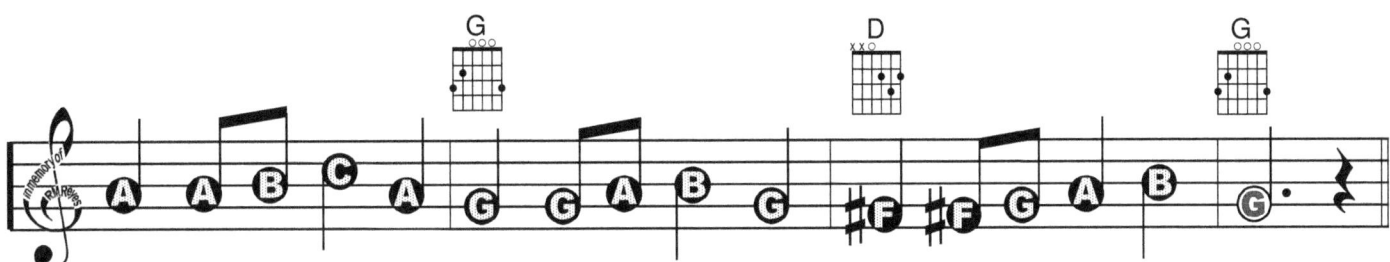

Earth's dark - est night will fade with the dawn - ing, Je - sus will soon ap - pear.

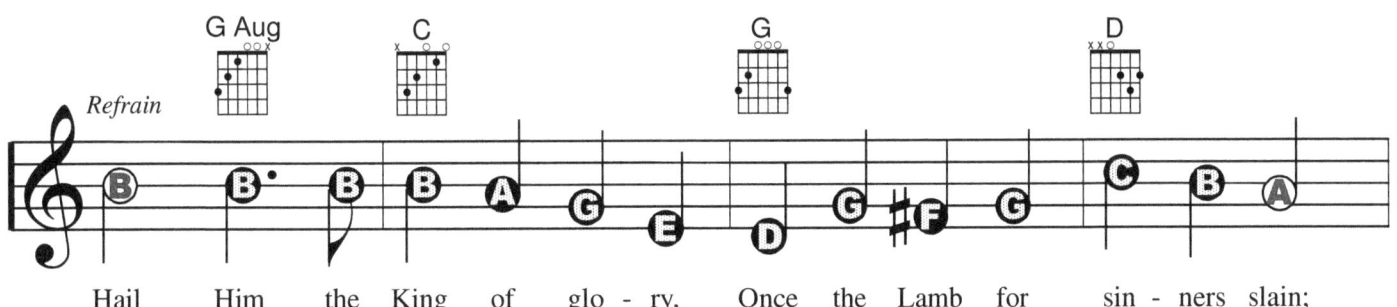

Refrain
Hail Him the King of glo - ry, Once the Lamb for sin - ners slain;

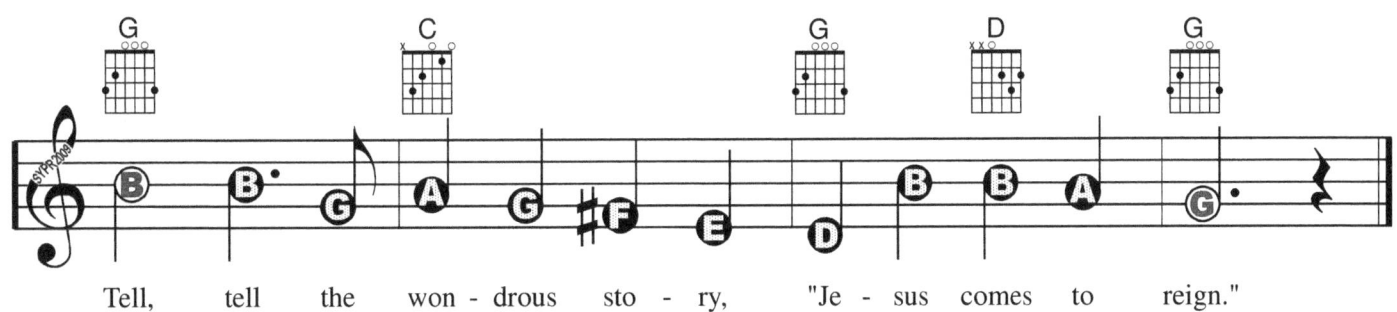

Tell, tell the won - drous sto - ry, "Je - sus comes to reign."

2. Nations again in strife and commotion,
   Warnings by the way;
   Signs in the heavens, unerring omens,
   Herald the glorious day.
   (Refrain)

3. Children of God look up with rejoicing;
   Shout and sing His praise;
   Blessed are they who, waiting and watching,
   Look for the dawning rays.
   (Refrain)

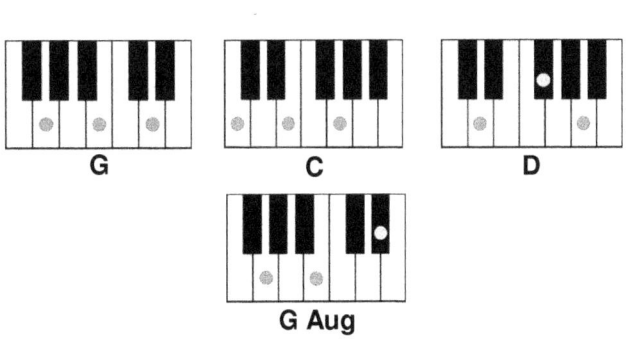

Hark! the Herald Angels Sing

Words by Charles Wesley

Tune by Felix Mendelssohn

2. Christ, by highest heav'n adored, Christ the everlasting Lord;
   In the manger born a king, While adoring angels sing,
   "Peace on earth, to men good will;" Bid the trembling soul be still,
   Christ on earth has come to dwell, Jesus, our Immanuel!
   (Refrain)

3. Hail! the heav'n-born Prince of Peace! Hail! the Sun of Righteousness!
   Life and light to all He brings, Ris'n with healing in His wings.
   Mild He lays His glory by, Born that man no more may die,
   Born to raise the sons of earth, Born to give them second birth,
   (Refrain)

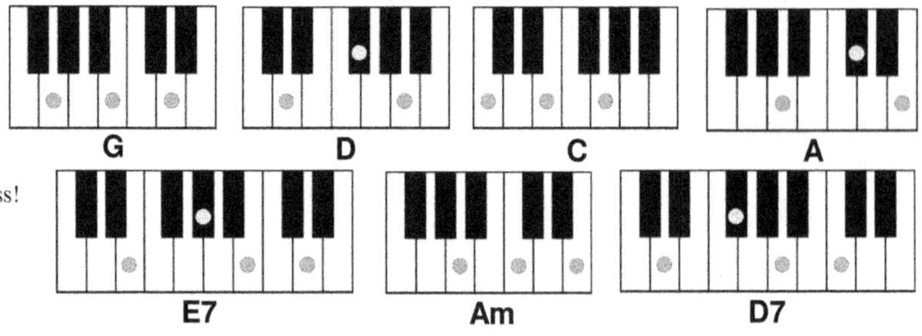

40

Have Thine Own Way, Lord

Words by Adelaide Pollard
Music by George Stebbins

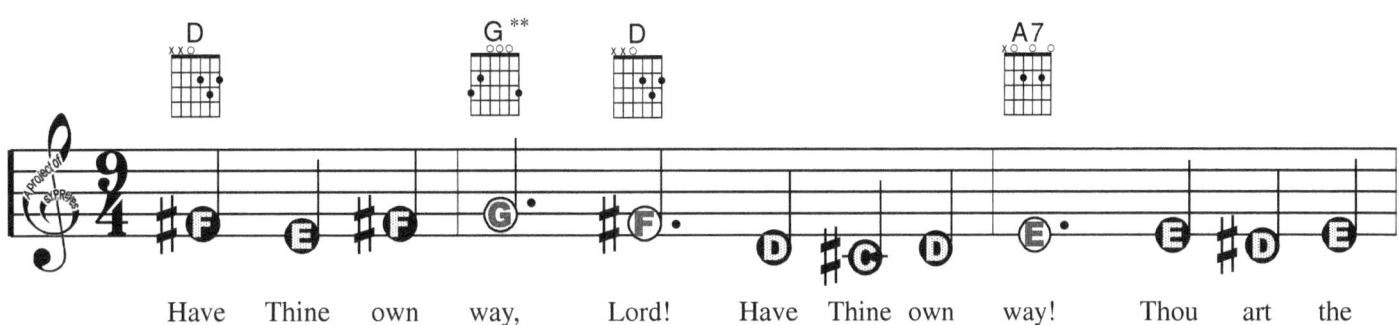

Have Thine own way, Lord! Have Thine own way! Thou art the

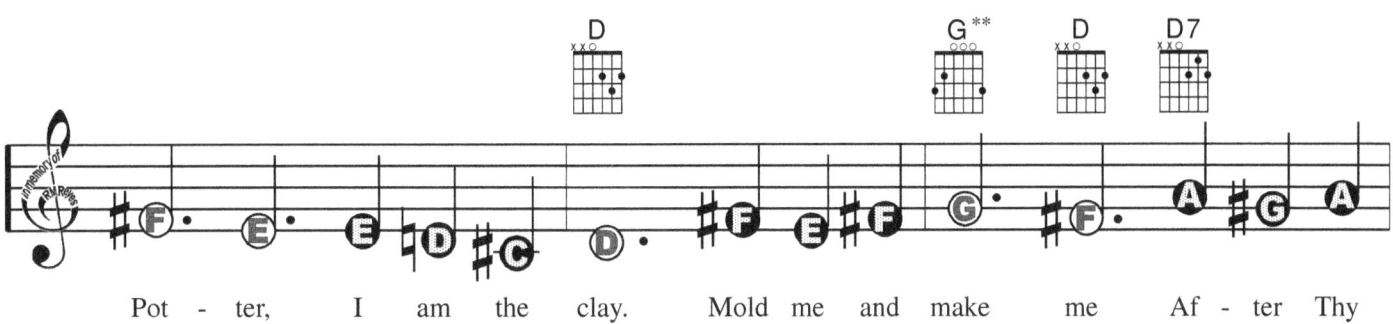

Pot - ter, I am the clay. Mold me and make me Af - ter Thy

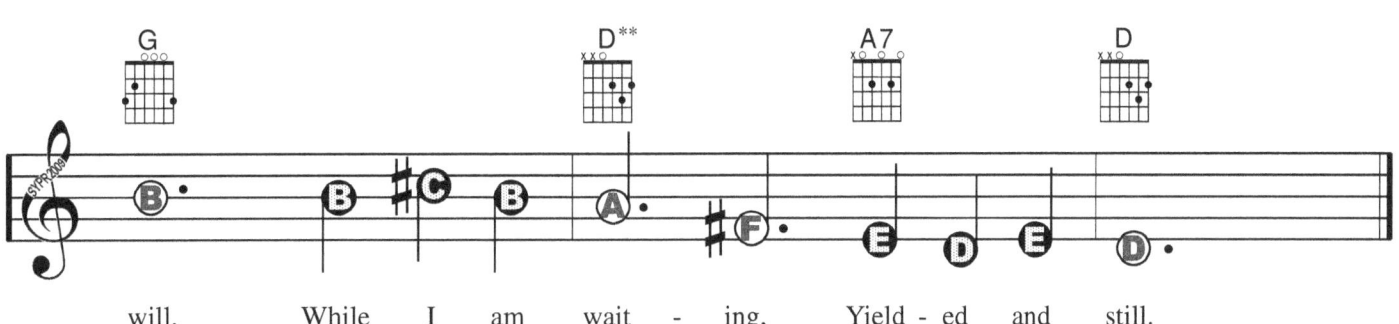

will, While I am wait - ing, Yield - ed and still.

2. Have Thine own way, Lord! Have Thine own way!
   Search me and try me, Master, today!
   Whiter than snow, Lord, Wash me just now,
   As in Thy presence Humbly I bow.

3. Have Thine own way, Lord! Have Thine own way!
   Wounded and weary Help me, I pray!
   Power--all power--Surely is Thine!
   Touch me and heal me, Savior divine!

4. Have Thine own way, Lord! Have Thine own way!
   Hold o'er my being Absolute sway!
   Fill with Thy Spirit Till all shall see
   Christ only, always, Living in me!

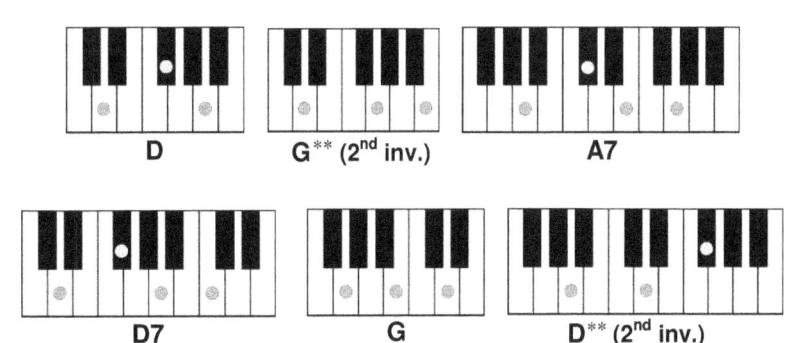

**On keyboard instrument, play second inversion

41

He Hideth My Soul

Words by Fanny Crosby
Music by William Kirkpatrick

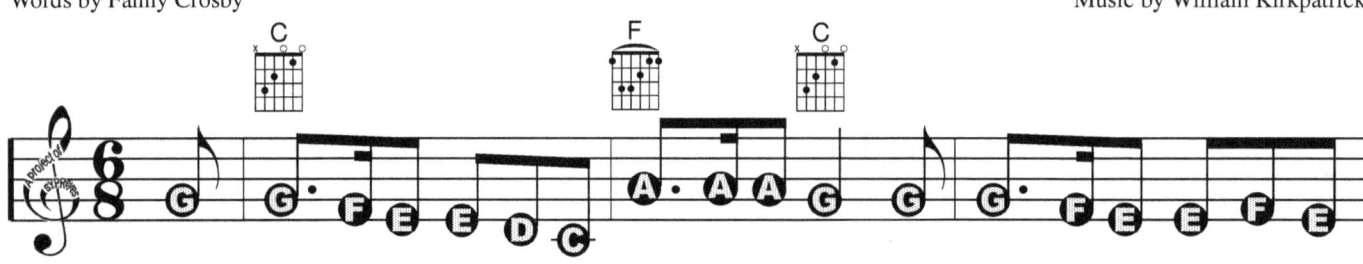
A won-der-ful Sav-ior is Je-sus my Lord, A won-der-ful Sav-ior to

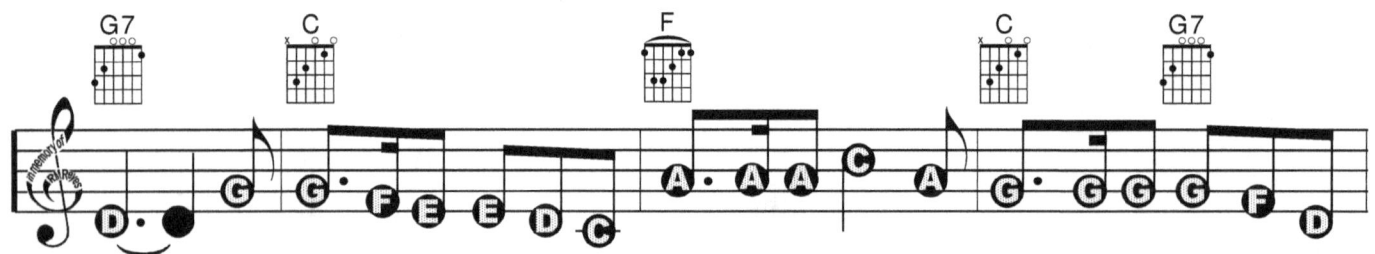
me, He hid-eth my soul in the cleft of the rock, Where riv-ers of plea-sure I

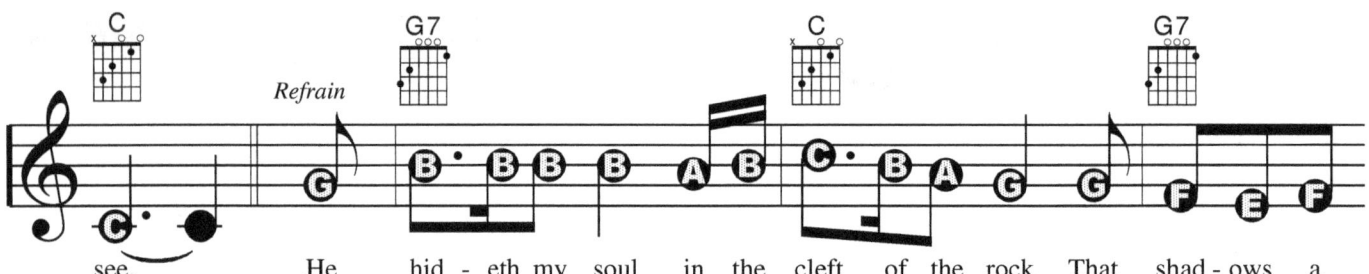
Refrain
see. He hid-eth my soul in the cleft of the rock That shad-ows a

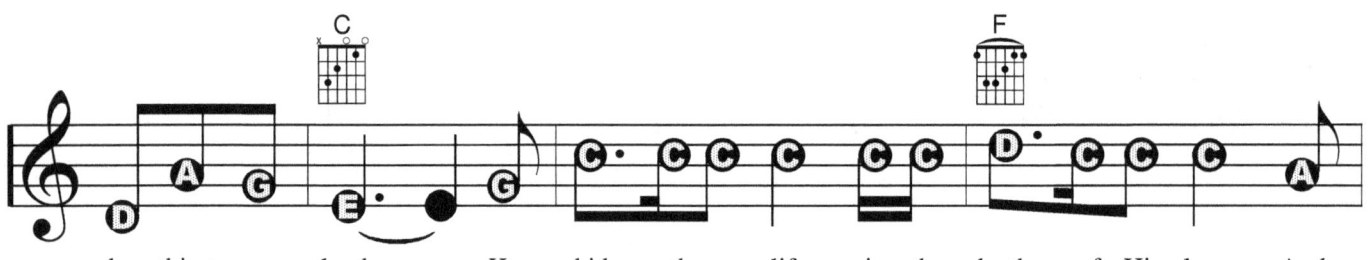
dry, thirst-y land; He hid-eth my life in the depths of His love, And

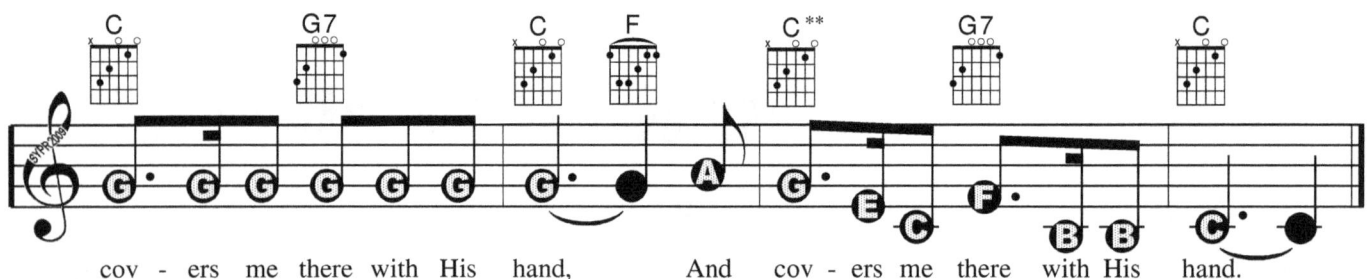
cov-ers me there with His hand, And cov-ers me there with His hand.

2. A wonderful Savior is Jesus my Lord, He taketh my burden away,
He holdeth me up, and I shall not be moved, He giveth me strength as my day.
(Refrain)

3. With numberless blessings each moment He crowns, And filled with His fullness divine,
I sing in my rapture, Oh glory to God For such a Redeemer as mine.
(Refrain)

4. When clothed in His brightness, transported I rise To meet Him in clouds of the sky,
His perfect salvation, His wonderful love, I'll shout with the millions on high.
(Refrain)

**On keyboard instrument, play second inversion

He Leadeth Me

Words by J. H. Gilmore
Music by William Bradbury

He lead-eth me! O bless-ed thought! O words with heav'n-ly com-fort fraught!

What-e'er I do, where-e'er I be, Still 'tis God's hand that lead-eth me.

Refrain

He lead-eth me, He lead-eth me, By His own hand He lead-eth me;

His faith-ful fol-lower I would be, For by His hand He lead-eth me.

2. Sometimes 'mid scenes of deepest gloom,
   Sometimes where Eden's bowers bloom,
   By waters still, o'er troubled sea--
   Still 'tis His hand that leadeth me!
   (Refrain)

3. Lord, I would clasp my hand in Thine,
   Nor ever murmur nor repine;
   Content, whatever lot I see,
   Since 'tis my God that leadeth me.
   (Refrain)

4. And when my task on earth is done,
   When, by Thy grace, the vict'ry's won,
   E'en death's cold wave I will not flee,
   Since God through Jordan leadeth me.
   (Refrain)

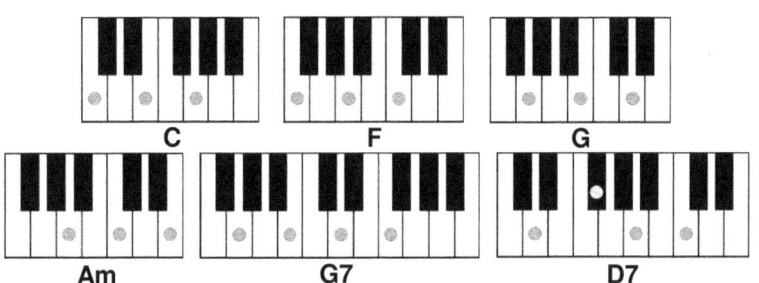

43

Higher Ground

Words by Johnson Oatman, Jr.
Music by Charles Gabriel

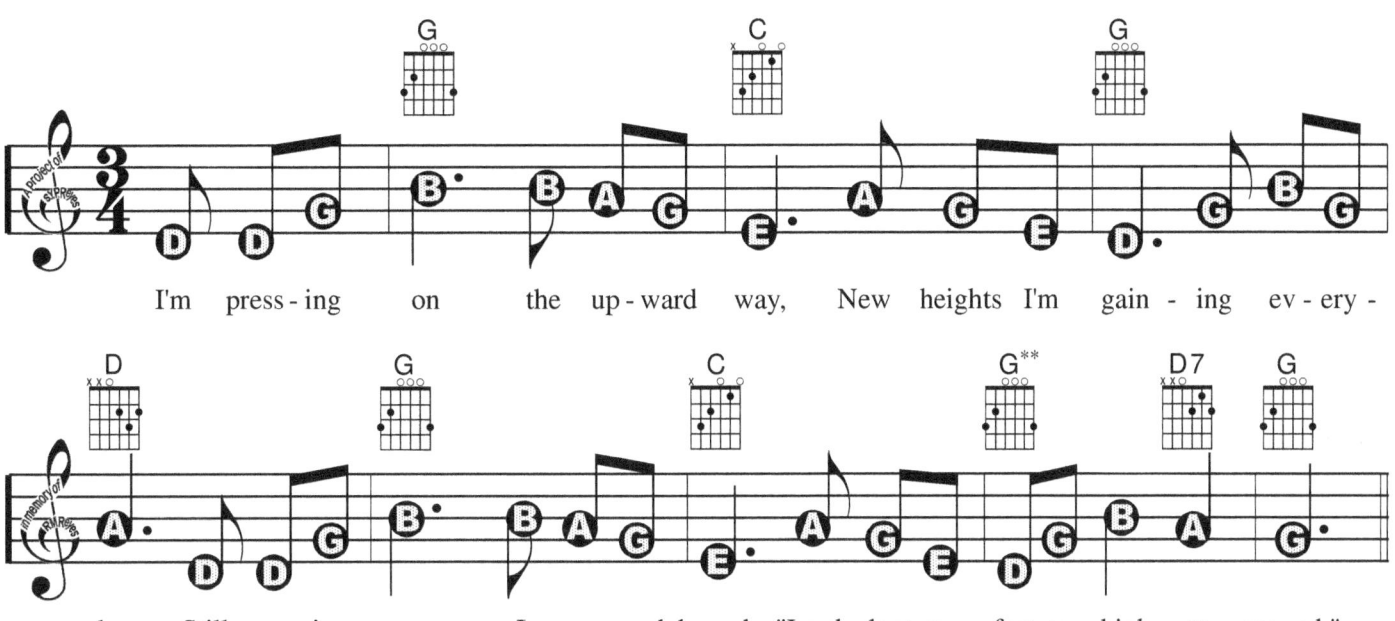

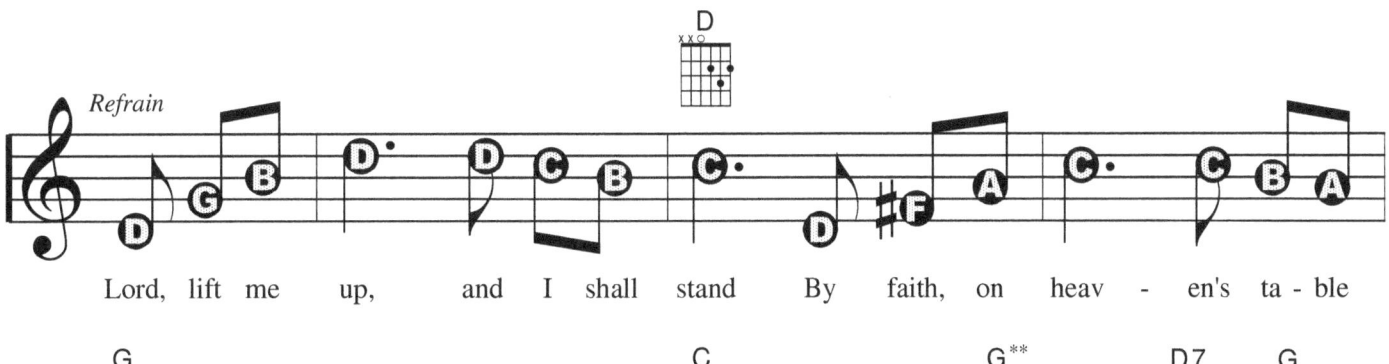

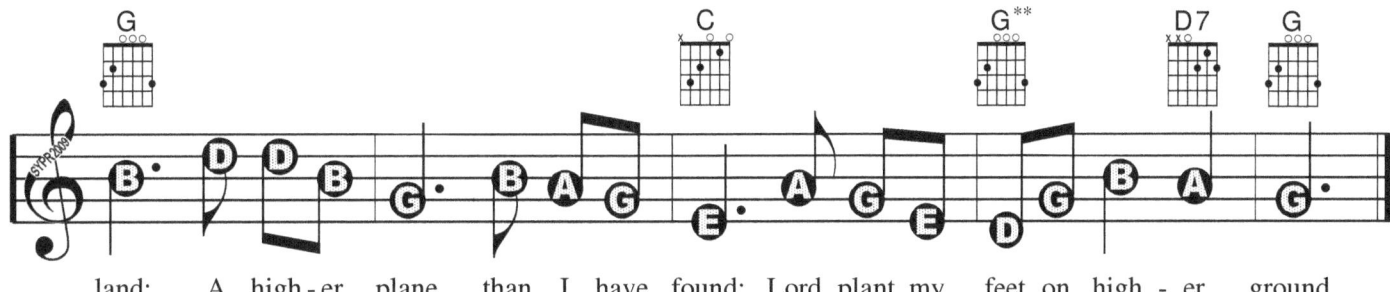

2. My heart has no desire to stay Where doubts arise and fears dismay;
Though some may dwell where these abound, My prayer, my aim is higher ground.
(Refrain)

3. I want to live above the world, Though Satan's darts at me are hurled;
For faith has caught a joyful sound, The song of saints on higher ground.
(Refrain)

4. I want to scale the utmost height, And catch a gleam of glory bright;
But still I'll pray till heaven I've found, "Lord, lead me on to higher ground."
(Refrain)

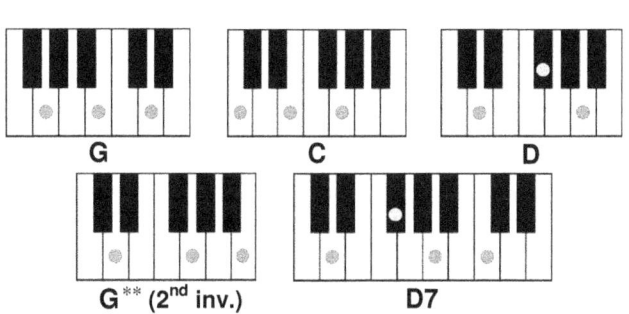

**On keyboard instrument, play second inversion

Hold Fast Till I Come

Words and music by F. E. Belden

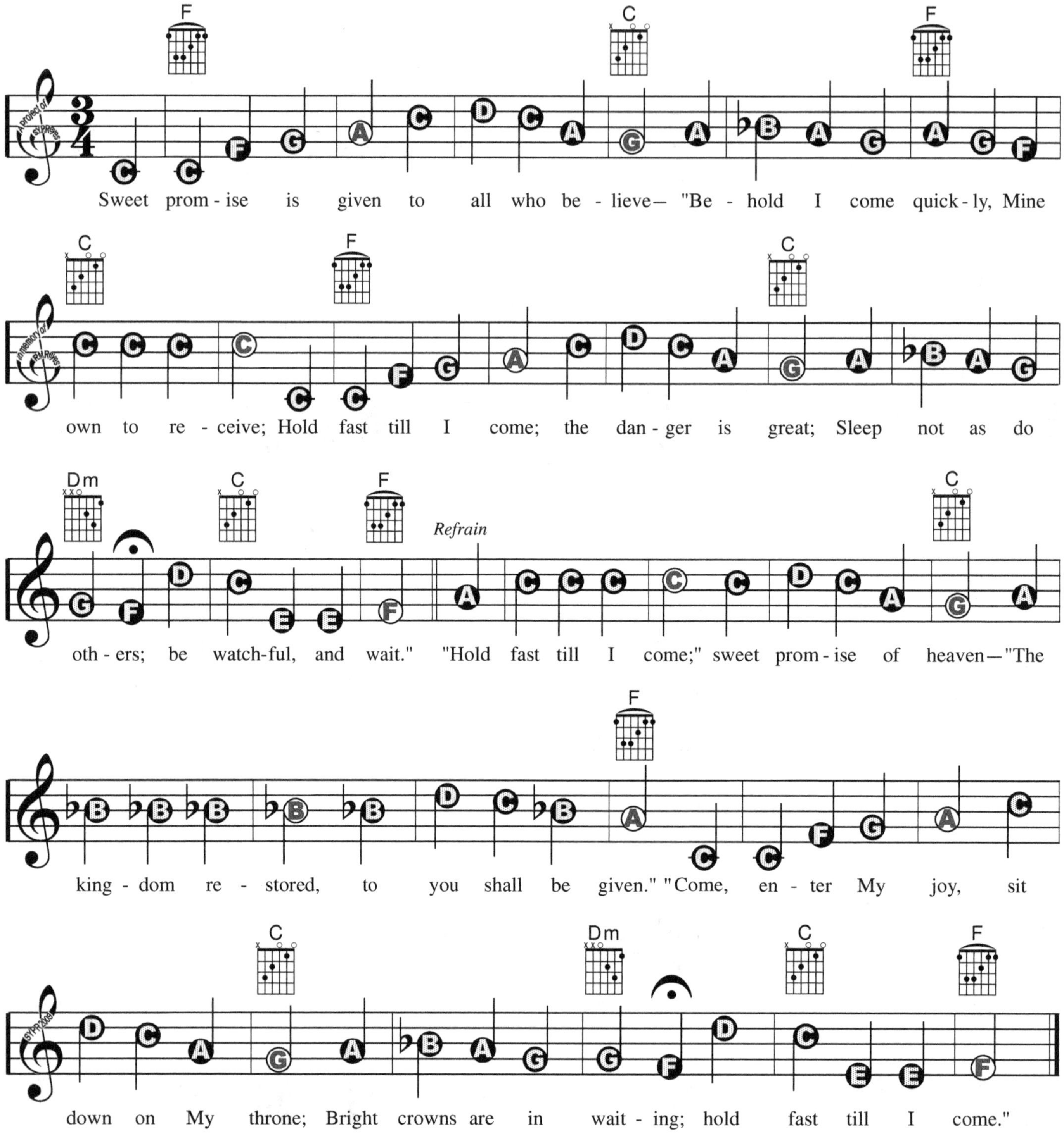

F C F
Sweet prom - ise is given to all who be - lieve— "Be - hold I come quick - ly, Mine
C F C
own to re - ceive; Hold fast till I come; the dan - ger is great; Sleep not as do
Dm C F C
Refrain
oth - ers; be watch-ful, and wait." "Hold fast till I come;" sweet prom - ise of heaven—"The
F
king - dom re - stored, to you shall be given." "Come, en - ter My joy, sit
C Dm C F
down on My throne; Bright crowns are in wait - ing; hold fast till I come."

2. We'll "watch unto prayer" with lamps burning bright;
He comes to all others a "thief in the night."
We know He is near, but know not the day--
As spring shows that summer is not far away.
(Refrain)

3. Yes! this is our hope, 'tis built on His word--
The glorious appearing of Jesus, our Lord;
Of promises all, it stands as the sum:
"Behold I come quickly, hold fast till I come."
(Refrain)

F
C
Dm

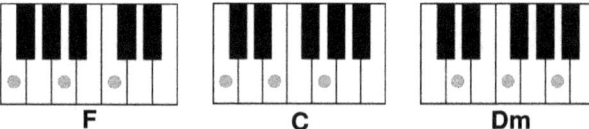

Holy, Holy, Holy

Words by Reginald Heber
Music by John Dykes

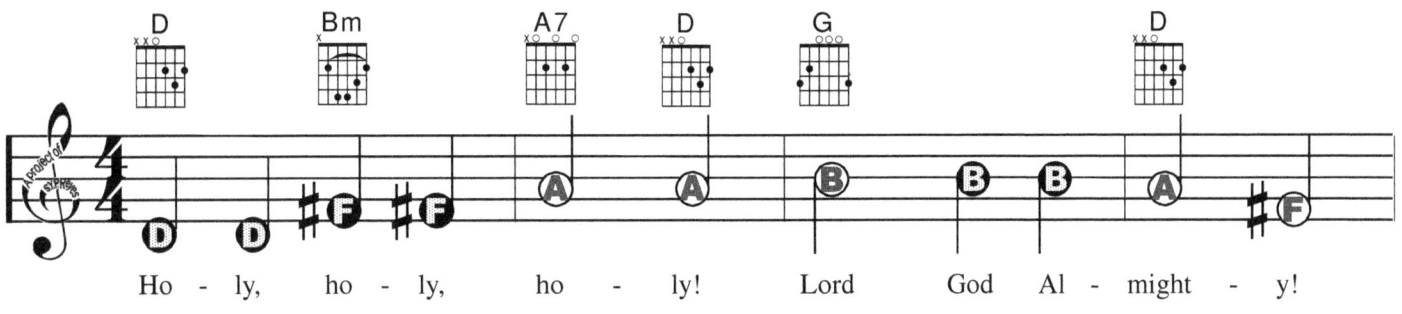
Ho - ly, ho - ly, ho - ly! Lord God Al - might - y!

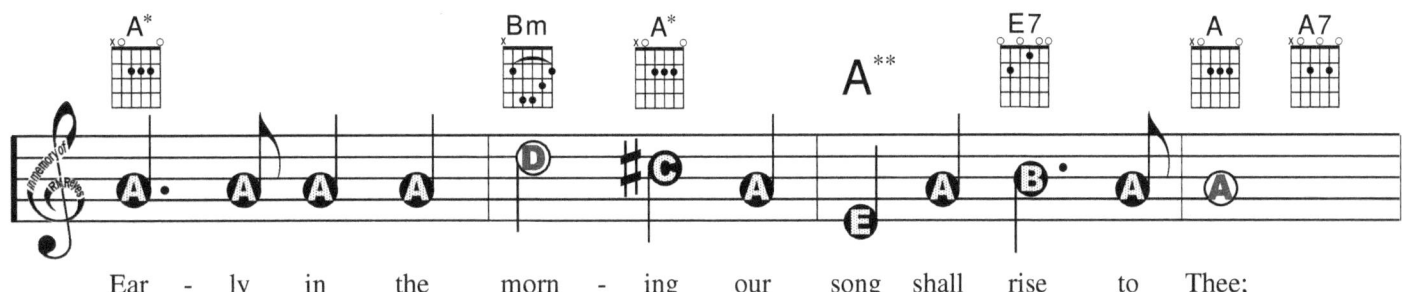
Ear - ly in the morn - ing our song shall rise to Thee;

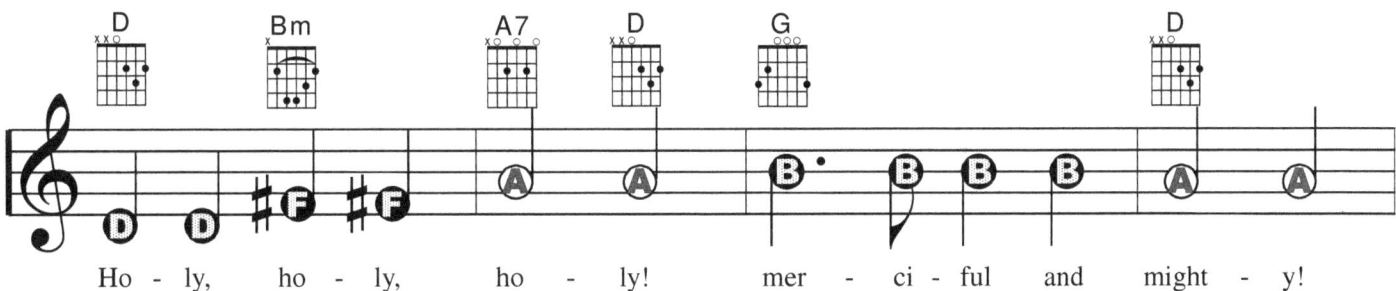
Ho - ly, ho - ly, ho - ly! mer - ci - ful and might - y!

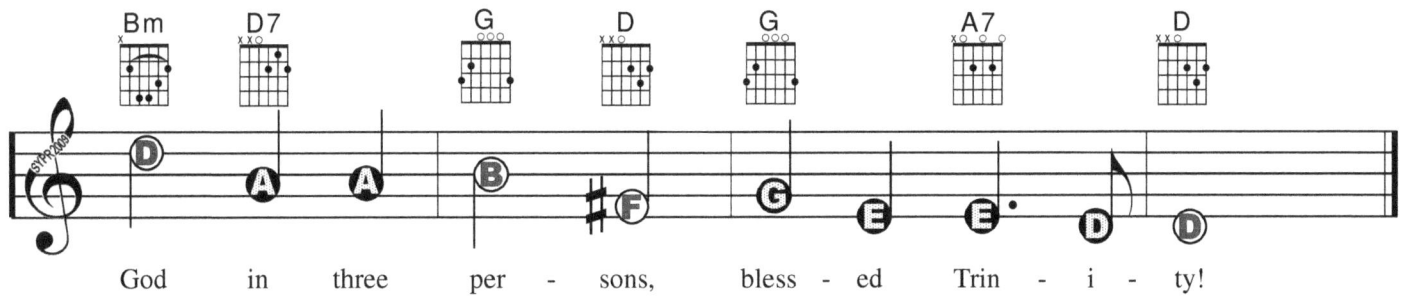
God in three per - sons, bless - ed Trin - i - ty!

2. Holy, holy, holy! Angels adore Thee,
   Casting down their bright crowns around the glassy sea;
   Thousands and ten thousands worship low before Thee,
   Which wert, and art, and evermore shalt be.

3. Holy, holy, holy! Though darkness hide Thee,
   Though the eye of man Thy great glory may not see;
   Only Thou art holy; there is none beside Thee,
   Perfect in pow'r, in love and purity.

4. Holy, holy, holy! Lord God Almighty!
   All Thy works shall praise Thy name in earth and sky and sea;
   Holy, holy, holy! Merciful and mighty!
   God in three persons, blessed Trinity!

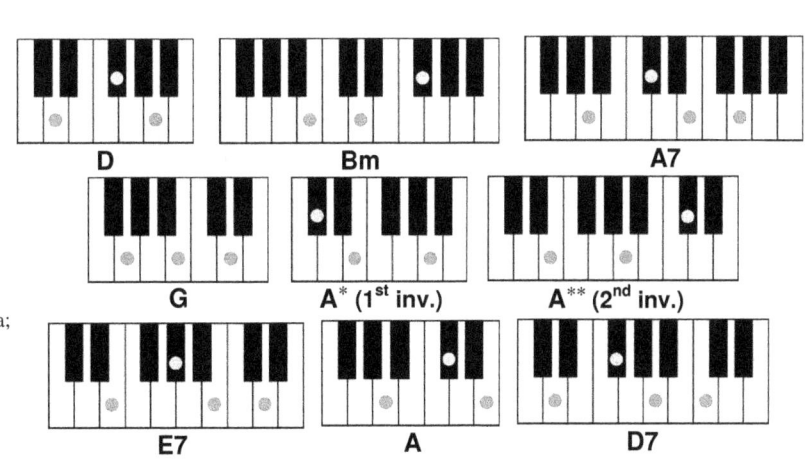

*On keyboard instrument, play first inversion
**On keyboard instrument, play second inversion

How Sweet Are the Tidings

Author unkonwn
Adapted from a tune by John Thomas

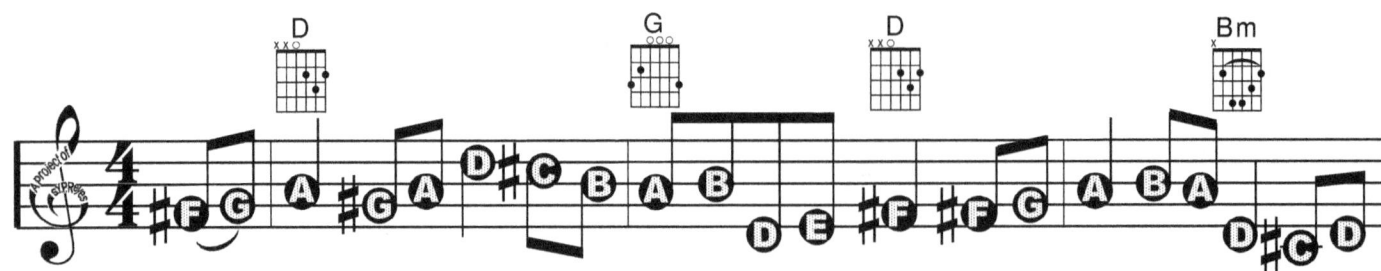

How sweet are the tid-ings that greet the pil-grim's ear, As he wan-ders in ex - ile from

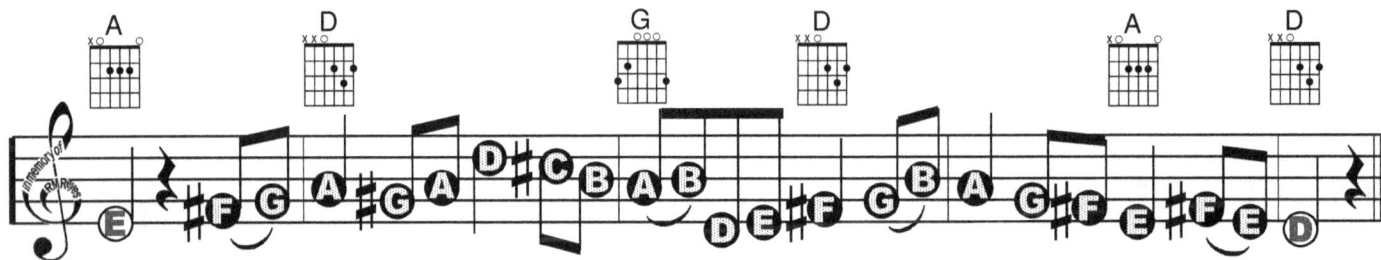

home! Soon, soon will the Sav-ior in glo - ry ap-pear, And soon will the king - dom come.

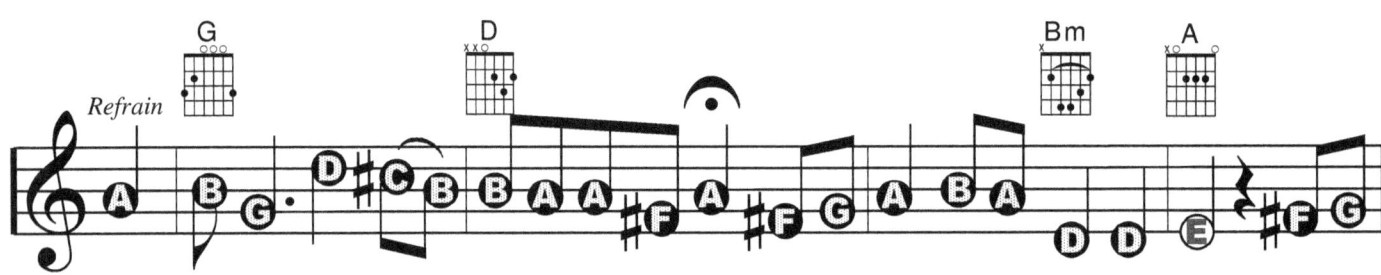

Refrain

He's com-ing, com - ing, com-ing soon I know, Com-ing back to this earth a - gain; and the

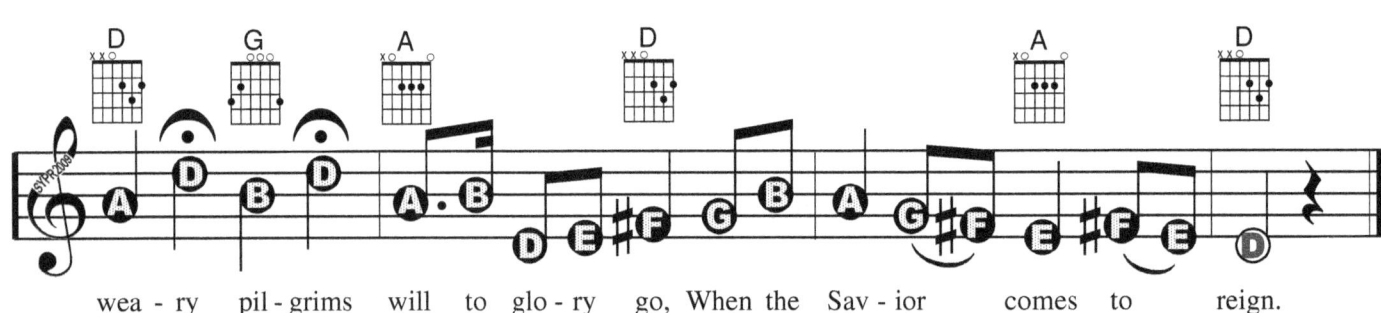

wea - ry pil - grims will to glo - ry go, When the Sav - ior comes to reign.

2. The mossy old graves where the pilgrims sleep
Shall be open as wide as before,
And the millions that sleep in the mighty deep
Shall live on this earth once more.
(Refrain)

3. There we'll meet ne'er to part in our happy Eden home,
Sweet songs of redemption we'll sing;
From the north, from the south, all the ransomed shall come,
And worship our heavenly King.
(Refrain)

4. Hallelujah, Amen! hallelujah again!
Soon, if faithful, we all shall be there;
O, be watchful, be hopeful, be joyful till then,
And a crown of bright glory we'll wear.
(Refrain)

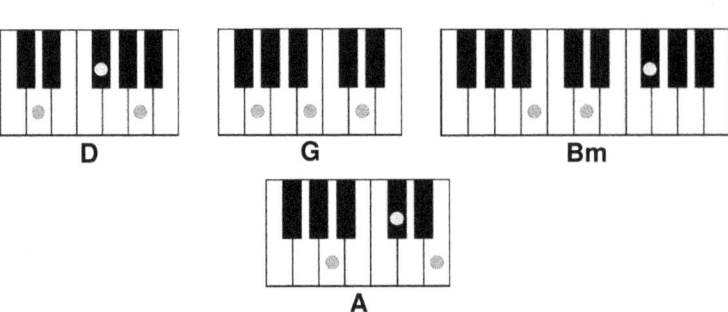

48

I Hear Thy Welcome Voice

Words and music by Lewis Hartsough

2. Though coming weak and vile, Thou dost my strength assure;
   Thou dost my vileness fully cleanse, Till spotless all, and pure.
   (Refrain)

3. 'Tis Jesus calls me on To perfect faith and love,
   To perfect hope, and peace, and trust, For earth and heav'n above.
   (Refrain)

4. All hail, atoning blood! All hail, redeeming grace!
   All hail! the gift of Christ, our Lord, Our Strength and Righteousness.
   (Refrain)

I Know Whom I Have Believed

Words by Daniel Whittle
Music by James McGranahan

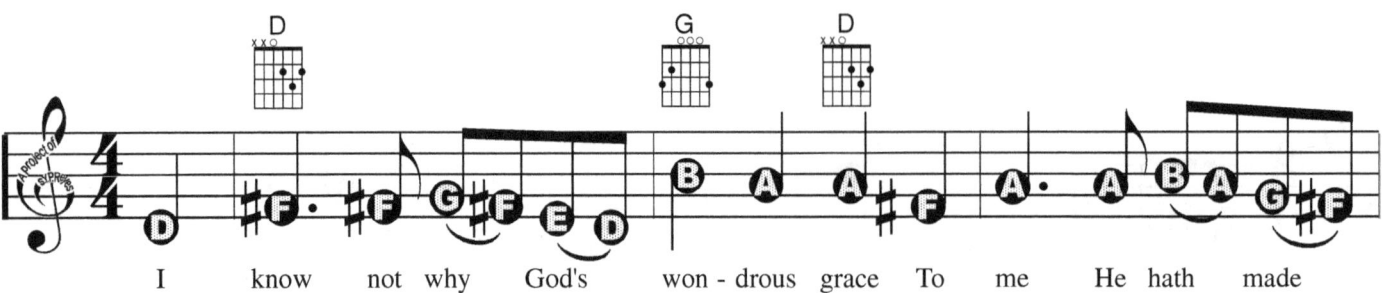
I know not why God's won-drous grace To me He hath made

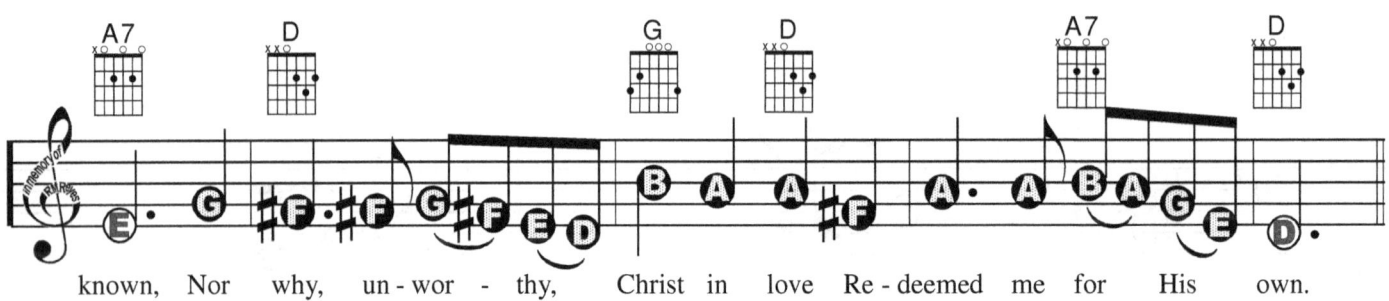
known, Nor why, un-wor-thy, Christ in love Re-deemed me for His own.

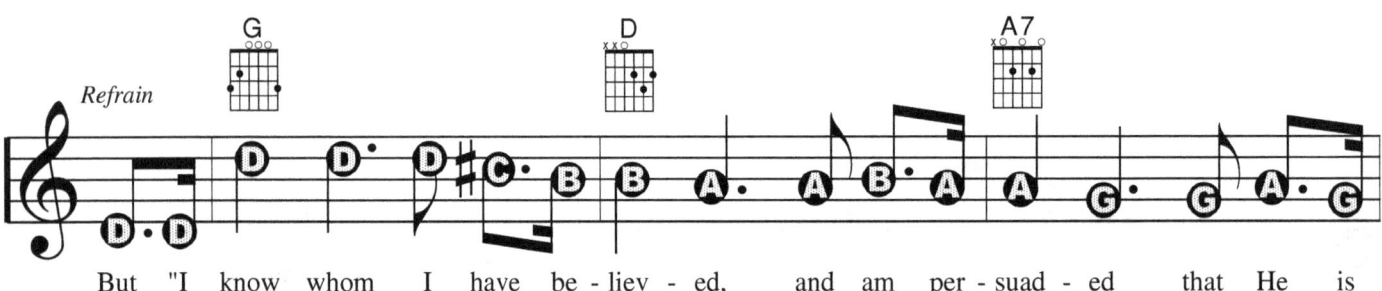
Refrain
But "I know whom I have be-liev-ed, and am per-suad-ed that He is

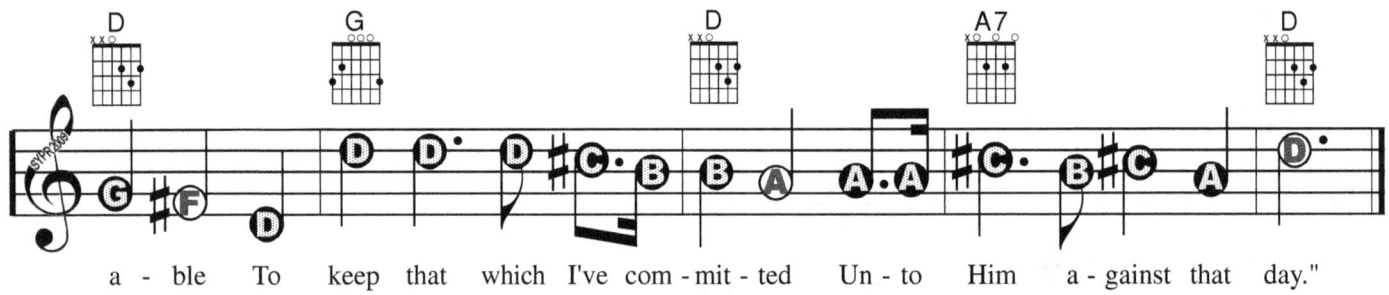
a-ble To keep that which I've com-mit-ted Un-to Him a-gainst that day."

2. I know not how this saving faith To me He did impart,
   Nor how believing in His word Wrought peace within my heart.
   (Refrain)

3. I know not how the Spirit moves, Convincing men of sin,
   Revealing Jesus through the word, Creating faith in Him.
   (Refrain)

4. I know not when my Lord may come, At night or noonday fair,
   Nor if I walk the vale with Him, Or meet Him in the air.
   (Refrain)

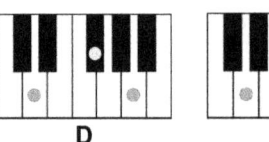
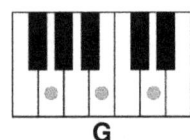
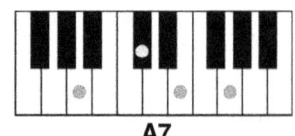

I Love to Tell the Story

Words by Katherine Hankey
Music by William Fischer

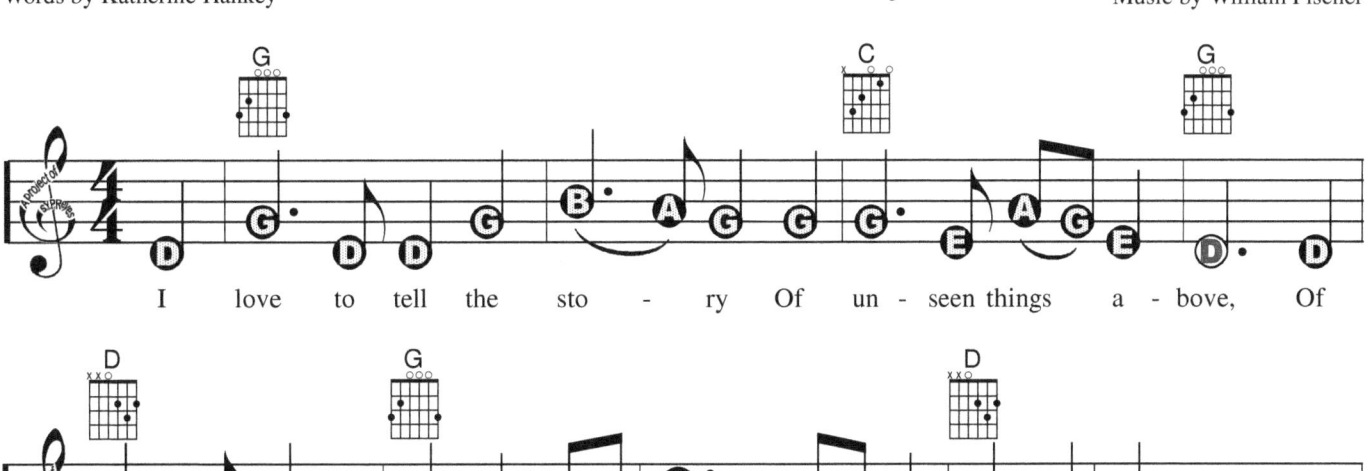

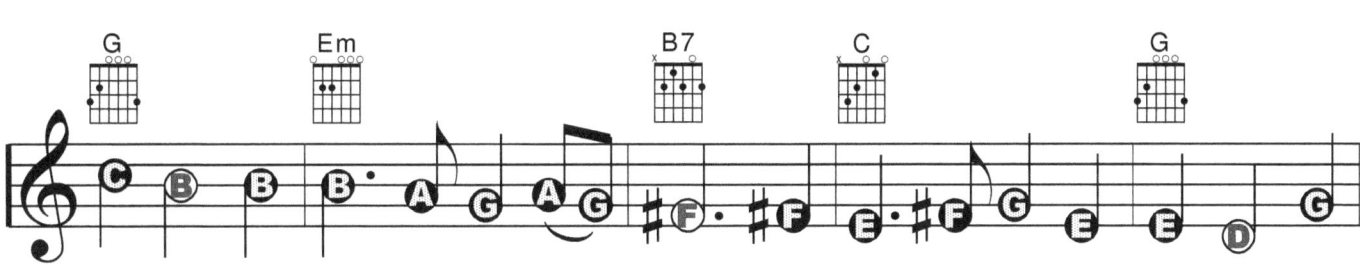

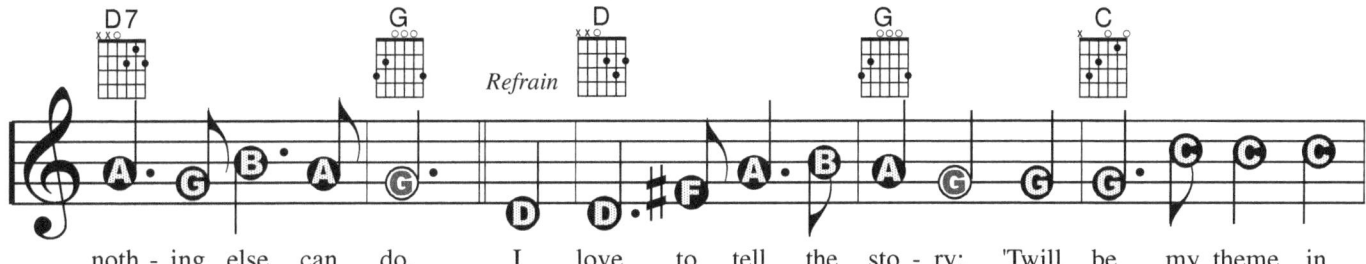

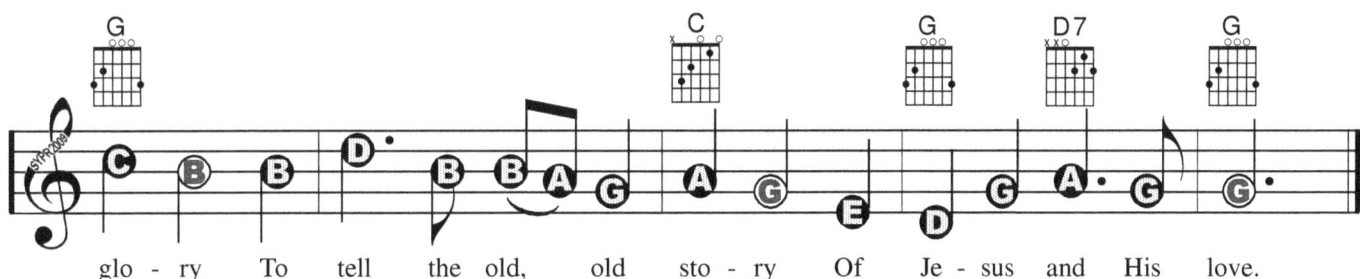

2. I love to tell the story; More wonderful it seems
Than all the golden fancies Of all our golden dreams;
I love to tell the story, It did so much for me,
And that is just the reason I tell it now to thee.
(Refrain)

3. I love to tell the story; 'Tis pleasant to repeat
What seems each time I tell it, More wonderfully sweet;
I love to tell the story, For some have never heard
The message of salvation From God's own holy word.
(Refrain)

4. I love to tell the story; For those who know it best
Seem hungering and thirsting To hear it like the rest;
And when in scenes of glory I sing the new, new song,
'Twill be the old, old story That I have loved so long.
(Refrain)

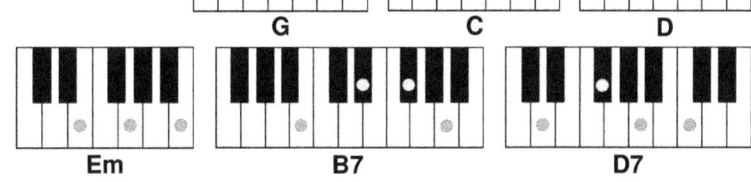

I Must Tell Jesus

Words and music by Elisha Hoffman

2. I must tell Jesus all of my troubles,
   He is a kind, compassionate Friend;
   If I but ask Him, He will deliver,
   Makes of my troubles quickly an end.
   (Refrain)

3. O how the world to evil allures me!
   O how my heart is tempted to sin!
   I must tell Jesus, and He will help me
   Over the world the vict'ry to win.
   (Refrain)

**On keyboard instrument, play second inversion

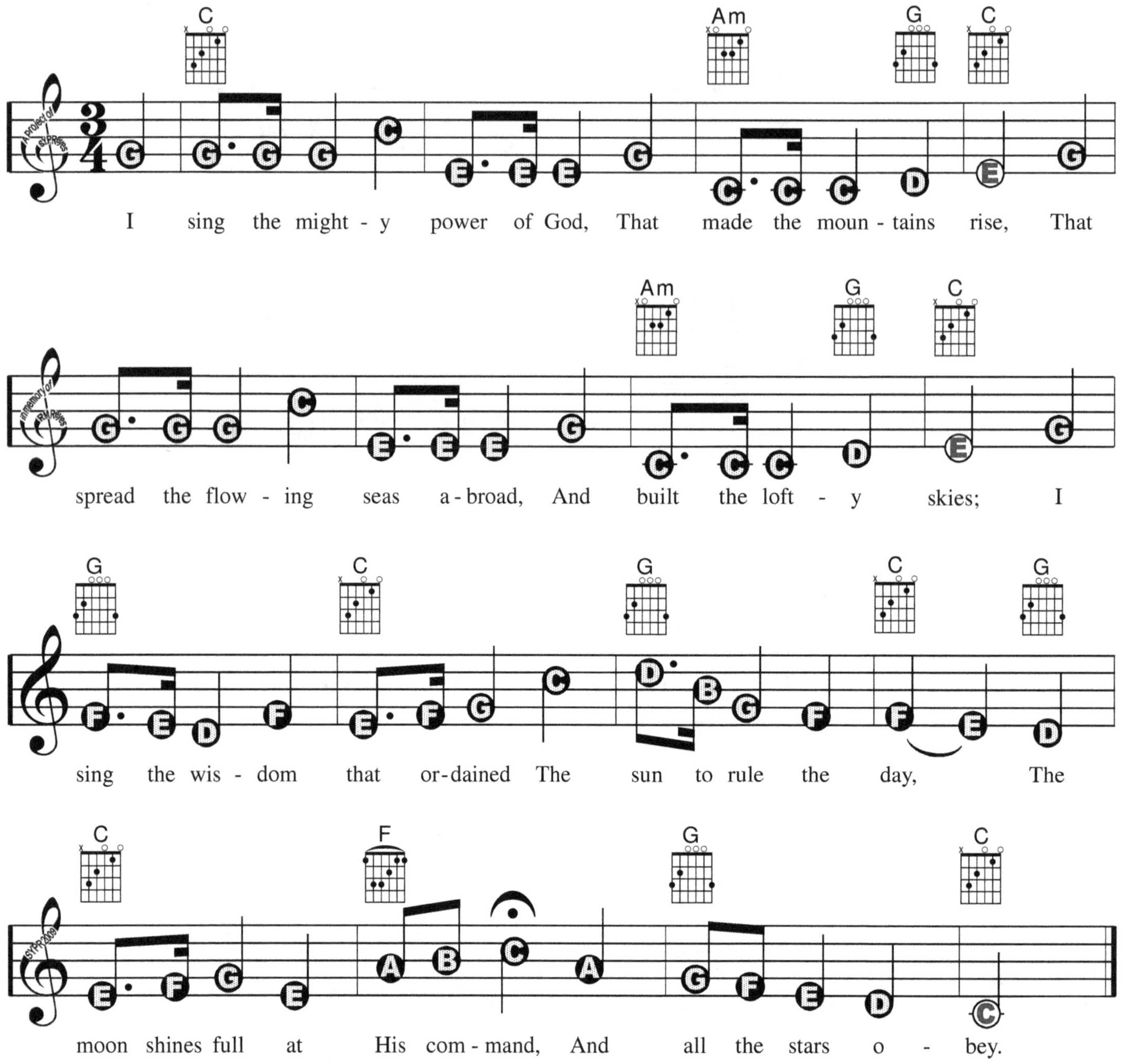

I Sing the Mighty Power of God

Words by Isaac Watts

Music by G. F. Root

C Am G C
I sing the might - y power of God, That made the moun - tains rise, That
Am G C
spread the flow - ing seas a - broad, And built the loft - y skies; I
G C G C G
sing the wis - dom that or - dained The sun to rule the day, The
C F G C
moon shines full at His com - mand, And all the stars o - bey.

2. I sing the goodness of the Lord, That filled the earth with food;
He formed the creatures with His word, And then pronounced them good.
Lord, how Thy wonders are displayed Where'er I turn my eye!
If I survey the ground I tread, Or gaze upon the sky!

3. There's not a plant or flower below But makes Thy glories known;
And clouds arise, and tempests blow, By order from Thy throne.
Creatures that borrow life from Thee Are subject to Thy care;
There's not a place where we can flee But God is present there.

C
Am
G
F

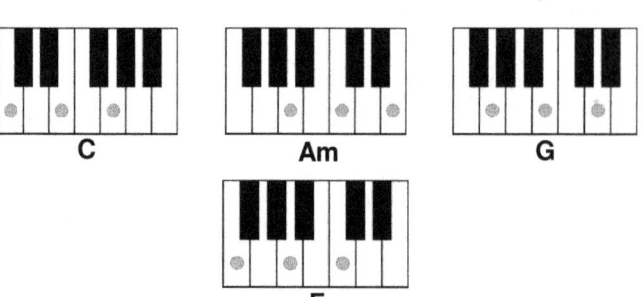

I Surrender All

Words by J. W. Van DeVenter
Music by W. S. Weeden

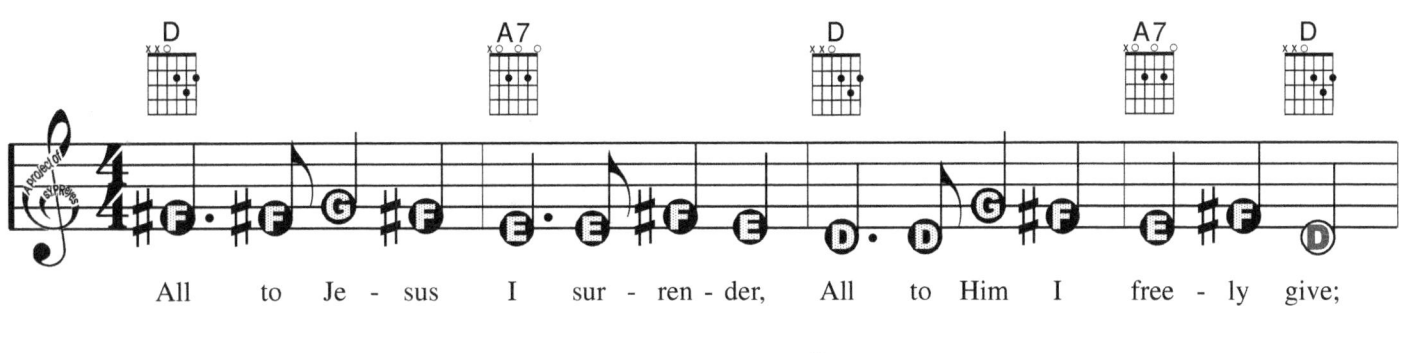

All to Je - sus I sur - ren - der, All to Him I free - ly give;

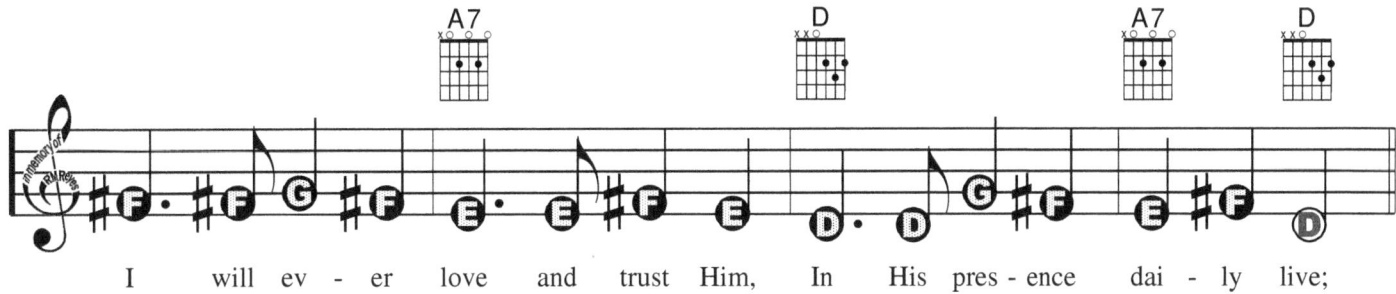

I will ev - er love and trust Him, In His pres - ence dai - ly live;

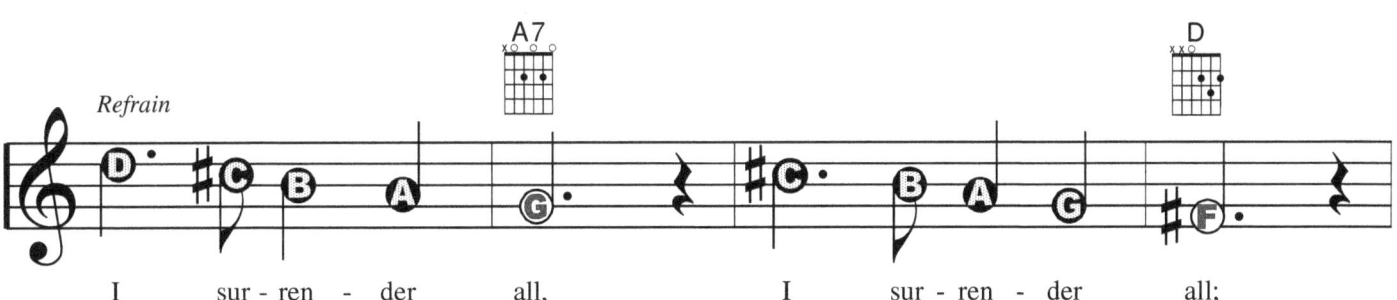

Refrain
I sur - ren - der all, I sur - ren - der all;

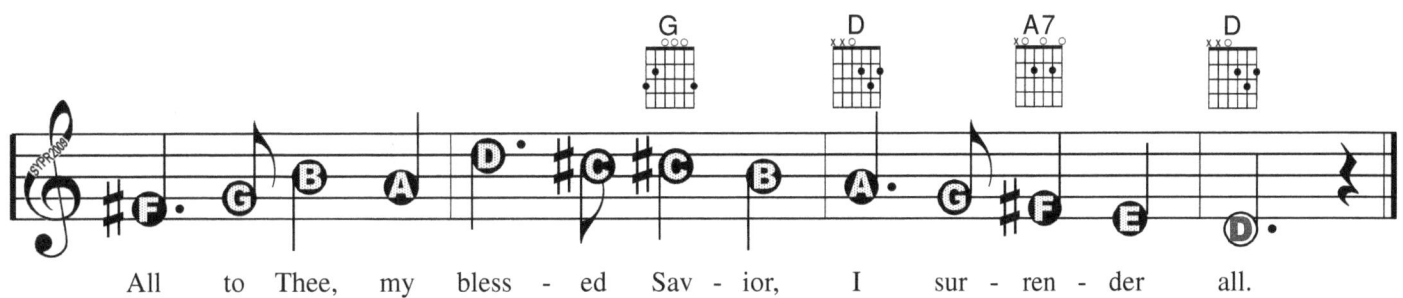

All to Thee, my bless - ed Sav - ior, I sur - ren - der all.

2. All to Jesus I surrender; Humbly at His feet I bow,
Worldly pleasures all forsaken; Take me, Jesus, take me now;
(Refrain)

3. All to Jesus I surrender; Make me, Savior, wholly Thine;
Let me feel the Holy Spirit, Truly know that Thou art mine;
(Refrain)

4. All to Jesus I surrender; Now I feel the sacred flame.
O the joy of full salvation! Glory, glory to His name!
(Refrain)

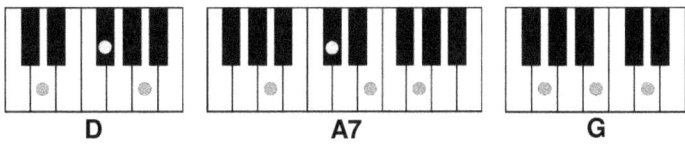

55

I Will Follow Thee

Words and music by James Lawson Elginburg

2. Though the road be rough and thorny, Trackless as the foaming sea,
Thou hast trod the way before me, And I'll gladly follow Thee.
(Refrain)

3. Though I meet with tribulations, Sorely tempted though I be;
I remember Thou wast tempted, And rejoice to follow Thee.
(Refrain)

4. Though Thou leadest me through affliction, Poor, forsaken though I be;
Thou wast destitute, afflicted, And I only follow Thee.
(Refrain)

5. Though to Jordan's rolling billows, Cold and deep, Thou leadest me,
Thou hast crossed the waves before me, And I still will follow Thee.
(Refrain)

**On keyboard instrument, play second inversion

In a Little While We're Going Home

Words and music by Eliza Hewitt

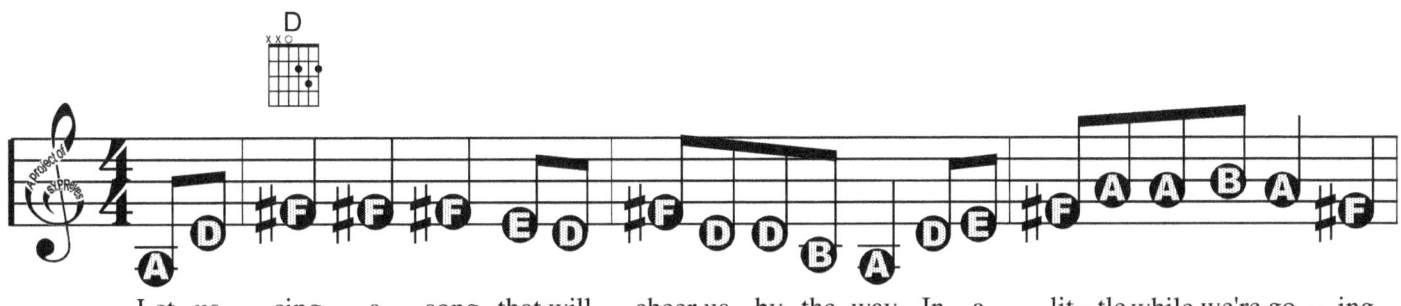
Let us sing a song that will cheer us by the way, In a lit-tle while we're go-ing

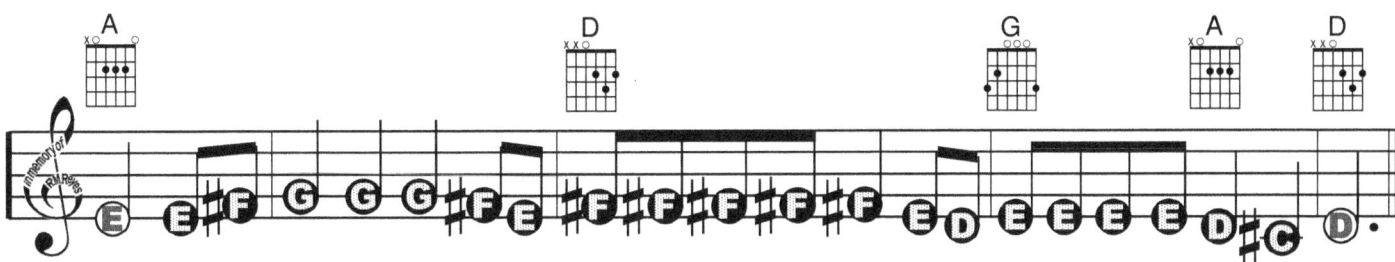
home; For the night will end in the ev-er-last-ing day, In a lit-tle while we're go-ing home.

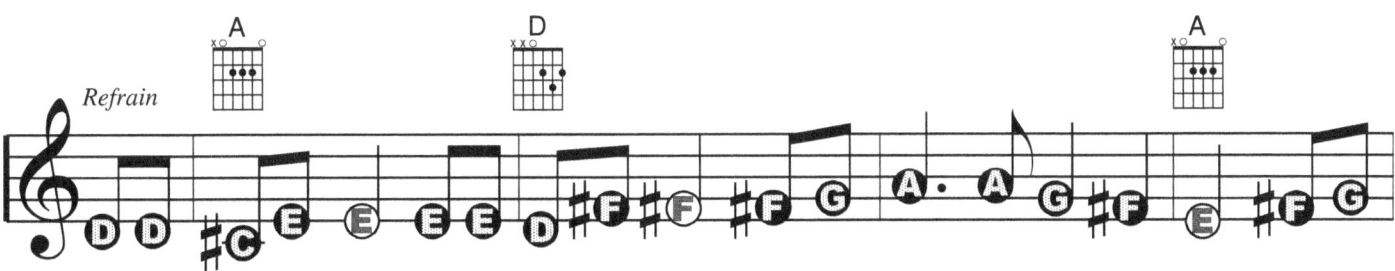
Refrain
In a lit-tle while, In a lit-tle while, We shall cross the bil-low's foam; we shall

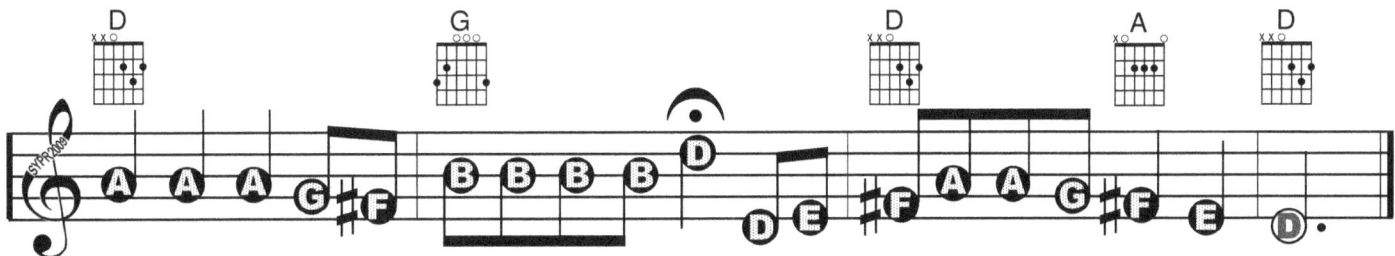
meet at last, When the storm-y winds are past, In a lit-tle while we're go-ing home.

2. We will do the work that our hands may find to do,
   In a little while we're going home;
   And the grace of God will our daily strength renew,
   In a little while we're going home.
   (Refrain)

3. We will smooth the path for some weary, way-worn feet,
   In a little while we're going home;
   And may loving hearts spread around an influence sweet!
   In a little while we're going home.
   (Refrain)

4. There's a rest beyond, there's relief from every care,
   In a little while we're going home;
   And no tears shall fall in that city bright and fair,
   In a little while we're going home.
   (Refrain)

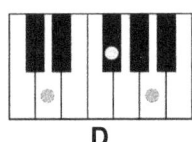
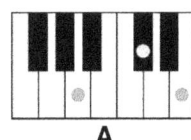
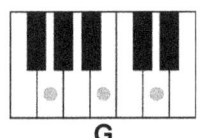

It Came Upon the Midnight Clear

Words by Edmund Sears
Music by Richard Willis

It came up-on the mid-night clear, That glo-rious song of old, From an-gels bend-ing near the earth To touch their harps of gold: "Peace on the earth, good will to men, From heav-en's all gra-cious King;" The world in sol-emn still-ness lay, To hear the an-gels sing.

2. Still through the cloven skies they come, With peaceful wings unfurled,
   And still their heavenly music floats O'er all the weary world;
   Above its sad and lowly plains They bend on hovering wing,
   And ever o'er its Babel sounds The blessed angels sing.

3. And ye, beneath life's crushing load, Whose forms are bending low,
   Who toil along the climbing way With painful steps and slow--
   Look now! for glad and golden hours Come swiftly on the wing;
   O rest beside the weary road, And hear the angels sing.

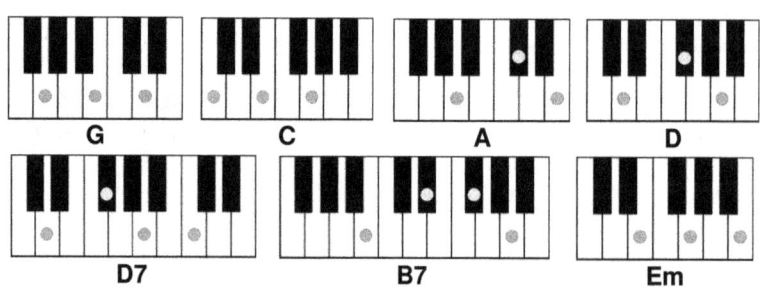

58

It Is Well With My Soul

Words by Horatio Spafford
Music by Philip Bliss

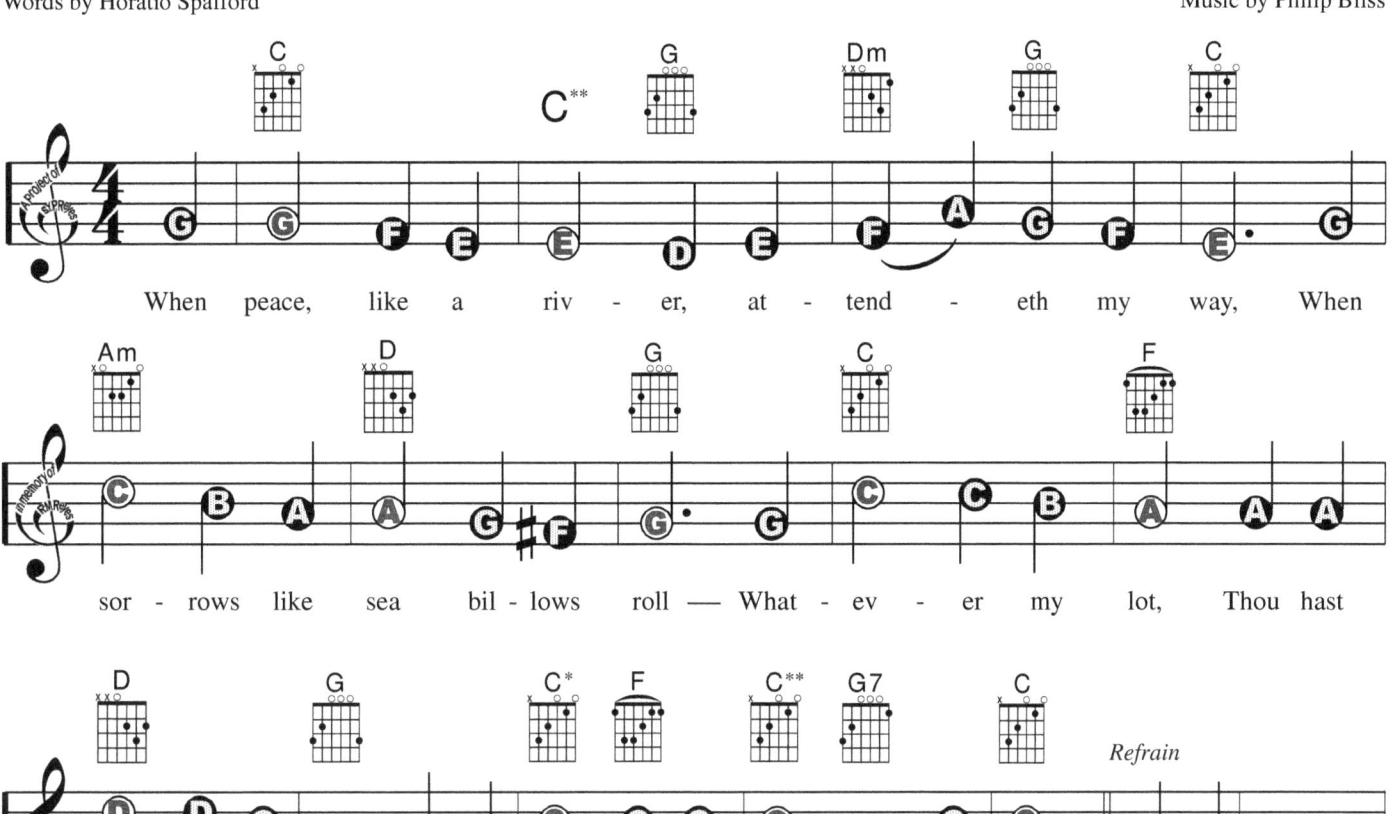

2. Though Satan should buffet, though trials should come,
   Let this blest assurance control,
   That Christ hath regarded My helpless estate
   And hath shed His own blood for my soul.
   (Refrain)

3. My sin--O, the bliss of this glorious thought!
   My sin, not in part, but the whole,
   Is nailed to the cross and I bear it no more,
   Praise the Lord, praise the Lord, oh, my soul!
   (Refrain)

4. And Lord, haste the day when my faith shall be sight,
   The clouds be rolled back as a scroll,
   The trump shall resound and the Lord shall descend,
   Even so, it is well with my soul.
   (Refrain)

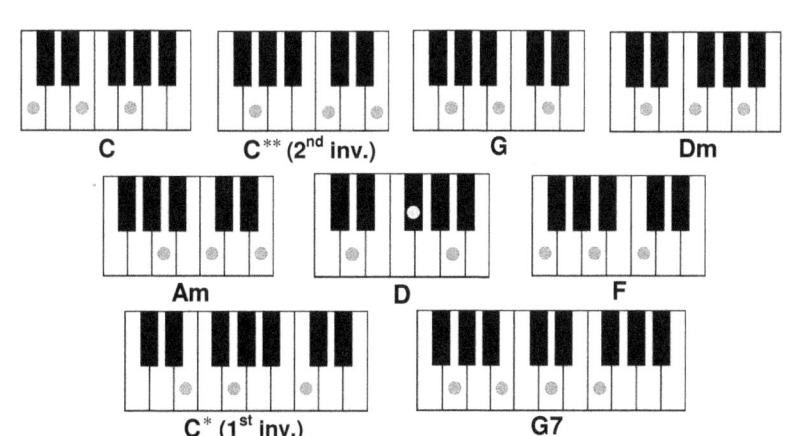

*On keyboard instrument, play first inversion
**On keyboard instrument, play second inversion

It May Be at Morn

Words by H. L. Turner
Music by James McGranahan

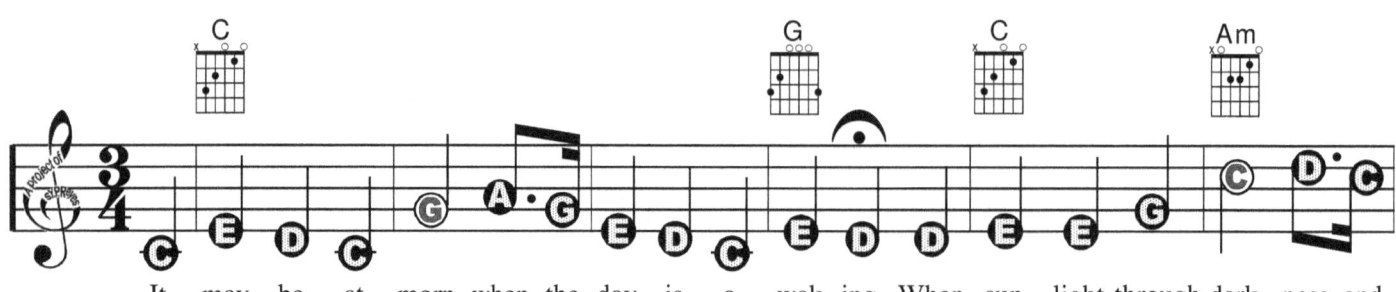

It may be at morn, when the day is a-wak-ing, When sun-light through dark-ness and

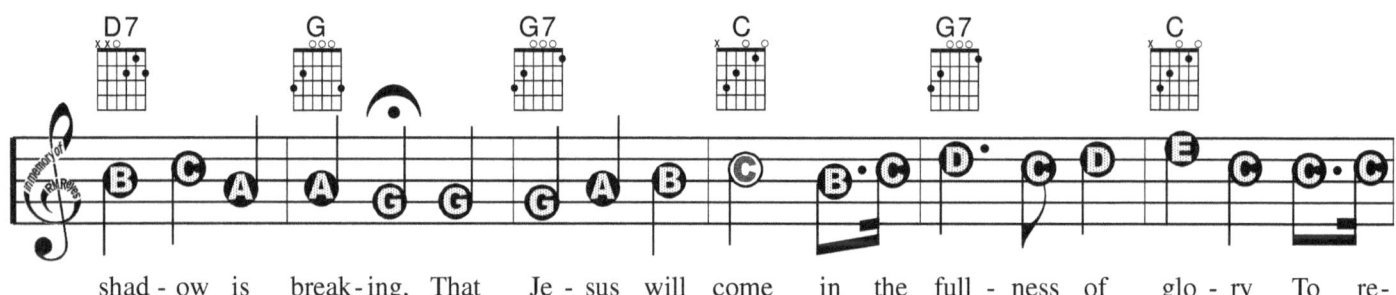

shad-ow is break-ing, That Je-sus will come in the full-ness of glo-ry To re-

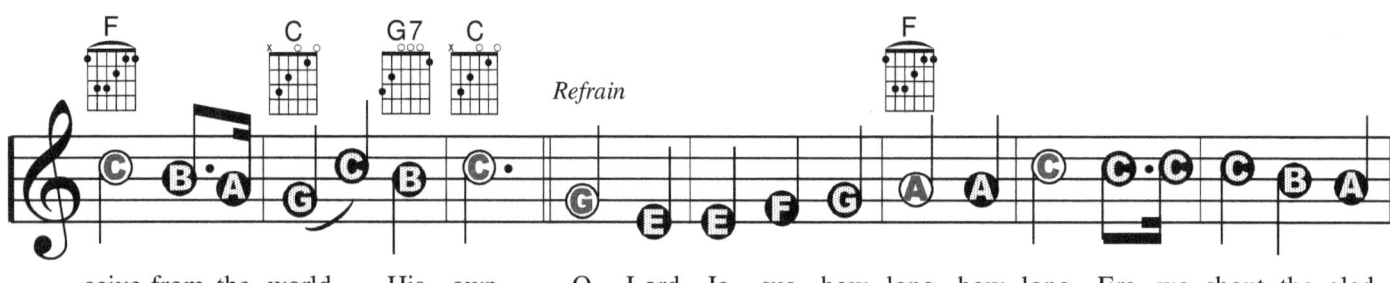

Refrain

ceive from the world His own. O Lord Je-sus, how long, how long Ere we shout the glad

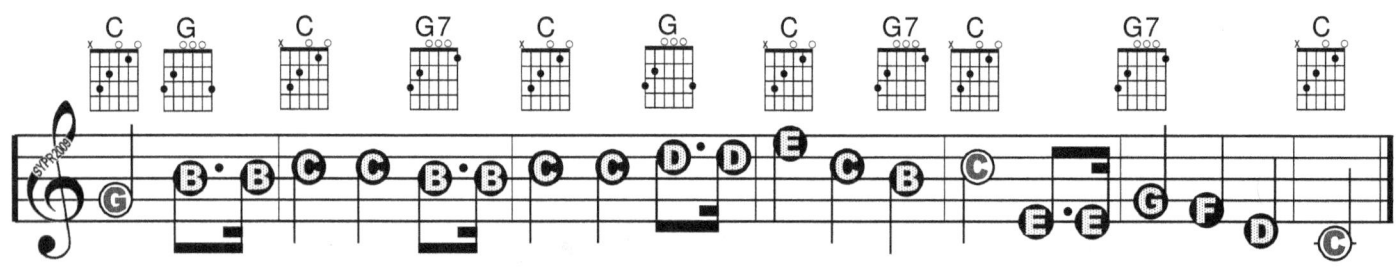

song? Christ re-turn-eth, Hal-le-lu-jah! hal-le-lu-jah! A-men, Hal-le-lu-jah! A-men.

2. It may be at midday, it may be at twilight
   It may be, perchance, that the blackness of midnight
   Will burst into light in the blaze of His glory,
   When Jesus receives His own.
   (Refrain)

3. O joy! O delight! should we go without dying,
   No sickness, no sadness, no dread, and no crying,
   Caught up through the clouds with our Lord into glory,
   When Jesus receives His own.
   (Refrain)

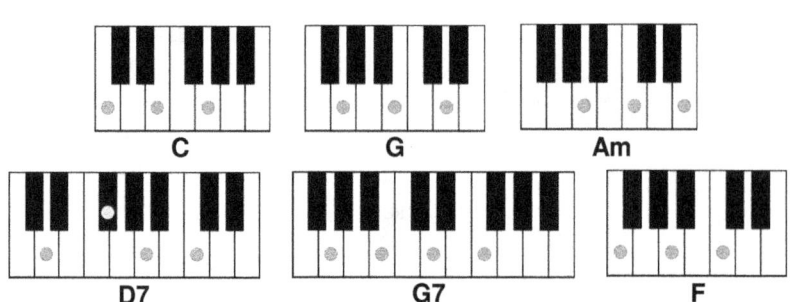

Jesus Is All the World to Me

Words and music by Will Thompson

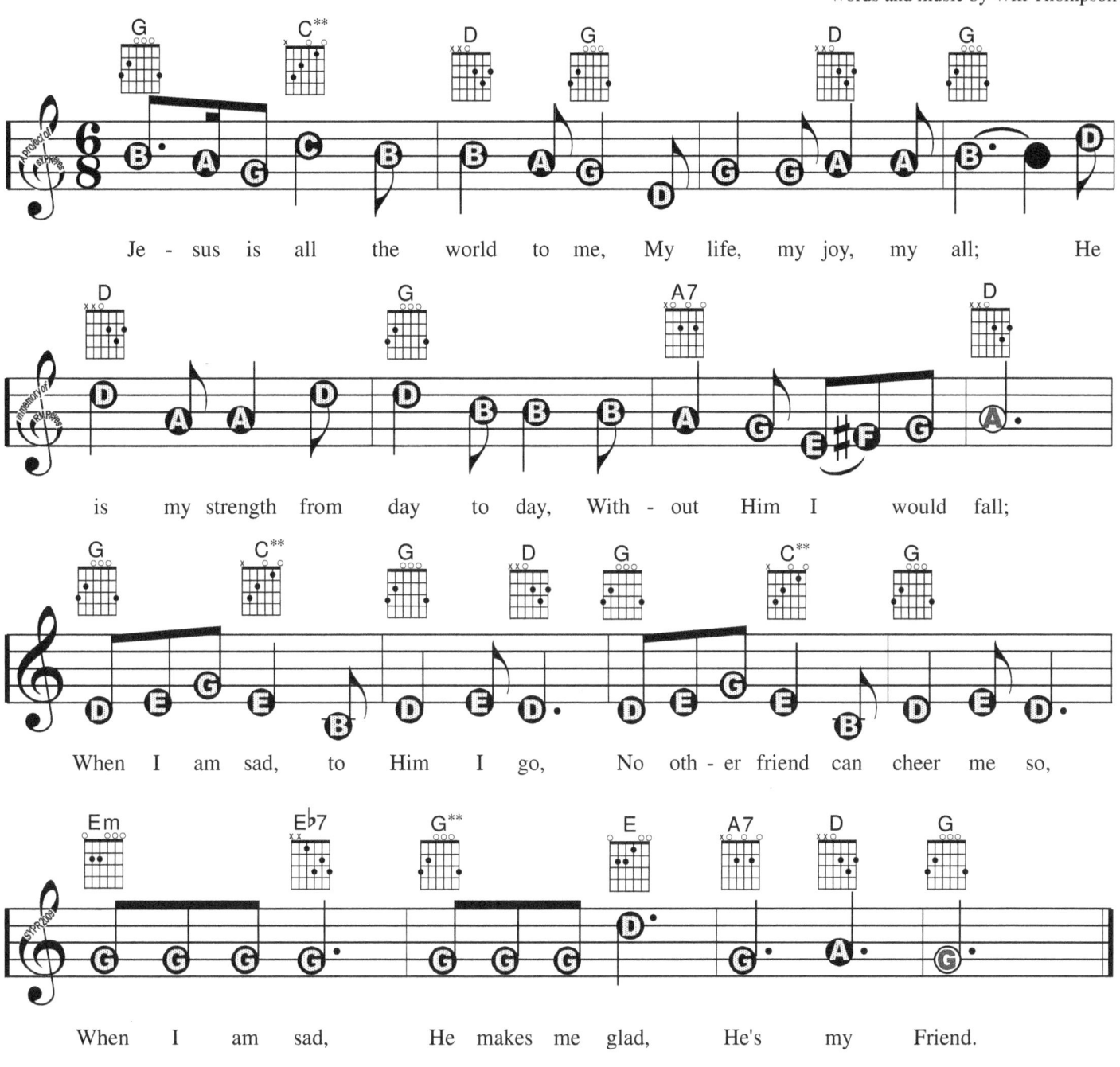

2. Jesus is all the world to me, My Friend in trials sore;
I go to Him for blessings, and He gives them o'er and o'er.
He sends the sunshine and the rain, He sends the harvest's golden grain;
Sunshine and rain, harvest of grain, He's my Friend.

3. Jesus is all the world to me, And true to Him I'll be;
O how could I this Friend deny, When He's so true to me?
Following Him I know I'm right, He watches o'er me day and night;
Following Him by day and night, He's my Friend.

4. Jesus is all the world to me, I want no better friend;
I trust Him now, I trust Him when Life's fleeting days shall end.
Beautiful life with such a Friend; Beautiful life that has no end;
Eternal life, eternal joy, He's my Friend.

**On keyboard instrument, play second inversion

Jesus Is Coming Again

Words by Jessie Strout
Music by George Lee

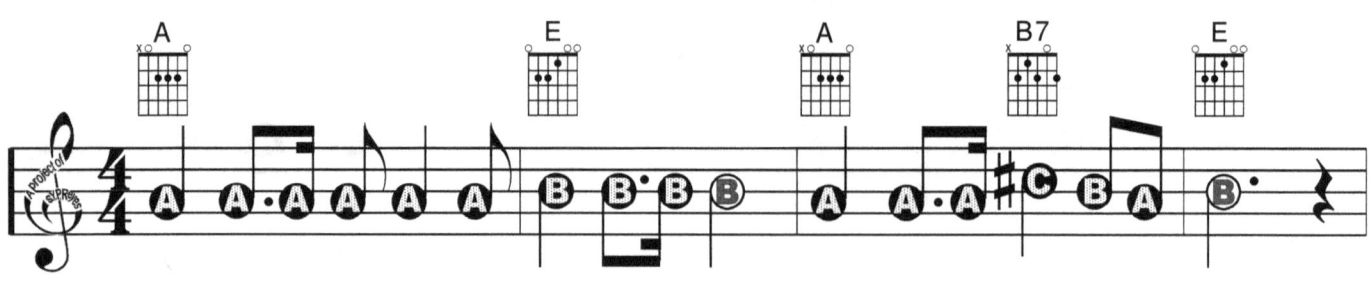

Lift up the trum-pet, and loud let it ring: Je-sus is com-ing a-gain!

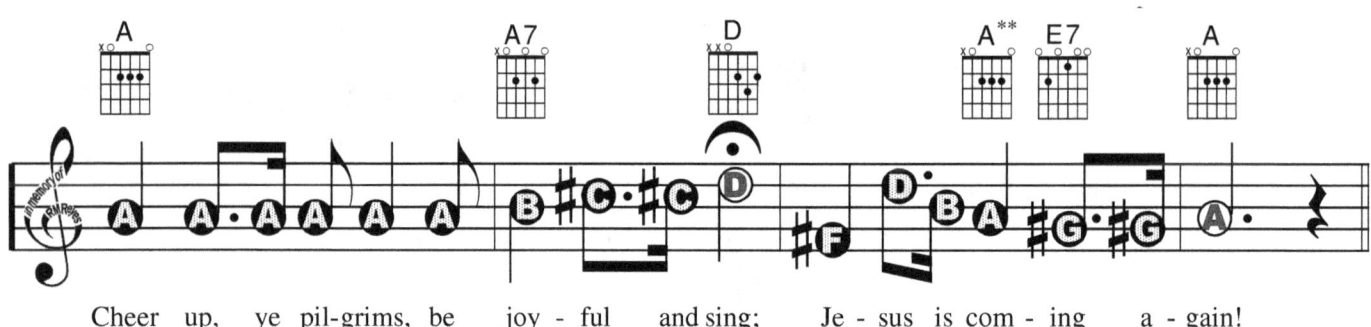

Cheer up, ye pil-grims, be joy-ful and sing; Je-sus is com-ing a-gain!

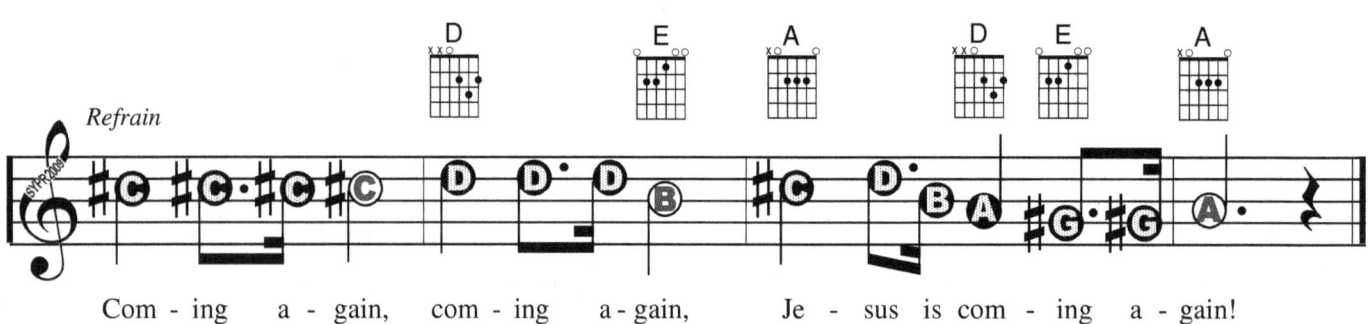

Refrain

Com-ing a-gain, com-ing a-gain, Je-sus is com-ing a-gain!

2. Echo it, hilltops; proclaim it, ye plains: Jesus is coming again!
   Coming in glory, the Lamb that was slain; Jesus is coming again!
   (Refrain)

3. Heavings of earth, tell the vast, wondering throng: Jesus is coming again!
   Tempests and whirlwinds, the anthem prolong; Jesus is coming again!
   (Refrain)

4. Nations are angry--by this we do know Jesus is coming again!
   Knowledge increases; men run to and fro; Jesus is coming again!
   (Refrain)

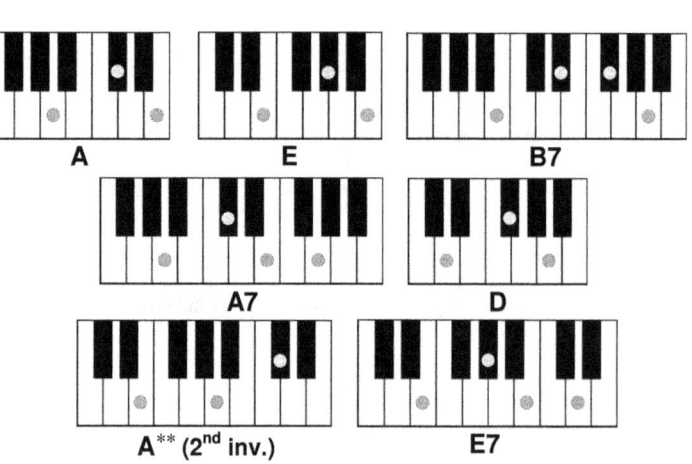

**On keyboard instrument, play second inversion

62

Jesus Paid It All

Words by Elvina Hall
Music by John Grape

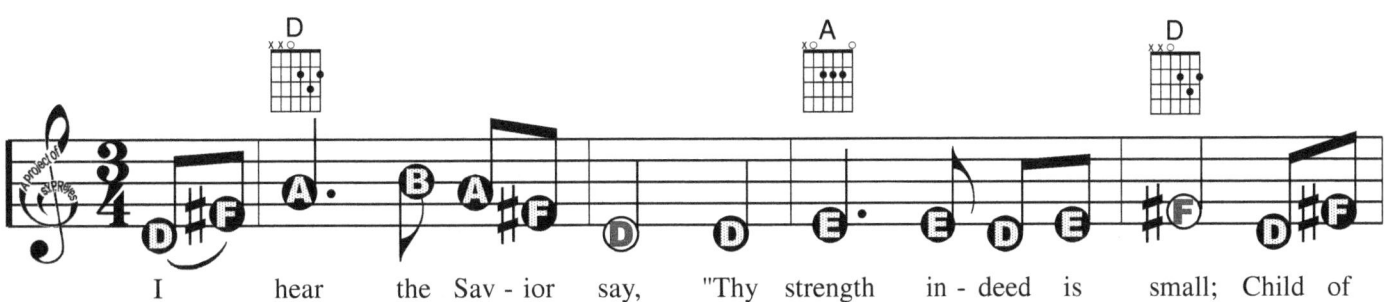
I hear the Sav-ior say, "Thy strength in-deed is small; Child of

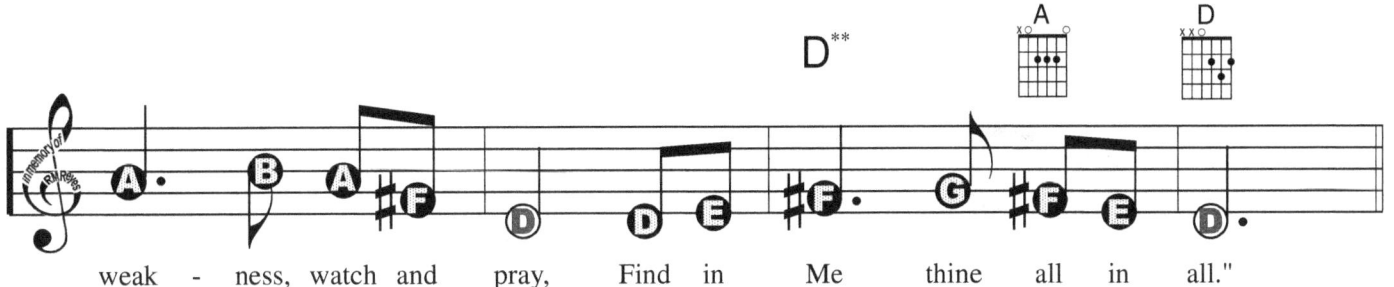
weak-ness, watch and pray, Find in Me thine all in all."

Refrain

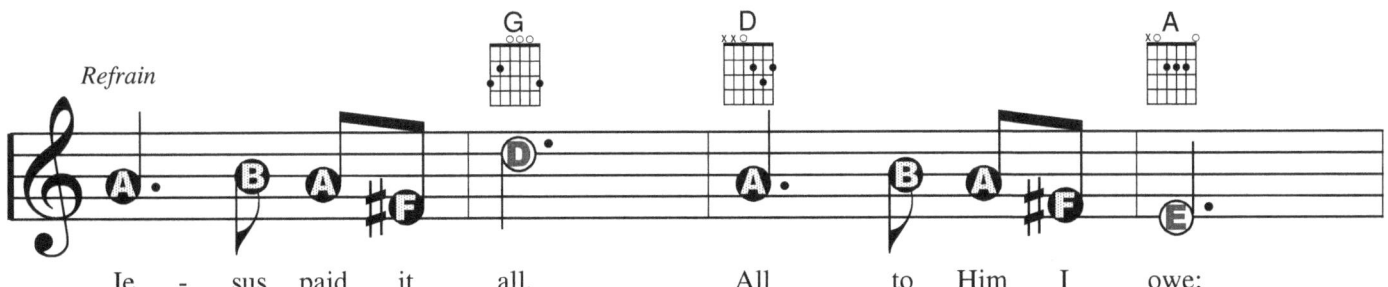
Je-sus paid it all, All to Him I owe;

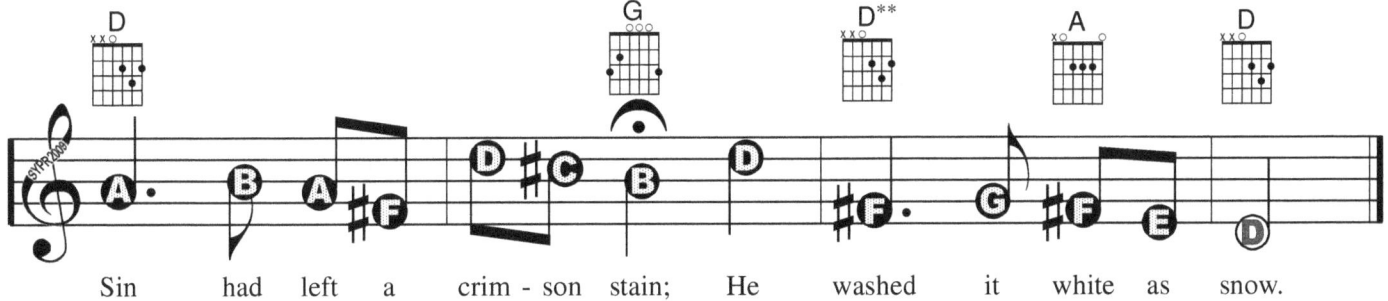
Sin had left a crim-son stain; He washed it white as snow.

2. Lord, now indeed I find Thy power, and Thine alone,
   Can change the leper's spots, And melt the heart of stone.
   (Refrain)

3. Since nothing good have I Whereby Thy grace to claim,
   I'll wash my garment white In the blood of Calvary's Lamb.
   (Refrain)

4. And when before the throne I stand in Him complete,
   I'll lay my trophies down, All down at Jesus' feet.
   (Refrain)

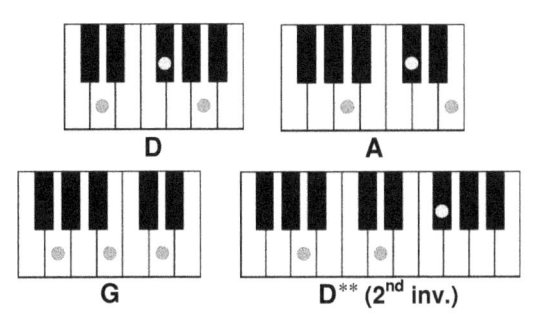

**On keyboard instrument, play second inversion

Jesus Saves

Words by Priscilla Owens
Music by William Kirkpatrick

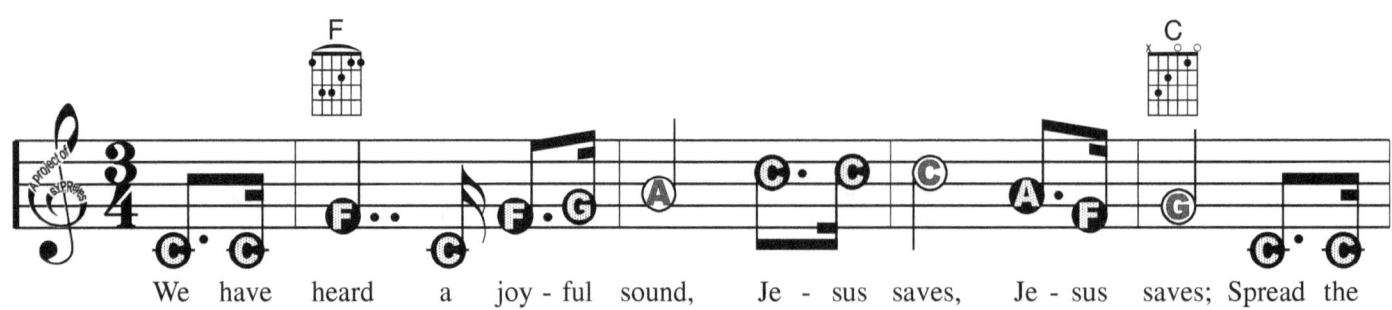
We have heard a joy-ful sound, Je-sus saves, Je-sus saves; Spread the

glad-ness all a-round, Je-sus saves, Je-sus saves; Bear the

news to ev-ery land, Climb the steeps and cross the waves, On-ward,

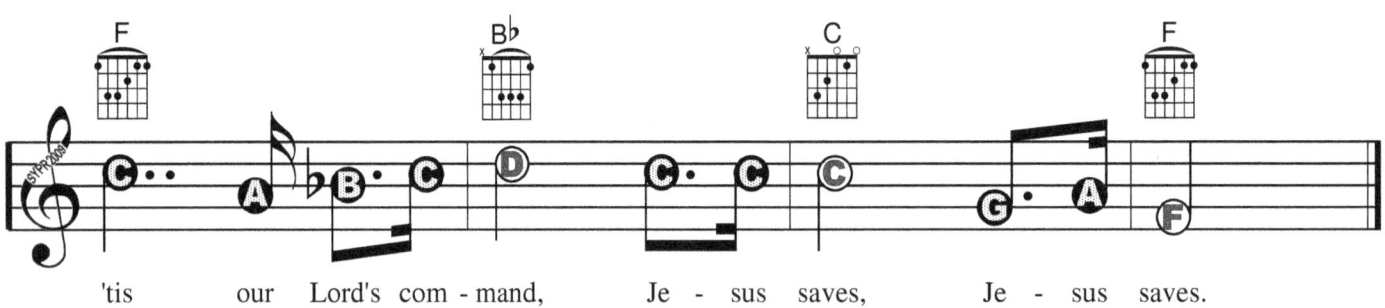
'tis our Lord's com-mand, Je-sus saves, Je-sus saves.

2. Waft it on the rolling tide, Jesus saves, Jesus saves;
Tell to sinners far and wide, Jesus saves, Jesus saves;
Sing, ye islands of the sea, Echo back, ye ocean caves;
Earth shall keep her jubilee, Jesus saves, Jesus saves.

3. Sing above the battle's strife, Jesus saves, Jesus saves;
By His death and endless life, Jesus saves, Jesus saves;
Sing it softly through the gloom, When the heart for mercy craves,
Sing in triumph o'er the tomb, Jesus saves, Jesus saves.

4. Give the winds a mighty voice, Jesus saves, Jesus saves;
Let the nations now rejoice, Jesus saves, Jesus saves;
Shout salvation full and free, Highest hills and deepest caves,
This our song of victory, Jesus saves, Jesus saves.

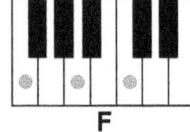
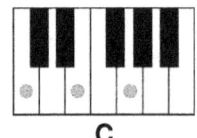
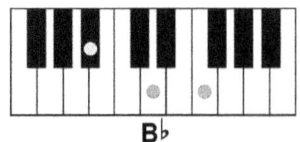

Jesus, Savior, Pilot Me

Words by Edward Hopper

Music by John Gould

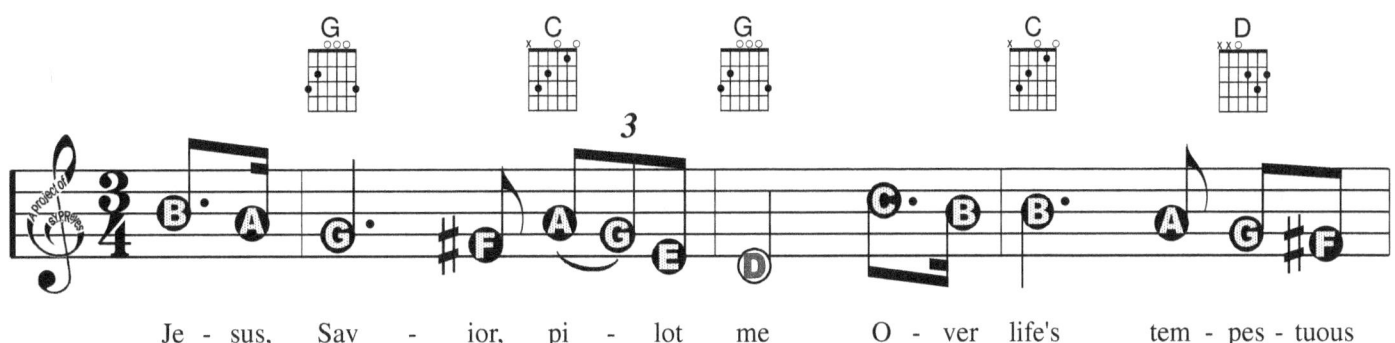

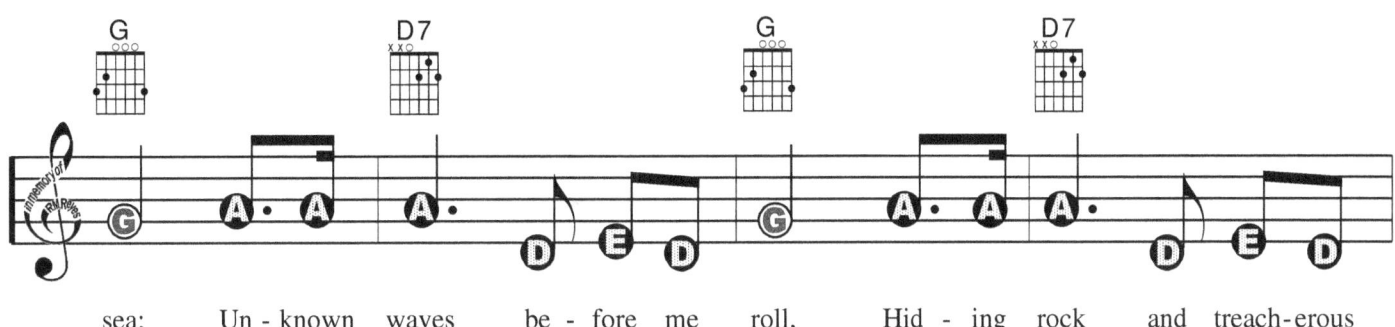

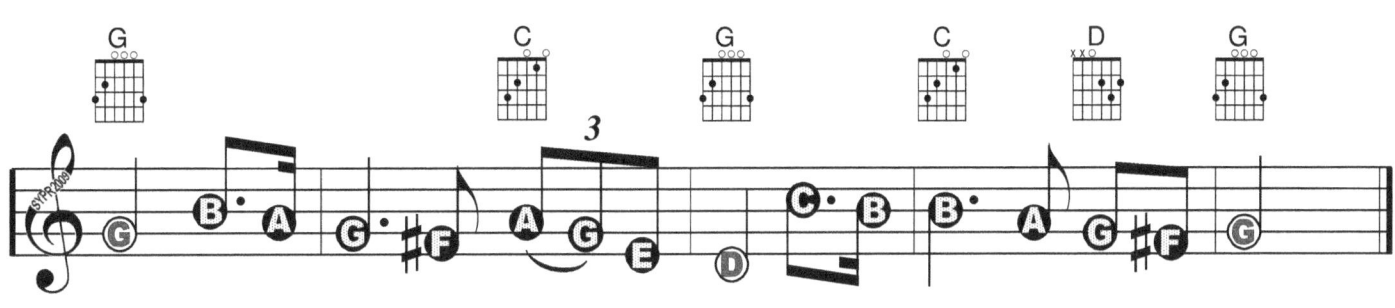

2. As a mother stills her child, Thou canst hush the ocean wild;
   Boisterous waves obey Thy will When Thou sayest to them, "Be still."
   Wondrous Sovereign of the sea, Jesus, Savior, pilot me.

3. When at last I near the shore, And the fearful breakers roar
   'Twixt me and the peaceful rest, Then, while leaning on Thy breast,
   May I hear Thee say to me, "Fear not, I will pilot Thee."

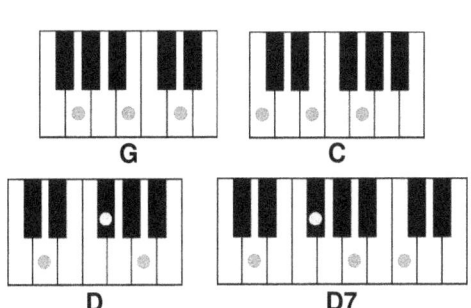

Jesus, the Very Thought of Thee

English translation by Edward Caswall
Music by John Dykes

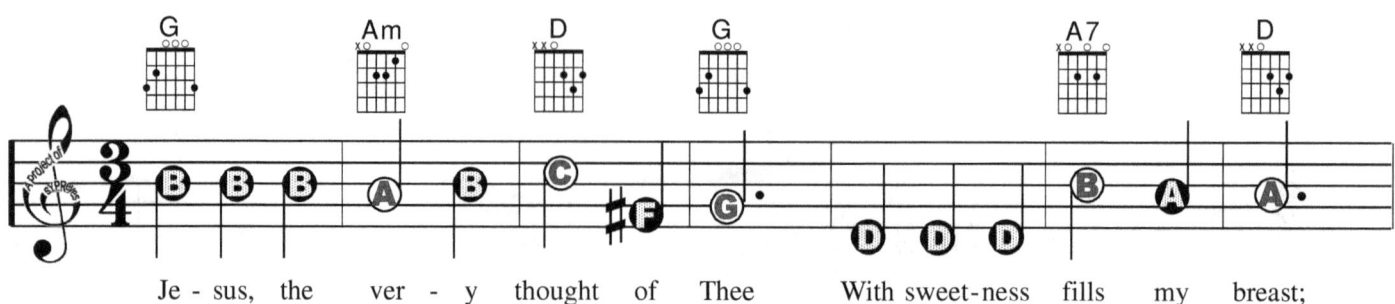

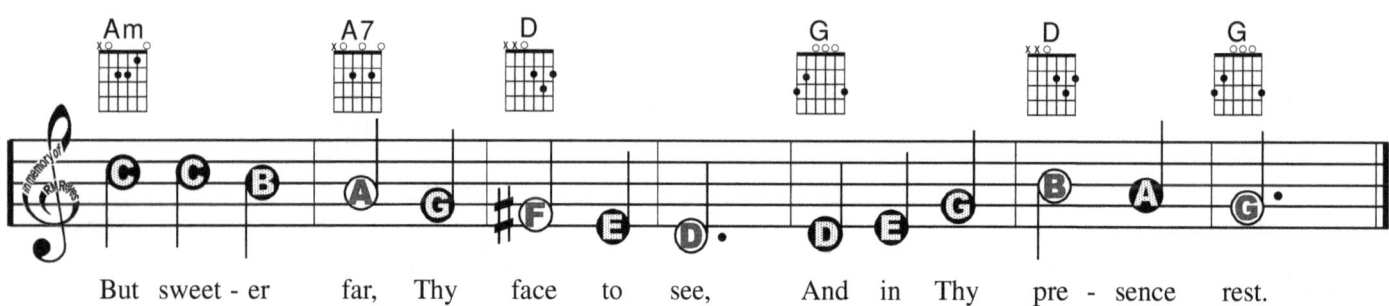

2. No voice can sing, no heart can frame, Nor can the memory find
   A sweeter sound than Jesus' name, The Savior of mankind.

3. O hope of every contrite heart! O joy of all the meek,
   To those who fall, how kind Thou art! How good to those who seek!

4. But what to those who find? Ah! this Nor tongue nor pen can show;
   The love of Jesus--what it is, None but His loved ones know.

5. Jesus, our only joy be Thou, As Thou our prize wilt be;
   In Thee be all our glory now, And through eternity.

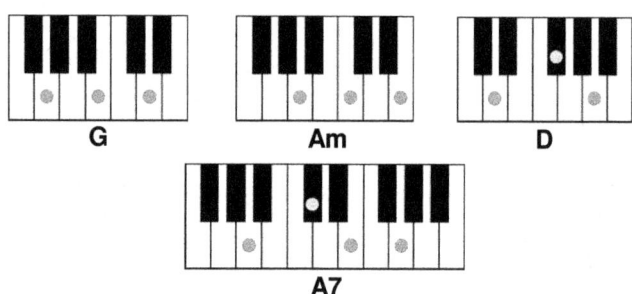

Happy the Home

(Same tune)
Words by Henry Ware

1. Happy the home when God is there, And love fills evey breast;
   When one their wish, and one their prayer, And one their heavenly rest.

2. Happy the home where Jesus' name Is sweet to every ear;
   Where children early lisp His fame, And parents hold Him dear.

3. Happy the home where prayer is heard, And praise is wont to rise;
   Where parents love the Sacred Word And all its wisdom prize.

4. Lord, let us in our homes agree This blessed peace to gain;
   Unite our hearts in love to Thee, And love to all will reign.

Joy to the World

Words by Isaac Watts

Music arranged from Handel's *Messiah*

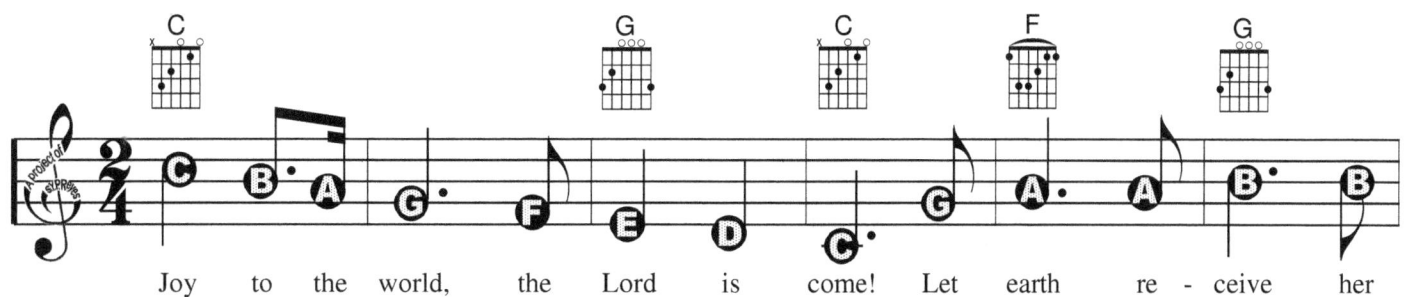
Joy to the world, the Lord is come! Let earth re-ceive her

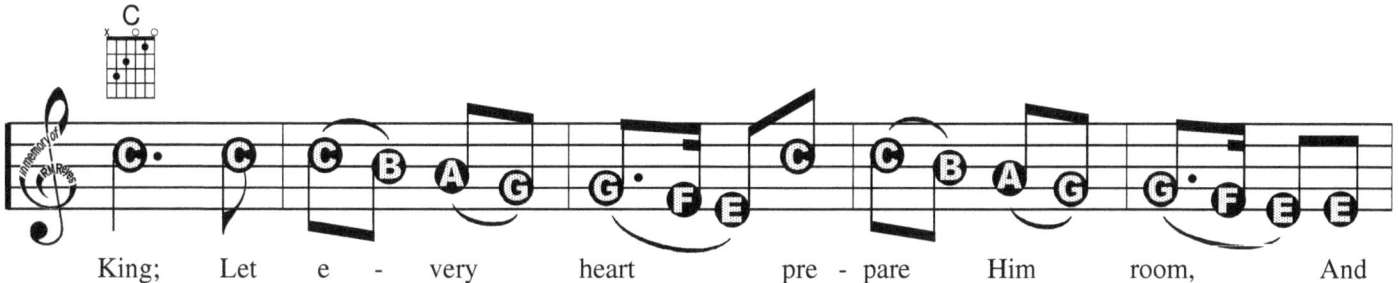
King; Let e - very heart pre-pare Him room, And

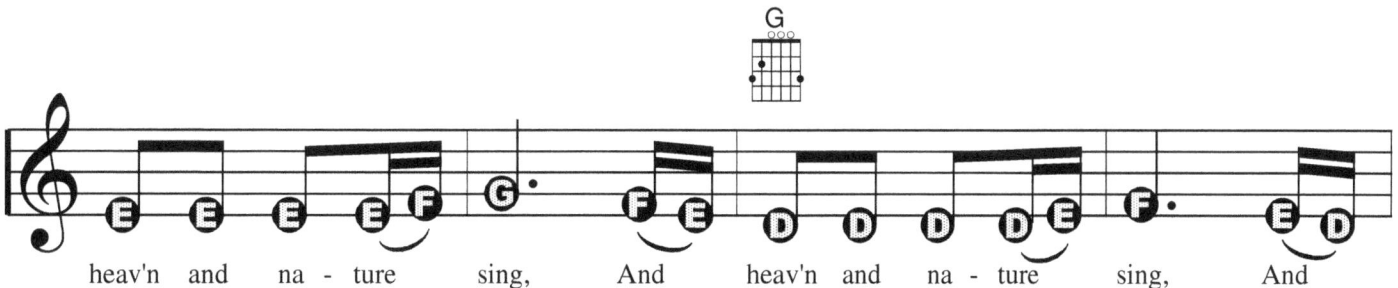
heav'n and na - ture sing, And heav'n and na - ture sing, And

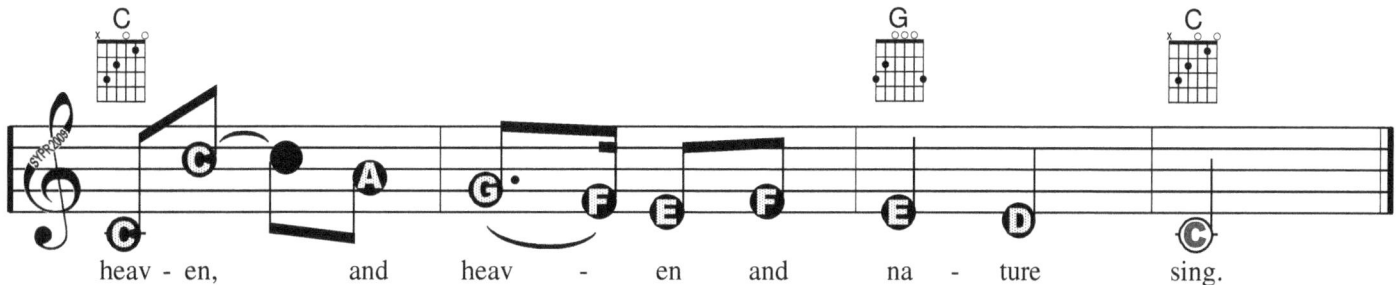
heav - en, and heav - en and na - ture sing.

2. Joy to the earth, the Savior reigns! Let men their songs employ;
   While fields and floods, rocks, hills, and plains,
   Repeat the sounding joy, Repeat the sounding joy,
   Repeat, repeat the sounding joy.

3. No more let sin and sorrow grow, Nor thorns infest the ground;
   He comes to make His blessings flow
   Far as the curse is found, Far as the curse is found,
   Far as, far as the curse is found.

4. He rules the world with truth and grace, And makes the nations prove
   The glories of His righteousness,
   And wonders of His love, And wonders of His love,
   And wonders, and wonders of His love.

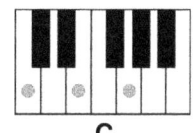
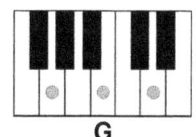
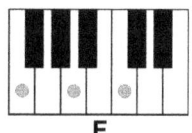

67

Just As I Am

Words by Charlotte Elliott

Music by William Bradbury

Just as I am, with-out one plea, But that Thy blood was shed for me, And that Thou bid'st me come to Thee, O Lamb of God, I come, I come.

2. Just as I am, and waiting not To rid my soul of one dark blot,
   To Thee whose blood can cleanse each spot, O Lamb of God, I come, I come.

3. Just as I am, though tossed about With many a conflict, many a doubt;
   "Fightings within, and fears without," O Lamb of God, I come, I come.

4. Just as I am, poor, wretched, blind; Sight, riches, healing of the mind,
   Yea, all I need, in Thee I find, O Lamb of God, I come, I come.

5. Just as I am, Thou wilt receive, Wilt welcome, pardon, cleanse, relieve;
   Because Thy promise I believe, O Lamb of God, I come, I come.

6. Just as I am, Thy love I own Has broken every barrier down;
   Now to be Thine, and Thine alone, O Lamb of God, I come, I come.

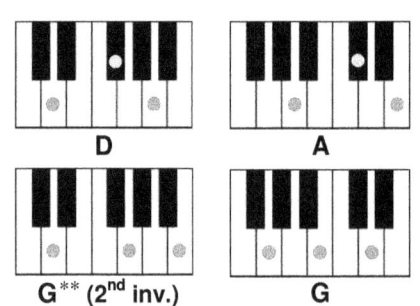

**On keyboard instrument, play second inversion

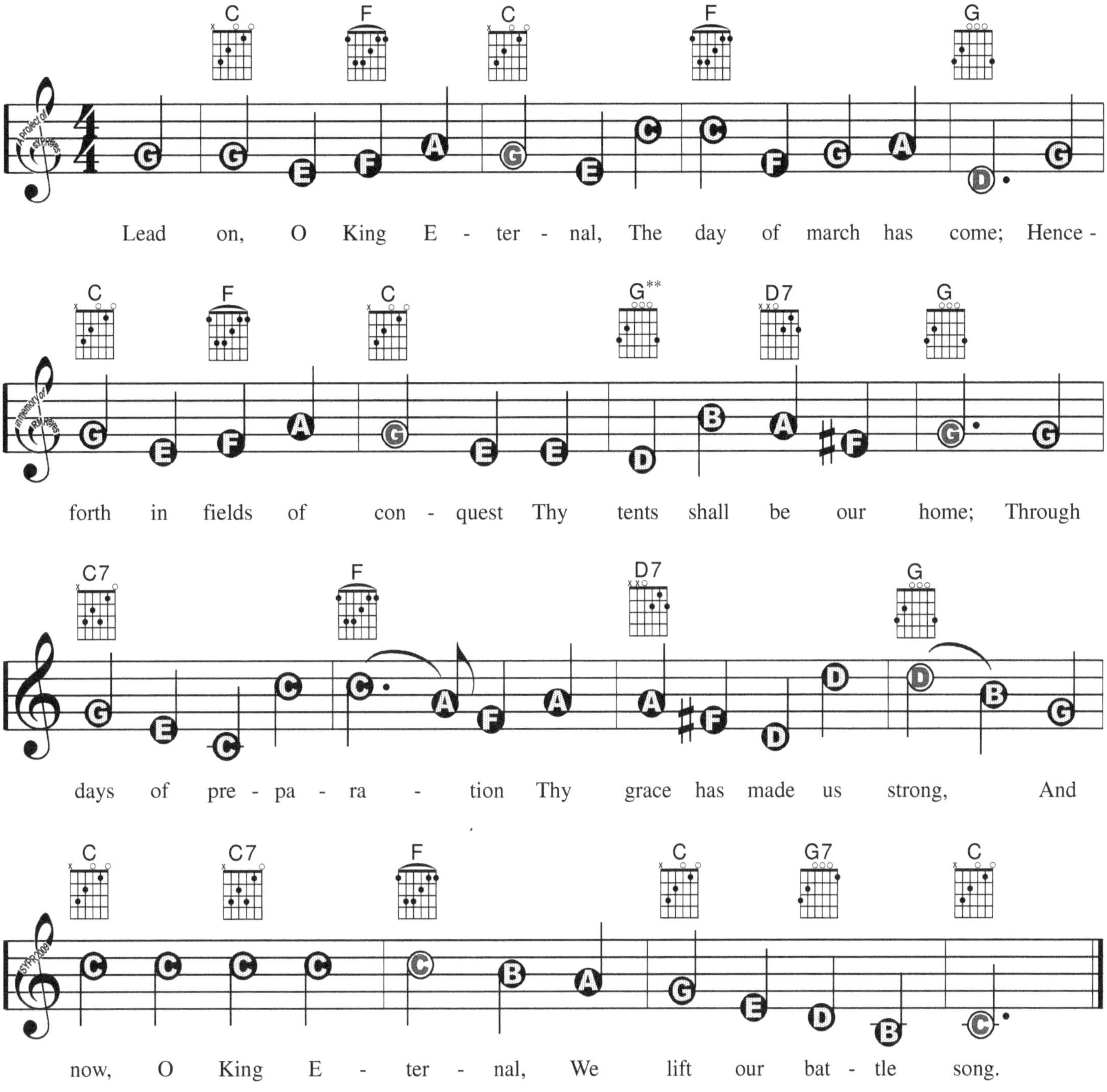

Lead On, O King Eternal

Words by Ernest Shurtleff

Music by Henry Smart

C F C F G
Lead on, O King E - ter - nal, The day of march has come; Hence -
C F C G** D7 G
forth in fields of con - quest Thy tents shall be our home; Through
C7 F D7 G
days of pre - pa - ra - tion Thy grace has made us strong, And
C C7 F C G7 C
now, O King E - ter - nal, We lift our bat - tle song.

2. Lead on O King Eternal, Till sin's fierce war shall cease,
And holiness shall whisper The sweet Amen of peace;
For not with swords, loud clashing, Nor roll of stirring drums,
With deeds of love and mercy, The heavenly kingdom comes.

3. Lead on O King Eternal, We follow, not with fears,
For gladness breaks like morning Where'er Thy face appears;
Thy cross is lifted o'er us; We journey in its light;
The crown awaits the conquest; Lead on, O God of might.

C
F
G
G** (2nd inv.)
D7
C7
G7

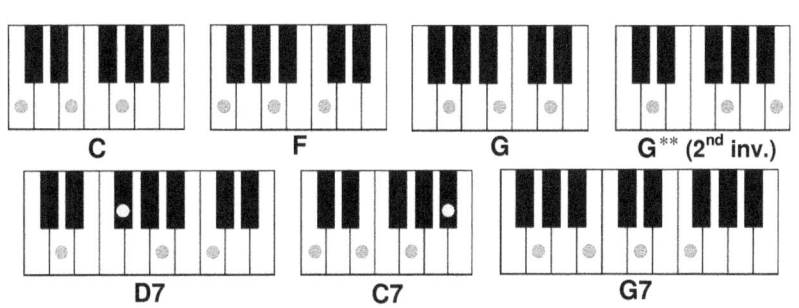

***On keyboard instrument, play second inversion*

Words by E. A. Hoffman
Leaning on the Everlasting Arms
Music by A. J. Showalter

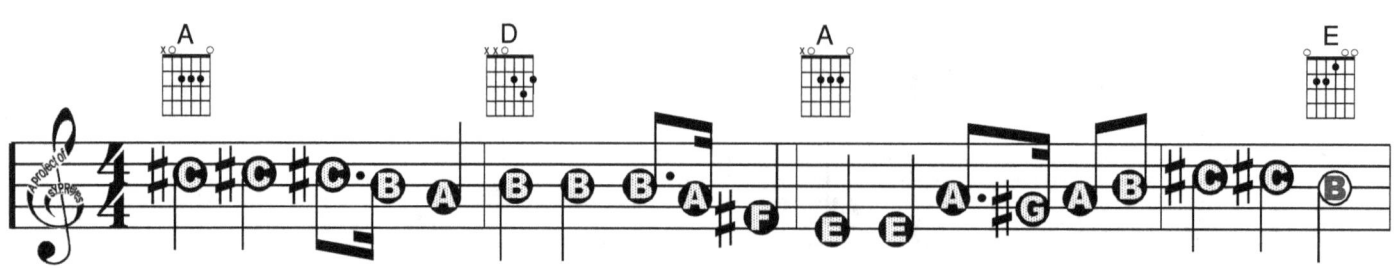

What a fel-low-ship, what a joy di-vine, Lean-ing on the ev-er-last-ing arms;

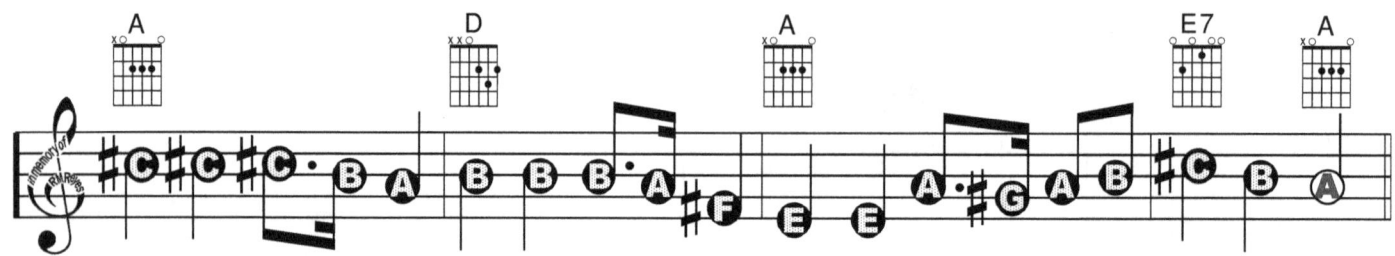

What a bless-ed-ness, what a peace is mine, Lean-ing on the ev-er-last-ing arms.

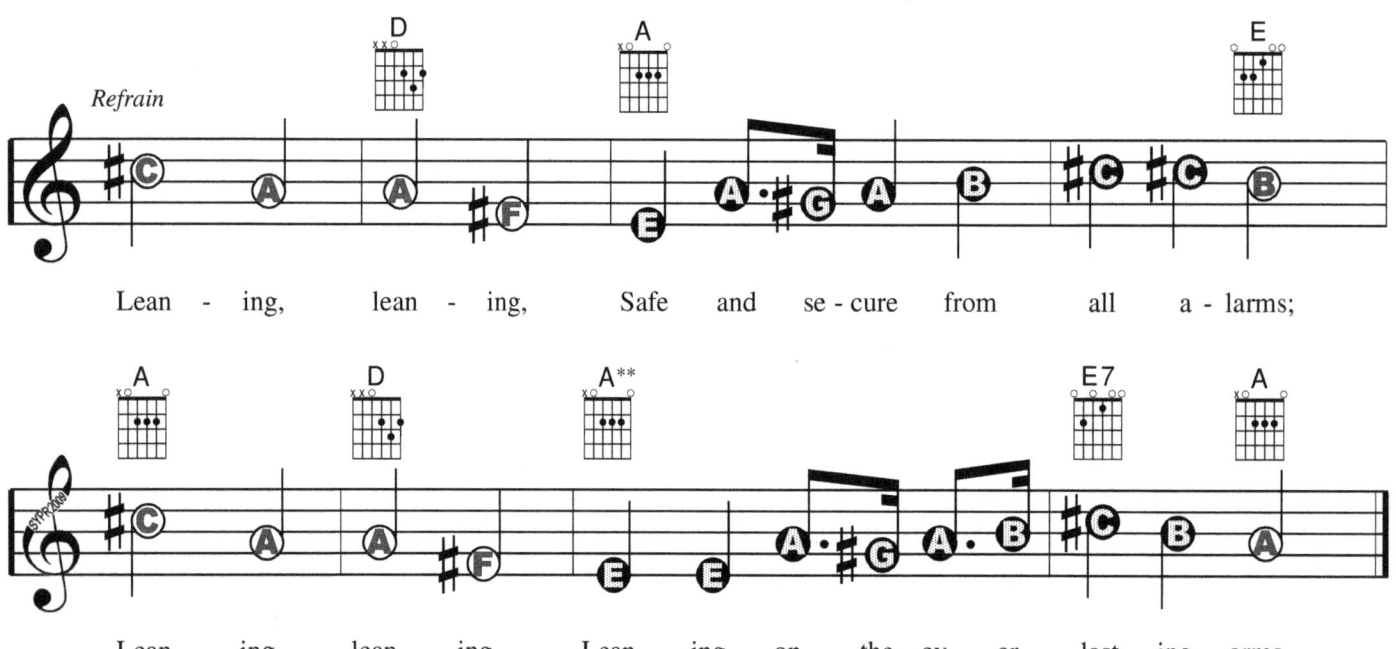

Refrain

Lean - ing, lean - ing, Safe and se - cure from all a - larms;

Lean - ing, lean - ing, Lean - ing on the ev - er - last - ing arms.

2. O how sweet to walk in this pilgrim way,
   Leaning on the everlasting arms;
   O how bright the path grows from day to day,
   Leaning on the everlasting arms.
   (Refrain)

3. What have I to dread, what have I to fear,
   Leaning on the everlasting arms?
   I have blessed peace with my Lord so near,
   Leaning on the everlasting arms.
   (Refrain)

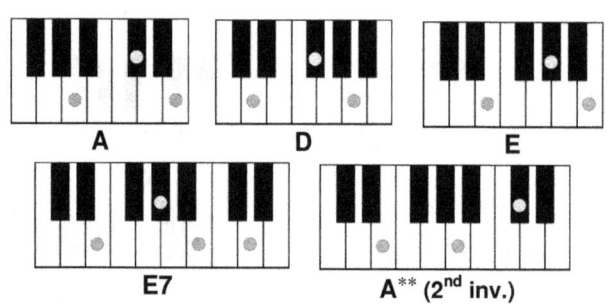

**On keyboard instrument, play second inversion*

Let All Mortal Flesh Keep Silence

Liturgy of St. James
Translated by Gerard Moultrie

17th century French carol

Lift Him Up

Words by May Warren
Music by D. S. Hakes

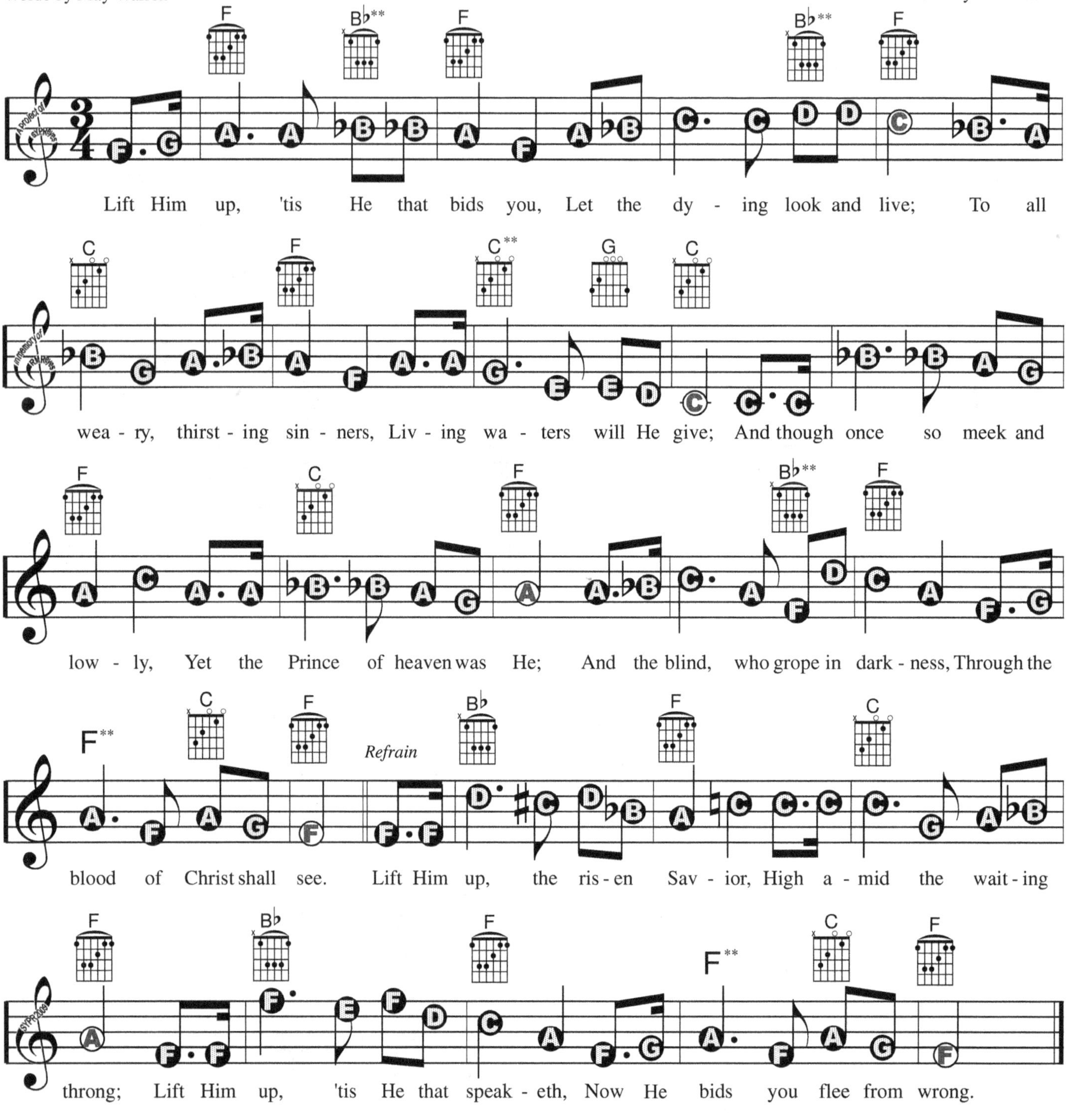

Lift Him up, 'tis He that bids you, Let the dy-ing look and live; To all wea-ry, thirst-ing sin-ners, Liv-ing wa-ters will He give; And though once so meek and low-ly, Yet the Prince of heaven was He; And the blind, who grope in dark-ness, Through the blood of Christ shall see.

Refrain
Lift Him up, the ris-en Sav-ior, High a-mid the wait-ing throng; Lift Him up, 'tis He that speak-eth, Now He bids you flee from wrong.

2. Lift Him up, this precious Savior, Let the multitude behold;
They with willing hearts shall seek Him, He will draw them to His fold;
They shall gather from the wayside, Hastening on with joyous feet,
They shall bear the cross of Jesus, And shall find salvation sweet.
(Refrain)

3. Lift Him up in all His glory, 'Tis the Son of God on high;
Lift Him up, His love shall draw them, E'en the careless shall draw nigh;
Let them hear again the story Of the cross, the death of shame;
And from tongue to tongue repeat it; Mighty throngs shall bless His name.
(Refrain)

4. O then lift Him up in singing, Lift the Savior up in prayer;
He, the glorious Redeemer, All the sins of men did bear;
Yes, the young shall bow before Him, And the old their voices raise;
All the deaf shall hear hosannah; And the dumb shall shout His praise.
(Refrain)

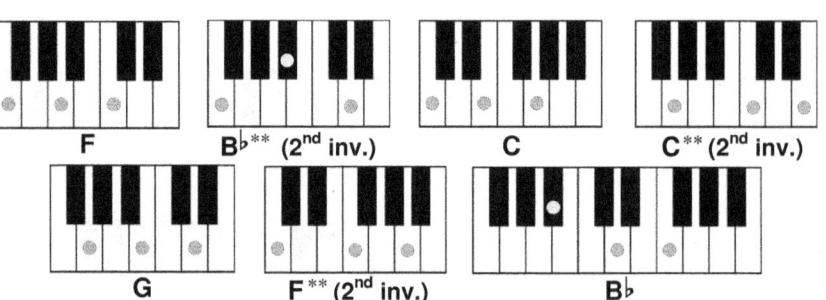

**On keyboard instrument, play second inversion

72

Lord, I'm Coming Home

Words and music by William Kirkpatrick

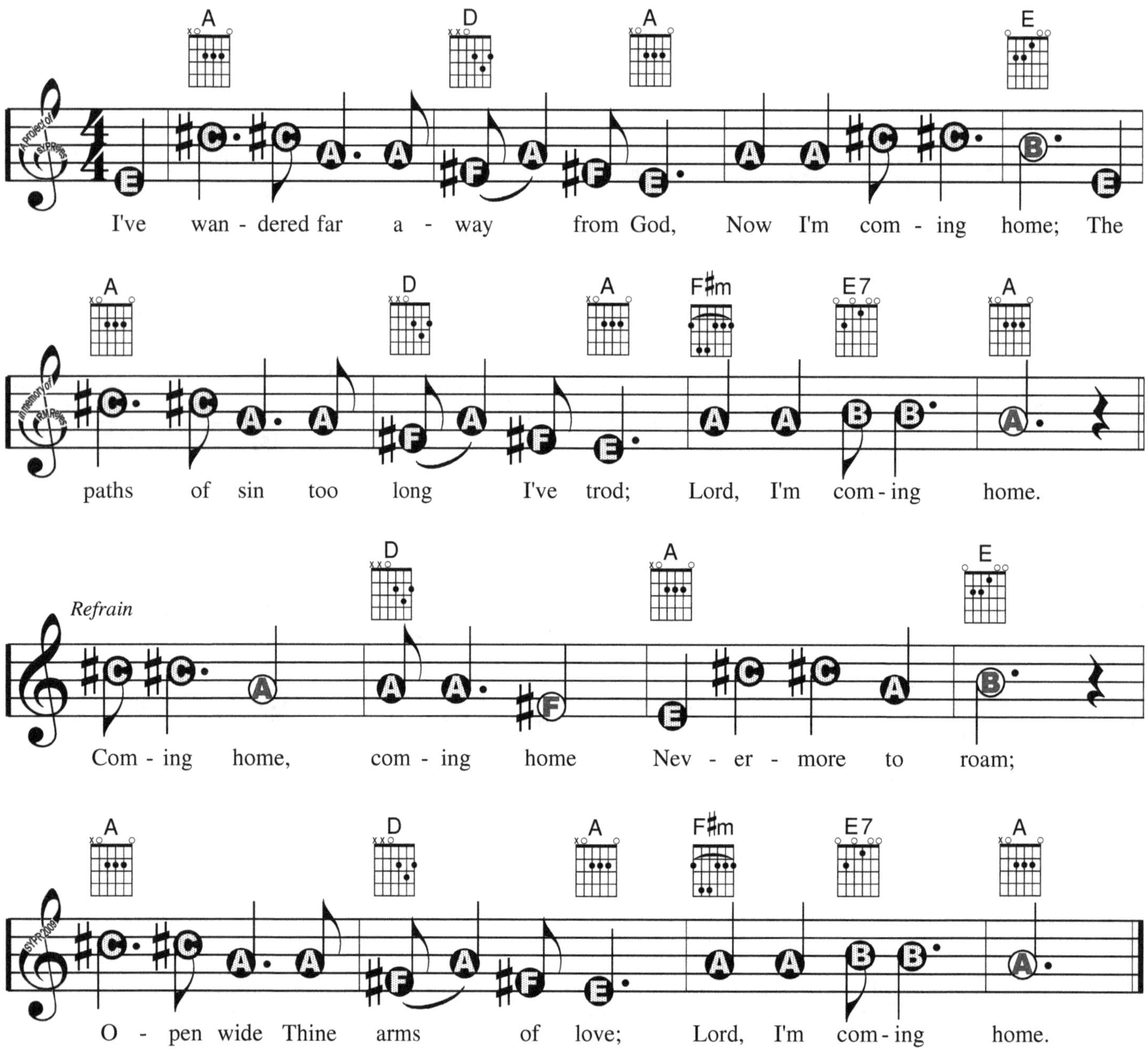

I've wan-dered far a-way from God, Now I'm com-ing home; The paths of sin too long I've trod; Lord, I'm com-ing home.

Refrain
Com-ing home, com-ing home Nev-er-more to roam; O-pen wide Thine arms of love; Lord, I'm com-ing home.

2. I've wasted many precious years, Now I'm coming home;
   I now repent with bitter tears; Lord, I'm coming home.
   (Refrain)

3. I'm tired of sin and straying, Lord, Now I'm coming home;
   I trust Thy love, believe Thy word; Lord, I'm coming home.
   (Refrain)

4. My only hope, my only plea, Now I'm coming home;
   That Jesus died, and died for me; Lord, I'm coming home.
   (Refrain)

5. I need His cleansing blood I know, Now I'm coming home;
   O wash me whiter than the snow; Lord, I'm coming home.
   (Refrain)

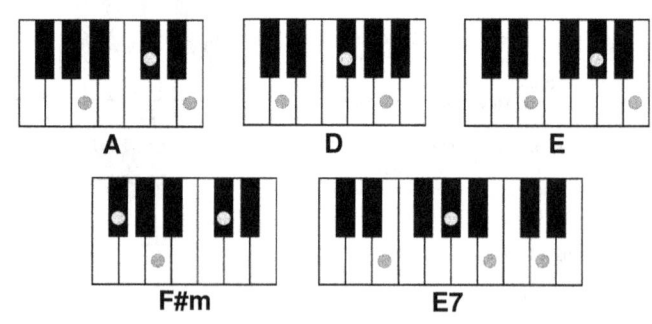

74

Love Divine, All Loves Excelling

Words by Charles Wesley
Music by John Zundel

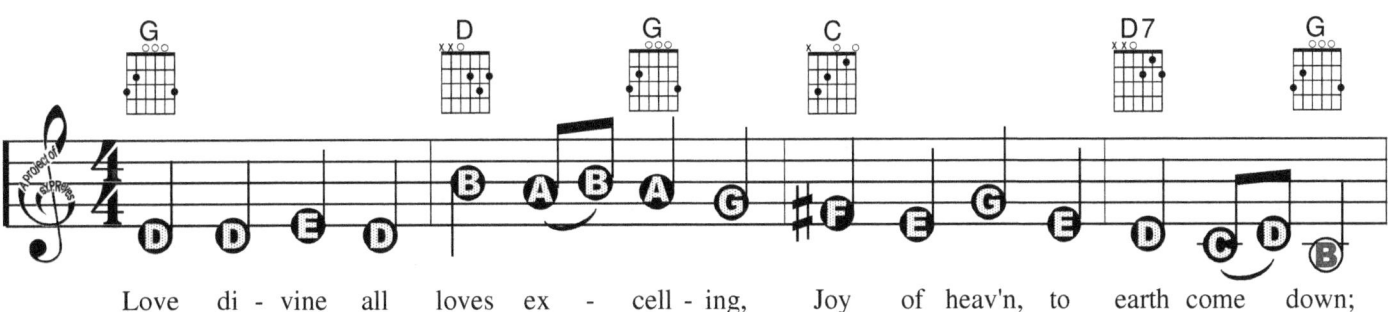

Love di-vine all loves ex-cell-ing, Joy of heav'n, to earth come down;

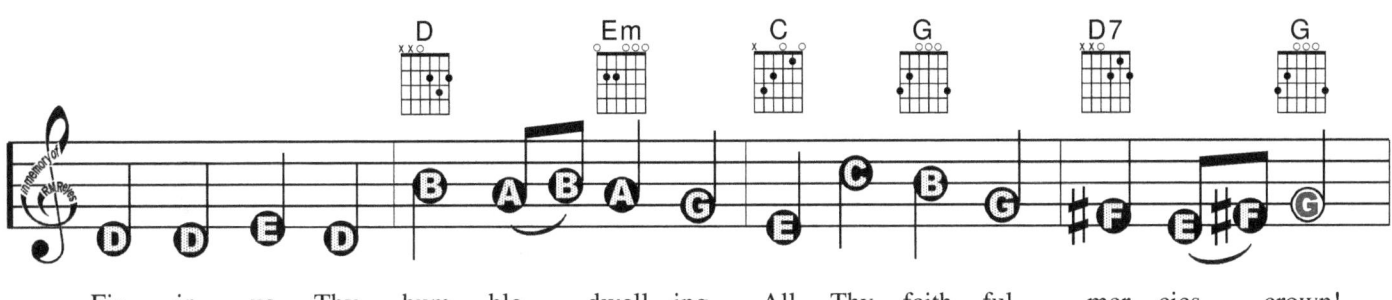

Fix in us Thy hum-ble dwell-ing, All Thy faith-ful mer-cies crown!

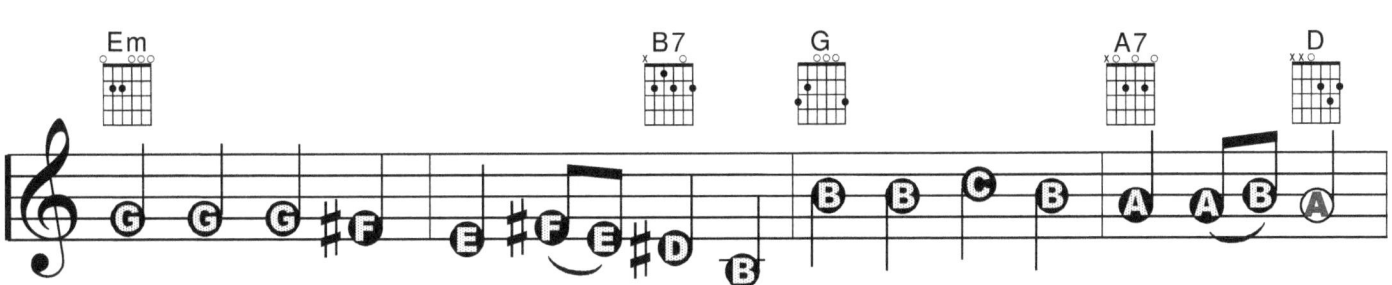

Je-sus, Thou art all com-pas-sion, Pure, un-bound-ed love Thou art;

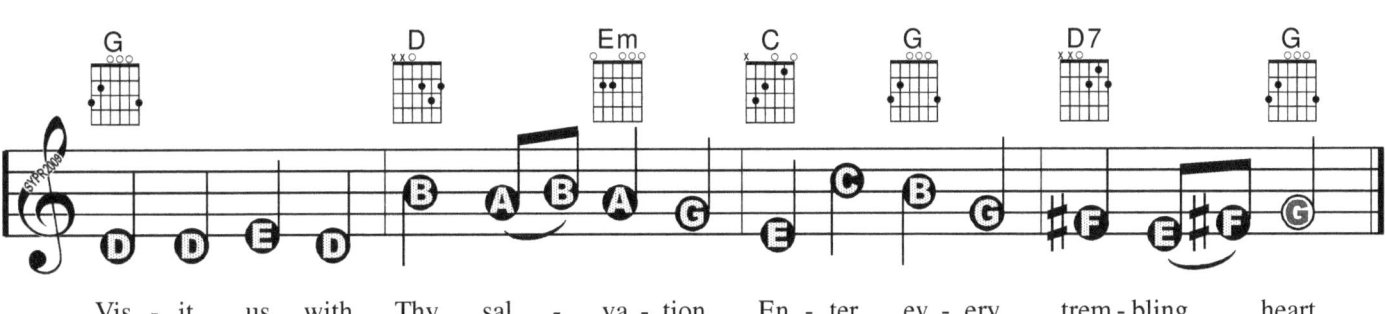

Vis-it us with Thy sal-va-tion, En-ter ev-ery trem-bling heart.

2. Breathe, O breathe Thy loving Spirit Into every troubled breast!
   Let us all in Thee inherit, Let us find the promised rest;
   Take away our bent to sinning; Alpha and Omega be;
   End of faith, as its beginning, Set our hearts at liberty.

3. Come, Almighty to deliver, Let us all Thy grace receive;
   Suddenly return, and never, Nevermore Thy temples leave.
   Thee we would be always blessing, Serve Thee as Thy hosts above,
   Pray, and praise Thee without ceasing, Glory in Thy perfect love.

4. Finish, then, Thy new creation; Pure and spotless let us be;
   Let us see Thy great salvation Perfectly restored in Thee:
   Changed from glory into glory, Till in heav'n we take our place,
   Till we cast our crowns before Thee, Lost in wonder, love, and praise.

Marching to Zion

Words by Isaac Watts
Music by Robert Lowry

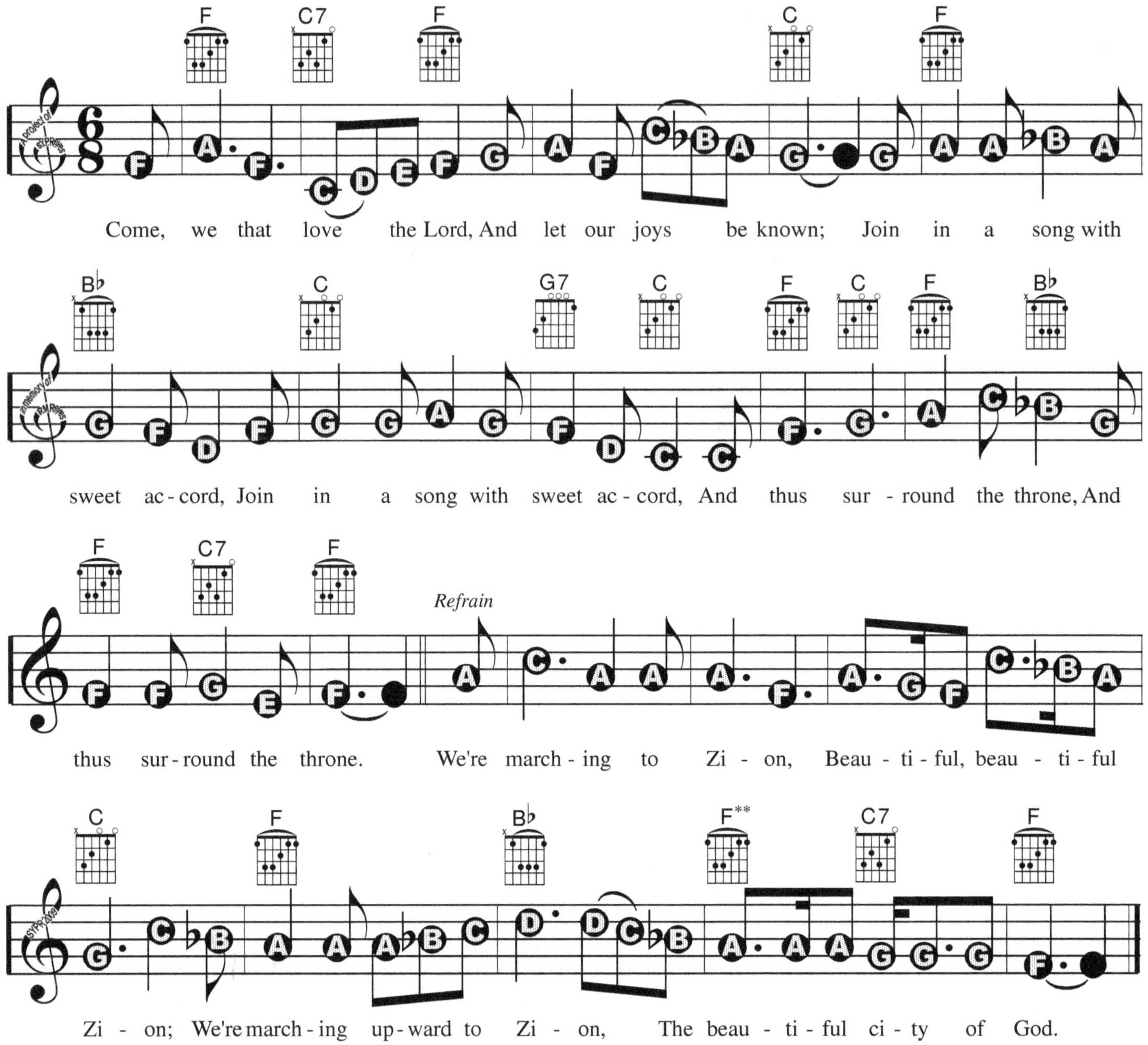

Come, we that love the Lord, And let our joys be known; Join in a song with sweet ac-cord, Join in a song with sweet ac-cord, And thus sur-round the throne, And thus sur-round the throne.

Refrain
We're march-ing to Zi-on, Beau-ti-ful, beau-ti-ful Zi-on; We're march-ing up-ward to Zi-on, The beau-ti-ful ci-ty of God.

2. Let those refuse to sing Who never knew our God;
   But children of the heavenly King,
   But children of the heavenly King,
   May speak their joys abroad, May speak their joys abroad.
   (Refrain)

3. The hill of Zion yields A thousand sacred sweets,
   Before we reach the heavenly fields,
   Before we reach the heavenly fields,
   Or walk the golden streets, Or walk the golden streets.
   (Refrain)

4. Then let our songs abound, And every tear be dry;
   We're marching through Immanuel's ground,
   We're marching through Immanuel's ground,
   To fairer worlds on high, To fairer worlds on high.
   (Refrain)

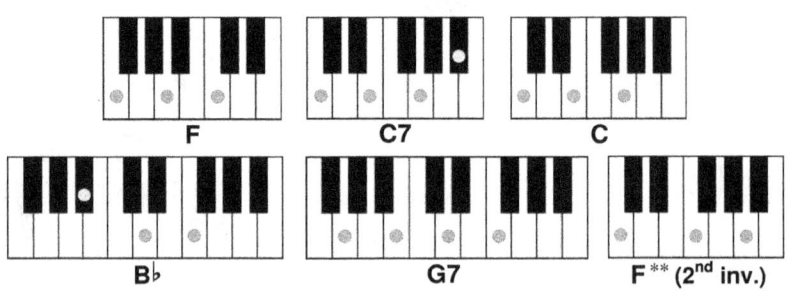

**On keyboard instrument, play second inversion

More About Jesus

Words by Eliza Hewitt

Music by John Sweney

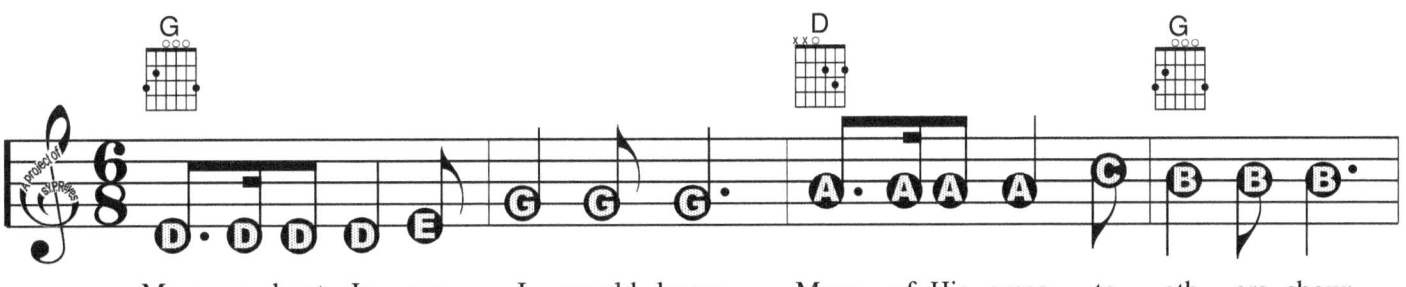

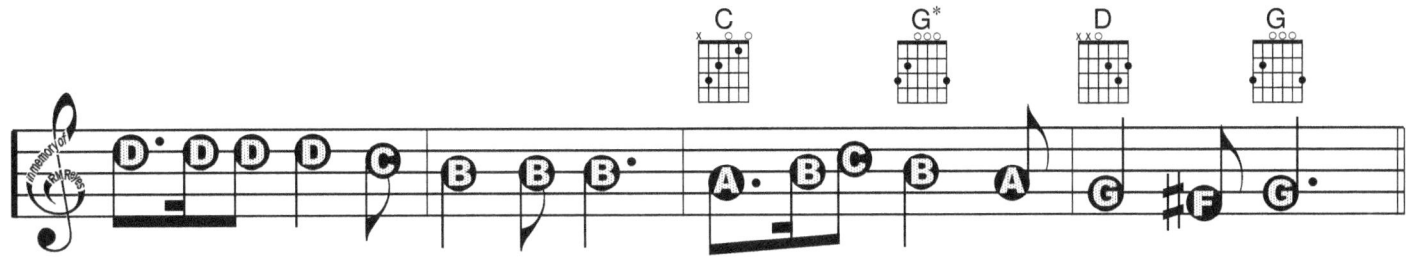

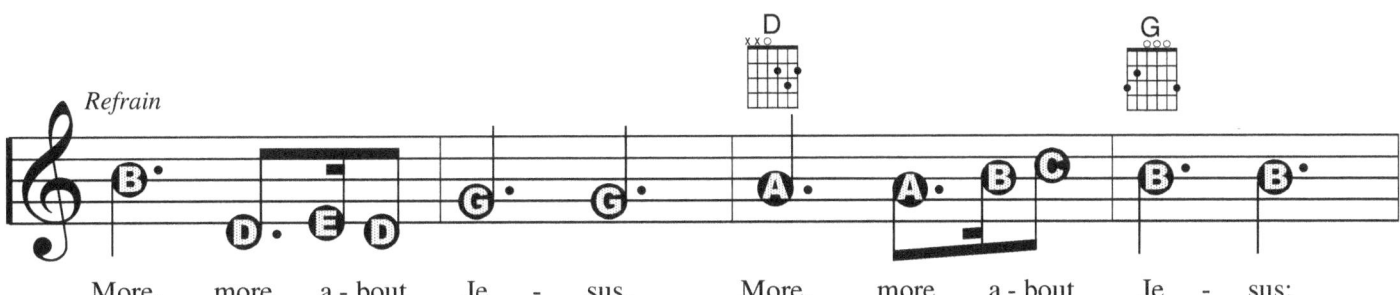

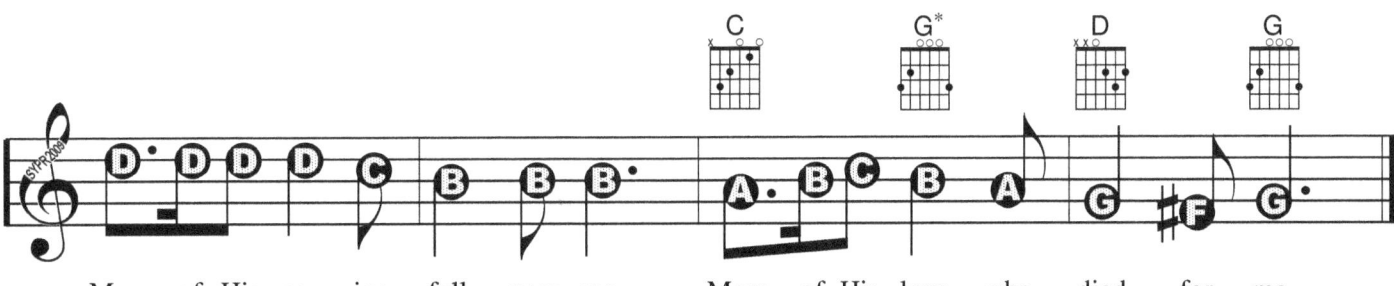

2. More about Jesus let me learn, More of His holy will discern;
   Spirit of God, my teacher be, Showing the things of Christ to me.
   (Refrain)

3. More about Jesus; in His word, Holding communion with my Lord,
   Hearing His voice in every line, Making each faithful saying mine.
   (Refrain)

4. More about Jesus; on His throne, Riches in glory all His own;
   More of His kingdom's sure increase; More of His coming, Prince of Peace.
   (Refrain)

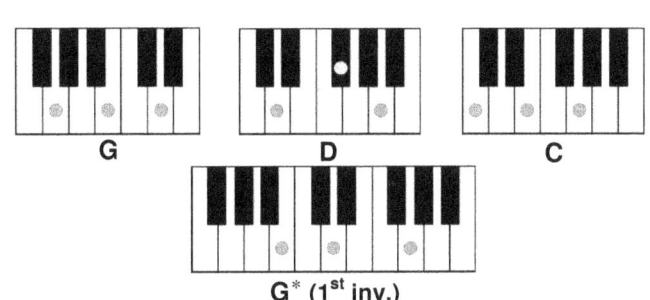

*On keyboard instrument, play first inversion

More Love to Thee

Words by Mrs. E. Prentiss
Music by William Doane

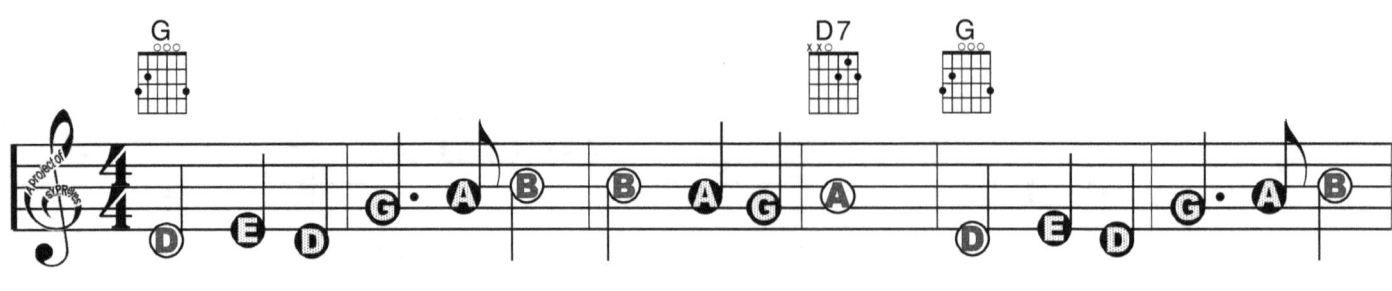

More love to Thee, O Christ! More love to Thee; Hear Thou the prayer I make

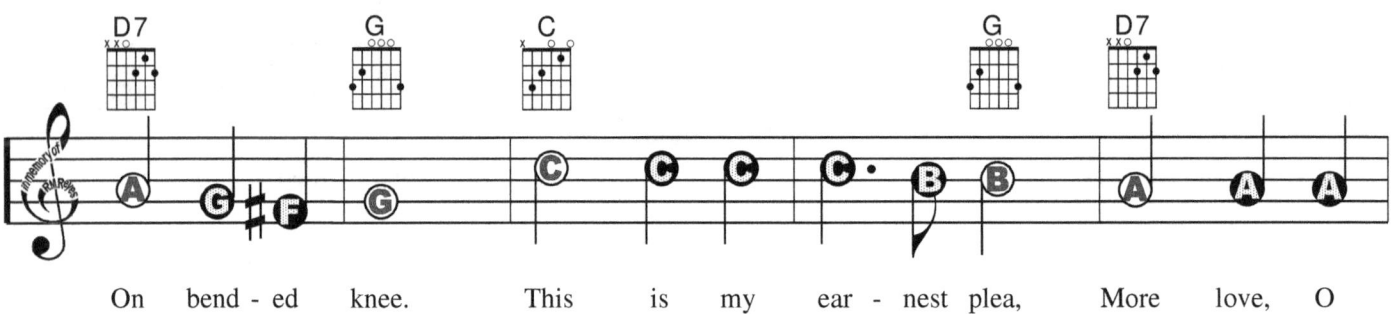

On bend-ed knee. This is my ear-nest plea, More love, O

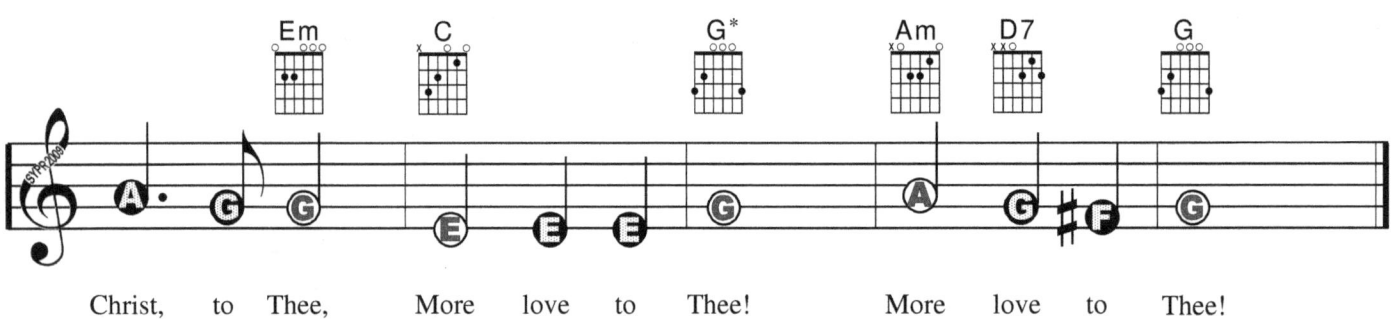

Christ, to Thee, More love to Thee! More love to Thee!

2. Once earthly joy I craved, Sought peace and rest;
   Now Thee alone I seek, Give what is best.
   This all my prayer shall be, More love, O Christ, to Thee,
   More love to Thee! More love to Thee!

3. Let sorrow do its work, Send grief or pain;
   Sweet are Thy messengers, Sweet their refrain,
   When they can sing with me, More love, O Christ, to Thee,
   More love to Thee! More love to Thee!

4. Then shall my latest breath Whisper Thy praise;
   This be the parting cry My heart shall raise,
   This still its prayer shall be: More love, O Christ, to Thee,
   More love to Thee! More love to Thee!

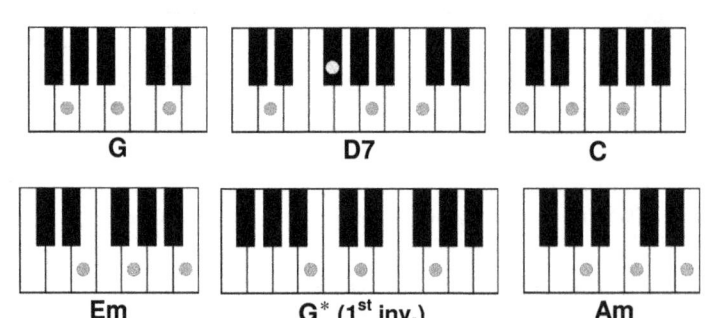

*On keyboard instrument, play first inversion

My Faith Looks Up to Thee

Words by Ray Palmer
Music by Lowell Mason

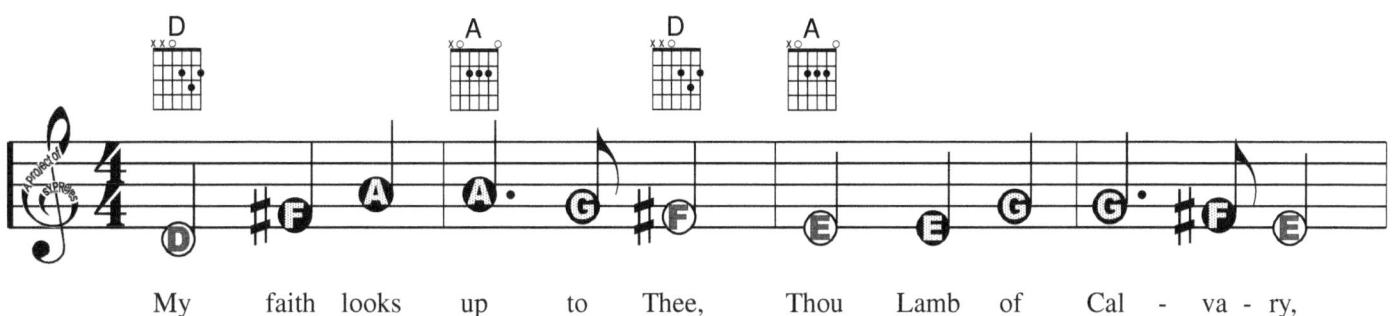

My faith looks up to Thee, Thou Lamb of Cal - va - ry,

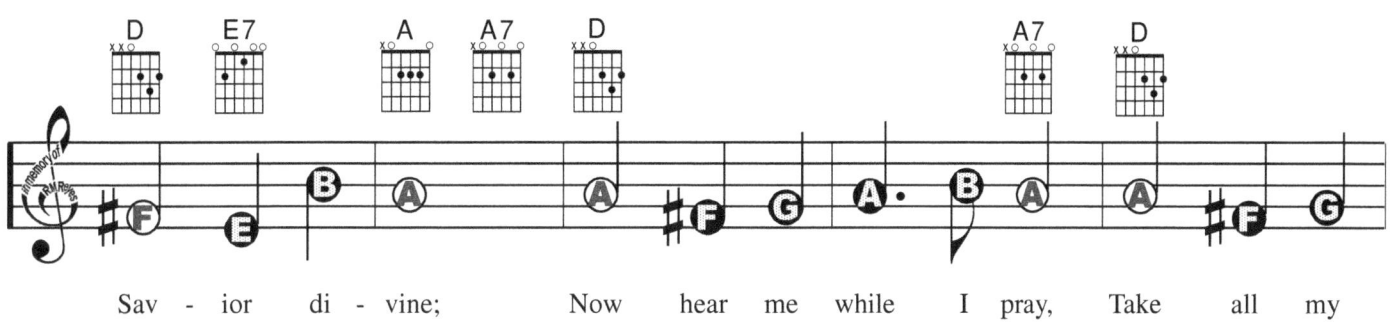

Sav - ior di - vine; Now hear me while I pray, Take all my

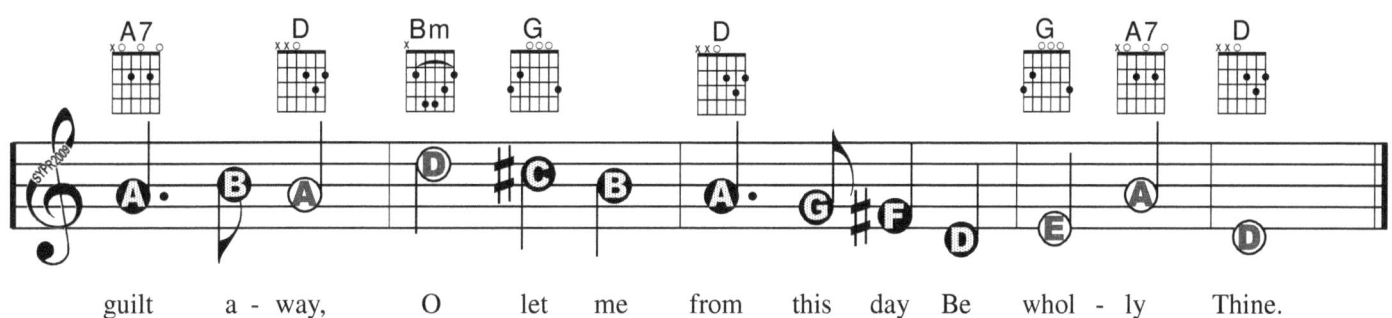

guilt a - way, O let me from this day Be whol - ly Thine.

2. May Thy rich grace impart Strength to my fainting heart,
My zeal inspire;
As Thou hast died for me, O may my love to Thee
Pure, warm, and changeless be, A living fire.

3. While life's dark maze I tread, And griefs around me spread,
Be Thou my Guide;
Bid darkness turn to day, Wipe sorrow's tears away.
Nor let me ever stray From Thee aside.

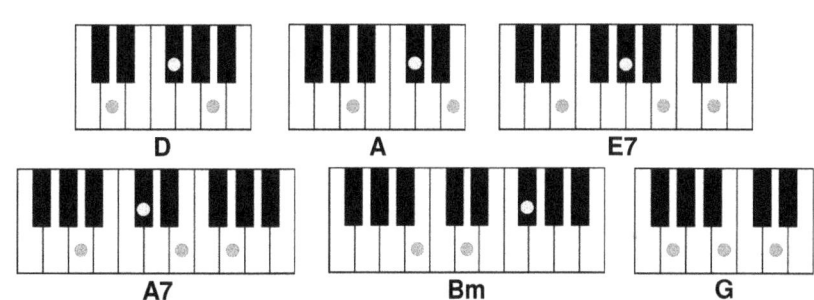

79

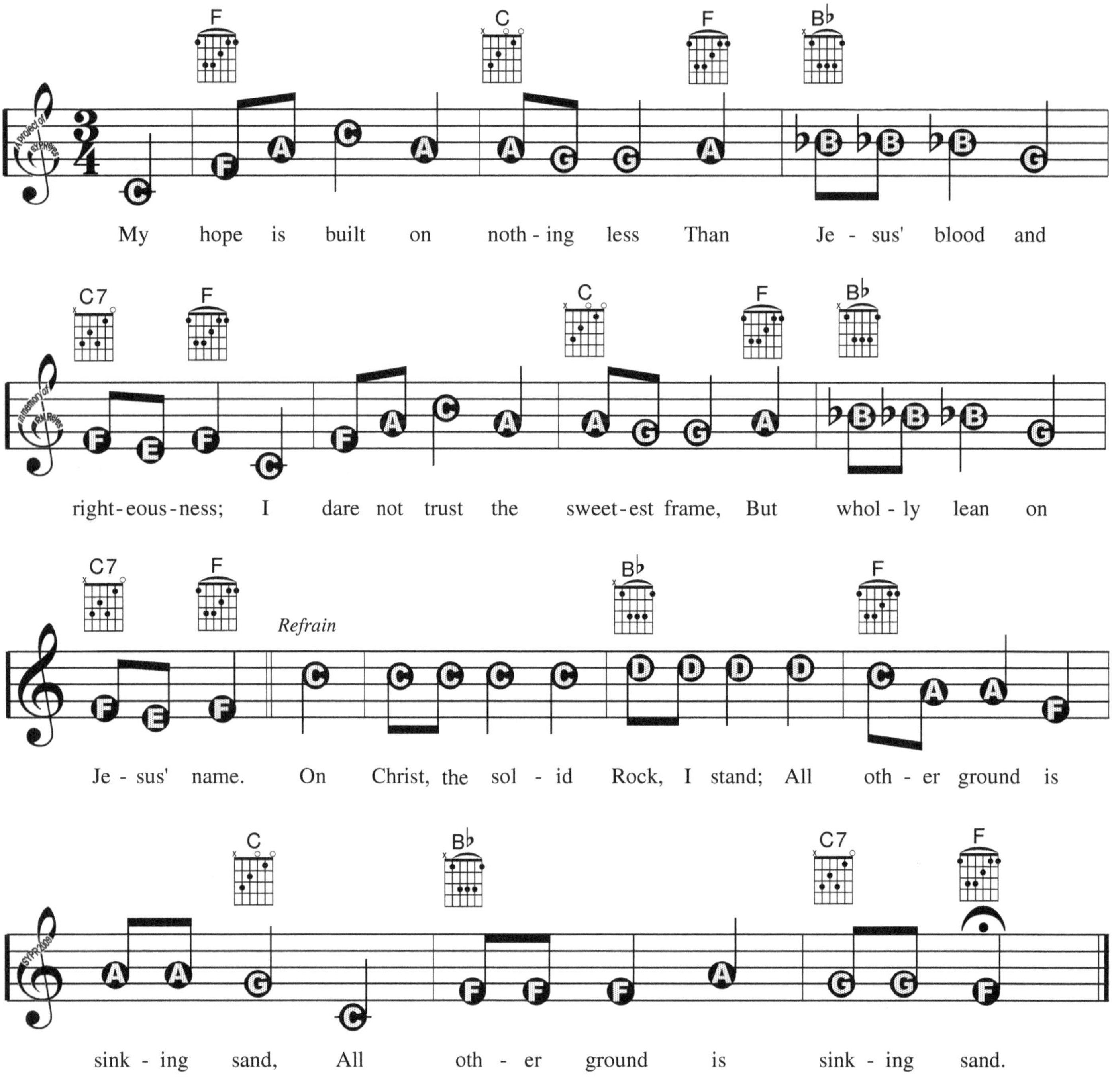

My Hope Is Built on Nothing Less

Words by Edward Mote

Music by William Bradbury

F C F B♭
My hope is built on noth - ing less Than Je - sus' blood and
C7 F C F B♭
right - eous - ness; I dare not trust the sweet - est frame, But whol - ly lean on
C7 F B♭ F
Refrain
Je - sus' name. On Christ, the sol - id Rock, I stand; All oth - er ground is
C B♭ C7 F
sink - ing sand, All oth - er ground is sink - ing sand.

2. When darkness seems to veil His face, I rest on His unchanging grace,
In every high and stormy gale My anchor holds within the veil.
(Refrain)

3. His oath, His covenant, and blood, Support me in the whelming flood;
When all around my soul gives way, He then is all my hope and stay.
(Refrain)

4. When He shall come in trumpet sound, O may I then in Him be found,
Clad in His righteousness alone, Faultless to stand before the throne.
(Refrain)

F
C
B♭
C7

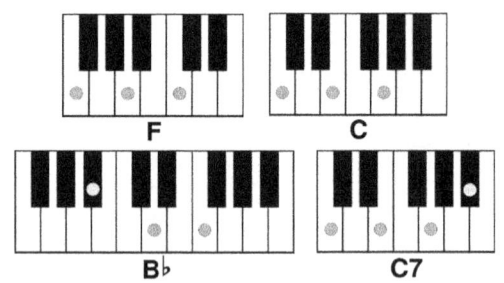

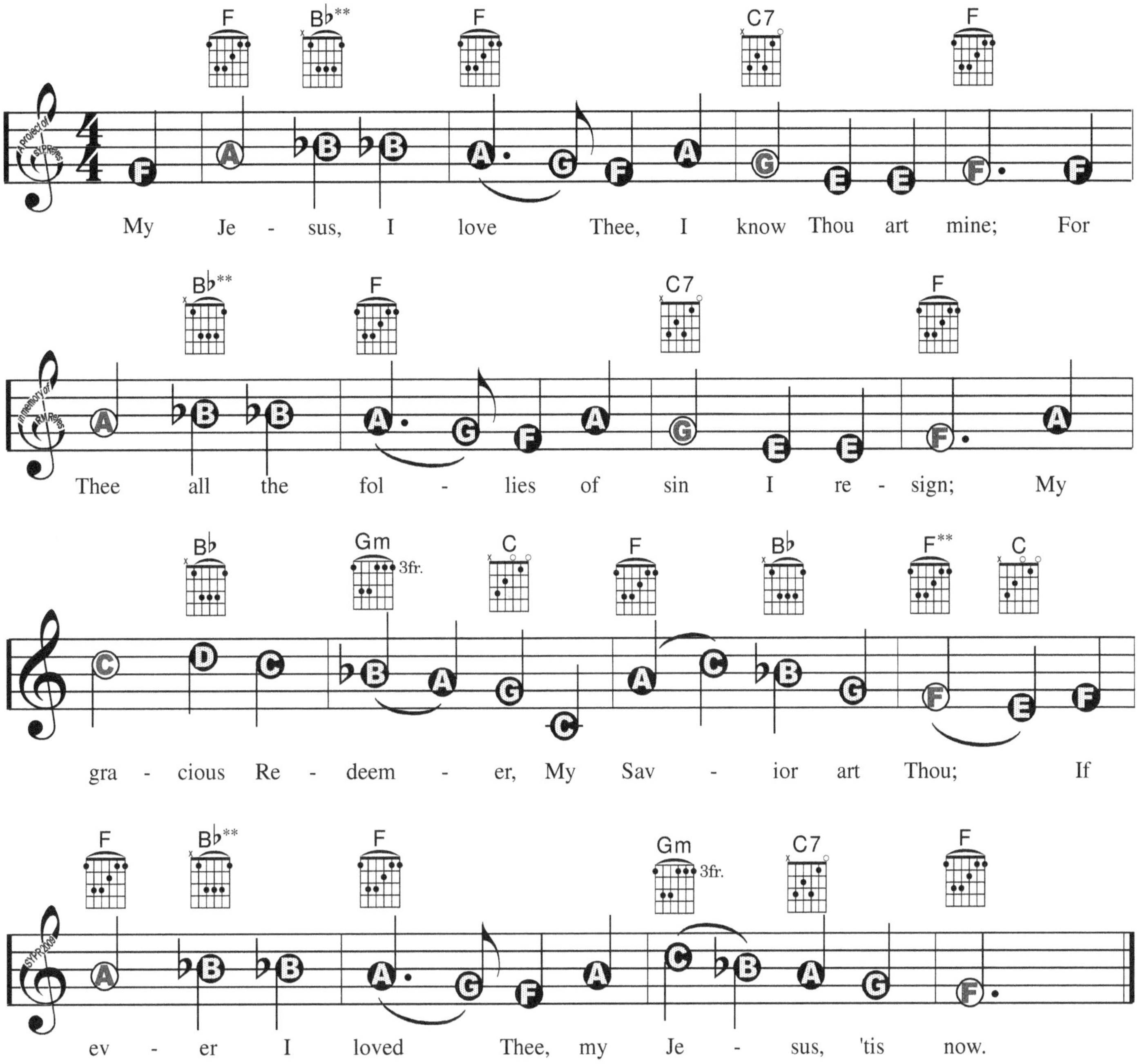

My Jesus, I Love Thee

Words by William Ralf Featherstone

Music by Adoniram Gordon

F Bb** F C7 F
My Je - sus, I love Thee, I know Thou art mine; For
Bb** F C7 F
Thee all the fol - lies of sin I re - sign; My
Bb Gm 3fr. C F Bb F** C
gra - cious Re - deem - er, My Sav - ior art Thou; If
F Bb** F Gm 3fr. C7 F
ev - er I loved Thee, my Je - sus, 'tis now.

2. I love Thee because Thou hast first loved me,
And purchased my pardon on Calvary's tree;
I love Thee for wearing the thorns on Thy brow;
If ever I loved Thee, my Jesus, 'tis now.

3. I'll love Thee in life, I will love Thee 'til death,
And praise Thee as long as Thou lendest me breath;
And say when the death dew lies cold on my brow,
If ever I loved Thee, my Jesus, 'tis now.

4. In mansions of glory and endless delight,
I'll ever adore Thee in heaven so bright;
I'll sing with the glittering crown on my brow,
If ever I loved Thee, my Jesus, 'tis now.

F
Bb** (2nd inv.)
C7
Bb
Gm
C
F** (2nd inv.)

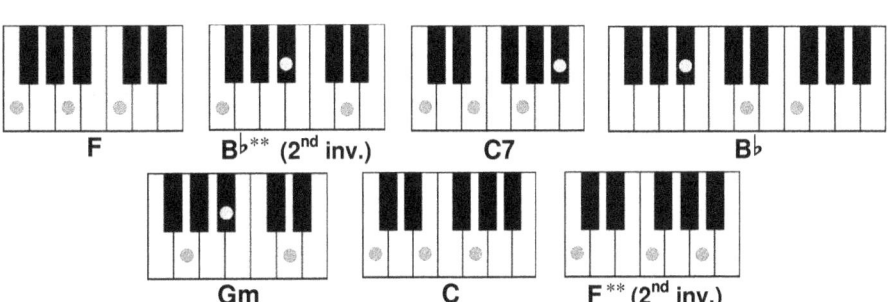

***On keyboard instrument, play second inversion*

My Maker and My King

Words by Anne Steele
Tune composer unknown

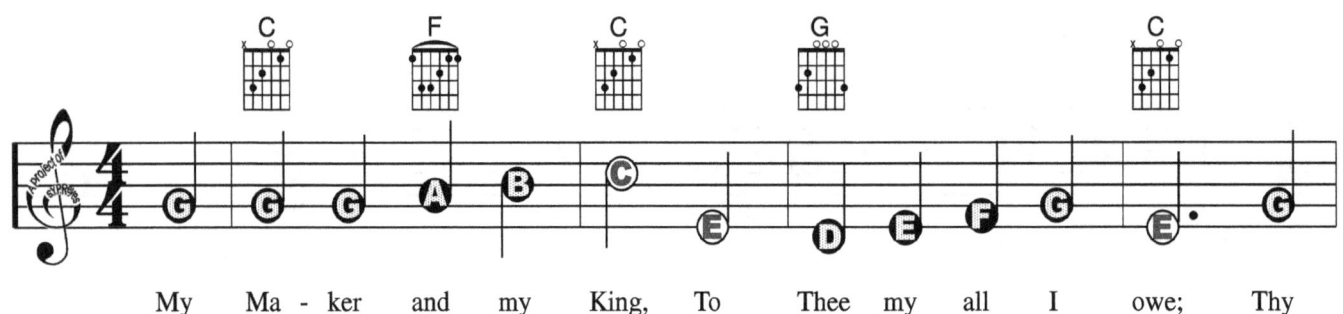

My Ma - ker and my King, To Thee my all I owe; Thy

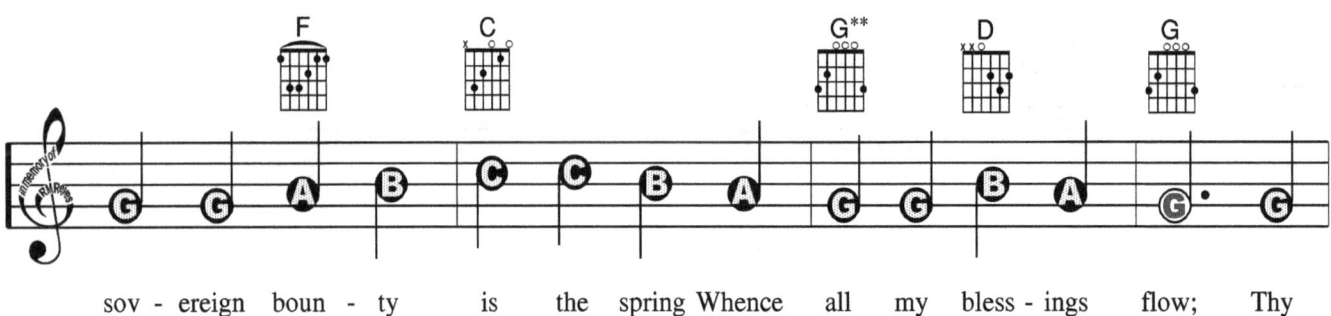

sov - ereign boun - ty is the spring Whence all my bless - ings flow; Thy

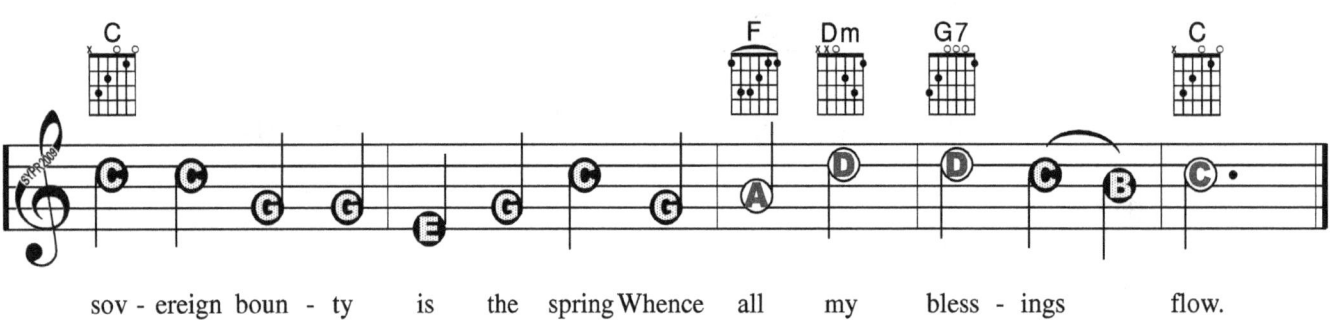

sov - ereign boun - ty is the spring Whence all my bless - ings flow.

2. The creature of Thy hand, On Thee alone I live;
My God, Thy benefits demand More praise than I can give.
My God, Thy benefits demand More praise than I can give.

3. Lord, what can I impart When all is Thine before?
Thy love demands a thankful heart; The gift alas! how poor.
Thy love demands a thankful heart; The gift alas! how poor.

4. O! let Thy grace inspire My soul with strength divine;
Let every word and each desire And all my days be Thine.
Let every word and each desire And all my days be Thine.

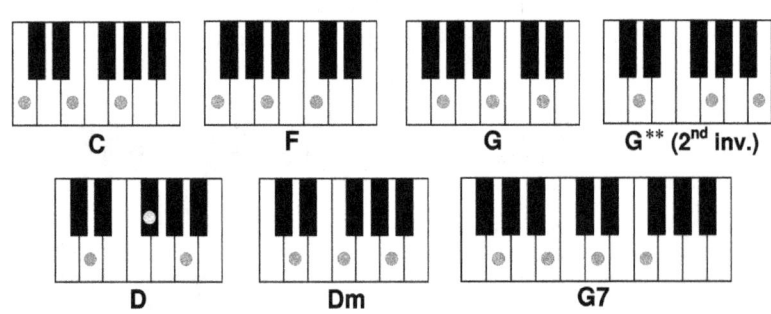

**On keyboard instrument, play second inversion*

Near the Cross

Words by Fanny Crosby

Music by William Doane

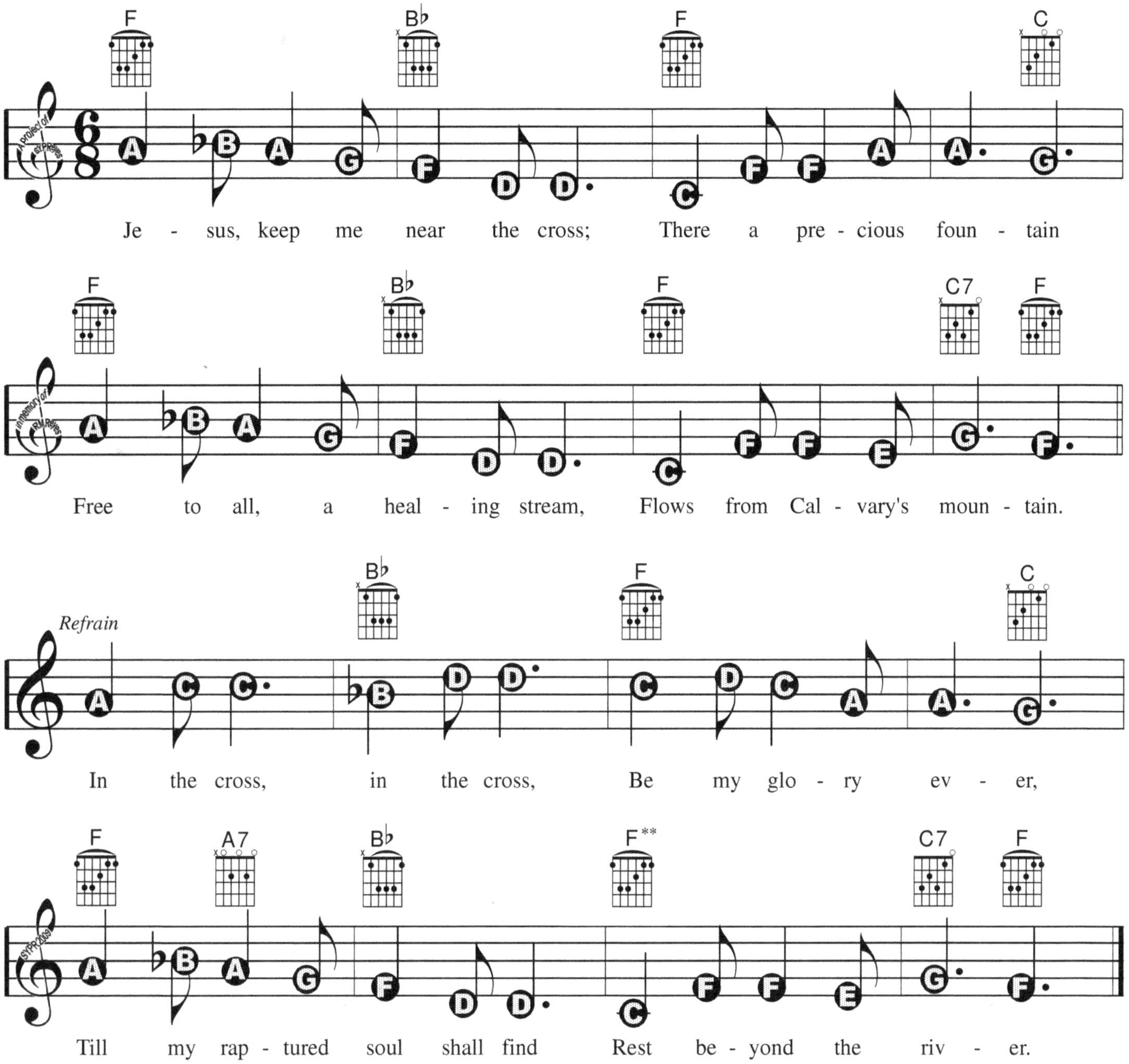

F Bb F C
Je - sus, keep me near the cross; There a pre - cious foun - tain
F Bb F C7 F
Free to all, a heal - ing stream, Flows from Cal - vary's moun - tain.
Refrain
Bb F C
In the cross, in the cross, Be my glo - ry ev - er,
F A7 Bb F** C7 F
Till my rap - tured soul shall find Rest be - yond the riv - er.

2. Near the cross, a trembling soul, Love and mercy found me;
   There the bright and Morning Star Sheds its beams around me.
   (Refrain)

3. Near the cross! O Lamb of God, Bring its scenes before me;
   Help me walk from day to day, With its shadows o'er me.
   (Refrain)

4. Near the cross I'll watch and wait, Hoping, trusting ever,
   Till I reach the golden strand, Just beyond the river.
   (Refrain)

F
Bb
C
C7
A7
F** (2nd inv.)

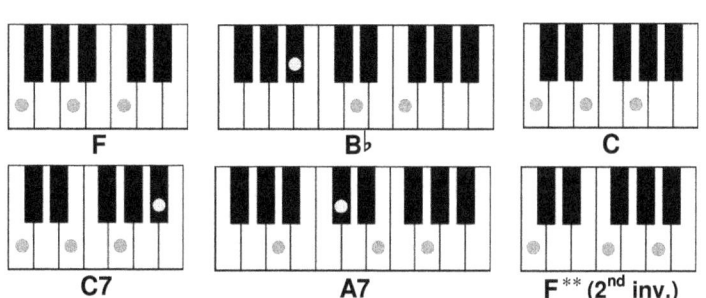

***On keyboard instrument, play second inversion*

Near to the Heart of God

Words and music by Cleland McAfee

There is a place of qui-et rest, Near to the heart of God, A place where sin can-not mo-lest, Near to the heart of

Refrain
God. O Je-sus, blest Re-deem-er, Sent from the heart of God, Hold us, who wait be-fore Thee, Near to the heart of God.

2. There is a place of comfort sweet, Near to the heart of God,
   A place where we our Savior meet, Near to the heart of God.
   (Refrain)

3. There is a place of full release, Near to the heart of God,
   A place where all is joy and peace, Near to the heart of God.
   (Refrain)

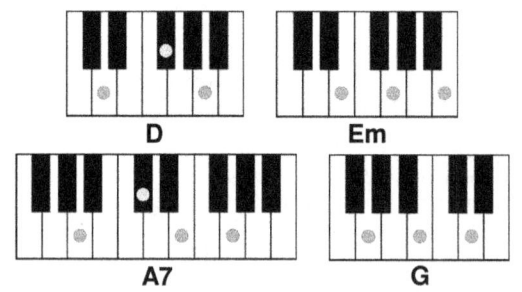

Nearer, My God, to Thee

Words by Sarah Adams
Music by Lowell Mason

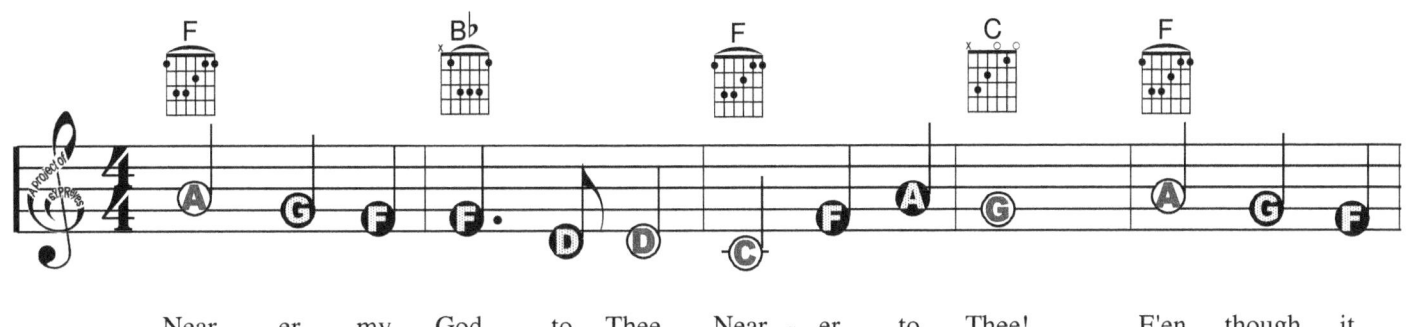

Near - er, my God, to Thee, Near - er to Thee! E'en though it

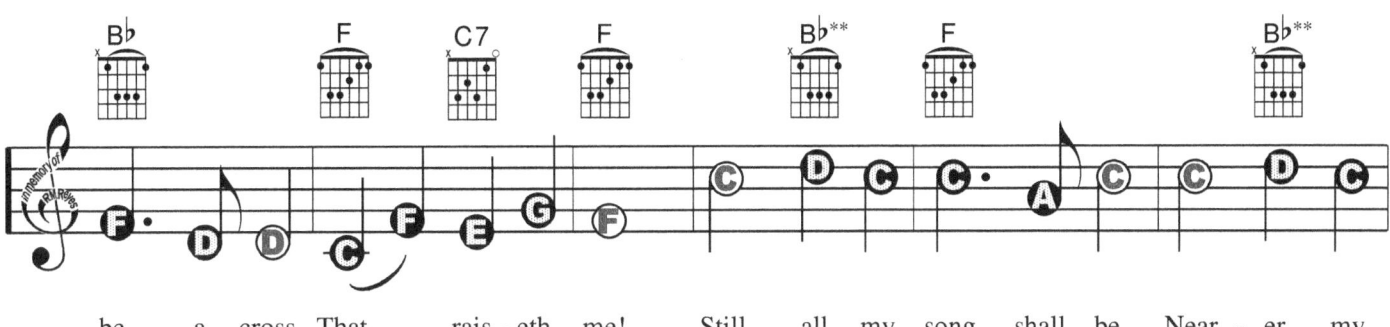

be a cross That rais - eth me! Still all my song shall be, Near - er, my

God, to Thee, Near - er, my God, to Thee, Near - er to Thee.

2. Though like a wanderer, Daylight all gone,
   Darkness be over me, My rest a stone;
   Yet in my dreams I'd be Nearer, my God, to Thee,
   Nearer, my God, to Thee, Nearer to Thee.

3. There let the way appear, Steps up to heaven;
   All that Thou sendest me, In mercy given;
   Angels to beckon me Nearer, my God, to Thee,
   Nearer, my God, to Thee, Nearer to Thee.

4. Then, with my waking thoughts Bright with Thy praise,
   Out of my stony griefs Bethel I'll raise;
   So by my woes to be Nearer, my God, to Thee,
   Nearer, my God, to Thee, Nearer to Thee.

5. Or if, on joyful wing Cleaving the sky,
   Sun, moon, and stars forgot, Upward I fly,
   Still all my song shall be Nearer, my God, to Thee,
   Nearer, my God, to Thee, Nearer to Thee.

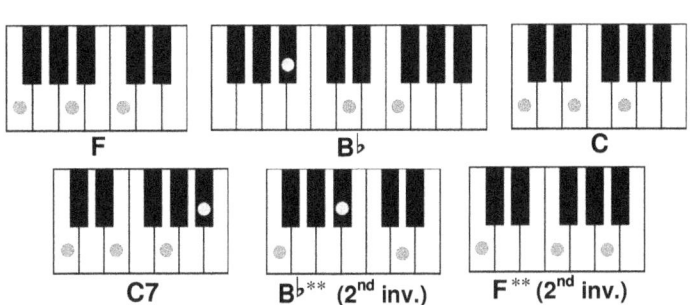

**On keyboard instrument, play second inversion

Nothing Between

Words and music by Charles Tindley

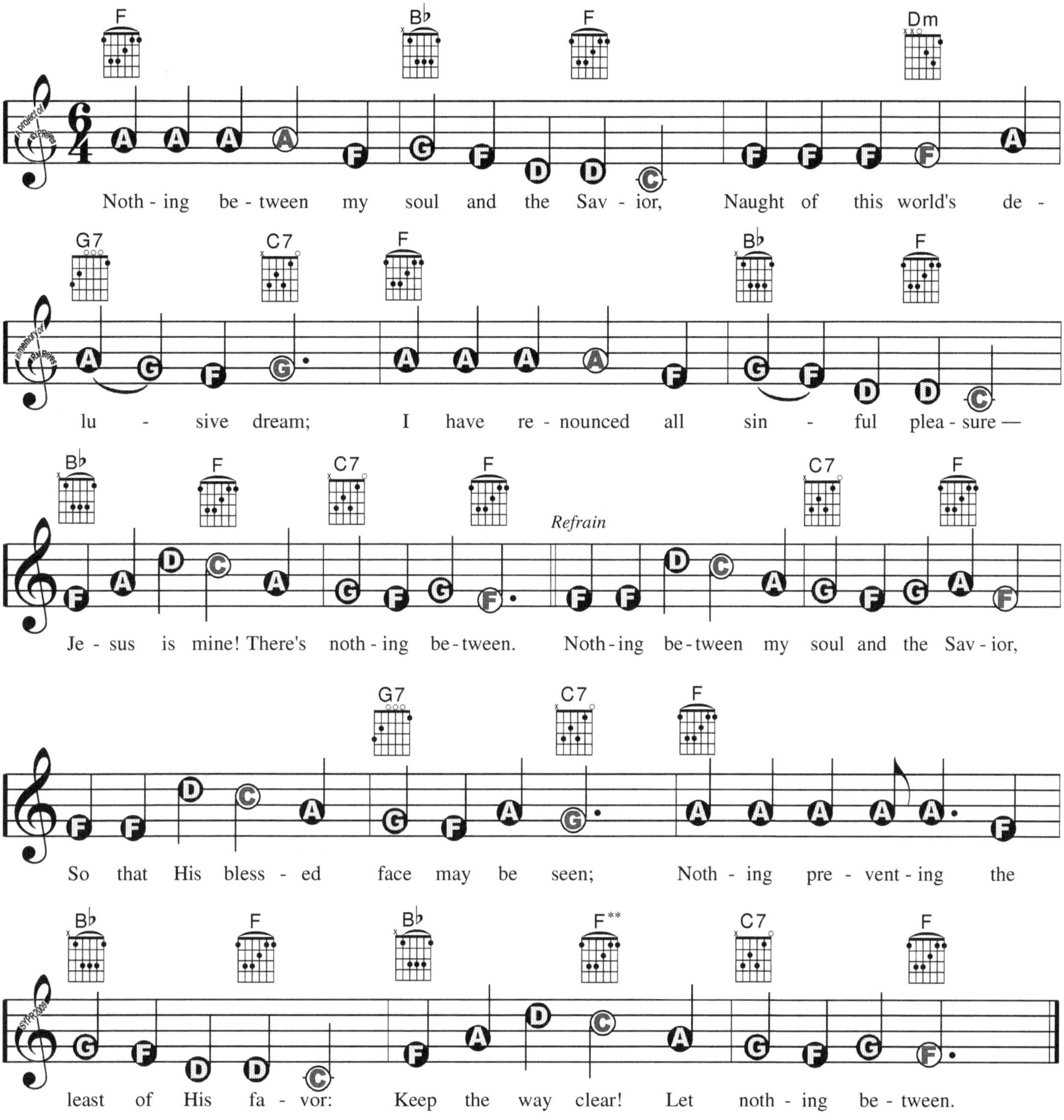

Nothing between my soul and the Savior, Naught of this world's delusive dream; I have renounced all sinful pleasure — Jesus is mine! There's nothing between.

Refrain
Nothing between my soul and the Savior, So that His blessed face may be seen; Nothing preventing the least of His favor: Keep the way clear! Let nothing between.

2. Nothing between, like worldly pleasure;
Habits of life, though harmless they seem,
Must not my heart from Him ever sever--
He is my all! There's nothing between.
(Refrain)

3. Nothing between, e'en many hard trials,
Though the whole world against me convene;
Watching with prayer and much self-denial--
Triumph at last, With nothing between!
(Refrain)

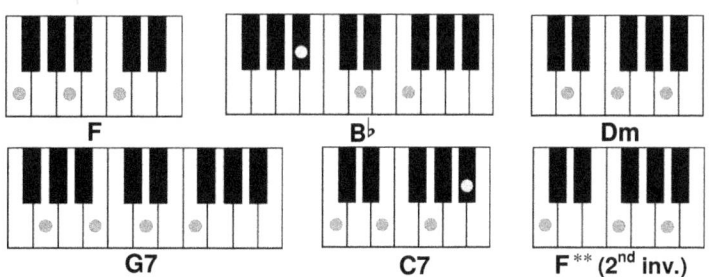

**On keyboard instrument, play second inversion

O Brother, Be Faithful

Words by Uriah Smith
Music by Isaac Woodbury

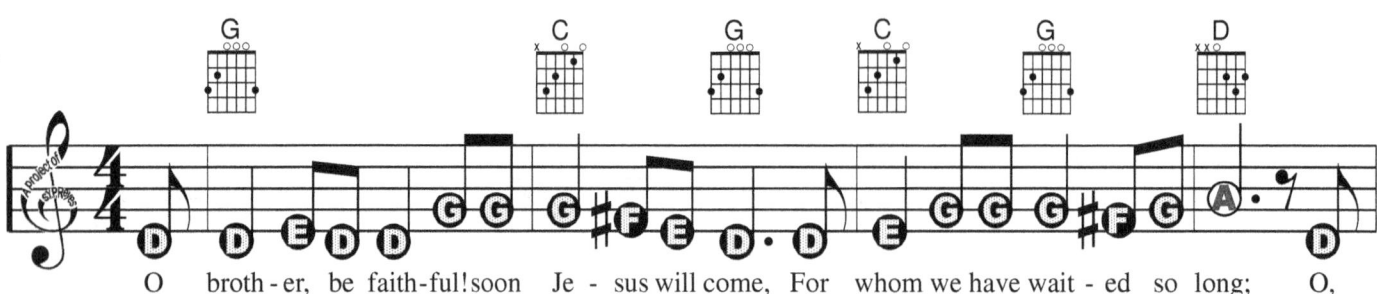
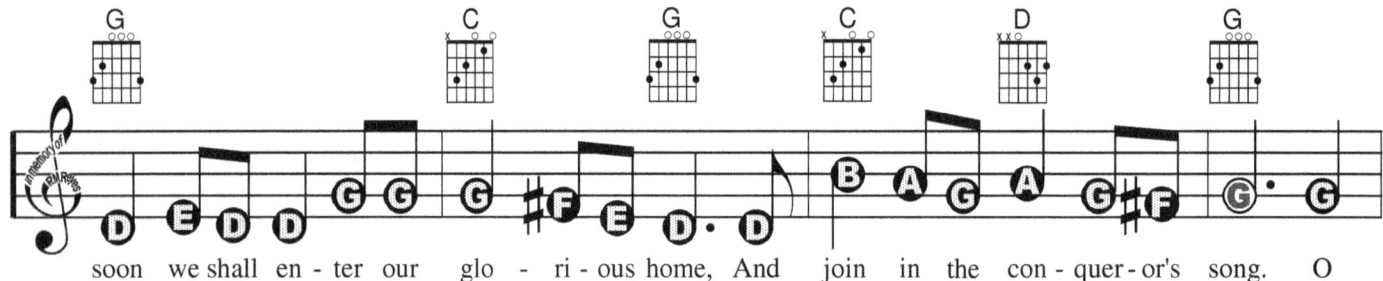
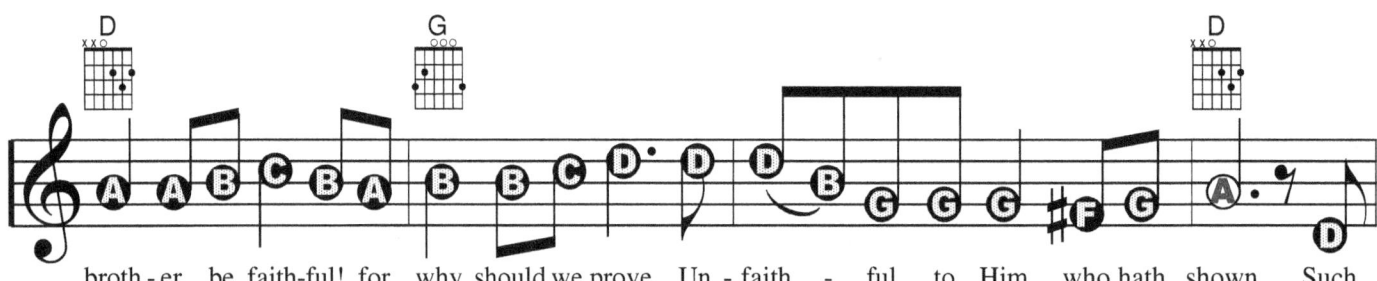
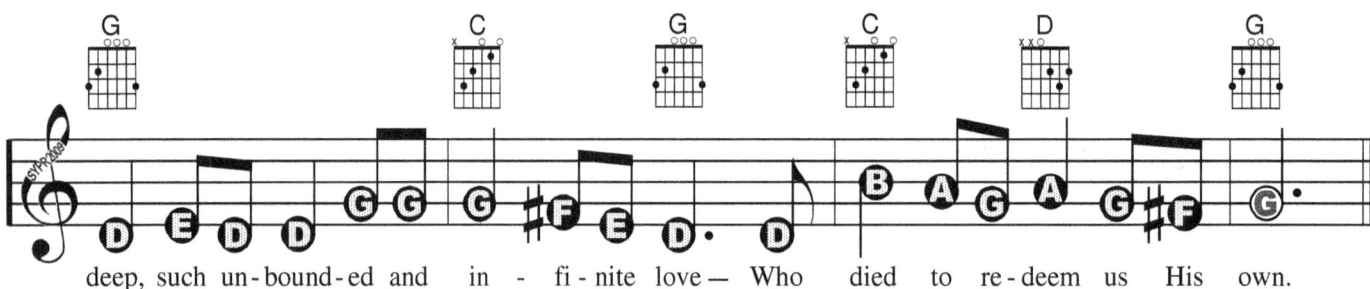

2. O brother. be faithful! the city of gold, Prepared for the good and the blest,
   Is waiting its portals of pearl to unfold, And welcome thee into thy rest.
   Then, brother, prove faithful! not long shall we stay In weariness here, and forlorn,
   Time's dark night of sorrow is wearing away, We haste to the glorious morn.

3. O brother, be faithful! He soon will descend, Creation's omnipotent King,
   While legions of angels His chariot attend, And palm wreaths of victory bring.
   O brother, be faithful! and soon shalt thou hear Thy Saviour pronounce the glad word,
   Well done, faithful servant, thy title is clear, To enter the joy of thy Lord.

4. O brother, be faithful! eternity's years Shall tell for thy faithfulness now,
   When bright smiles of gladness shall scatter thy tears, A coronet gleam on thy brow.
   O brother, be faithful! the promise is sure, That waits for the faithful and tried;
   To reign with the ransomed, immortal and pure, And ever with Jesus abide.

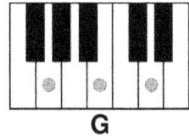
G

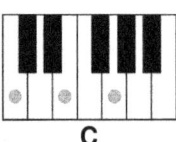
C

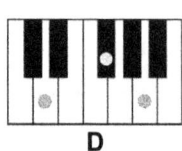
D

O Come, All Ye Faithful

Translated from Latin by Frederick Oakeley

Music by John Wade

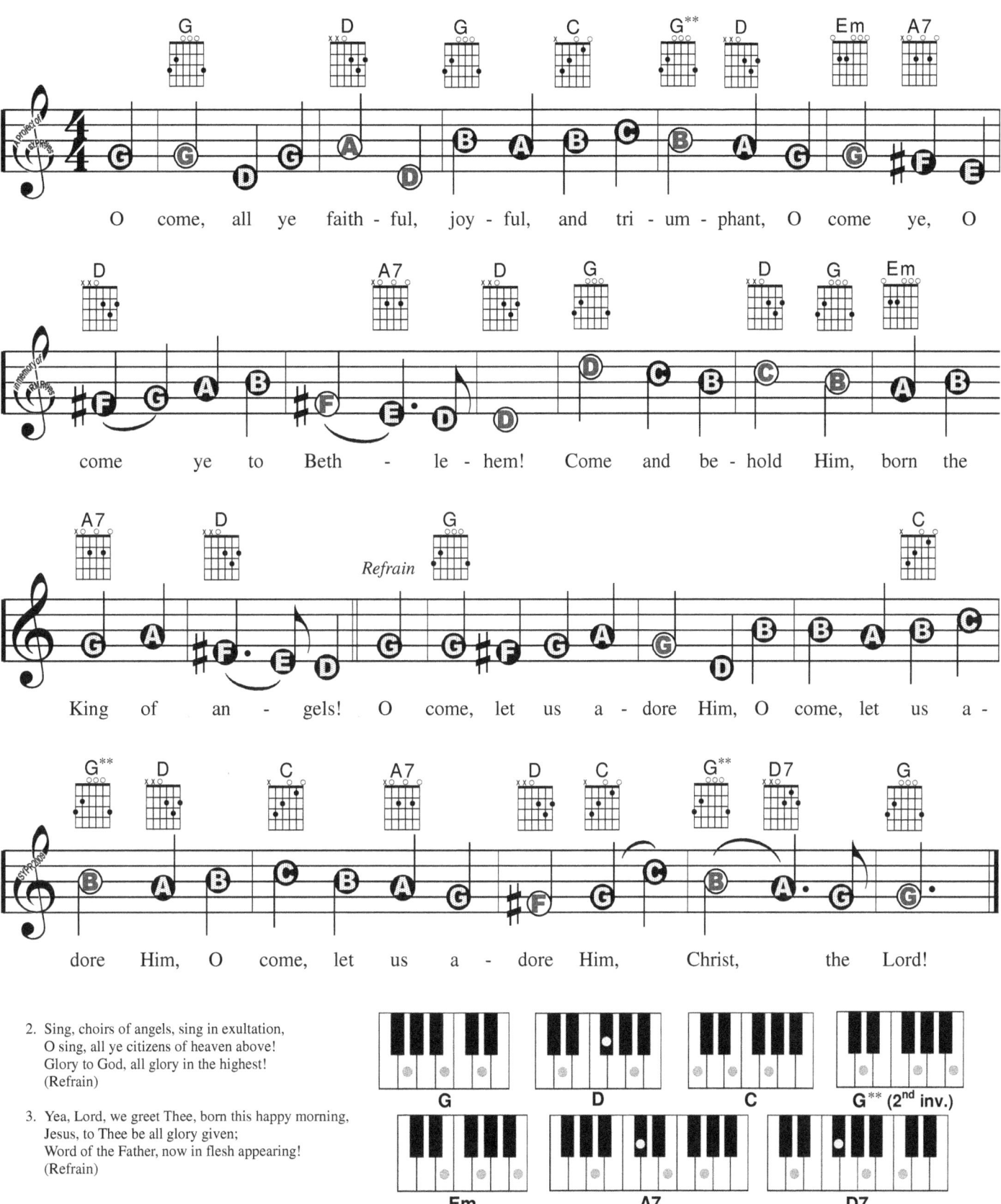

2. Sing, choirs of angels, sing in exultation,
   O sing, all ye citizens of heaven above!
   Glory to God, all glory in the highest!
   (Refrain)

3. Yea, Lord, we greet Thee, born this happy morning,
   Jesus, to Thee be all glory given;
   Word of the Father, now in flesh appearing!
   (Refrain)

**On keyboard instrument, play second inversion*

O Day of Rest and Gladness

Words by Christopher Wordsworth

German Melody

O day of rest and gladness, O day of joy and light, O
balm of care and sadness, Most beautiful, most bright; On
thee, the high and lowly, Who bend before the throne, Sing,
Holy, holy, holy, To the Eternal One.

2. Thou art a port protected From storms that round us rise,
   A garden intersected With streams of Paradise;
   Thou art a cooling fountain In life's dry, dreary sand,
   From thee, like Pisgah's mountain, We view our promised land.

3. A day of sweet reflection Thou art, a day of love;
   A day to raise affection From earth to things above.
   New graces ever gaining From this our day of rest,
   We seek the rest remaining In mansions of the blest.

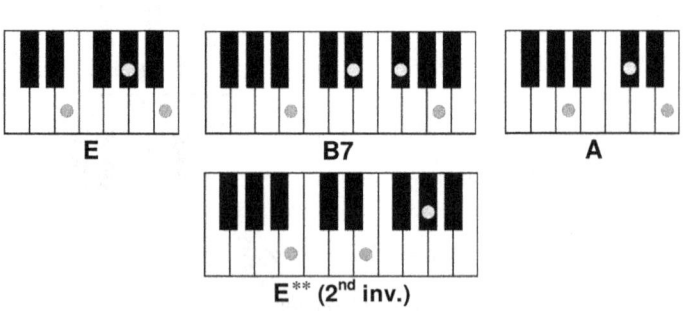

**On keyboard instrument, play second inversion

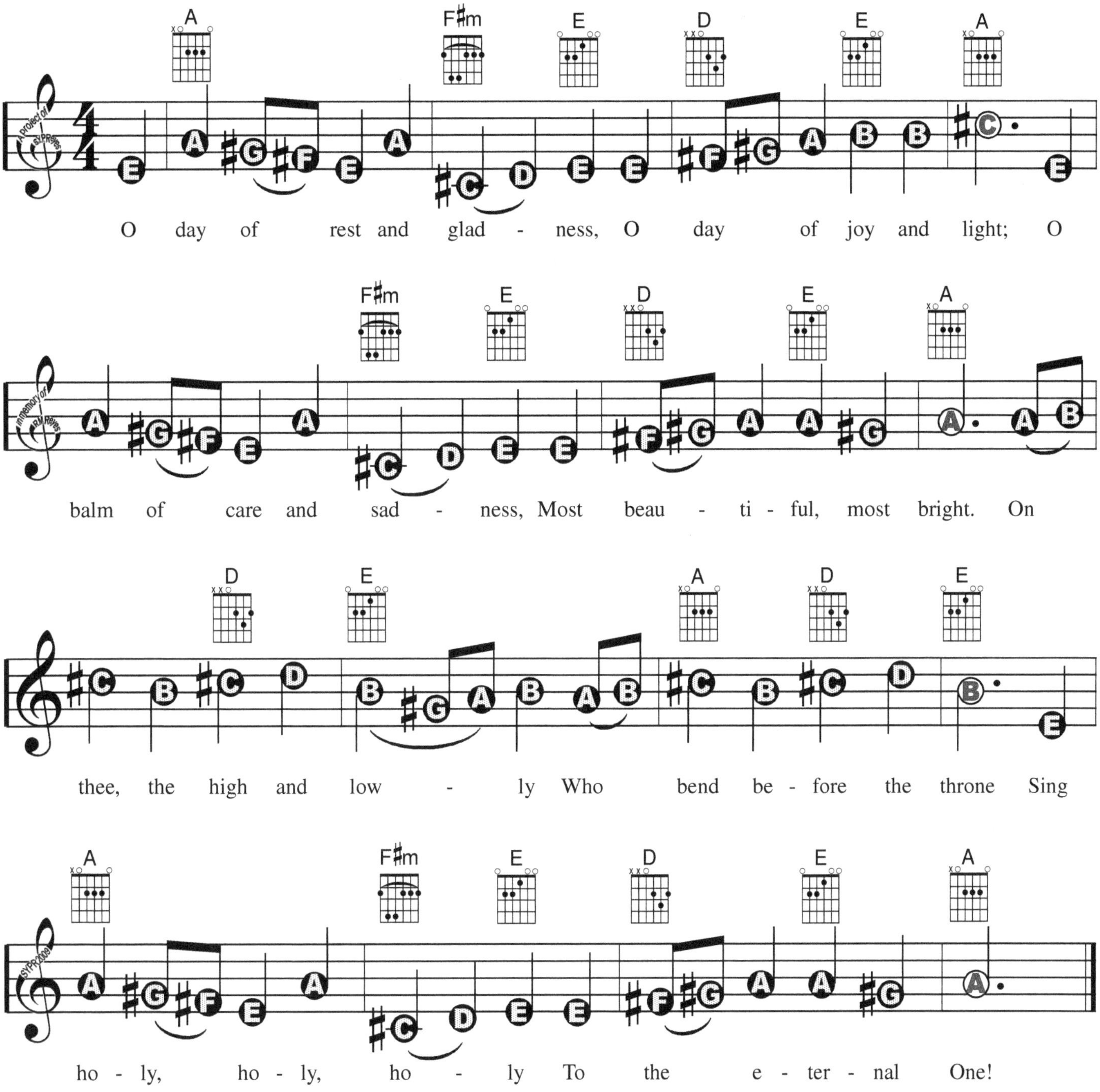

O Day of Rest and Gladness

Words by Christopher Wordsworth

(Alternate tune)

Music from *Gesangbuch der Herzogl*

A F♯m E D E A
O day of rest and glad - ness, O day of joy and light; O
F♯m E D E A
balm of care and sad - ness, Most beau - ti - ful, most bright. On
D E A D E
thee, the high and low - ly Who bend be - fore the throne Sing
A F♯m E D E A
ho - ly, ho - ly, ho - ly To the e - ter - nal One!

A
F#m
E
D

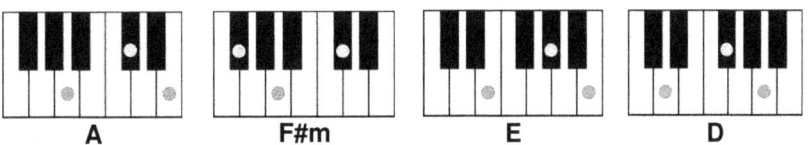

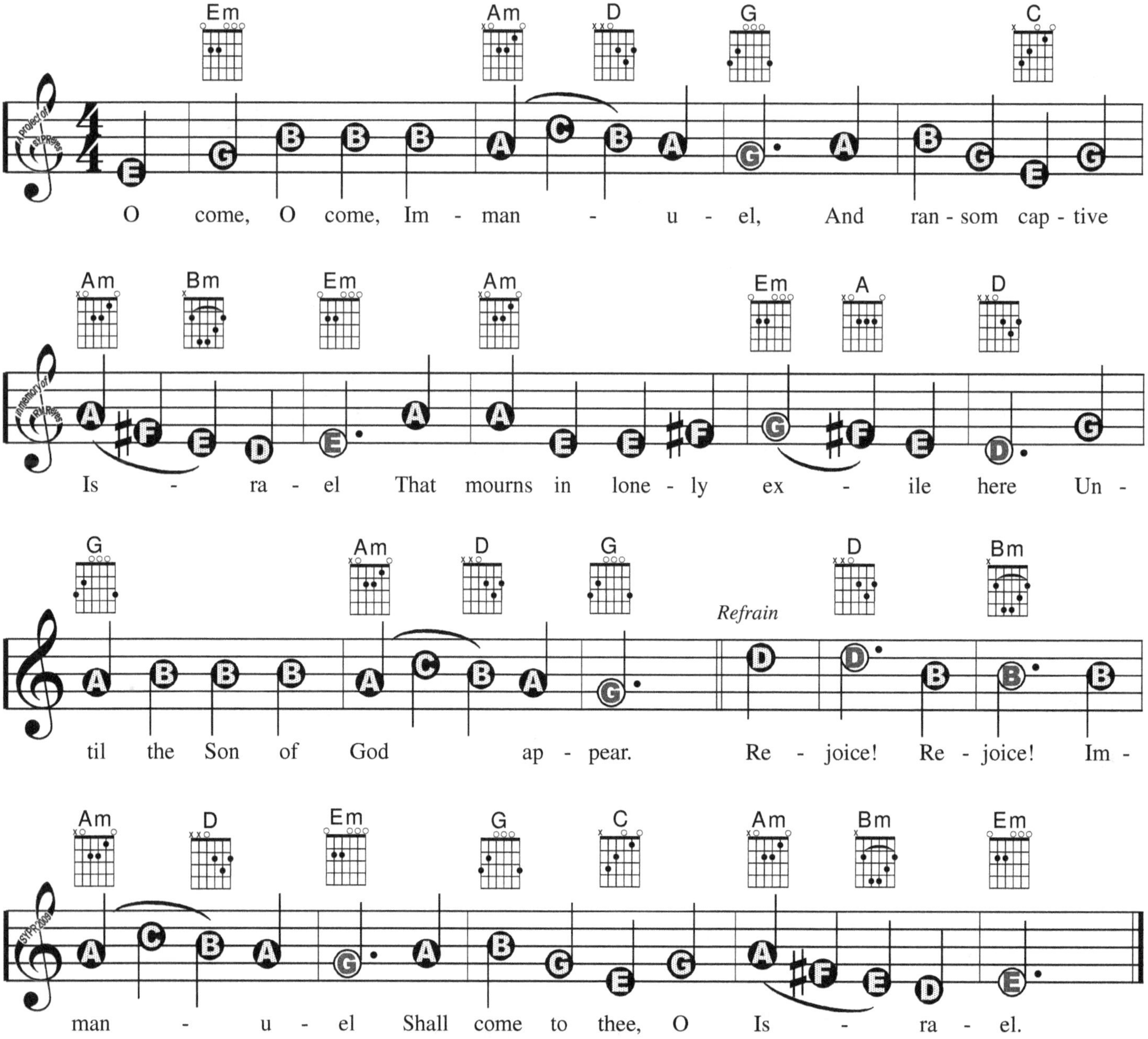

O Come, O Come, Immanuel

From 9th Century Latin text
Translated by John Neale and Henry Coffin

15th Century French Processional

Em Am D G C
O come, O come, Im - man - u - el, And ran - som cap - tive
Am Bm Em Am Em A D
Is - ra - el That mourns in lone - ly ex - ile here Un -
G Am D G D Bm
Refrain
til the Son of God ap - pear. Re - joice! Re - joice! Im -
Am D Em G C Am Bm Em
man - u - el Shall come to thee, O Is - ra - el.

2. O come, Thou Wisdom from on high,
   And order all things, far and nigh;
   To us the path of knowledge show,
   And cause us in her ways to go.
   (Refrain)

3. O come, Desire of nations, bind
   All peoples in one heart and mind;
   Bid envy, strife, and quarrels cease;
   Fill the whole world with heaven's peace.
   (Refrain)

Em
Am
D
G
C
Bm
A

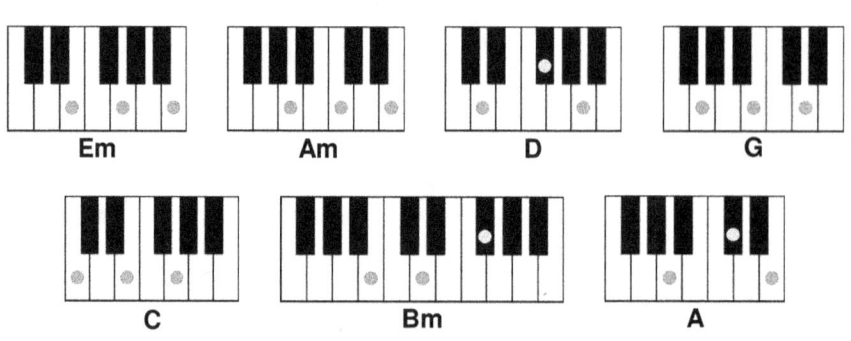

O, How I Love Jesus

Words by Frederick Whitfield
19th century American melody

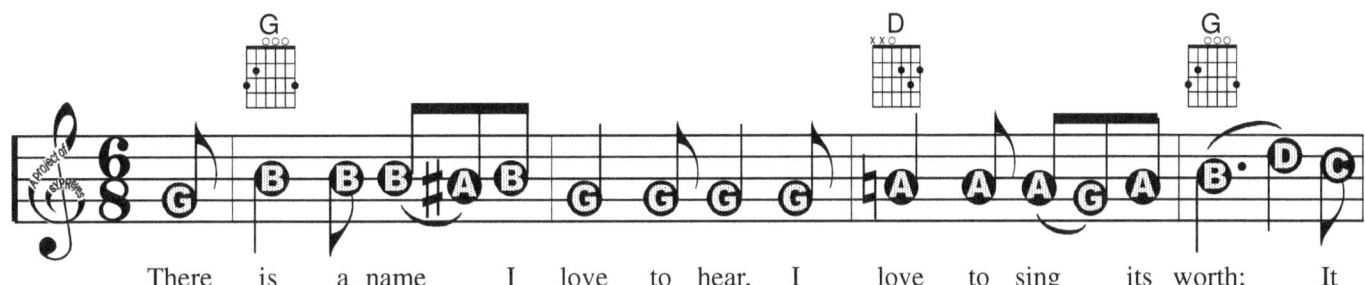

There is a name I love to hear, I love to sing its worth; It

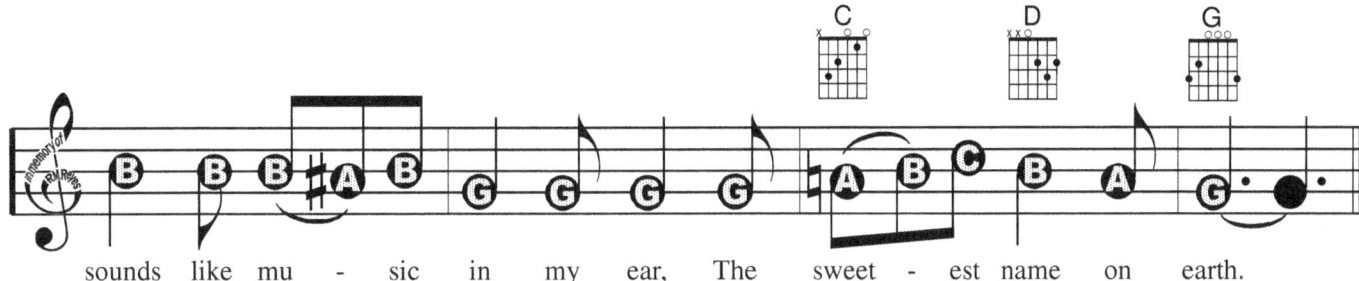

sounds like mu-sic in my ear, The sweet-est name on earth.

Refrain

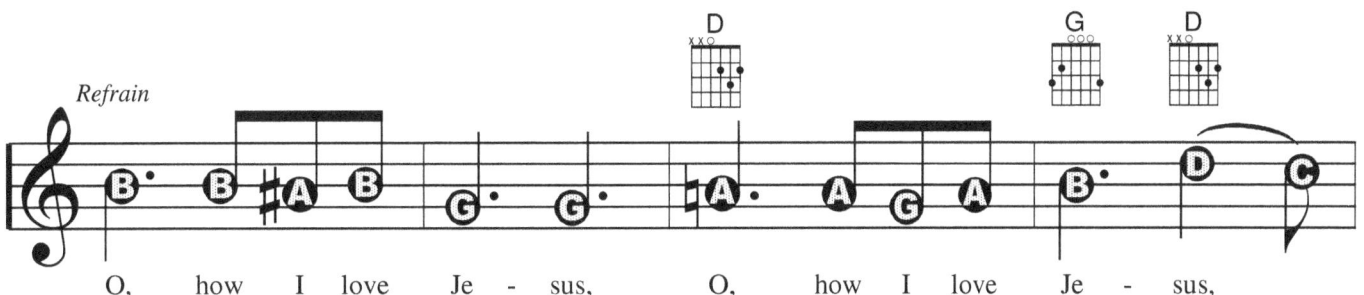

O, how I love Je-sus, O, how I love Je-sus,

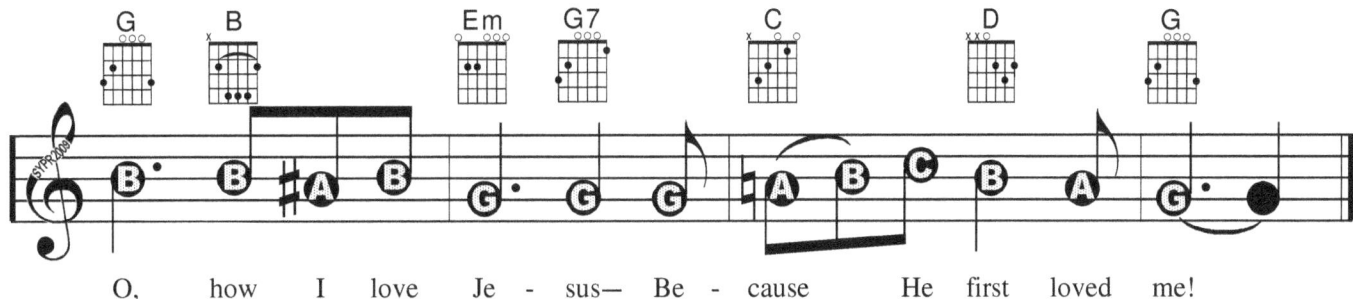

O, how I love Je-sus— Be-cause He first loved me!

2. It tells me of a Savior's love, Who died to set me free;
It tells me of His precious blood, The sinner's perfect plea.
(Refrain)

3. It tells of One whose loving heart Can feel my deepest woe,
Who in each sorrow bears a part That none can bear below.
(Refrain)

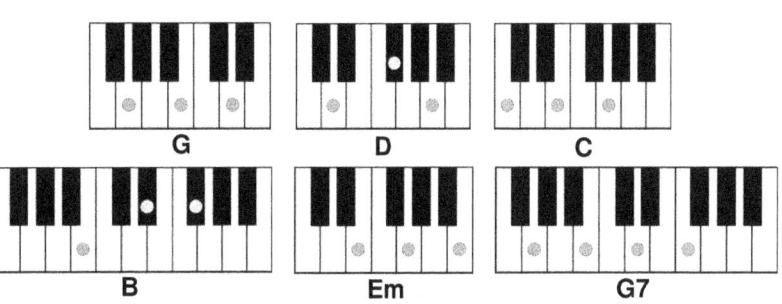

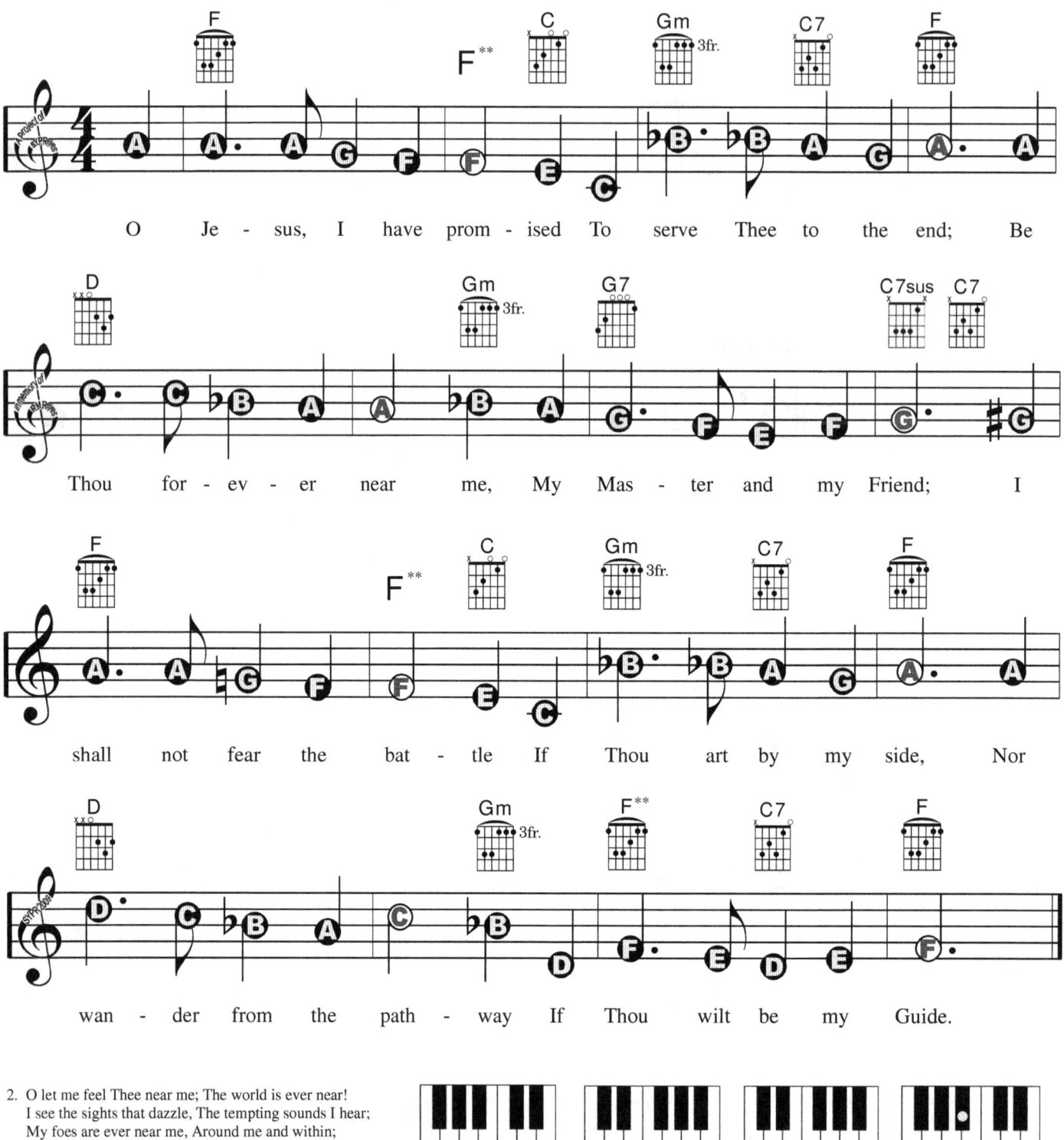

O Let Me Walk With Thee

Words by L. D. Avery Stuttle
Music by Edwin Barnes

O let me walk with Thee, my God, As E-noch walked in days of old; Place Thou my trem-bling hand in Thine, And sweet com-mun-ion with Thee hold; E'en though the path I may not see, Yet, Je-sus, let me walk with Thee.

2. I cannot, dare not, walk alone; The tempest rages in the sky,
   A thousand snares beset my feet, A thousand foes are lurking nigh.
   Still Thou the raging of the sea O Master! let me walk with Thee.

3. If I may rest my hand in Thine, I'll count the joys of earth but loss,
   And firmly, bravely journey on; I'll bear the banner of the cross
   Till Zion's glorious gates I see; Yet, Saviour, let me walk with Thee.

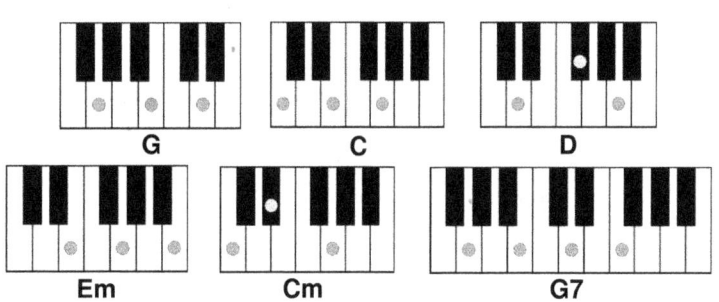

O Little Town of Bethlehem

Words by Phillips Brooks
Music by L. H. Redner

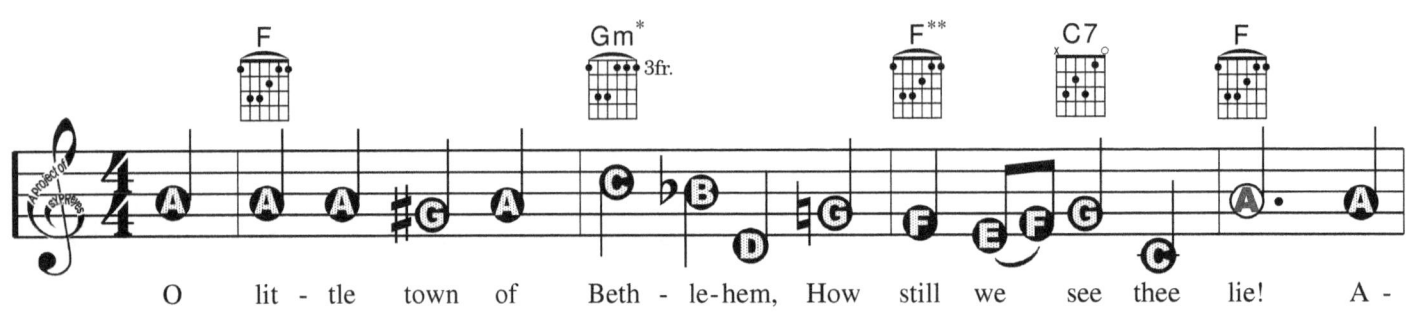

O lit-tle town of Beth-le-hem, How still we see thee lie! A-

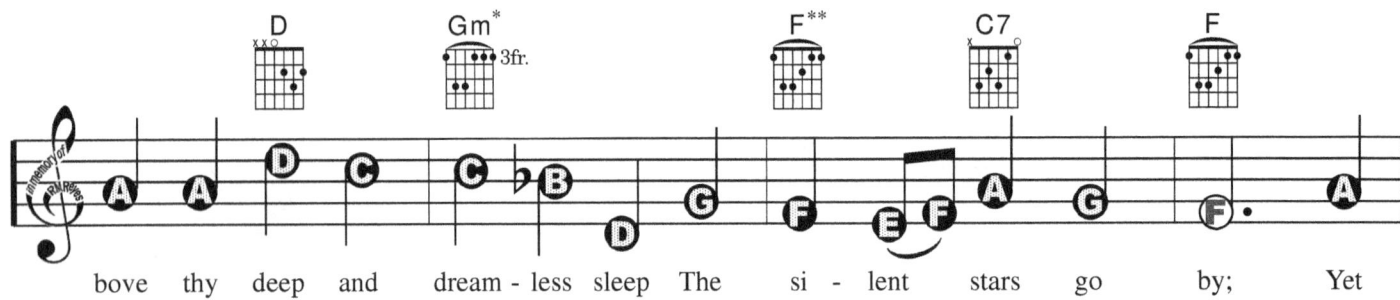

bove thy deep and dream-less sleep The si-lent stars go by; Yet

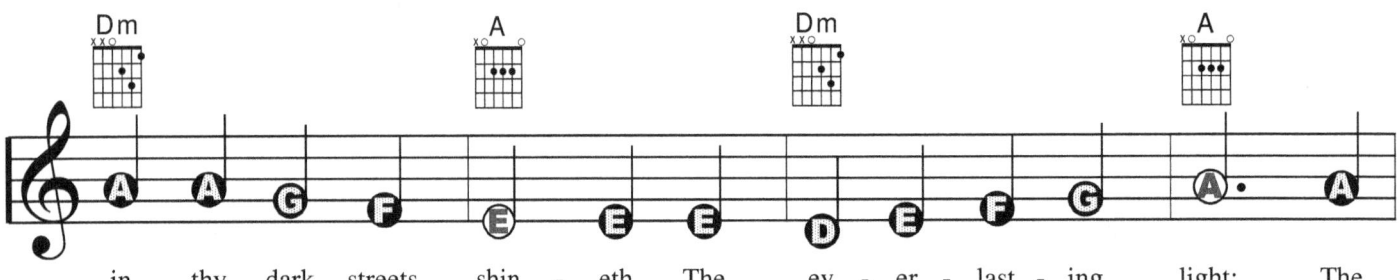

in thy dark streets shin-eth The ev-er-last-ing light; The

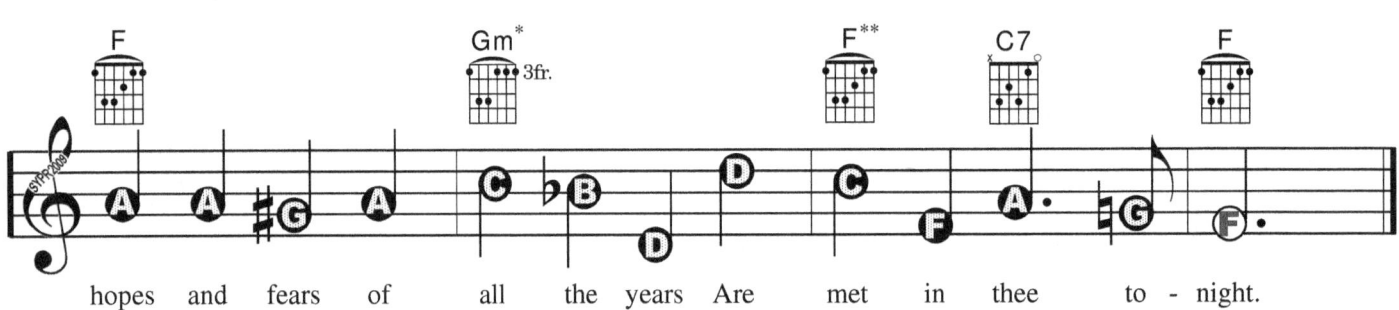

hopes and fears of all the years Are met in thee to-night.

2. For Christ is born of Mary; And gathered all above,
While mortals sleep, the angels keep Their watch of wondering love.
O morning stars, together Proclaim the holy birth!
And praises sing to God the King, And peace to men on earth.

3. How silently, how silently The wondrous gift is given!
So God imparts to human hearts The blessings of His heaven.
No ear may hear His coming; But in this world of sin,
Where meek souls will receive Him still, The dear Christ enters in.

4. O holy Child of Bethlehem, Descend to us, we pray;
Cast out our sin and enter in--Be born in us today.
We hear the Christmas angels The great glad tidings tell--
O come to us, abide with us, Our Lord Immanuel!

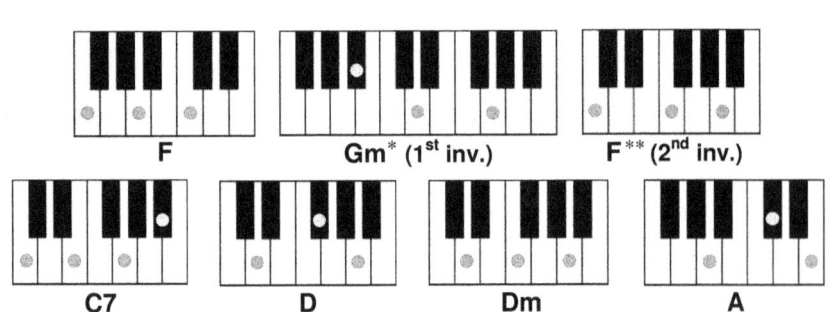

*On keyboard instrument, play first inversion
**On keyboard instrument, play second inversion

O Worship the King

Words by Robert Grant
Music by J. Michael Haydn

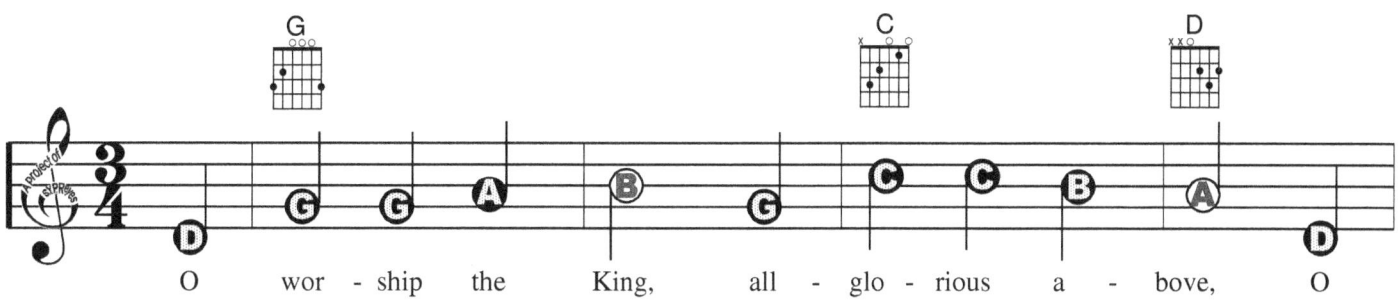

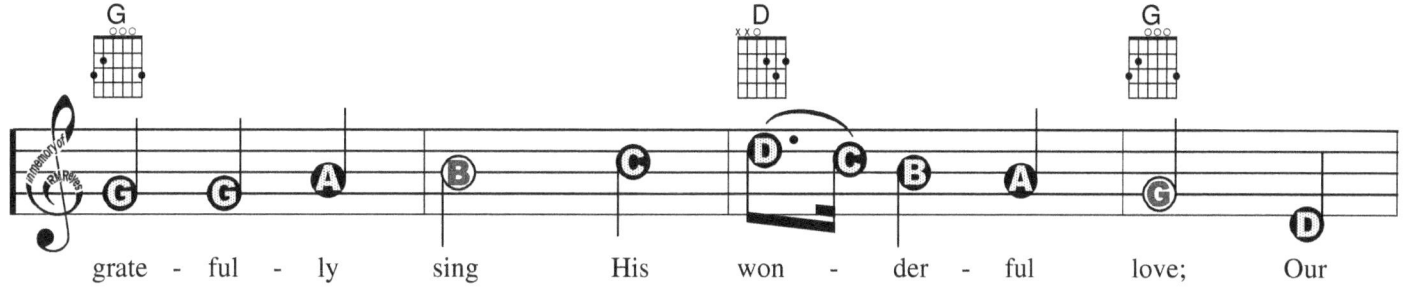

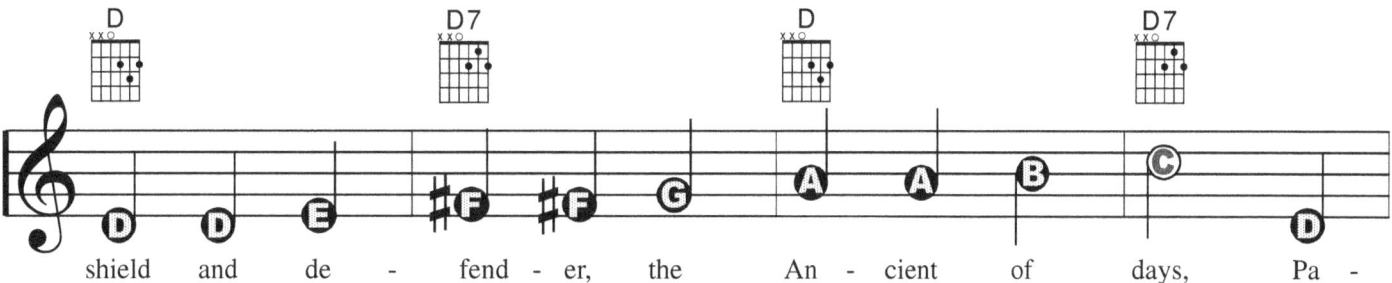

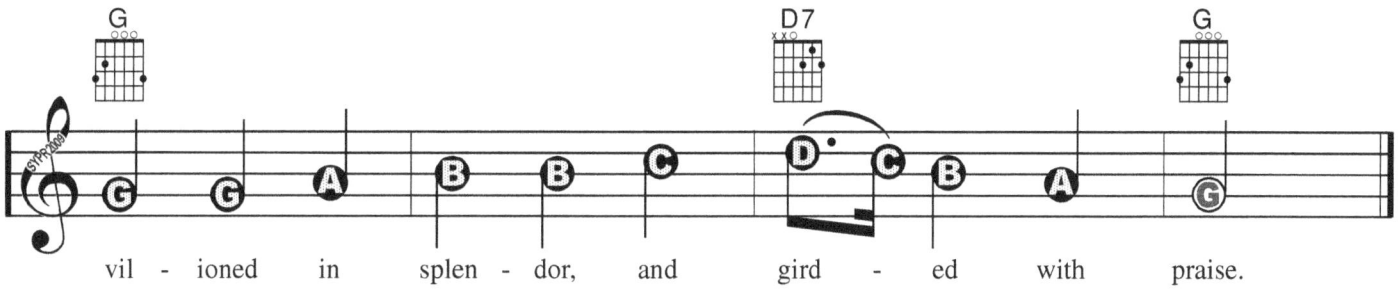

2. O tell of His might, O sing of His grace,
   Whose robe is the light, whose canopy space;
   His chariots of wrath the deep thunderclouds form,
   And dark is His path on the wings of the storm.

3. Thy bountiful care, what tongue can recite?
   It breathes in the air, it shines in the light;
   It streams from the hills, it descends to the plain,
   And sweetly distills in the dew and the rain.

4. Frail children of dust, and feeble as frail,
   In Thee do we trust, nor find Thee to fail;
   Thy mercies, how tender! how firm to the end!
   Our Maker, Defender, Redeemer, and Friend!

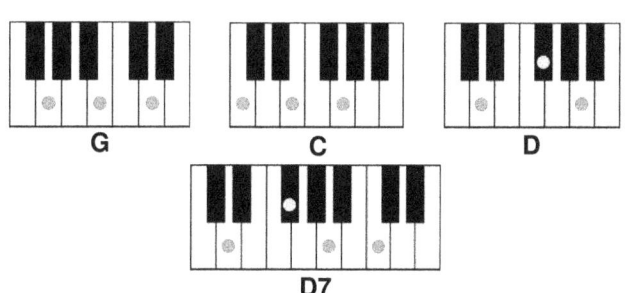

O Zion, Haste

Words by Mary Thomson

Music by James Walch

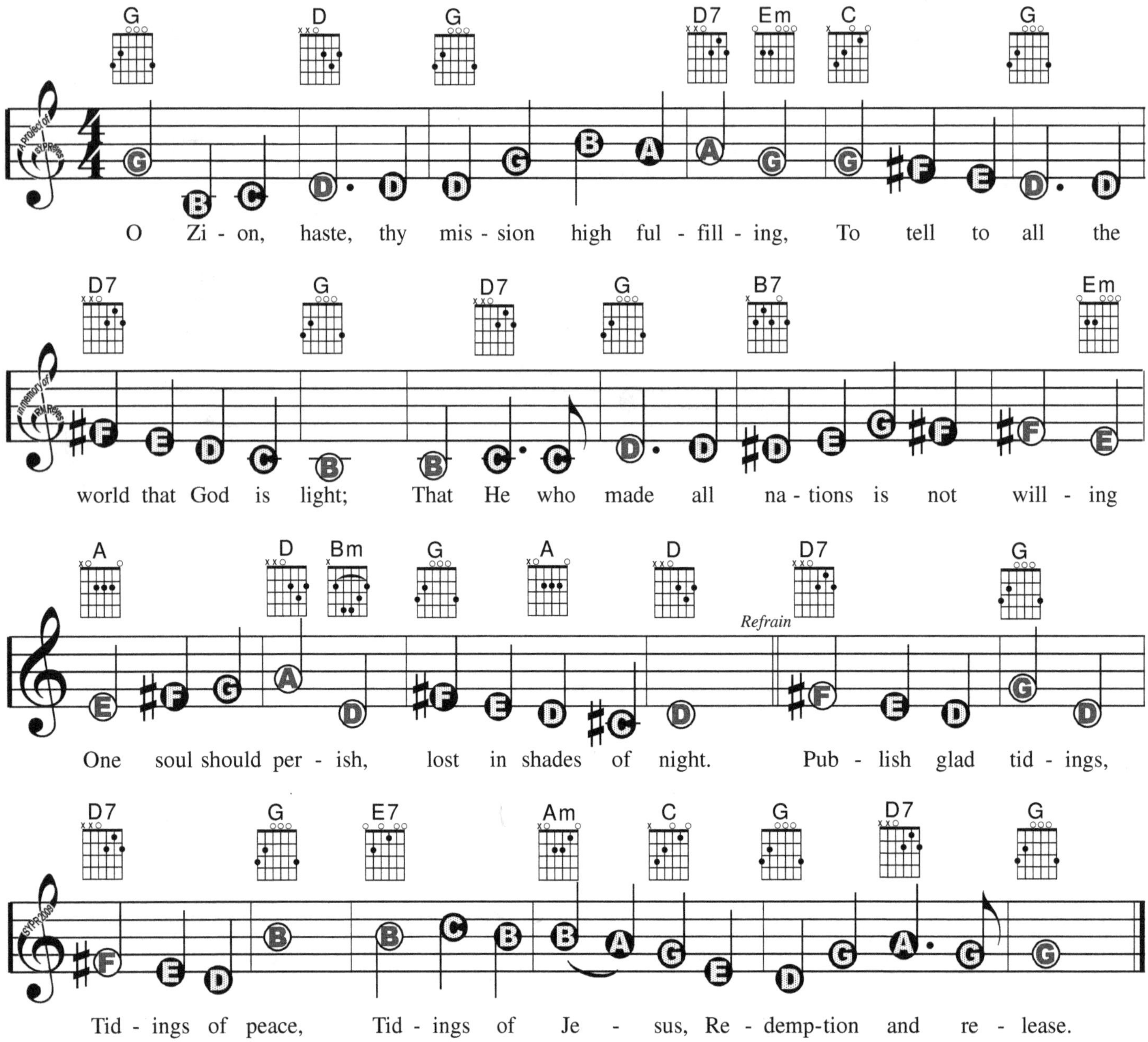

G D G D7 Em C G
O Zi - on, haste, thy mis - sion high ful - fill - ing, To tell to all the
D7 G D7 G B7 Em
world that God is light; That He who made all na - tions is not will - ing
A D Bm G A D D7 G
Refrain
One soul should per - ish, lost in shades of night. Pub - lish glad tid - ings,
D7 G E7 Am C G D7 G
Tid - ings of peace, Tid - ings of Je - sus, Re - demp-tion and re - lease.

2. Proclaim to every people, tongue, and nation
That God, in whom they live and move, is love;
Tell how He stooped to save His lost creation,
And died on earth that man might live above.
(Refrain)

3. Give of thy sons to bear the message glorious;
Give of thy wealth to speed them on their way;
Pour out thy soul for them in prayer victorious;
And all thou spendest Jesus will repay.
(Refrain)

4. He comes again; O Zion, ere thou meet Him,
Make known to every heart His saving grace;
Let none whom He hath ransomed fail to greet Him,
Through thy neglect, unfit to see His face.
(Refrain)

G
D
Em
C
D7
B7
A
Bm
E7
Am

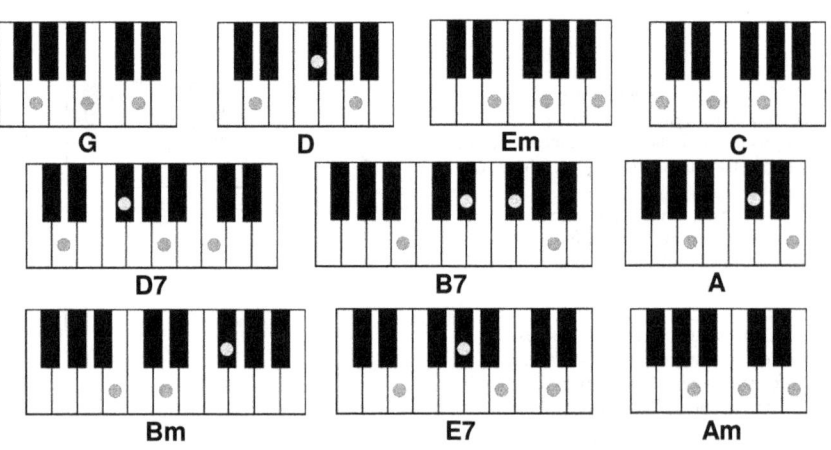

Only Trust Him

Words and music by J. H. Stockton

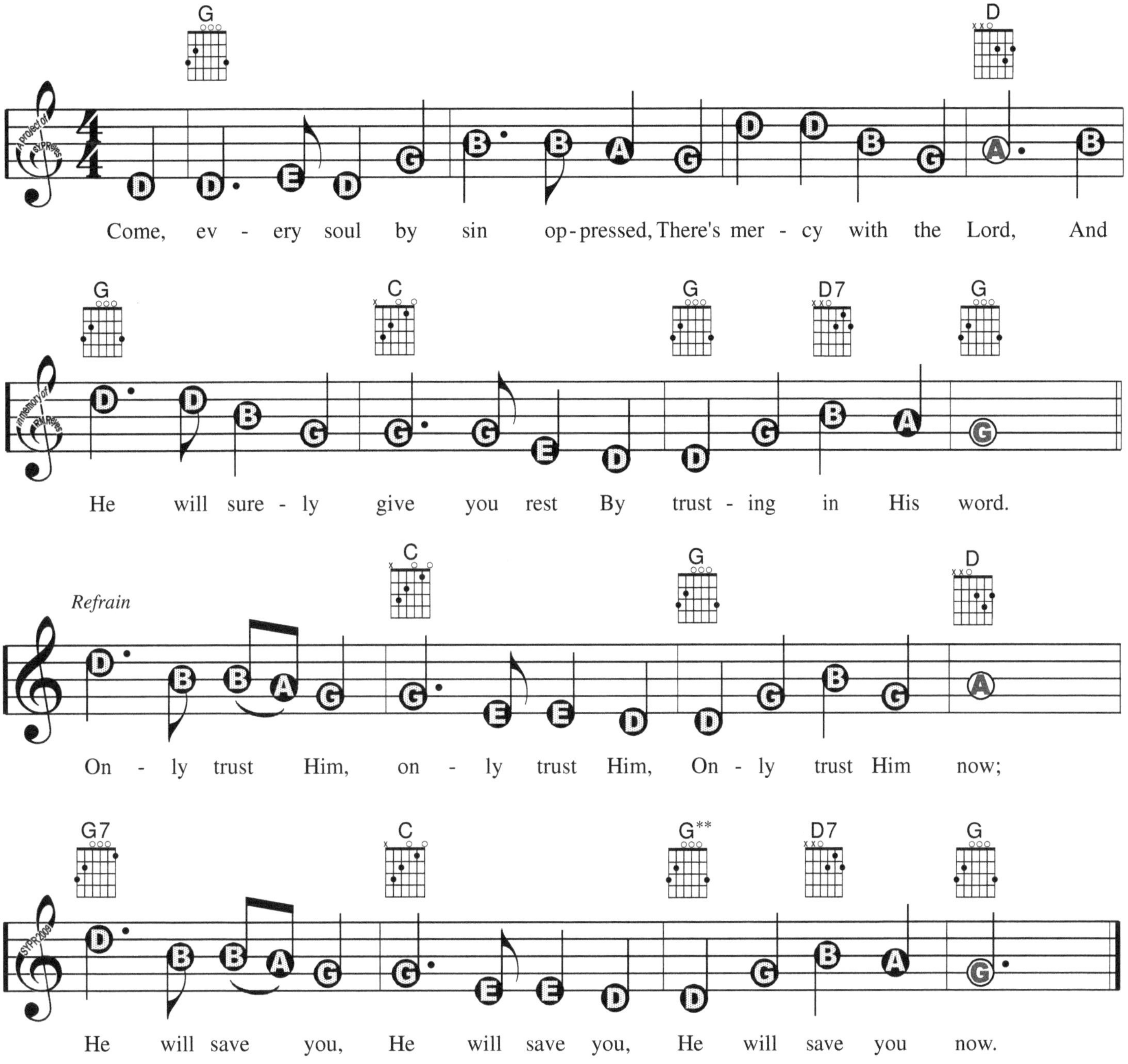

G
D
Come, ev - ery soul by sin op-pressed, There's mer - cy with the Lord, And
G
C
G
D7
G
He will sure - ly give you rest By trust - ing in His word.
Refrain
C
G
D
On - ly trust Him, on - ly trust Him, On - ly trust Him now;
G7
C
G**
D7
G
He will save you, He will save you, He will save you now.

2. For Jesus shed His precious blood Rich blessings to bestow;
Plunge now into the crimson flood That washes white as snow.
(Refrain)

3. Yes, Jesus is the truth, the way, That leads you into rest;
Believe in Him without delay, And you are fully blest.
(Refrain)

4. Come, then, and join this holy band, And on to glory go,
To dwell in that celestial land, Where joys immortal flow.
(Refrain)

G
D
C
D7
G7
G** (2nd inv.)

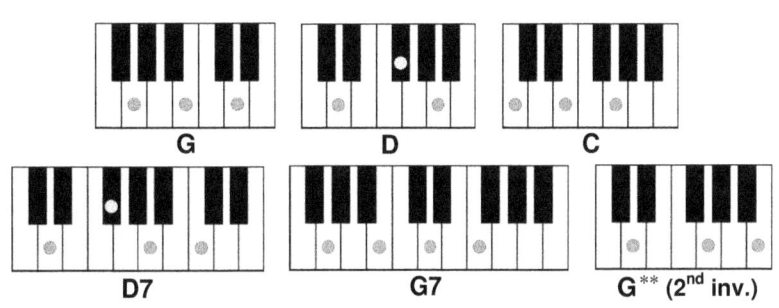

**On keyboard instrument, play second inversion*

Onward, Christian Soldiers!

Words by Sabine Baring-Gould
Music by Arthur Sullivan

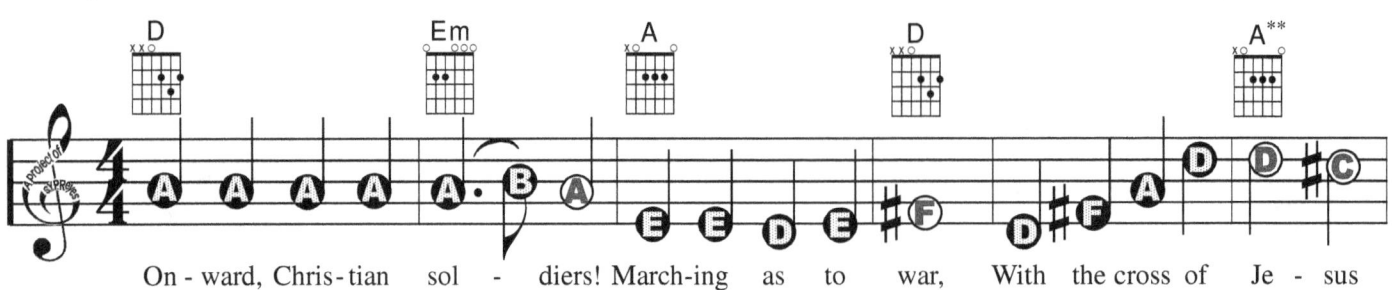

On - ward, Chris - tian sol - diers! March-ing as to war, With the cross of Je - sus

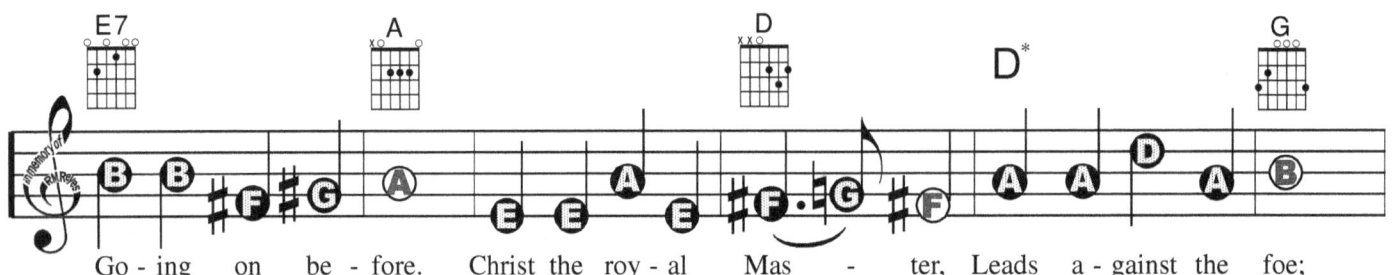

Go - ing on be - fore. Christ the roy - al Mas - ter, Leads a - gainst the foe;

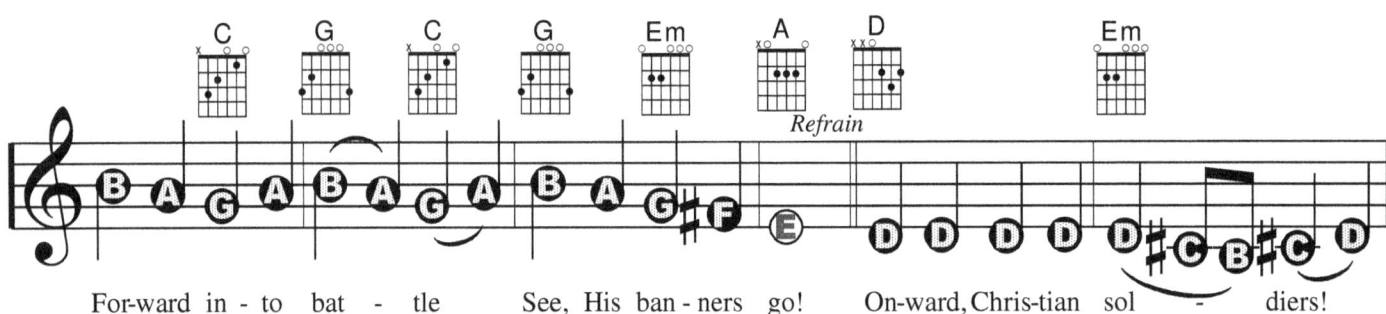

For - ward in - to bat - tle See, His ban - ners go! On - ward, Chris - tian sol - diers!

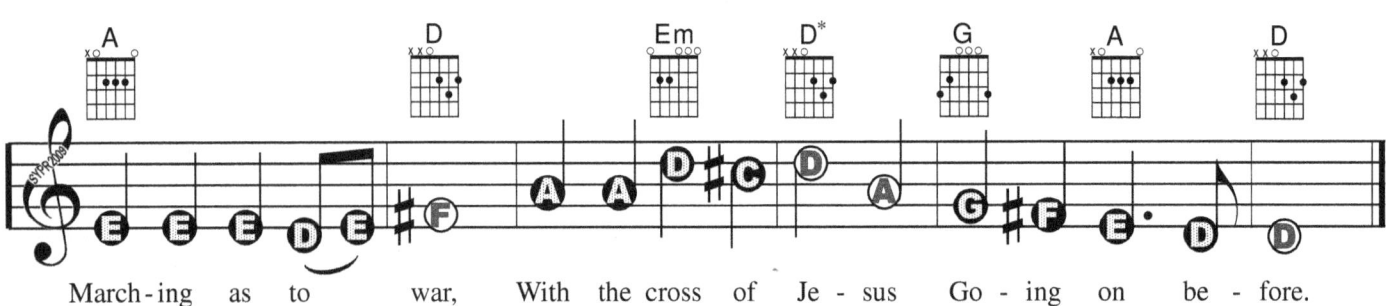

March - ing as to war, With the cross of Je - sus Go - ing on be - fore.

2. Like a mighty army Moves the church of God;
Christians, we are treading Where the saints have trod;
We are not divided, All one body we,
One in hope and doctrine, One in charity.
(Refrain)

3. Crowns and thrones have perished, Kingdoms rise and wane,
But the church of Jesus Constant will remain.
Gates of hell can never 'Gainst the church prevail;
We have Christ's own promise, That can never fail.
(Refrain)

4. Onward, then, ye people! Join our happy throng,
Blend with ours your voices In the triumph song;
Glory, praise, and honor Unto Christ the King,
This through countless ages Men and angels sing.
(Refrain)

*On keyboard instrument, play first inversion
**On keyboard instrument, play second inversion

Pass Me Not, O Gentle Savior

Words by Fanny Crosby

Music by William Doane

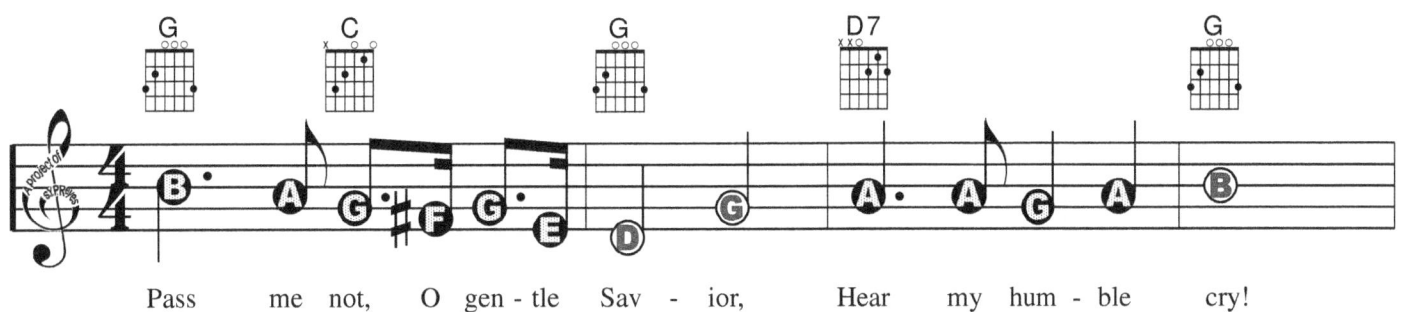

Pass me not, O gen-tle Sav - ior, Hear my hum - ble cry!

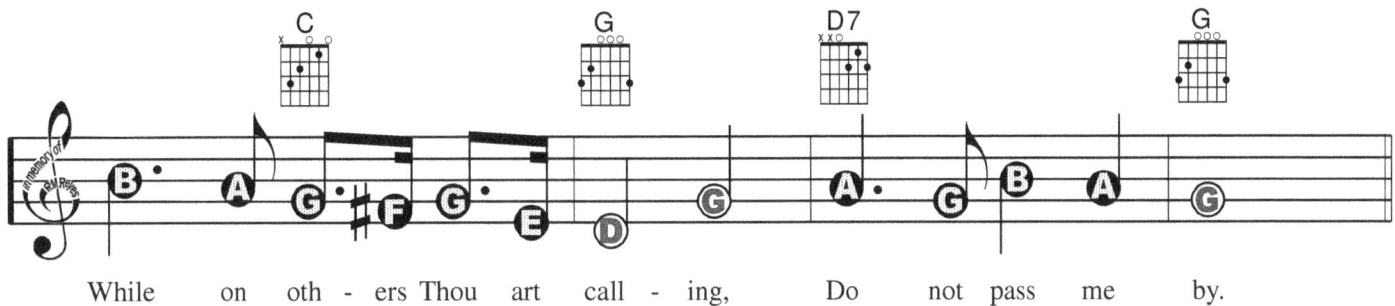

While on oth - ers Thou art call - ing, Do not pass me by.

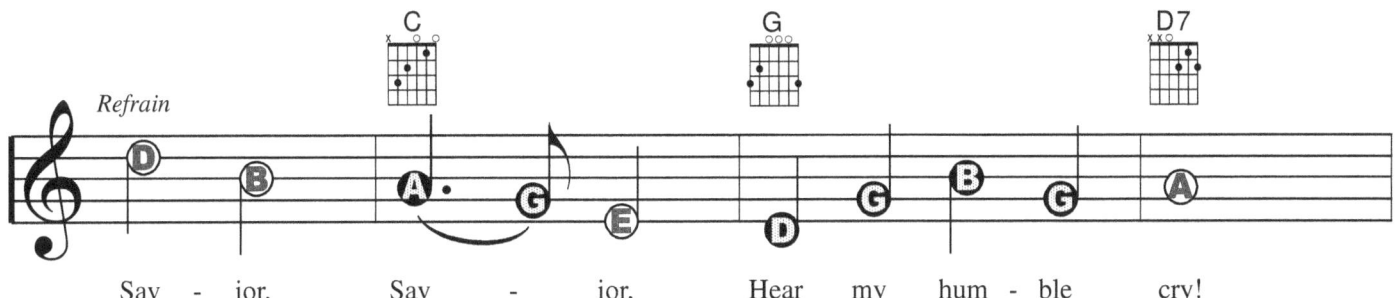

Refrain

Sav - ior, Sav - ior, Hear my hum - ble cry!

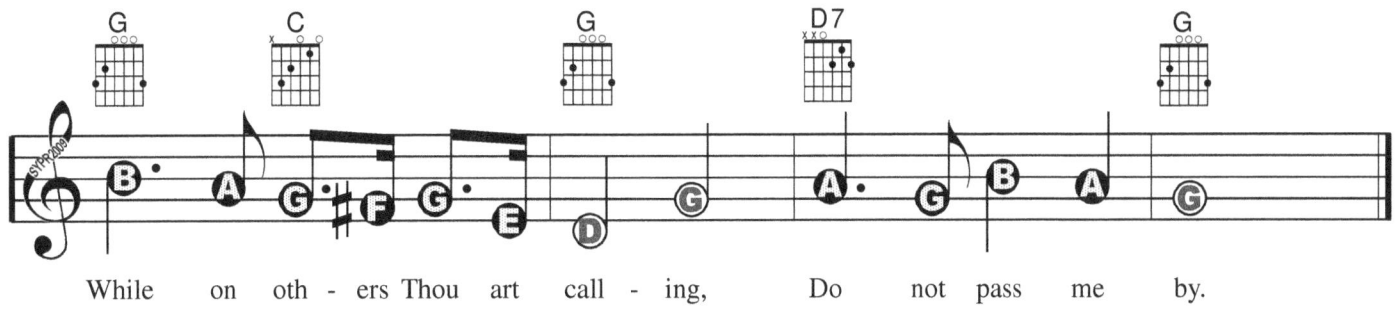

While on oth - ers Thou art call - ing, Do not pass me by.

2. Let me at Thy throne of mercy Find a sweet relief;
   Kneeling there in deep contrition, Help my unbelief.
   (Refrain)

3. Trusting only in Thy merit, Would I seek Thy face;
   Heal my wounded, broken spirit, Save me by Thy grace.
   (Refrain)

4. Thou the spring of all my comfort, More than life to me;
   Whom have I on earth beside Thee? whom in heaven but Thee?
   (Refrain)

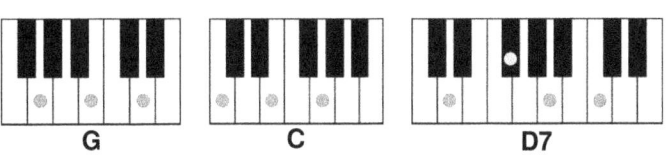

101

Power in the Blood

Words and music by Lewis Jones

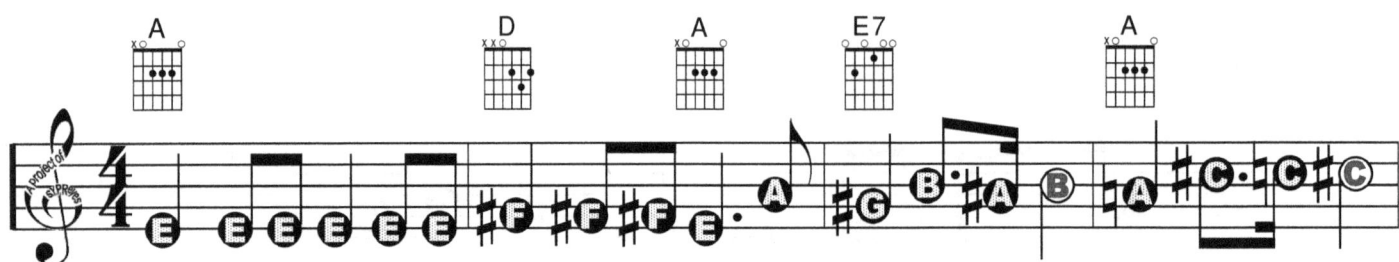

Would you be free from the bur-den of sin? There's pow'r in the blood, pow'r in the blood;

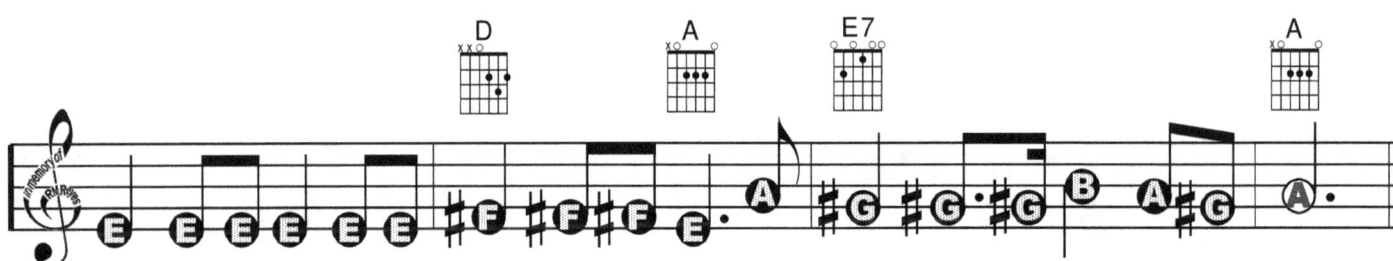

Would you o'er e-vil a vic-to-ry win? There's won-der-ful pow'r in the blood.

Refrain

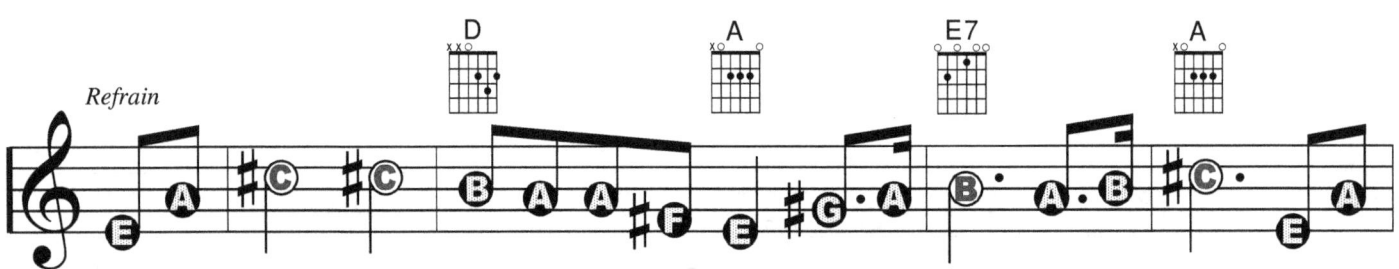

There is pow'r, pow'r, won-der-work-ing pow'r In the blood of the Lamb, There is

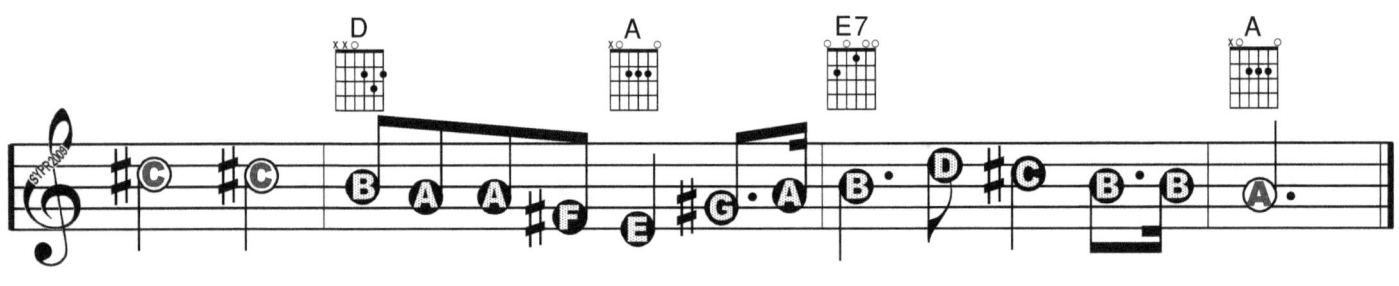

pow'r, pow'r, won-der-work-ing pow'r In the pre-cious blood of the Lamb.

2. Would you be free from your passion and pride?
   There's pow'r in the blood, pow'r in the blood;
   Come for a cleansing to Calvary's tide?
   There's wonderful pow'r in the blood.
   (Refrain)

3. Would you do service for Jesus your King?
   There's pow'r in the blood, pow'r in the blood;
   Would you live daily His praises to sing?
   There's wonderful pow'r in the blood.
   (Refrain)

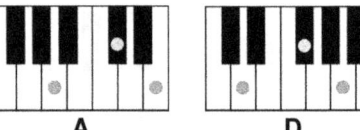

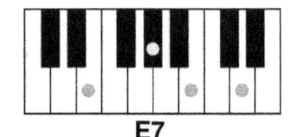

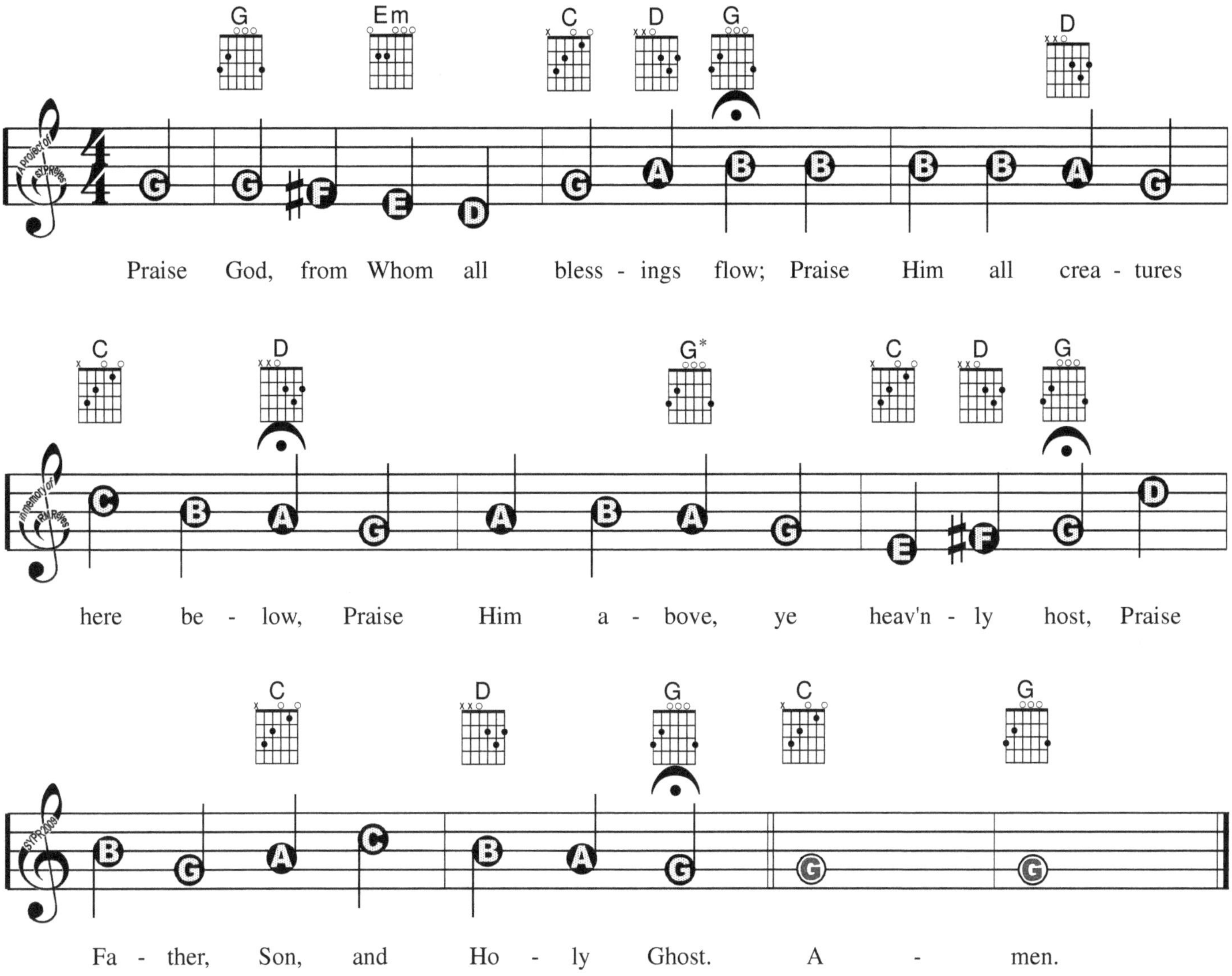

Praise God, From Whom All Blessings Flow

Words by Thomas Ken

Music by Louis Bourgeois

G Em C D G D
Praise God, from Whom all bless - ings flow; Praise Him all crea - tures
C D G* C D G
here be - low, Praise Him a - bove, ye heav'n - ly host, Praise
C D G C G
Fa - ther, Son, and Ho - ly Ghost. A - men.

G
Em
C
D
G* (1st inv.)

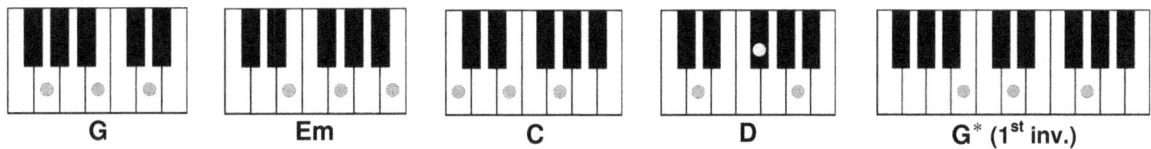

*On keyboard instrument, play first inversion

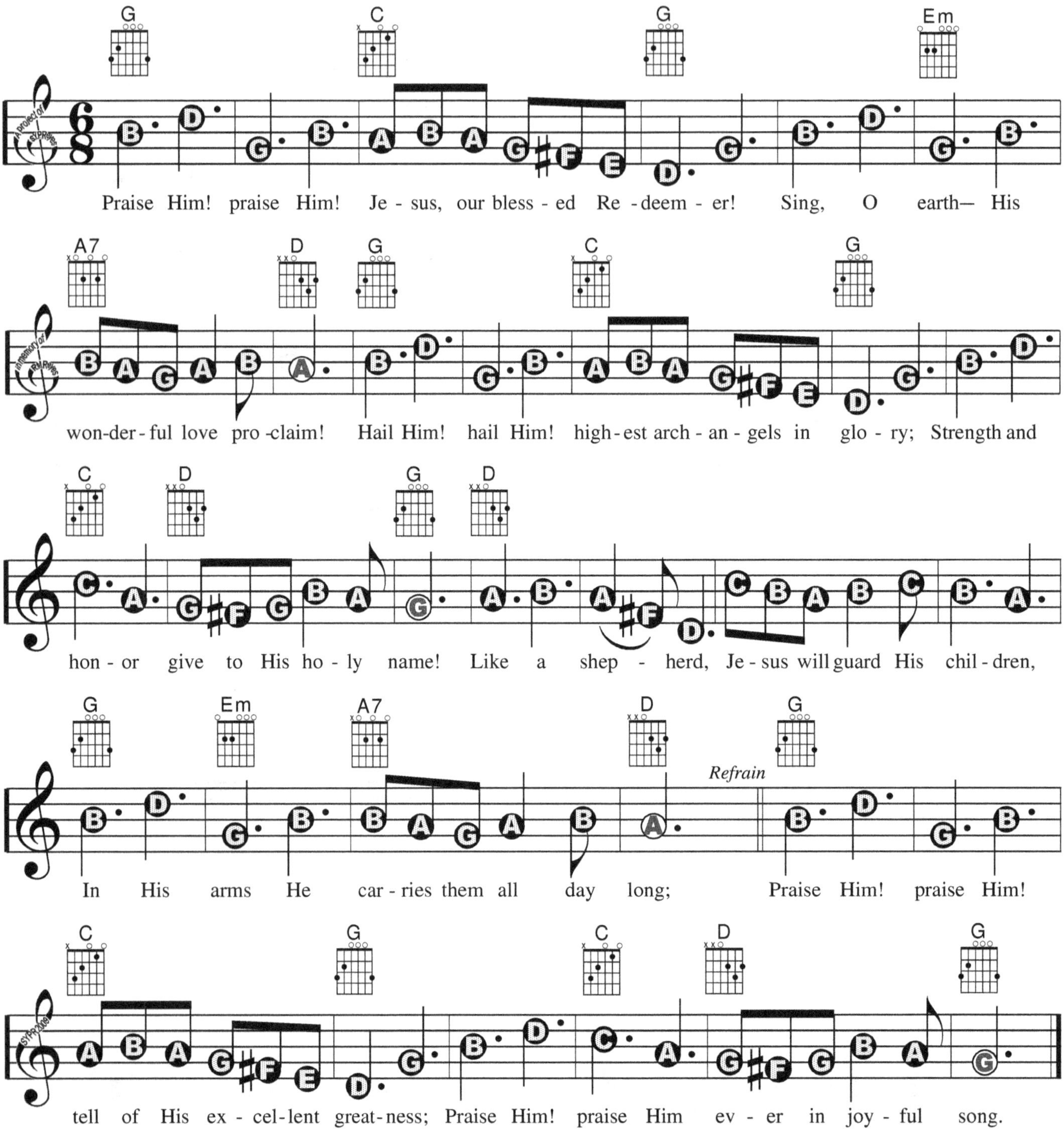

Praise Him! Praise Him!

Words by Fanny Crosby

Music by Chester Allen

G C G Em
Praise Him! praise Him! Je - sus, our bless - ed Re - deem - er! Sing, O earth— His
A7 D G C G
won-der - ful love pro - claim! Hail Him! hail Him! high-est arch - an - gels in glo - ry; Strength and
C D G D
hon - or give to His ho - ly name! Like a shep - herd, Je - sus will guard His chil - dren,
G Em A7 D G
Refrain
In His arms He car - ries them all day long; Praise Him! praise Him!
C G C D G
tell of His ex - cel - lent great - ness; Praise Him! praise Him ev - er in joy - ful song.

2. Praise Him! praise Him! Jesus, our blessed Redeemer!
For our sins He suffered, and bled, and died;
He--our Rock, our hope of eternal salvation,
Hail Him! hail Him! Jesus, the crucified.
Sound His praises! Jesus who bore our sorrows,
Love unbounded, wonderful, deep, and strong;
(Refrain)

3. Praise Him! praise Him! Jesus, our blessed Redeemer!
Heavenly portals, loud with hosannas ring!
Jesus, Savior, reigneth forever and ever;
Crown Him! crown Him! Prophet, and Priest, and King!
Christ is coming over the world victorious,
Power and glory unto the Lord belong;
(Refrain)

G
C
Em
A7
D

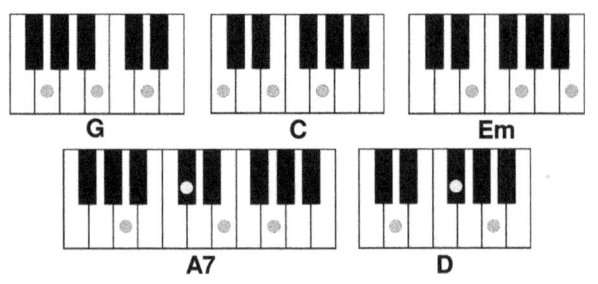

Redeemed!

Words by Fanny Crosby
Music by William Kirkpatrick

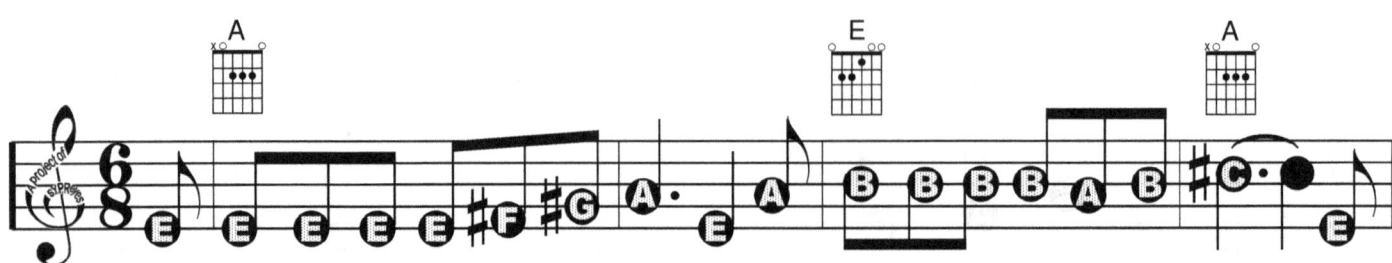

Re-deemed! how I love to pro-claim it! Re-deemed by the blood of the Lamb; Re-

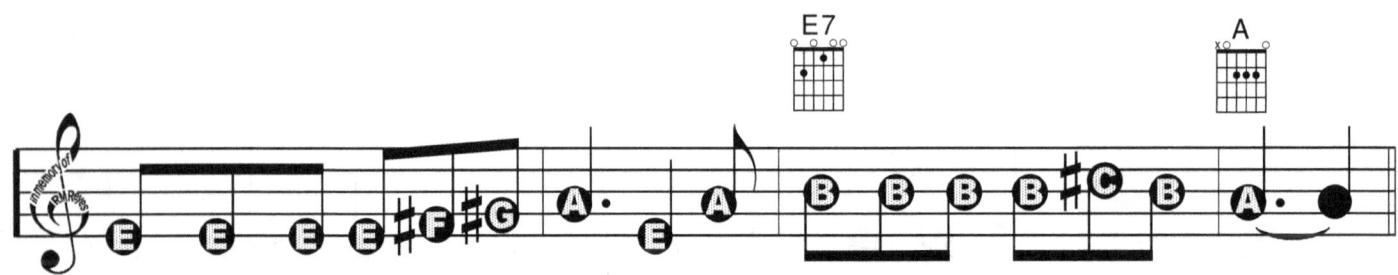

deemed through His in-fi-nite mer-cy, His child, and for-ev-er, I am.

Refrain

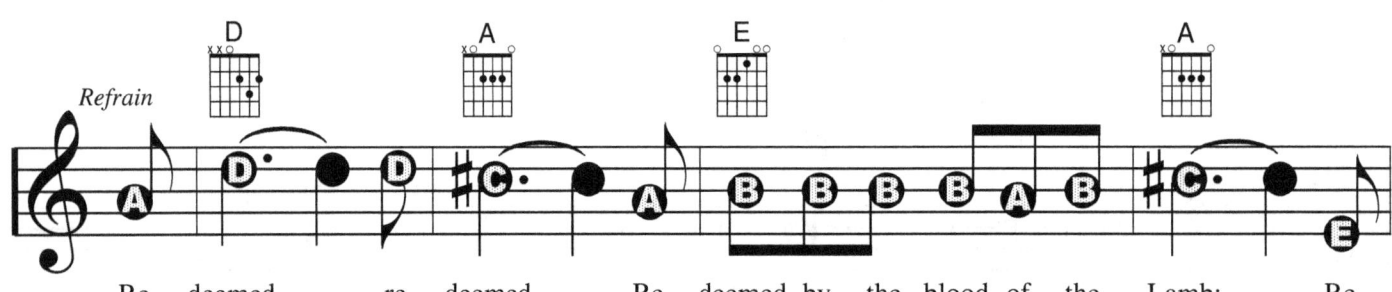

Re-deemed, re-deemed, Re-deemed by the blood of the Lamb; Re-

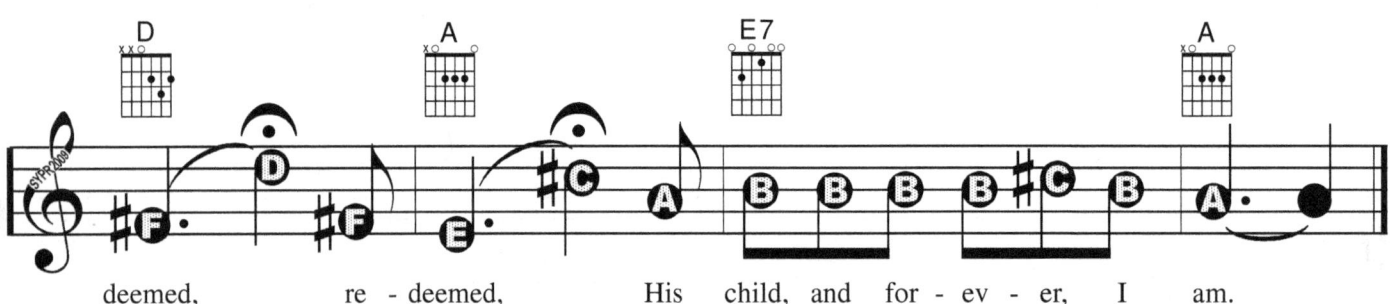

deemed, re-deemed, His child, and for-ev-er, I am.

2. Redeemed! and so happy in Jesus! No language my rapture can tell;
   I know that the light of His presence With me doth continually dwell.
   (Refrain)

3. I think of my blessed Redeemer, I think of Him all the day long;
   I sing, for I cannot be silent; His love is the theme of my song.
   (Refrain)

4. I know I shall see in His beauty The King in whose law I delight,
   Who lovingly guardeth my footsteps, And giveth me songs in the night.
   (Refrain)

5. I know there's a crown that is waiting In yonder bright mansion for me;
   And soon, with the saints made perfect, At home with the Lord I shall be.
   (Refrain)

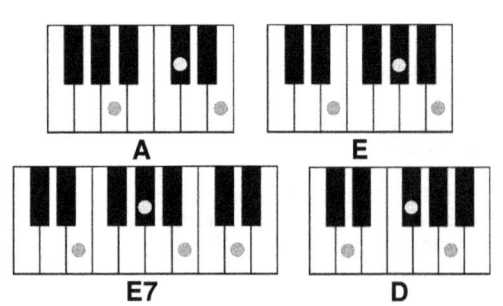

Rejoice! the Lord is King

Words by Charles Wesley
Music by John Darwall

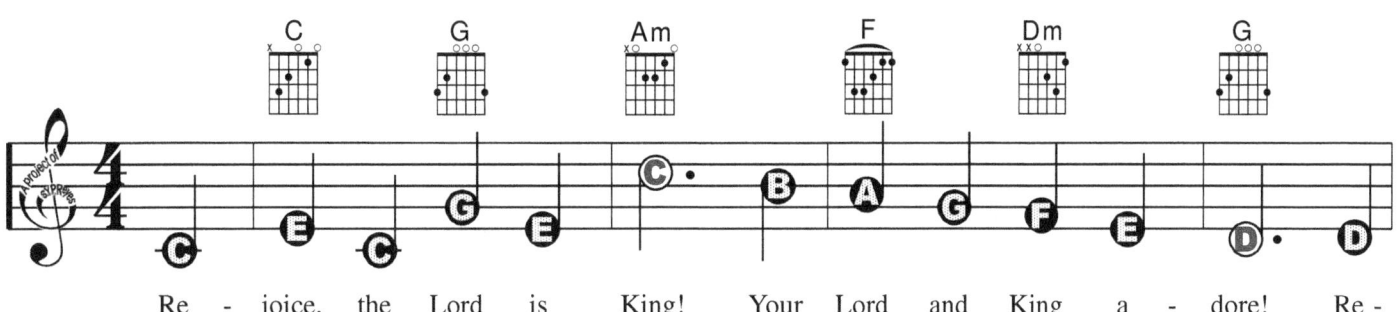

Re - joice, the Lord is King! Your Lord and King a - dore! Re -

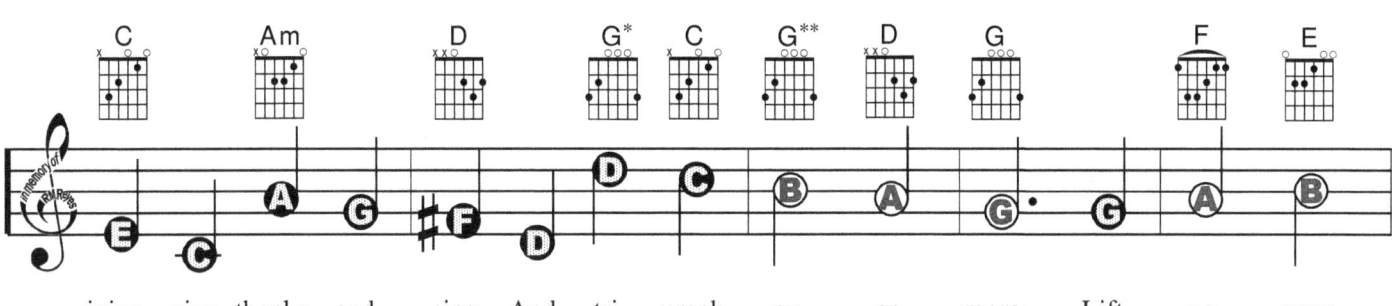

joice, give thanks, and sing, And tri - umph ev - er - more: Lift up your

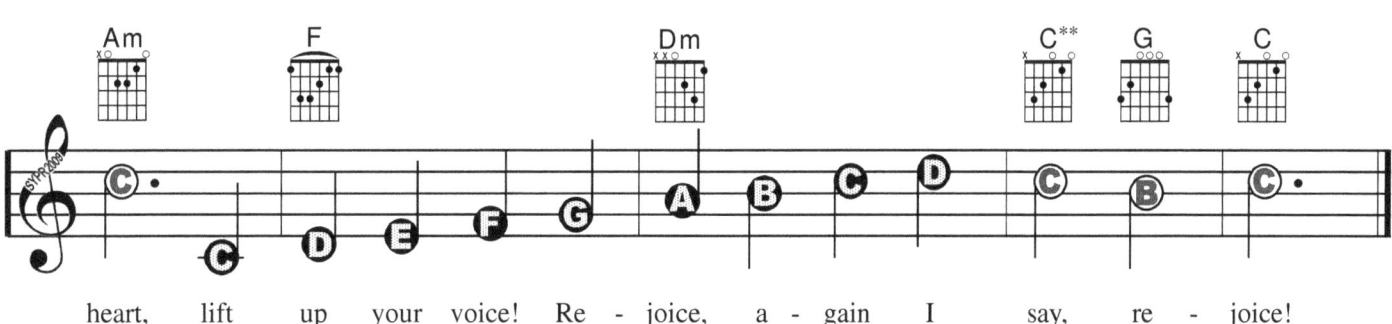

heart, lift up your voice! Re - joice, a - gain I say, re - joice!

2. Jesus, the Savior, reigns, The God of truth and love;
When He had purged our stains, He took His seat above:
Lift up your heart, lift up your voice!
Rejoice, again I say, rejoice!

3. His kingdom cannot fail, He rules o'er earth and heav'n;
The keys of death and grave Are to our Jesus giv'n:
Lift up your heart, lift up your voice!
Rejoice, again I say, rejoice!

4. Rejoice, in glorious hope! Our Lord the judge shall come,
And take His servants up To their eternal home:
Lift up your heart, lift up your voice!
Rejoice, again I say, rejoice!

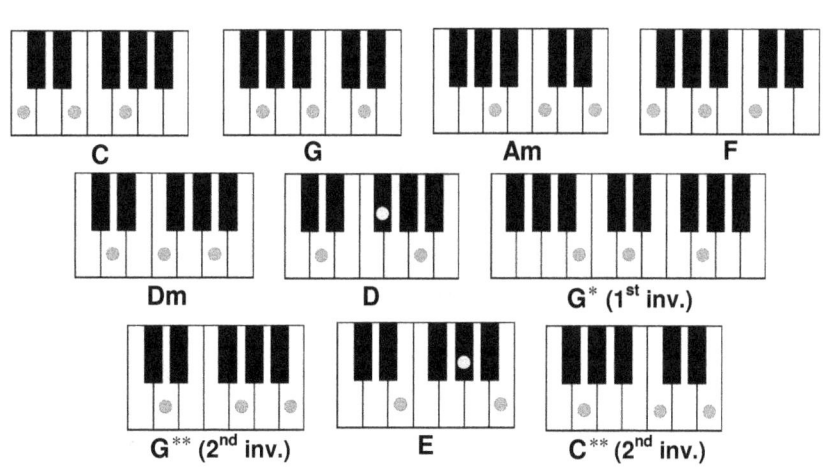

*On keyboard instrument, play first inversion
**On keyboard instrument, play second inversion

Rejoice, Ye Pure in Heart

Words by Edward Plumptre
Music by Arthur Messiter

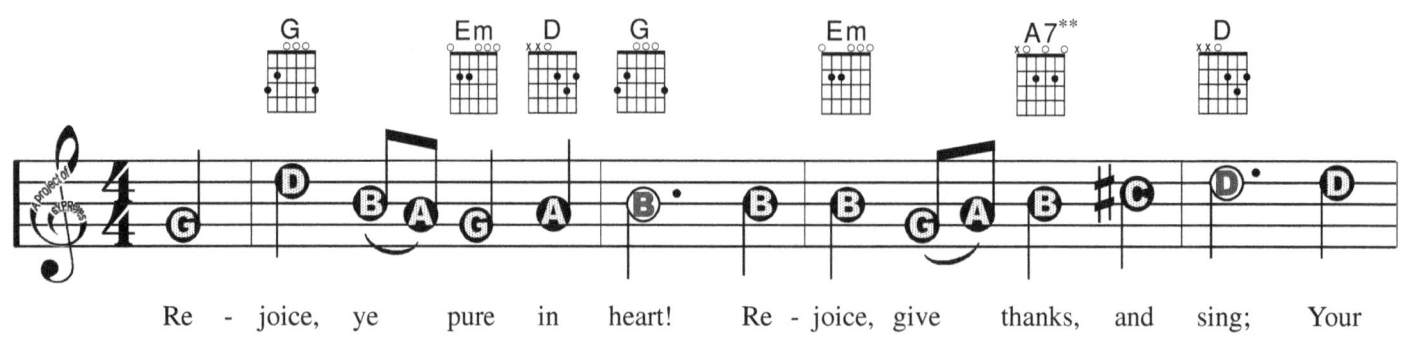

Re - joice, ye pure in heart! Re - joice, give thanks, and sing; Your

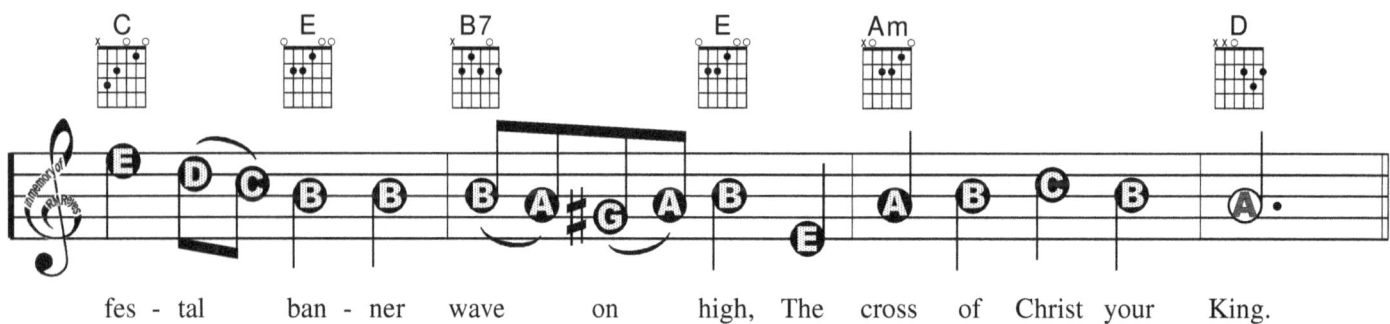

fes - tal ban - ner wave on high, The cross of Christ your King.

Refrain

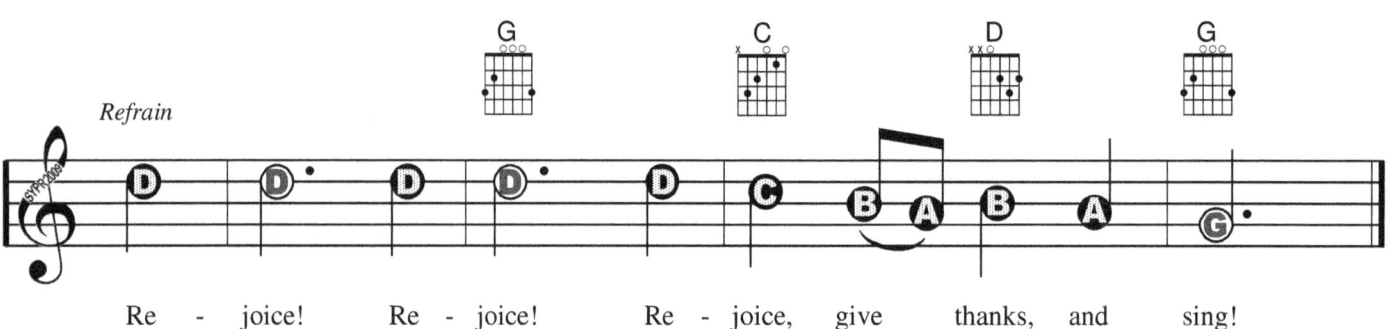

Re - joice! Re - joice! Re - joice, give thanks, and sing!

2. With voice as full and strong As ocean's surging praise,
Send forth the sturdy hymns of old, The psalms of ancient days.
(Refrain)

3. With all the angel choirs, With all the saints on earth,
Pour out the strains of joy and bliss, True rapture, noblest mirth.
(Refrain)

4. Yes, on through life's long path, Still chanting as ye go;
From youth to age, by night and day, In gladness and in woe.
(Refrain)

5. Praise Him who reigns on high, The Lord whom we adore
The Father, Son, and Holy Ghost, One God forevermore.
(Refrain)

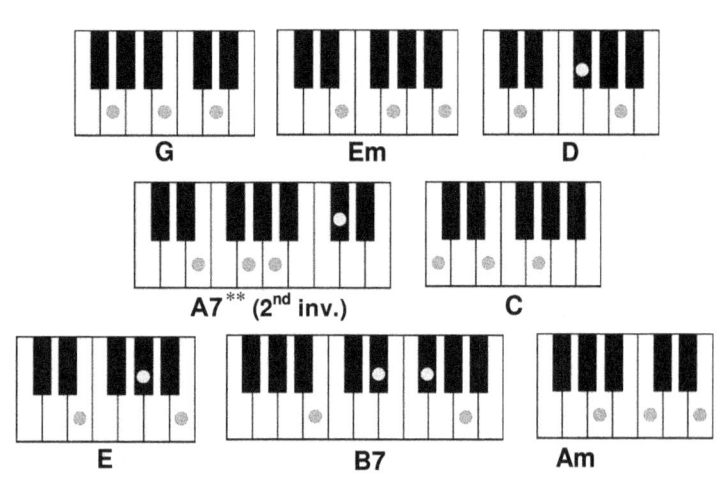

**On keyboard instrument, play second inversion*

Rescue the Perishing

Words by Fanny Crosby

Music by W. H. Doane

Res - cue the per - ish - ing, Care for the dy - ing; Snatch them in pit - y from

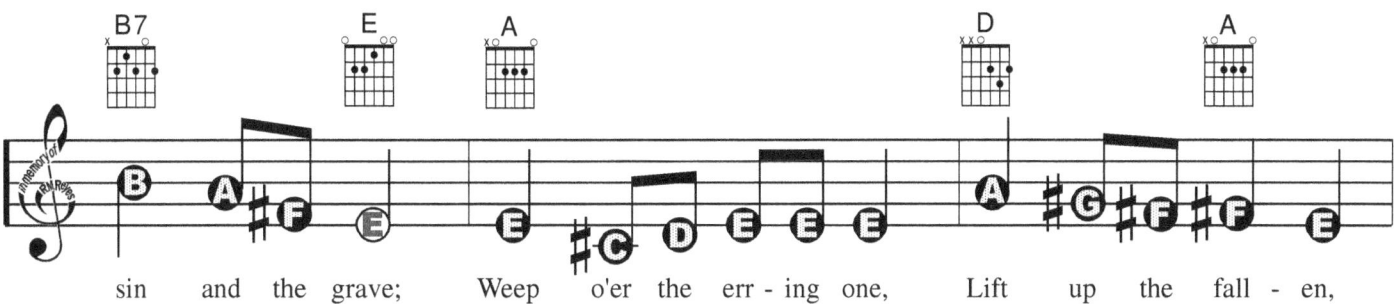
sin and the grave; Weep o'er the err - ing one, Lift up the fall - en,

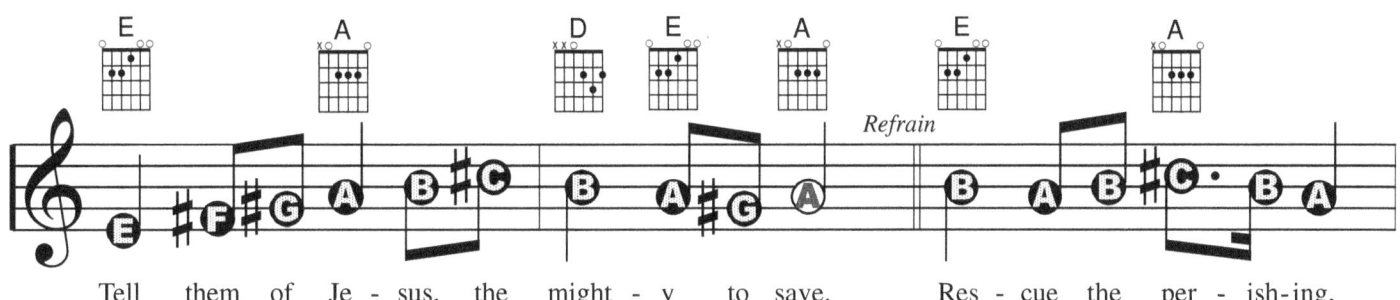
Tell them of Je - sus, the might - y to save. Res - cue the per - ish - ing,

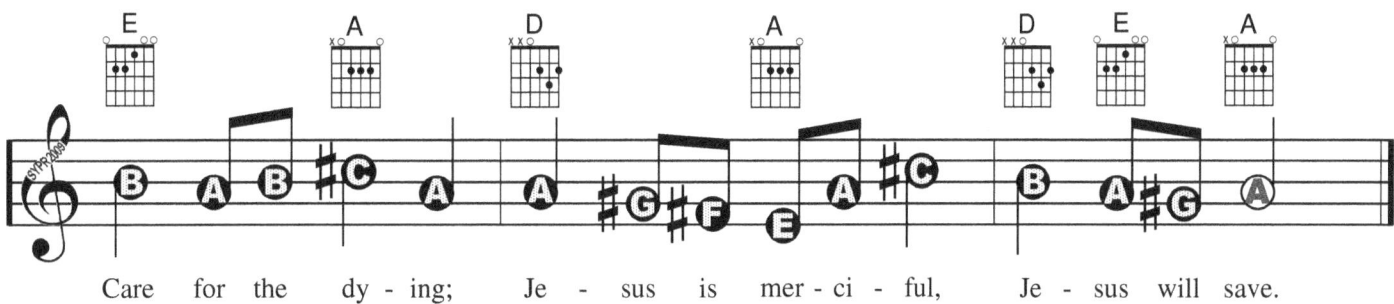
Care for the dy - ing; Je - sus is mer - ci - ful, Je - sus will save.

2. Though they are slighting Him, Still He is waiting,
   Waiting the penitent child to receive.
   Plead with them earnestly, Plead with them gently;
   He will forgive if they only believe.
   (Refrain)

3. Rescue the perishing, Duty demands it;
   Strength for thy labor the Lord will provide;
   Back to the narrow way Patiently win them;
   Tell the poor wanderer a Savior has died.
   (Refrain)

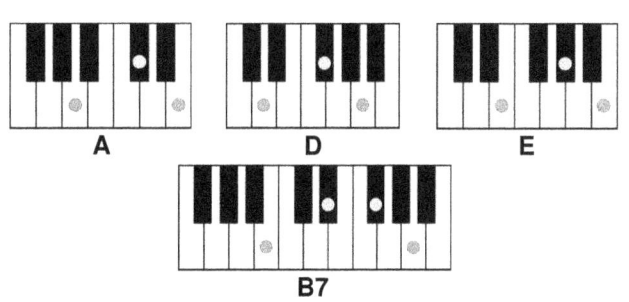

109

Rock of Ages

Words by Augustus Toplady
Music by Thomas Hastings

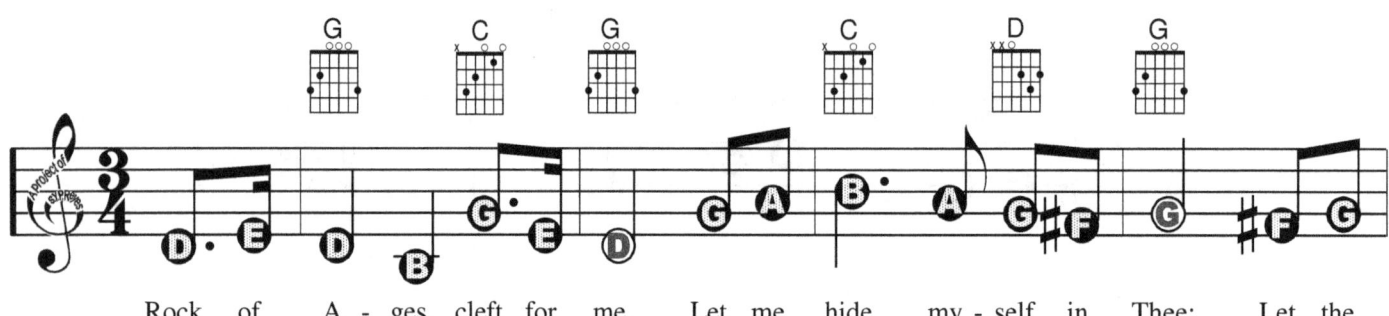

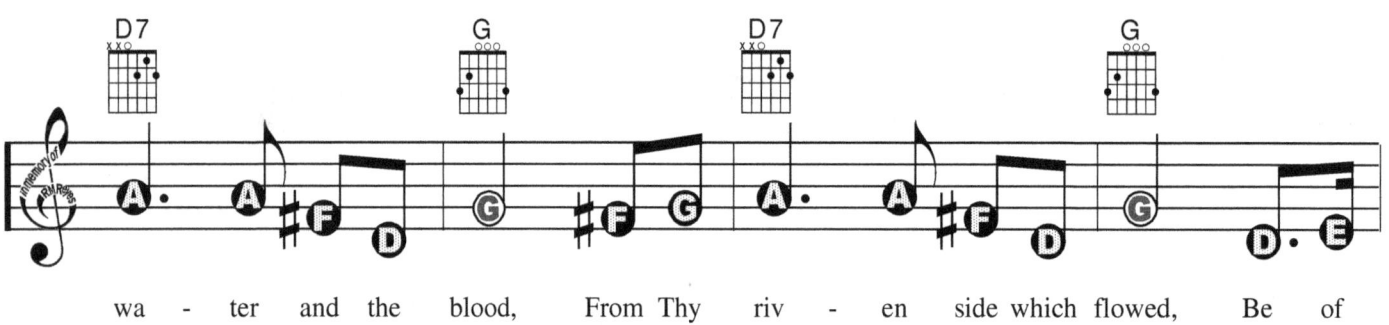

2. Not the labors of my hands Can fulfill Thy law's demands;
Could my zeal no respite know, Could my tears forever flow,
All for sin could not atone; Thou must save, and Thou alone.

3. When my pilgrimage I close, Victor o'er the last of foes,
When I soar to worlds unknown, See Thee on Thy judgment throne,
Rock of Ages, cleft for me, Let me hide myself in Thee.

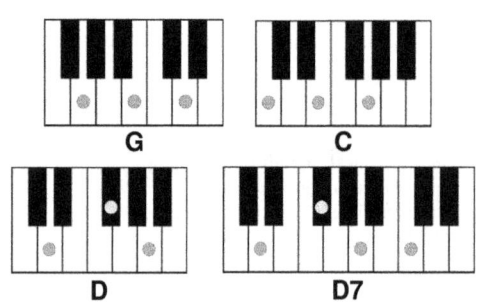

Safely Through Another Week

Words by John Newton
Music by Lowell Mason

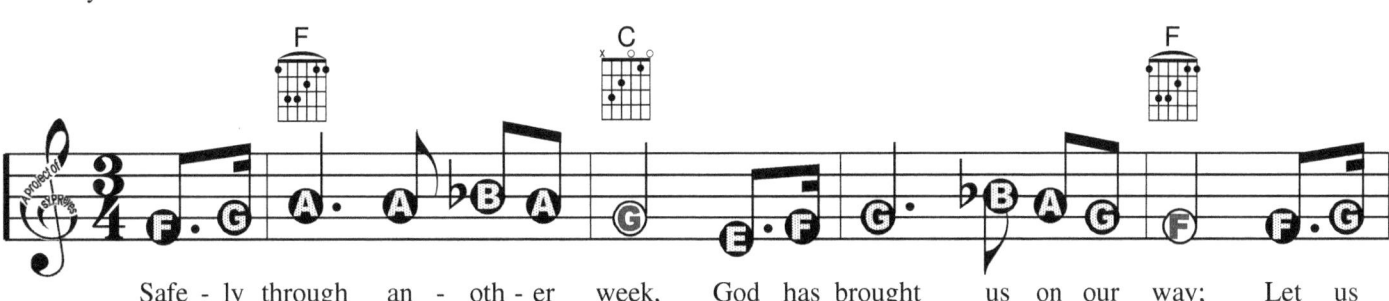
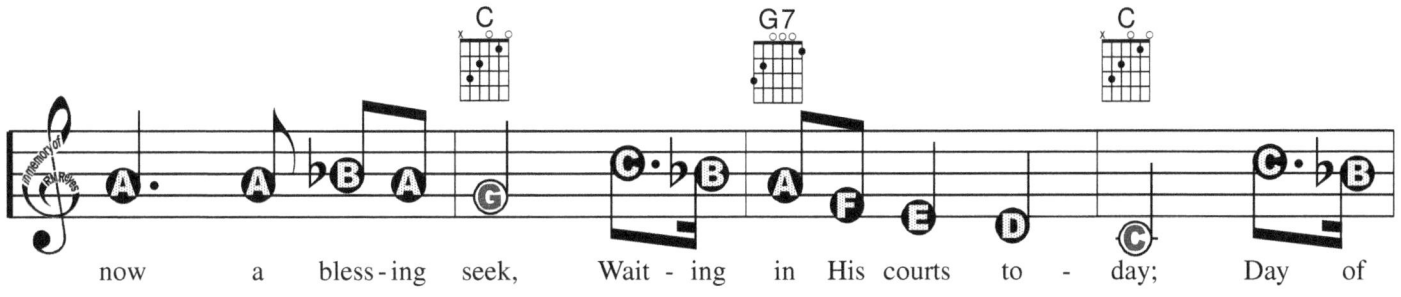
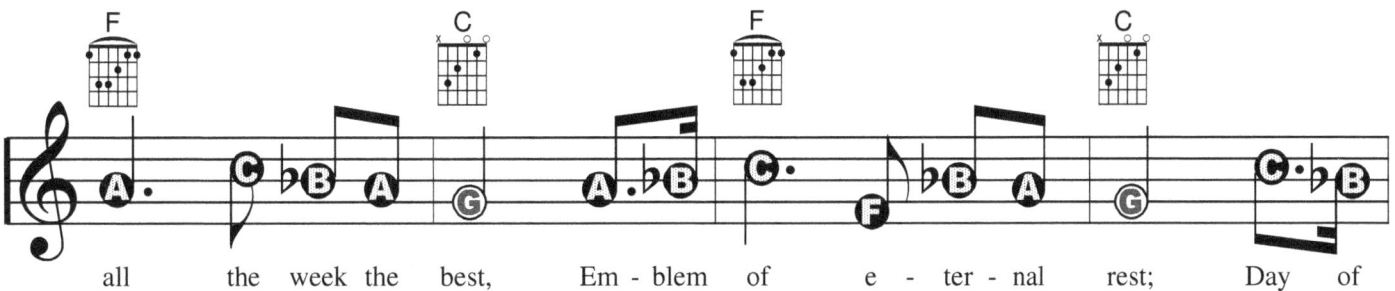
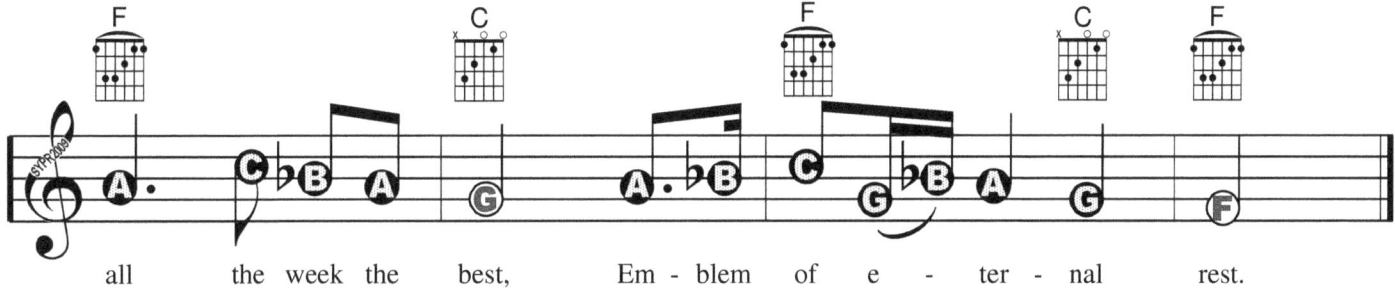

2. While we seek supplies of grace Through the dear Redeemer's name,
   Show Thy reconciling face, Take away our sin and shame;
   From our worldly cares set free May we rest this day in Thee.
   From our worldly cares set free May we rest this day in Thee.

3. When the morn shall bid us rise, May we feel Thy presence near,
   May Thy glory meet our eyes When we in Thy house appear;
   Here afford us, Lord, a taste Of our everlasting feast.
   Here afford us, Lord, a taste Of our everlasting feast.

4. May the gospel's joyful sound Conquer sinners, comfort saints;
   Make the fruits of grace abound, Bring relief to all complaints;
   Thus may all our Sabbaths be Till we rise to reign with Thee.
   Thus may all our Sabbaths be Till we rise to reign with Thee.

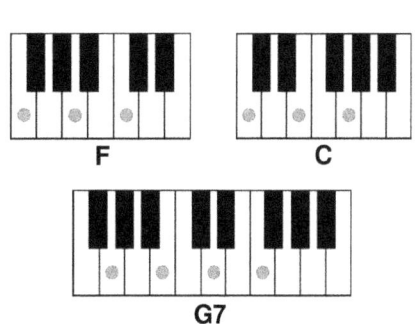

111

Savior, Like a Shepherd Lead Us

Music by William Bradbury

Sav - ior, like a Shep-herd lead us, Much we need Thy ten-derest care;
In Thy pleas-ant pas-tures feed us, For our use Thy folds pre - pare. Bless-ed
Je - sus, bless-ed Je - sus, Thou hast bought us, Thine we are, Bless-ed
Je - sus, bless-ed Je - sus, Thou hast bought us, Thine we are.

2. We are Thine; do Thou befriend us, Be the Guardian of our way;
Keep Thy flock, from sin defend us, Seek us when we go astray.
Blessed Jesus, blessed Jesus, Hear, O hear us, when we pray!
Blessed Jesus, blessed Jesus, Hear, O hear us, when we pray!

3. Thou hast promised to receive us, Poor and sinful though we be;
Thou hast mercy to relieve us, Grace to cleanse, and power to free.
Blessed Jesus, blessed Jesus, We will early turn to Thee;
Blessed Jesus, blessed Jesus, We will early turn to Thee.

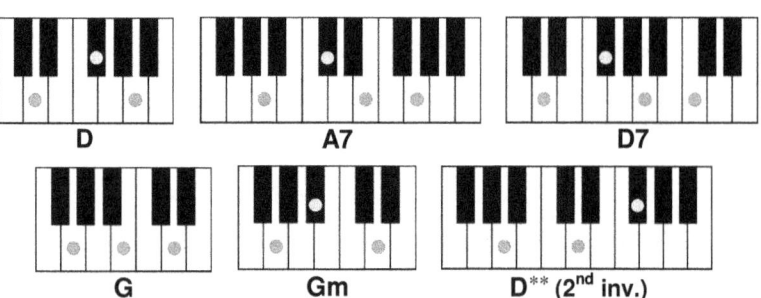

**On keyboard instrument, play second inversion

Showers of Blessing

Words by Daniel Whittle
Music by James McGranahan

"There shall be show-ers of bless-ing;" This is the prom-ise of love;
There shall be sea-sons re-fresh-ing, Sent from the Sav-ior a-bove.

Refrain
Show — ers of bless-ing, Show-ers of bless-ing we need;
Mer-cy drops round us are fall-ing, But for the show-ers we plead.

2. "There shall be showers of blessing;" Precious reviving again;
Over the hills and the valleys, Sound of abundance of rain.
(Refrain)

3. "There shall be showers of blessing;" Send them upon us, O Lord;
Grant to us now a refreshing; Come, and now honor Thy word.
(Refrain)

4. "There shall be showers of blessing;" O that today they might fall,
Now as to God we're confessing, Now as on Jesus we call!
(Refrain)

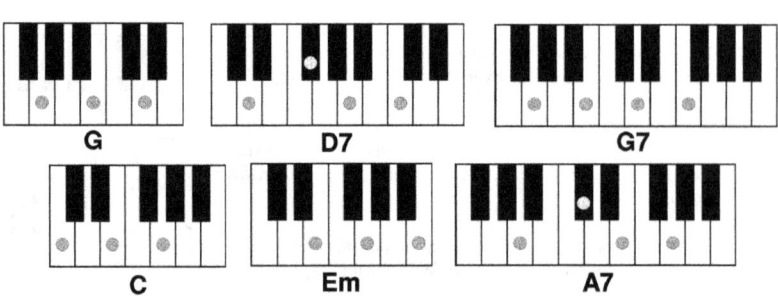

114

Silent Night

Words by Joseph Mohr
English translation by John Young

Music by Franz Gruber

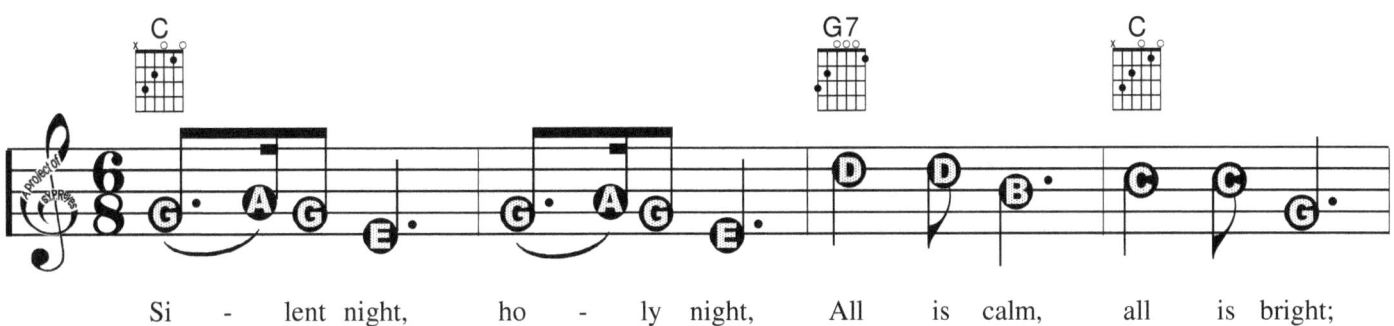
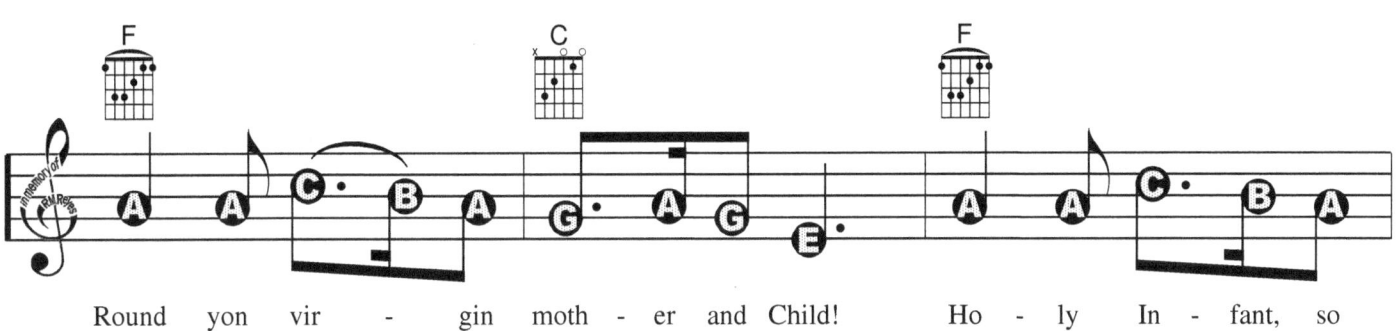
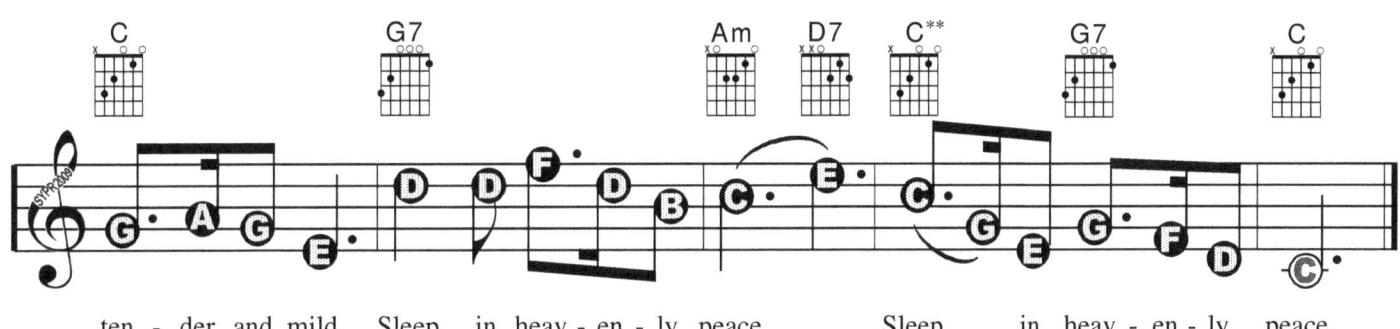

2. Silent night, holy night, Darkness flies, all is light;
Shepherds hear the angels sing, "Alleluia! hail the King!
Christ the Savior is born, Christ the Savior is born."

3. Silent night, holy night, Son of God, love's pure light;
Radiant beams from Thy holy face, With the dawn of redeeming grace,
Jesus, Lord, at Thy birth, Jesus, Lord, at Thy birth.

4. Silent night, holy night, Wondrous star, lend thy light;
With the angels let us sing, Alleluia to our King;
Christ the Savior is born, Christ the Savior is born.

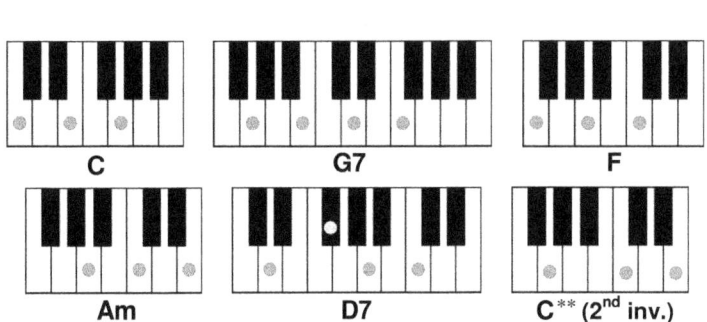

**On keyboard instrument, play second inversion*

Softly and Tenderly

Words and music by Will Thompson

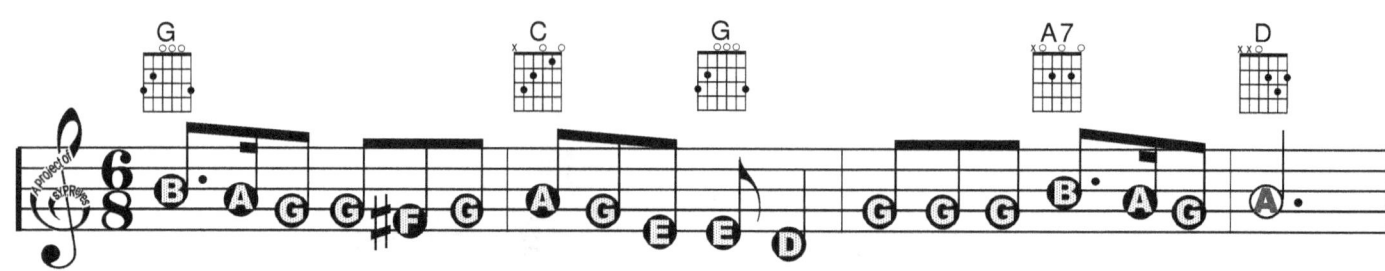

Soft-ly and ten-der-ly Je-sus is call-ing, Call-ing for you and for me;

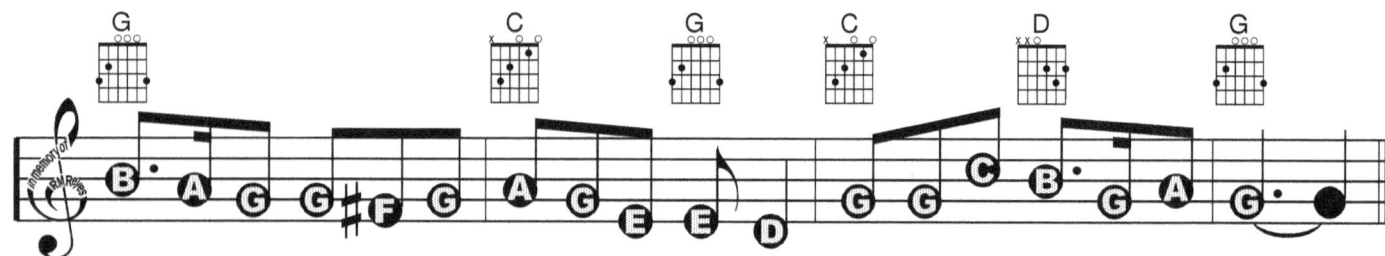

At the heart's por-tal He's wait-ing and watch-ing, Watch-ing for you and for me.

Refrain

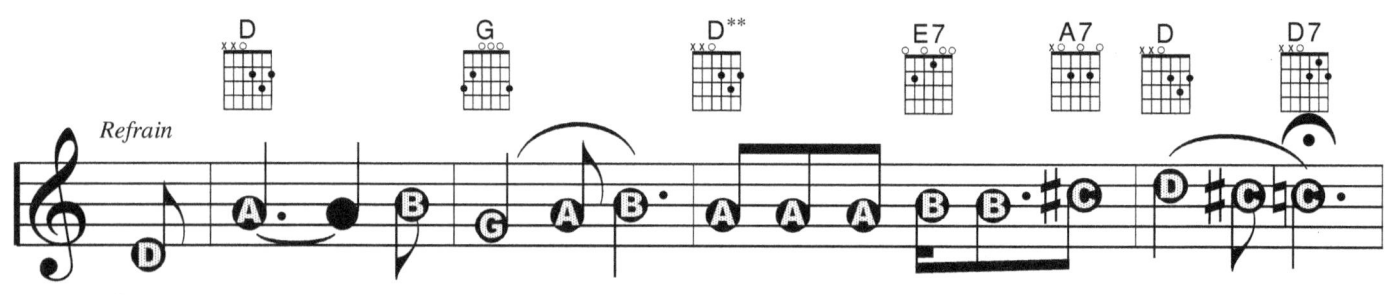

Come home, come home, Ye who are wea-ry, come home;

Ear-nest-ly, ten-der-ly Je-sus is call-ing, Call-ing, O sin-ner, come home!

2. Why should we tarry when Jesus is pleading,
   Pleading for you and for me?
   Why should we linger and heed not His mercies,
   Mercies for you and for me?
   (Refrain)

3. Think of the wonderful love He has promised,
   Promised for you and for me;
   Though we have sinned, He has mercy and pardon,
   Pardon for you and for me.
   (Refrain)

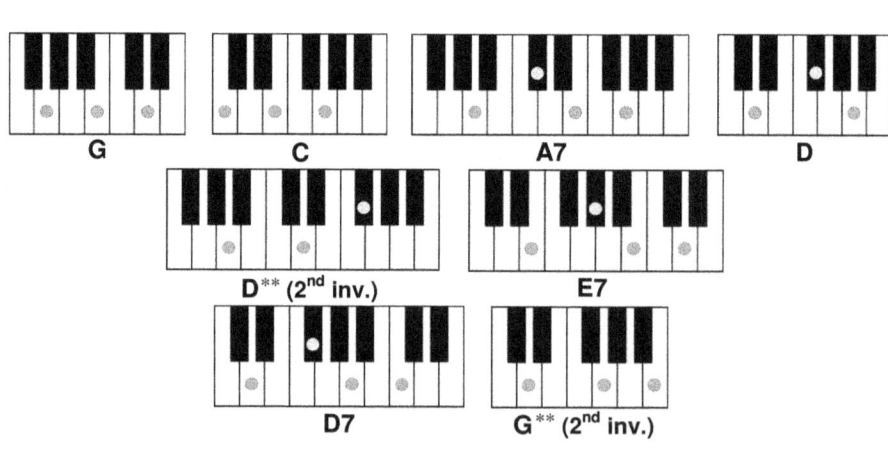

**On keyboard instrument, play second inversion

Sound the Battle Cry

Words and music by William Sherwin

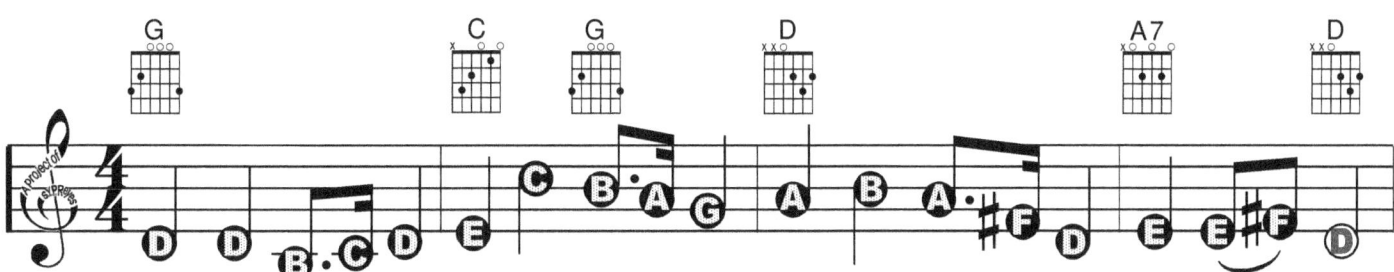

Sound the bat-tle cry! See! the foe is nigh; Raise the stand-ard high For the Lord;

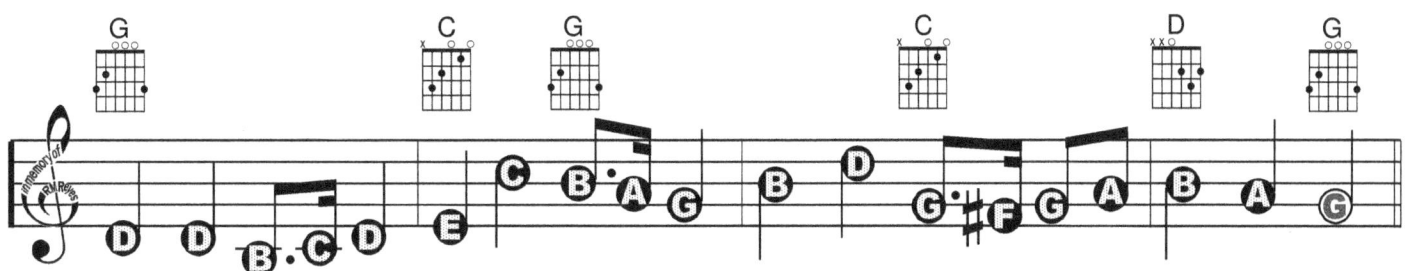

Gird your ar-mor on, Stand firm, ev-ery one, Rest your cause up-on His ho-ly word.

Refrain

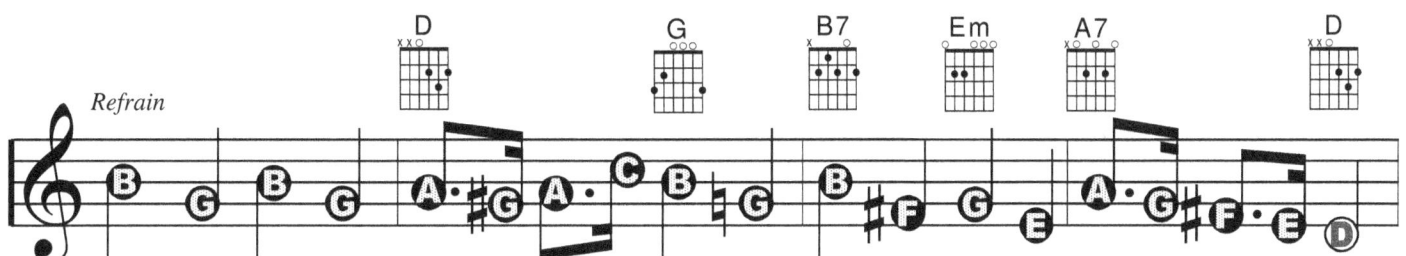

Rouse, then, sol-diers! ral-ly round the ban-ner! Read-y, stead-y, pass the word a-long;

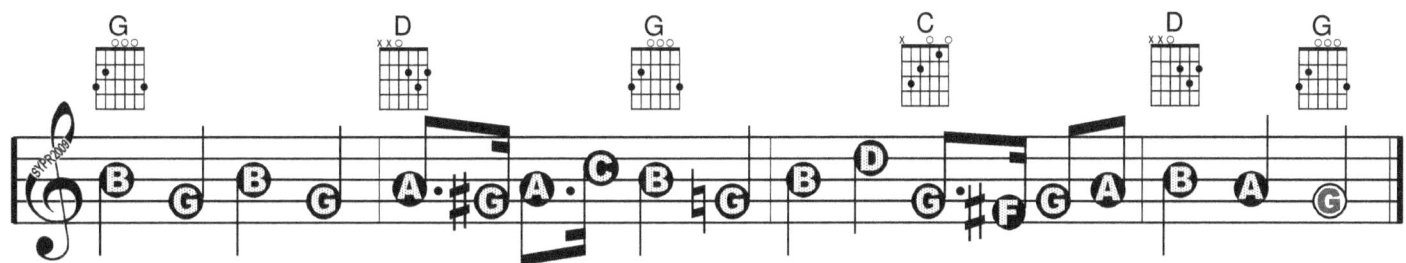

On-ward, for-ward, shout a-loud ho-san-na! Christ is Cap-tain of the might-y throng.

2. Strong to meet the foe, Marching on we go,
   While our cause we know Must prevail;
   Shield and banner bright, Gleaming in the light,
   Battling for the right, We ne'er can fail.
   (Refrain)

3. O Thou God of all, Hear us when we call,
   Help us, one and all, By Thy grace;
   When the battle's done, And the victory won,
   May we wear the crown Before Thy face.
   (Refrain)

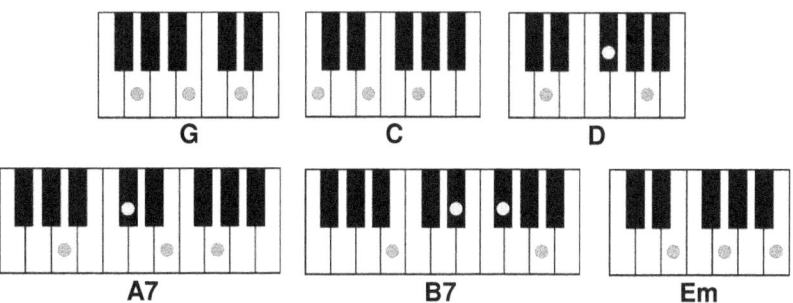

117

Stand Like the Brave

Words by Fanny Crosby

Music by William Bradbury and Philip Philipps

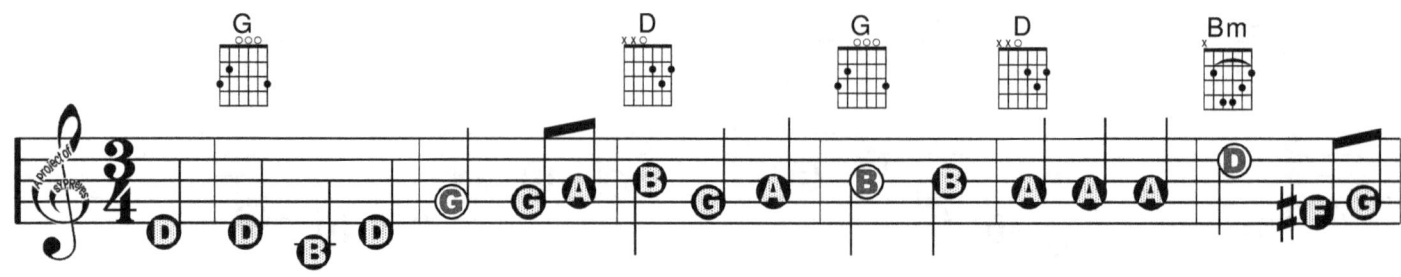

O Christian, a-wake! 'tis the Master's command; With helmet and shield, and a

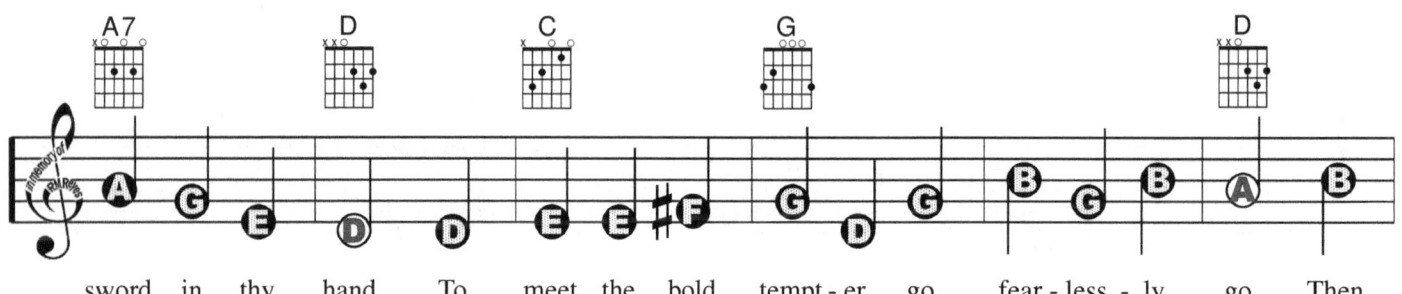

sword in thy hand, To meet the bold tempt-er, go, fear-less-ly go, Then

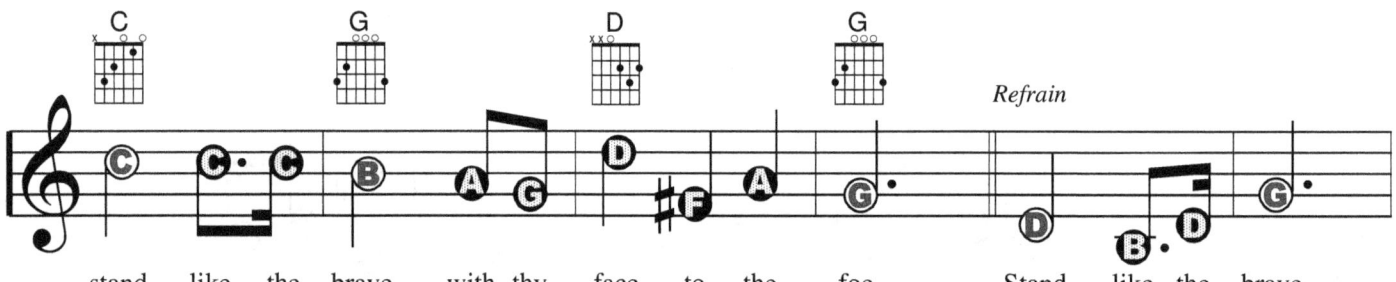

stand like the brave, with thy face to the foe. Stand like the brave,

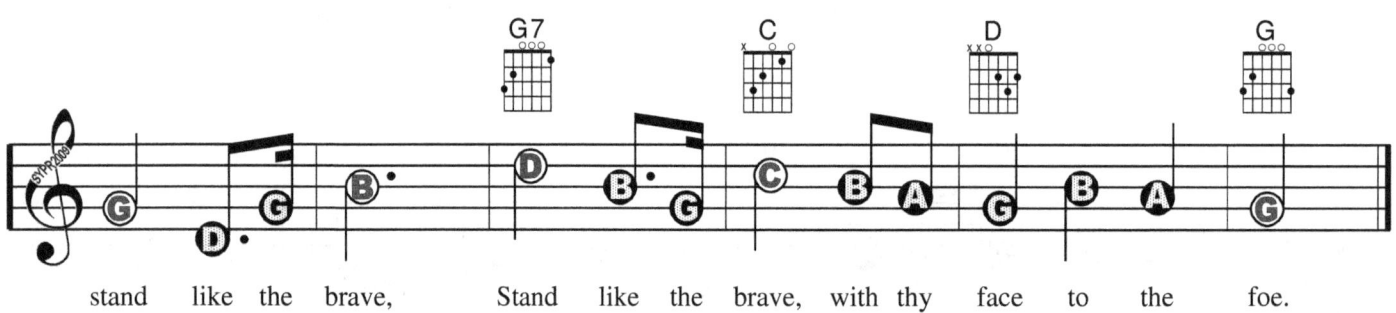

stand like the brave, Stand like the brave, with thy face to the foe.

2. The cause of thy Master with vigor defend;
   Be watchful, be zealous, and fight to the end;
   Wherever He leads thee, go, valiantly go,
   Then stand like the brave, with thy face to the foe.
   (Refrain)

3. Press on, never doubting, thy Captain is near,
   With grace to supply, and with comfort to cheer;
   His love, like a stream in the desert will flow;
   Then stand like the brave, with thy face to the foe.
   (Refrain)

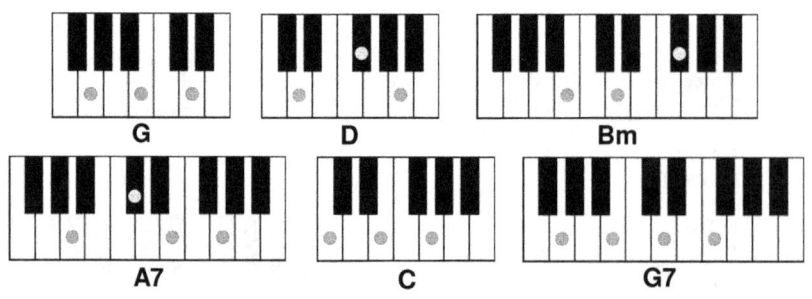

Stand Up! Stand Up for Jesus!

Words by George Duffield
Music by George Webb

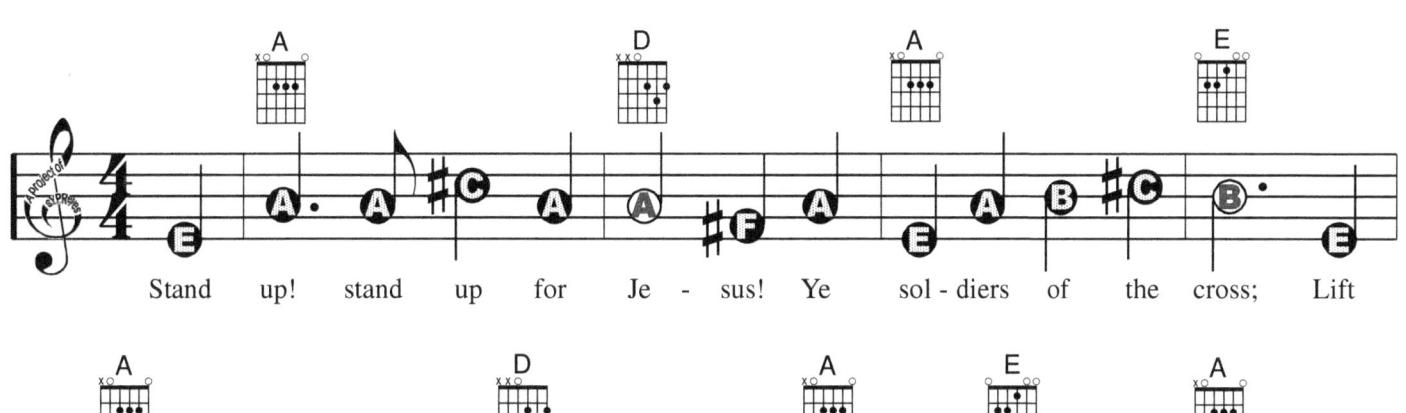

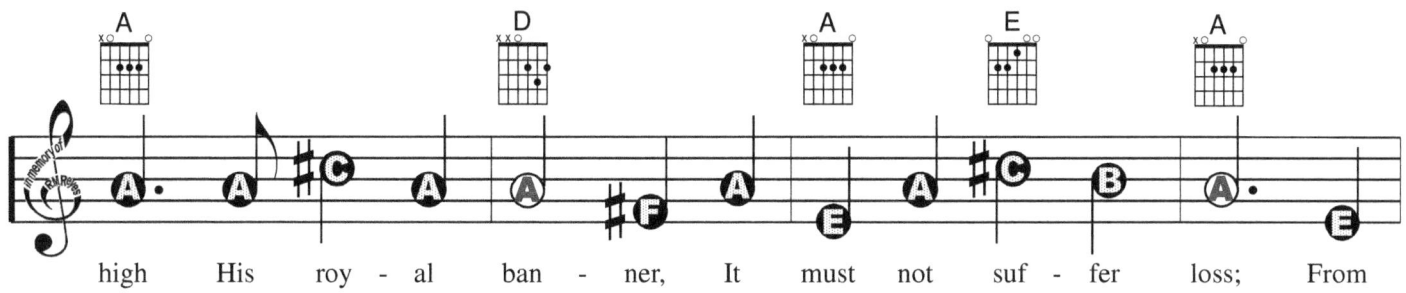

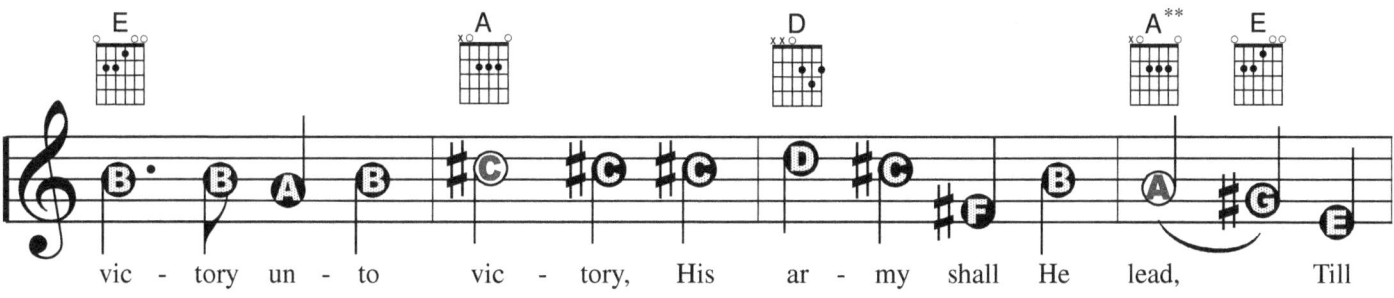

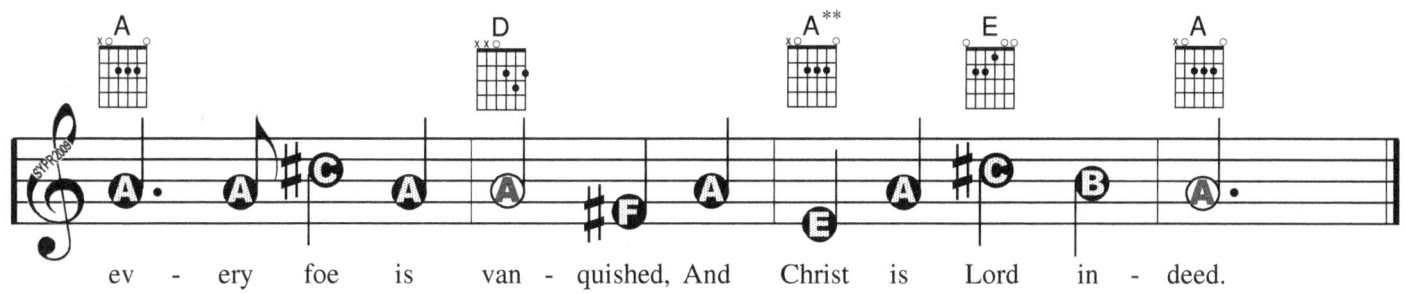

2. Stand up! stand up for Jesus! The trumpet call obey;
   Forth to the mighty conflict, In this His glorious day.
   Ye that are men now serve Him Against unnumbered foes;
   Let courage rise with danger, And strength to strength oppose.

3. Stand up! stand up for Jesus! Stand in His strength alone;
   The arm of flesh will fail you; Ye dare not trust your own.
   Put on the gospel armor, And watching unto prayer,
   Where duty calls, or danger, Be never wanting there.

4. Stand up! stand up for Jesus! The strife will not be long;
   This day the noise of battle, The next the victor's song.
   To him that overcometh, A crown of life shall be;
   He with the King of glory Shall reign eternally.

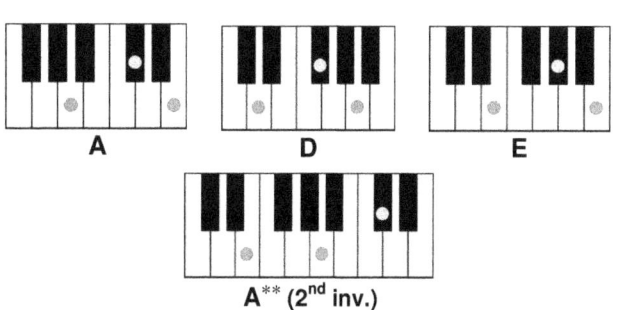

**On keyboard instrument, play second inversion

Standing on the Promises

Words and music by R. Kelso Carter

2. Standing on the promises that cannot fail,
   When the howling storms of doubt and fear assail,
   By the living word of God I shall prevail,
   Standing on the promises of God.
   (Refrain)

3. Standing on the promises of Christ the Lord,
   Bound to Him eternally by love's strong cord,
   Overcoming daily with the Spirit's sword,
   Standing on the promises of God.
   (Refrain)

**On keyboard instrument, play second inversion

Sweet By and By

Words by S. F. Bennett
Music by J. P. Webster

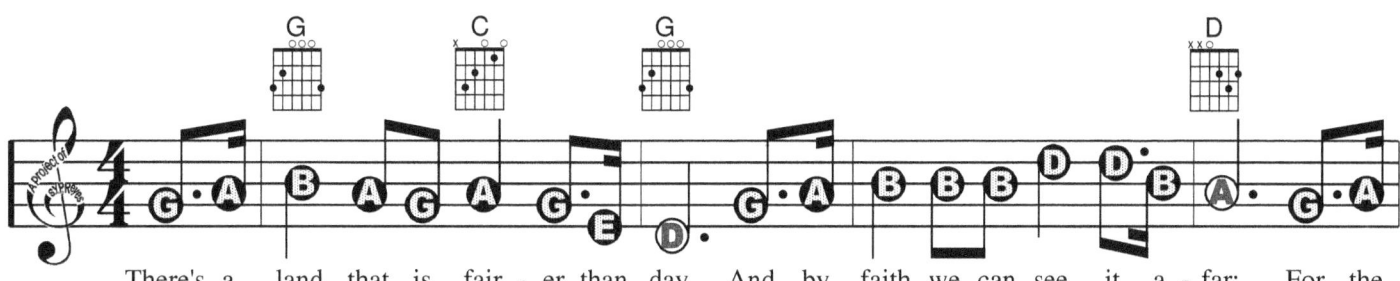

There's a land that is fair-er than day, And by faith we can see it a-far; For the

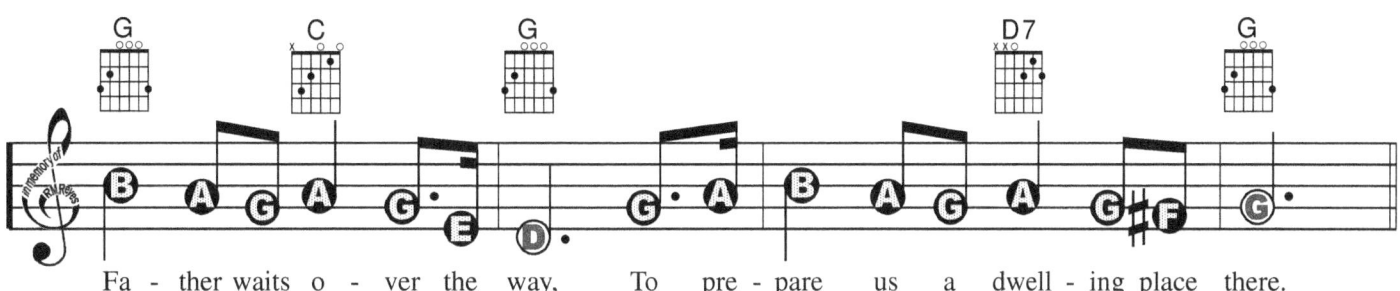

Fa-ther waits o-ver the way, To pre-pare us a dwell-ing place there.

Refrain

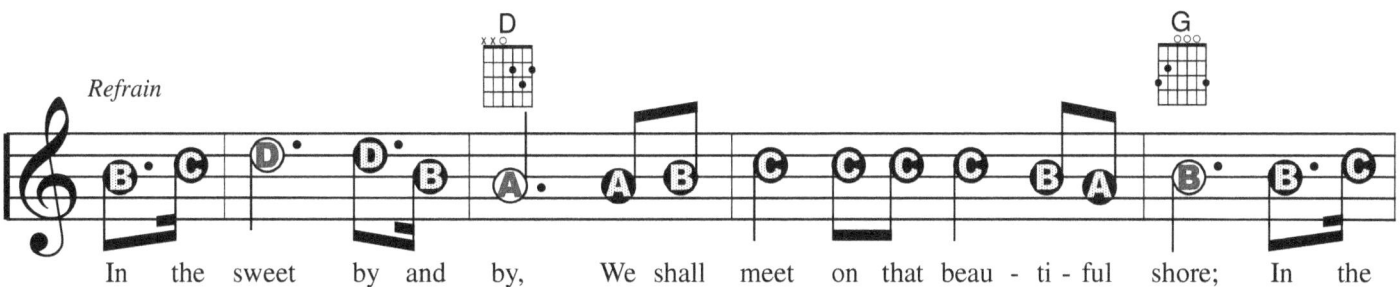

In the sweet by and by, We shall meet on that beau-ti-ful shore; In the

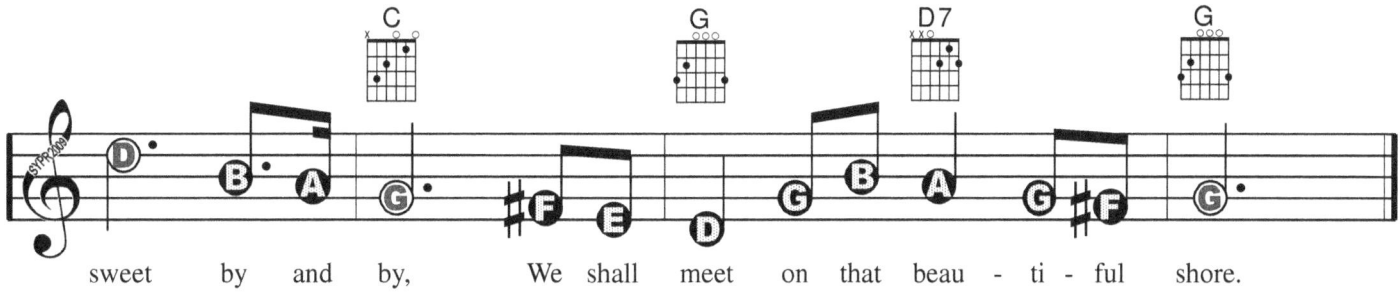

sweet by and by, We shall meet on that beau-ti-ful shore.

2. We shall sing on that beautiful shore The melodious songs of the blest,
   And our spirits shall sorrow no more, Not a sigh for the blessing of rest.
   (Refrain)

3. To our bountiful Father above, We will offer a tribute of praise,
   For the glorious gift of His love, And the blessings that hallow our days.
   (Refrain)

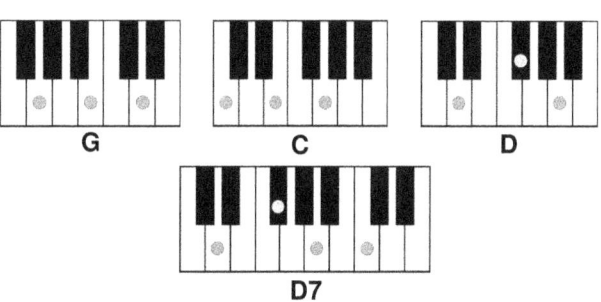

121

Sweet Hour of Prayer

Words by William Walford
Music by William Bradbury

Sweet hour of prayer, sweet hour of prayer, That calls me from a world of care And bids me, at my Father's throne, Make all my wants and wish-es known! In sea-sons of dis-tress and grief, My soul has of-ten found re-lief, And oft es-caped the tempt-er's snare By thy re-turn sweet hour of prayer.

2. Sweet hour of prayer! sweet hour of prayer! Thy wings shall my petition bear
   To Him whose truth and faithfulness Engage the waiting soul to bless.
   And since He bids me seek His face, Believe His word, and trust His grace,
   I'll cast on Him my every care, And wait for thee, sweet hour of prayer.

3. Sweet hour of prayer! sweet hour of prayer! May I thy consolation share
   Till from Mount Pisgah's lofty height I view my home and take my flight.
   In my immortal flesh I'll rise To seize the everlasting prize.
   And shout while passing through the air, "Farewell, farewell, sweet hour of prayer!"

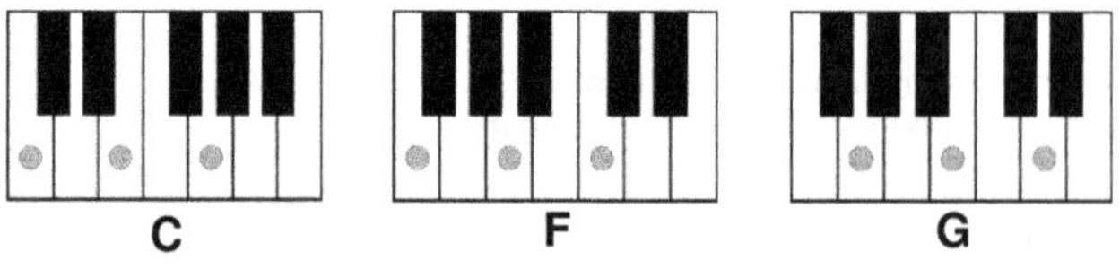

122

Take My Life and Let It Be

Words by Frances Ridley Havergal

Music by H. A. Cesar Malan

Take my life, and let it be Con - se - crat - ed,
Lord, to Thee; Take my hands, and let them move At the im - pulse
of Thy love, At the im - pulse of Thy love.

2. Take my feet, and let them be Swift and beautiful for Thee;
   Take my voice, and let me sing
   Always, only, for my King, Always, only, for my King.

3. Take my lips, and let them be Filled with messages from Thee;
   Take my silver and my gold,
   Not a mite would I withhold, Not a mite would I withhold.

4. Take my will and make it Thine; It shall be no longer mine;
   Take my heart, it is Thine own!
   It shall be Thy royal throne, It shall be Thy royal throne.

5. Take my love; my Lord, I pour At Thy feet its treasure store;
   Take myself, and I will be,
   Ever, only, all for Thee, Ever, only, all for Thee.

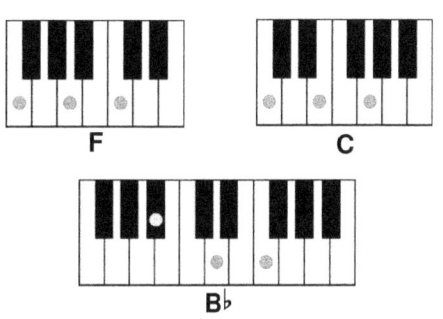

123

Take the Name of Jesus With You

Words by Lillian Baxter
Music by William Doane

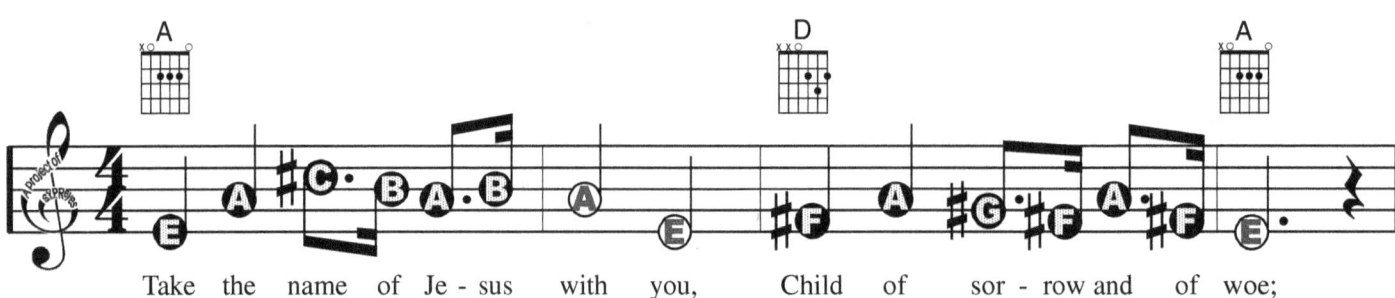
Take the name of Je - sus with you, Child of sor - row and of woe;

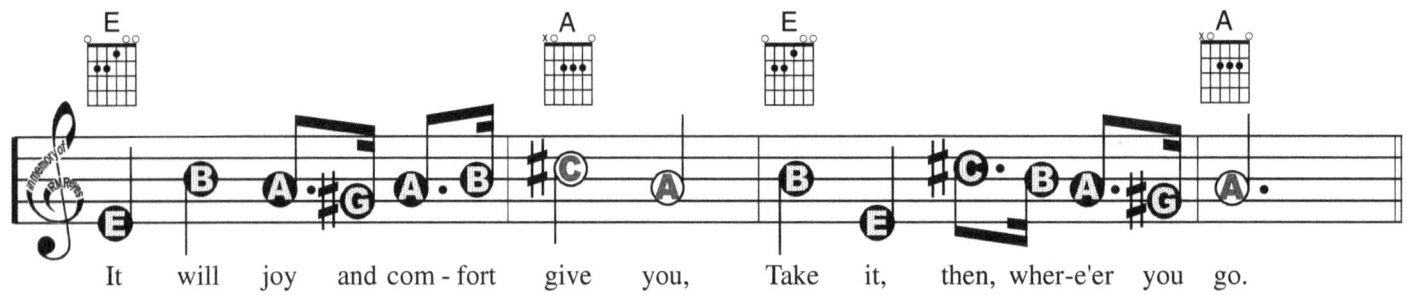
It will joy and com - fort give you, Take it, then, wher-e'er you go.

Refrain

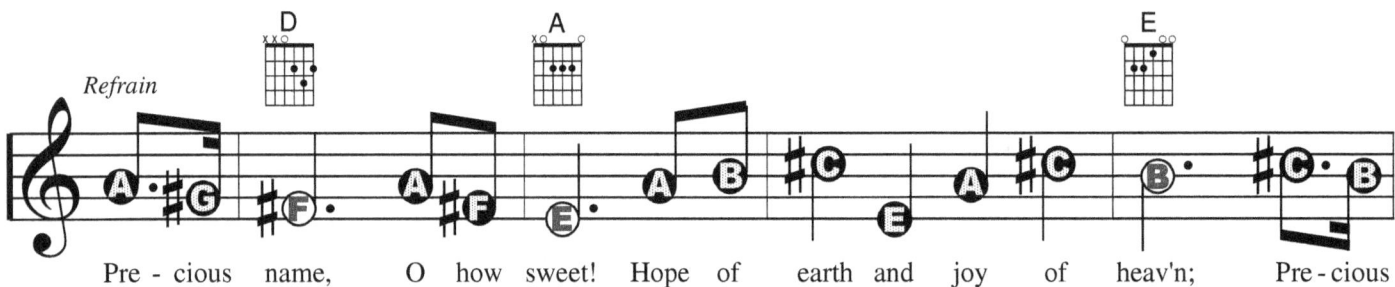
Pre - cious name, O how sweet! Hope of earth and joy of heav'n; Pre - cious

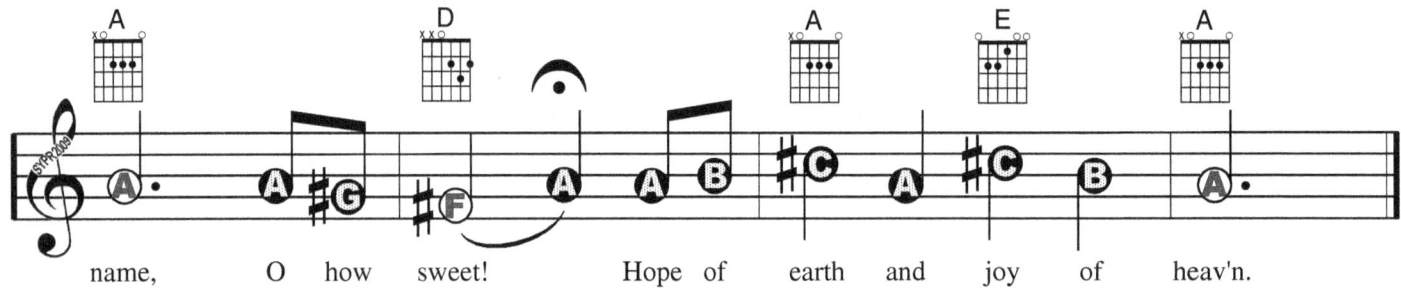
name, O how sweet! Hope of earth and joy of heav'n.

2. Take the name of Jesus ever, As a shield from every snare;
   If temptations round you gather, Breathe that holy name in prayer.
   (Refrain)

3. O the precious name of Jesus! How it thrills our souls with joy,
   When His loving arms receive us, And His songs our tongues employ!
   (Refrain)

4. At the name of Jesus bowing, Falling prostrate at His feet,
   King of kings in heaven we'll crown Him, When our journey is complete.
   (Refrain)

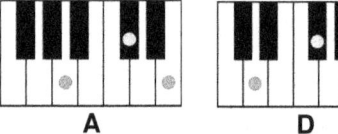 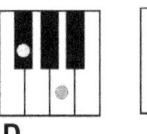 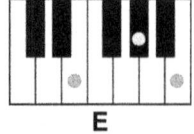

124

Take the World, but Give Me Jesus

Words by Fanny Crosby
Music by John Sweney

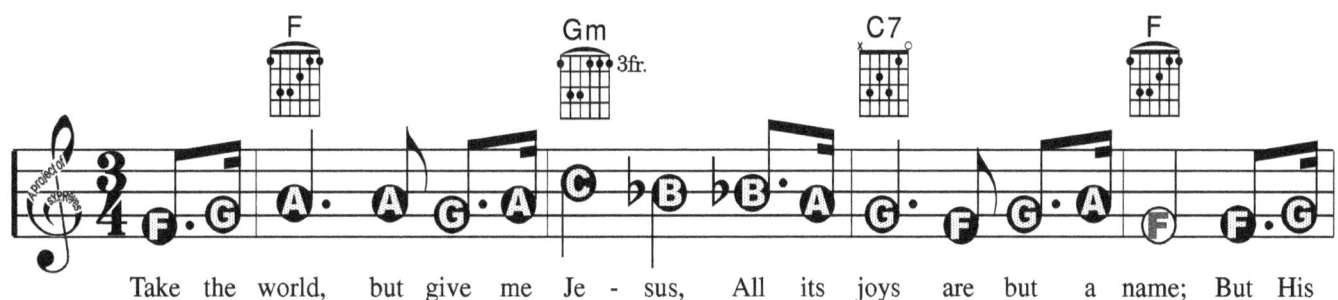

Take the world, but give me Je-sus, All its joys are but a name; But His

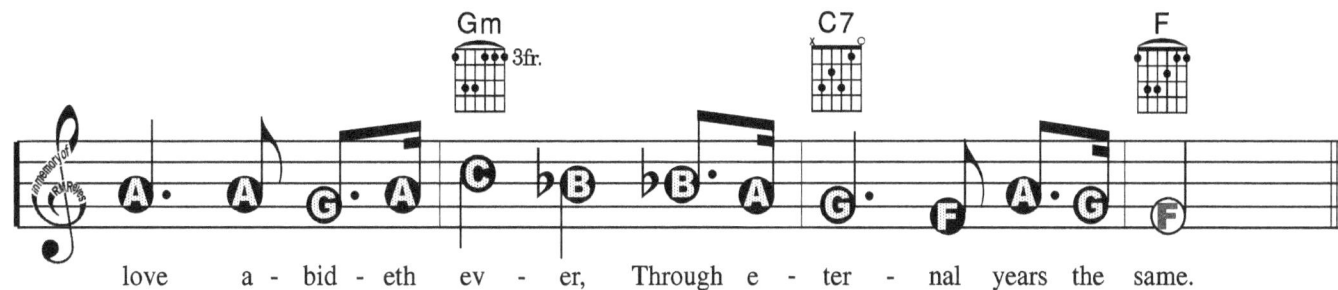

love a-bid-eth ev-er, Through e-ter-nal years the same.

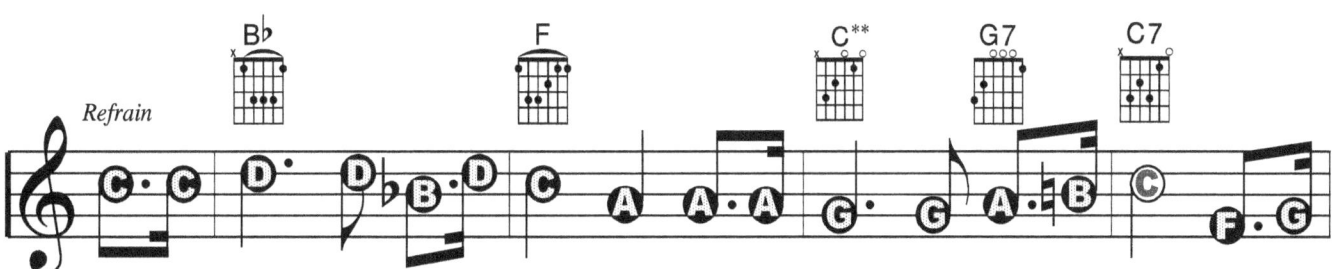

Refrain
Oh, the height and depth of mer-cy! Oh, the length and breadth of love! Oh, the

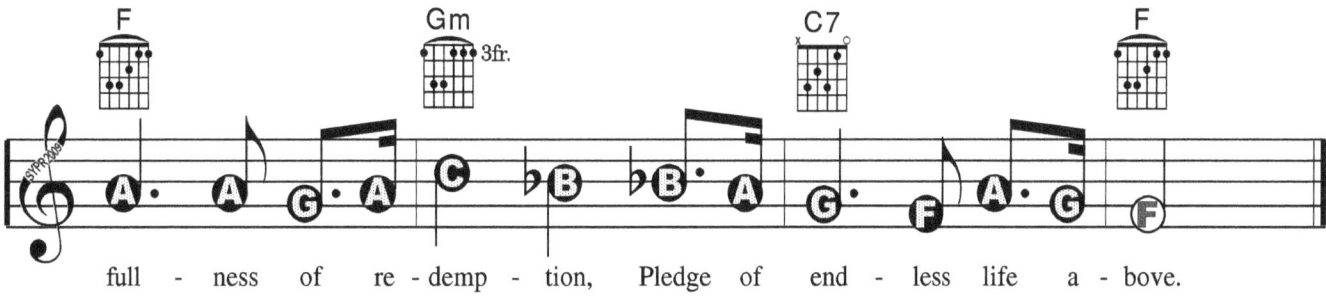

full-ness of re-demp-tion, Pledge of end-less life a-bove.

2. Take the world, but give me Jesus, Sweetest comfort to my soul;
With my Savior watching o'er me, I can sing, though billows roll.
(Refrain)

3. Take the world, but give me Jesus; Let me view His constant smile;
Then throughout my pilgrim journey Light will cheer me all the while.
(Refrain)

4. Take the world, but give me Jesus; In His cross my trust shall be,
Till, with clearer, brighter vision, Face to face my Lord I see.
(Refrain)

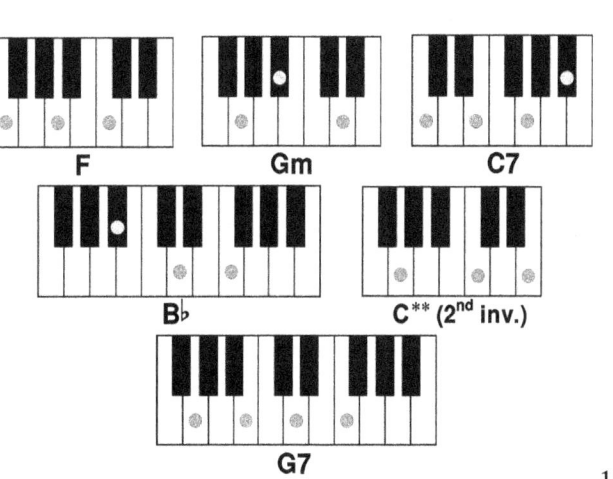

**On keyboard instrument, play second inversion

Tell Me the Old, Old Story

Words by Katherine Hankey
Music by William Doane

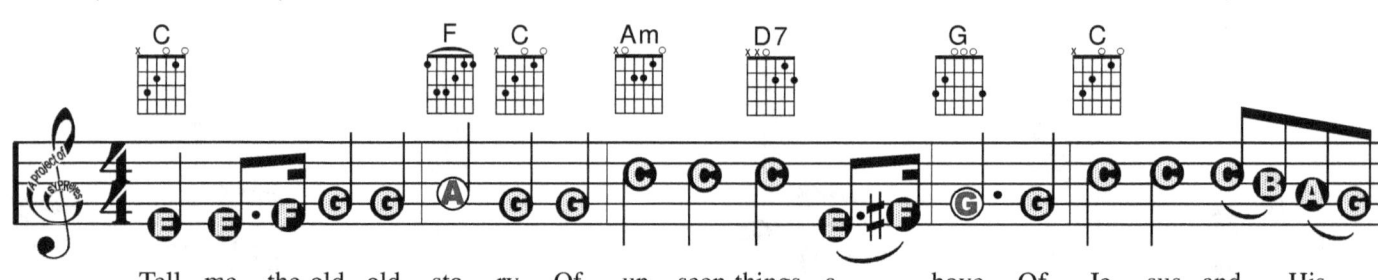
Tell me the old, old story, Of un-seen things a - bove, Of Je-sus and His

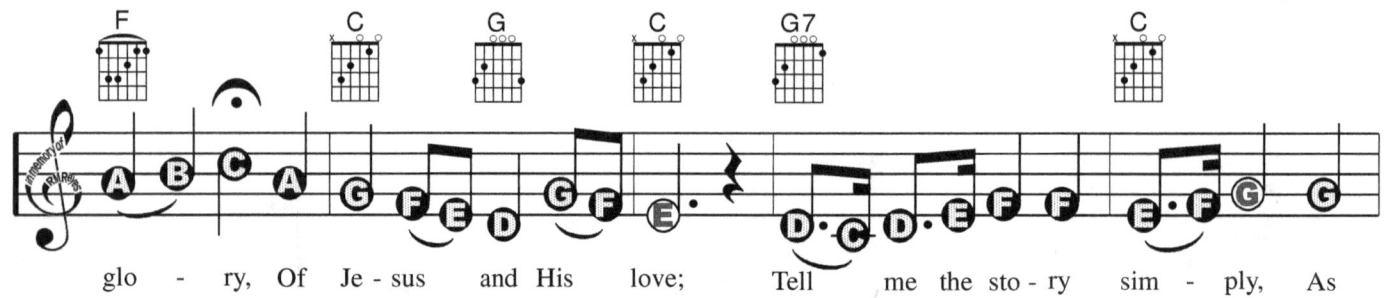
glo - ry, Of Je - sus and His love; Tell me the sto - ry sim - ply, As

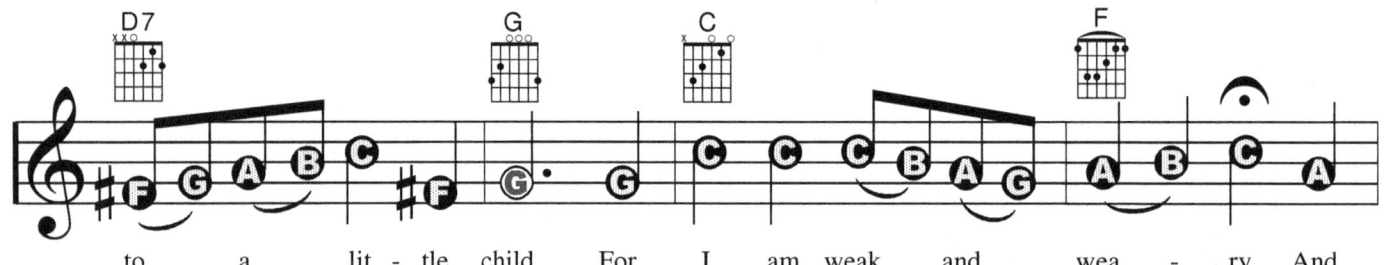
to a lit - tle child, For I am weak and wea - ry, And

Refrain
help-less and de - filed. Tell me the old, old sto - ry, Tell me the old, old

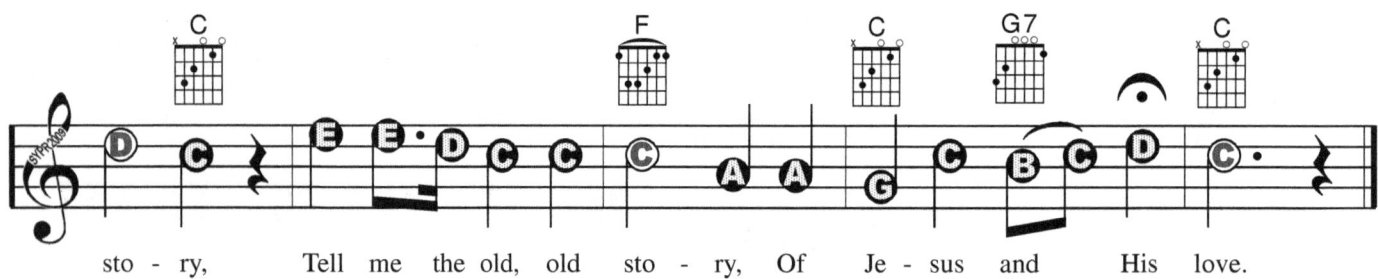
sto - ry, Tell me the old, old sto - ry, Of Je - sus and His love.

2. Tell me the story softly, With earnest tones and grave;
Remember I'm the sinner Whom Jesus came to save;
Tell me the story always, If you would really be,
In any time of trouble, A comforter to me.
(Refrain)

3. Tell me the same old story, When you have cause to fear
That this world's empty glory Is costing me too dear;
Yes, and when that world's glory Is dawning on my soul,
Tell me the old, old story: "Christ Jesus makes thee whole."
(Refrain)

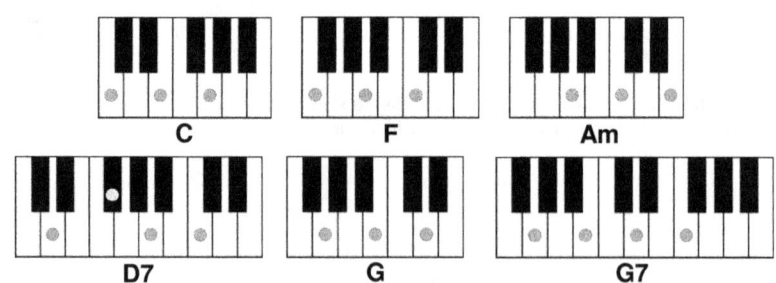

Tell Me the Story of Jesus

Words by Fanny Crosby
Music by John Sweney

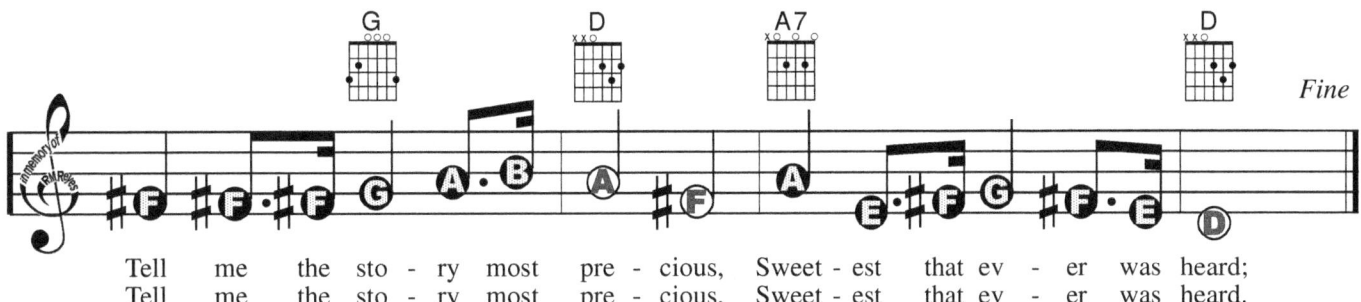
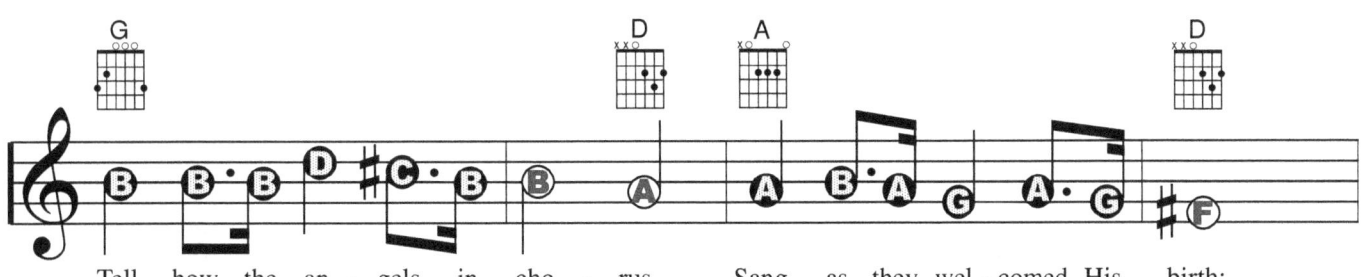
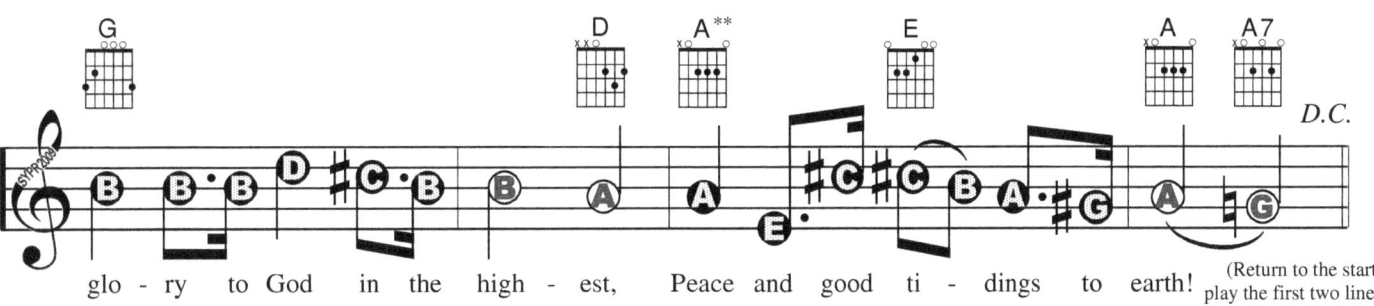

2. Fasting alone in the desert, Tell of the days that He passed,
   How for our sins He was tempted, Yet was triumphant at last;
   Tell of the years of His labor, Tell of the sorrow He bore,
   He was despised and afflicted, Homeless, rejected and poor.
   (Refrain)

3. Tell of the cross where they nailed Him, Writhing in anguish and pain;
   Tell of the grave where they laid Him, Tell how He liveth again;
   Love in that story so tender, Clearer than ever I see;
   Stay, let me weep while you whisper, Love paid the ransom for me.
   (Refrain)

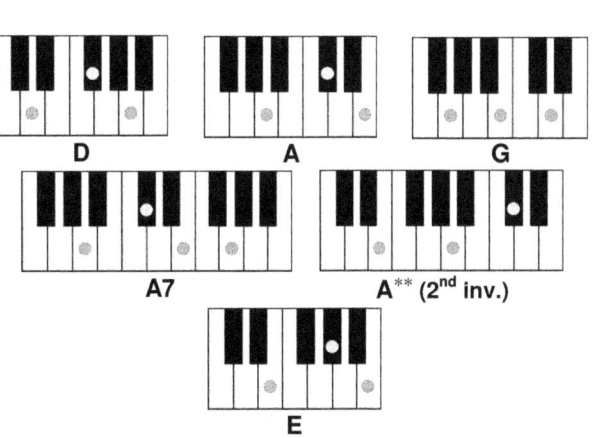

**On keyboard instrument, play second inversion

127

The First Noel

Traditional English carol

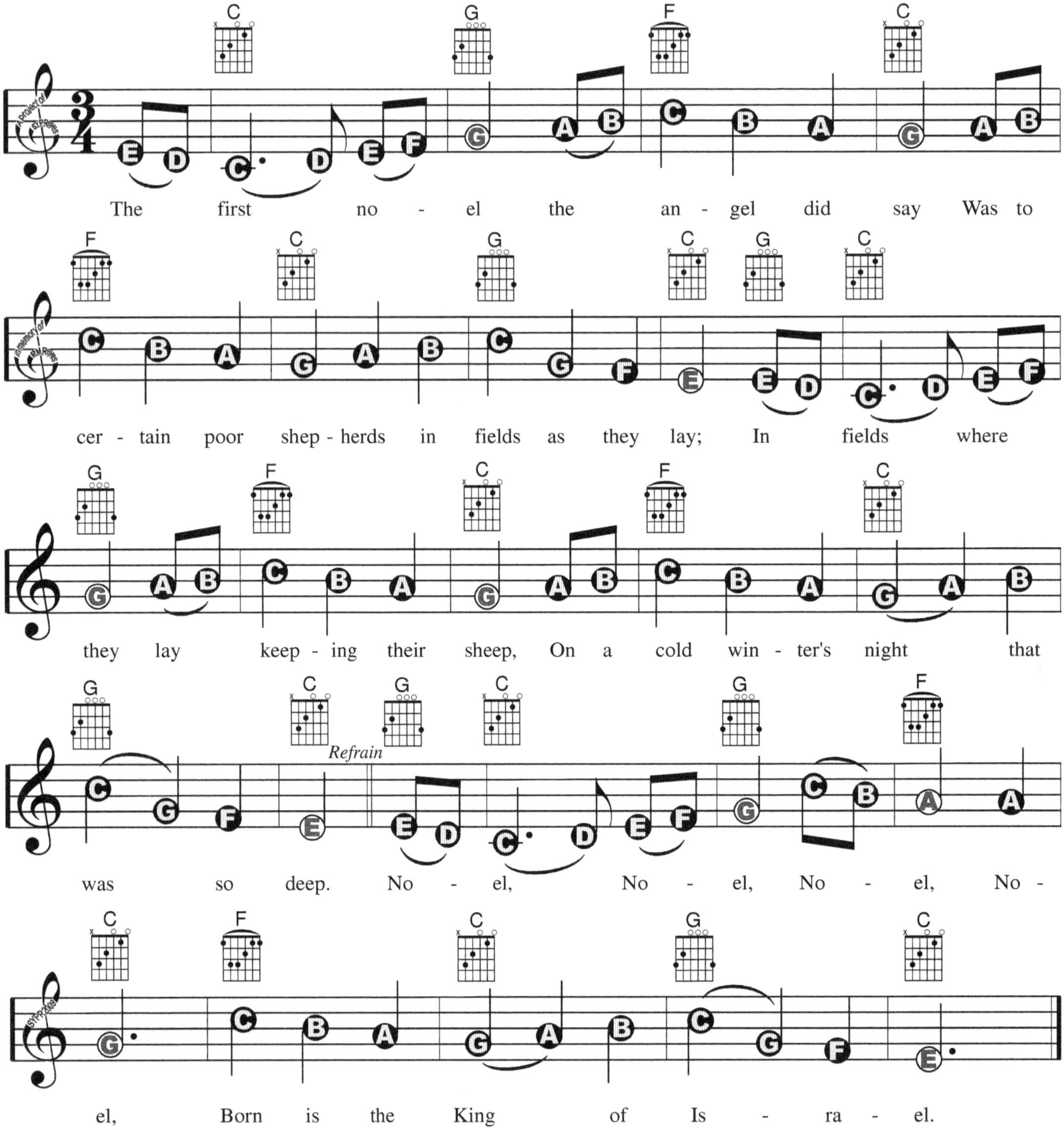

The first no-el the an-gel did say Was to cer-tain poor shep-herds in fields as they lay; In fields where they lay keep-ing their sheep, On a cold win-ter's night that was so deep.

Refrain
No-el, No-el, No-el, No-el, Born is the King of Is-ra-el.

2. They looked up and saw a star Shining in the east, beyond them far,
   And to the earth it gave great light, And so it continued both day and night.
   (Refrain)

3. And by the light of that same star, Three wise men came from country far;
   To seek for a king was their intent, And to follow the star wherever it went.
   (Refrain)

4. This star drew nigh to the northwest, O'er Bethlehem it took its rest,
   And there it did both stop and stay, Right over the place where Jesus lay.
   (Refrain)

5. Then entered in those wise men three, Full reverently upon the knee,
   And offered there, in His presence, Their gold, and myrrh, and frankincense.
   (Refrain)

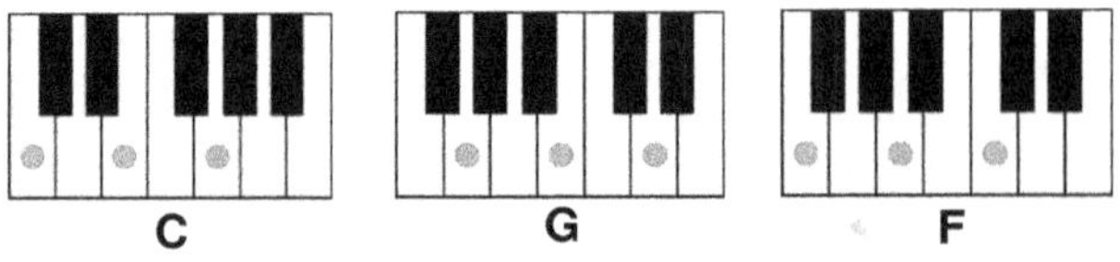

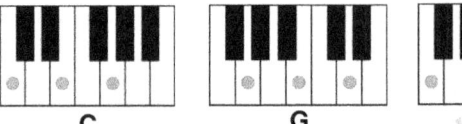

128

The Lord in Zion Reigneth

Words by Fanny Crosby

Music by Hart Danks

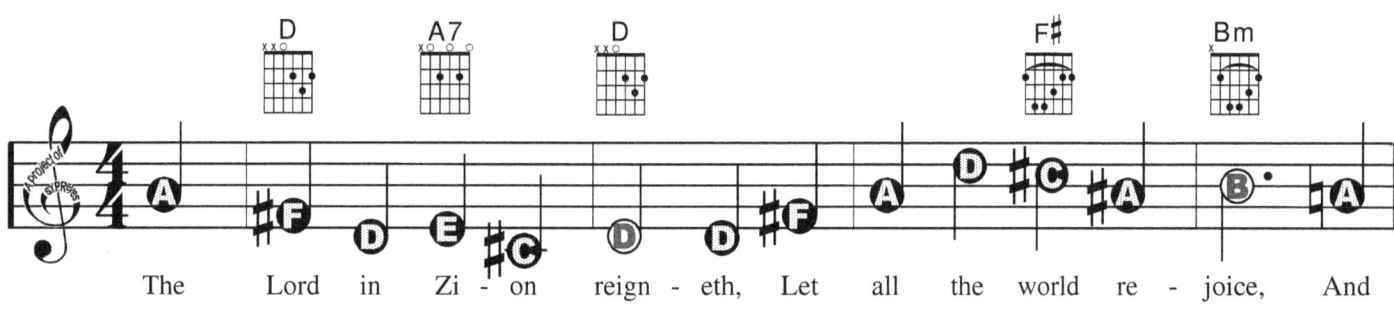

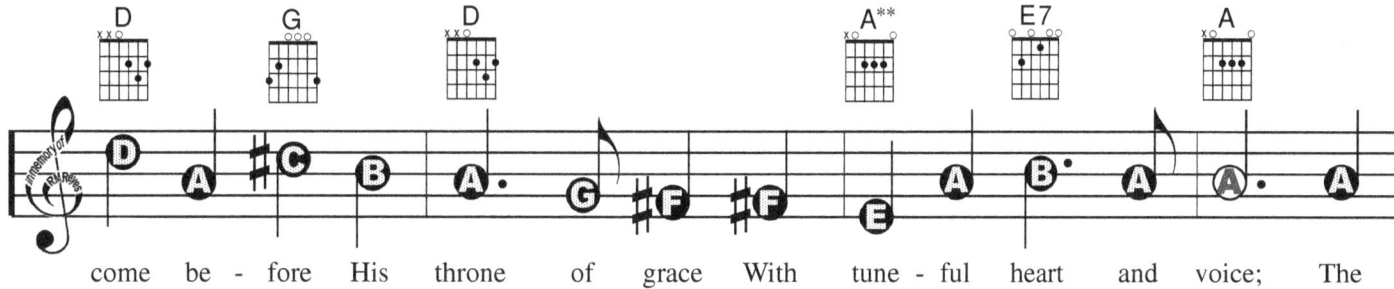

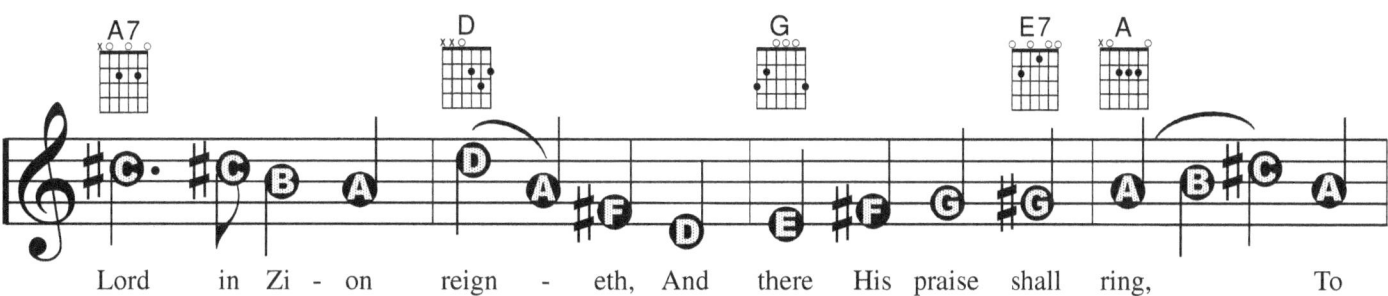

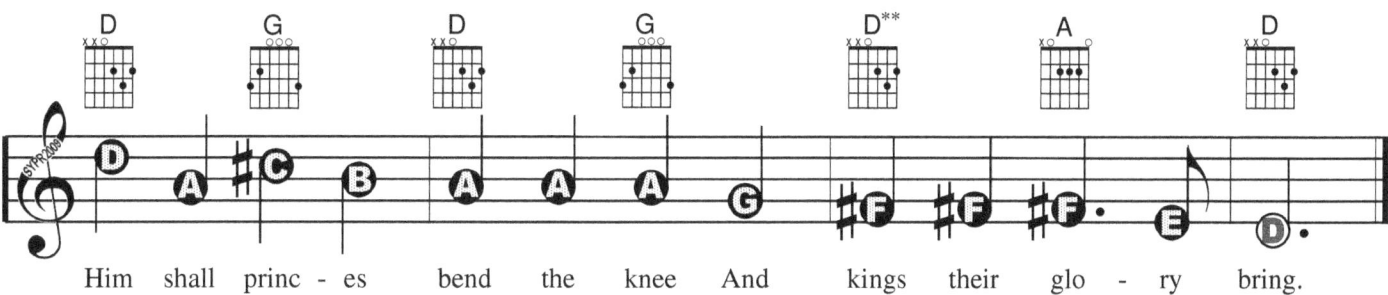

2. The Lord in Zion reigneth And who so great as He?
   The depths of earth are in His hands; He rules the mighty sea
   O crown His name with honour, And let His standard wave,
   Till distant isles beyond the deep Shall own His power to save.

3. The Lord in Zion reigneth, These hours to Him belong;
   O enter now His temple gates And fill His courts with song;
   Beneath His royal banner Let every creature fall
   Exalt the King of heaven and earth And crown Him Lord of all.

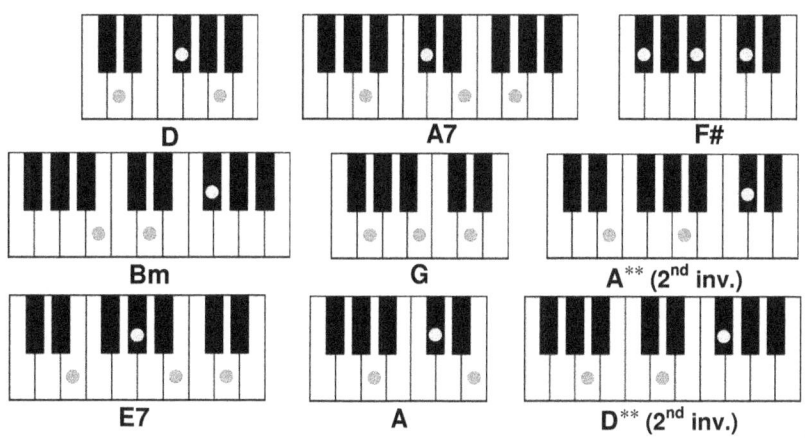

**On keyboard instrument, play second inversion

The Lord Is My Light

Words by James Nicholson
Music by J. W. Bischoff

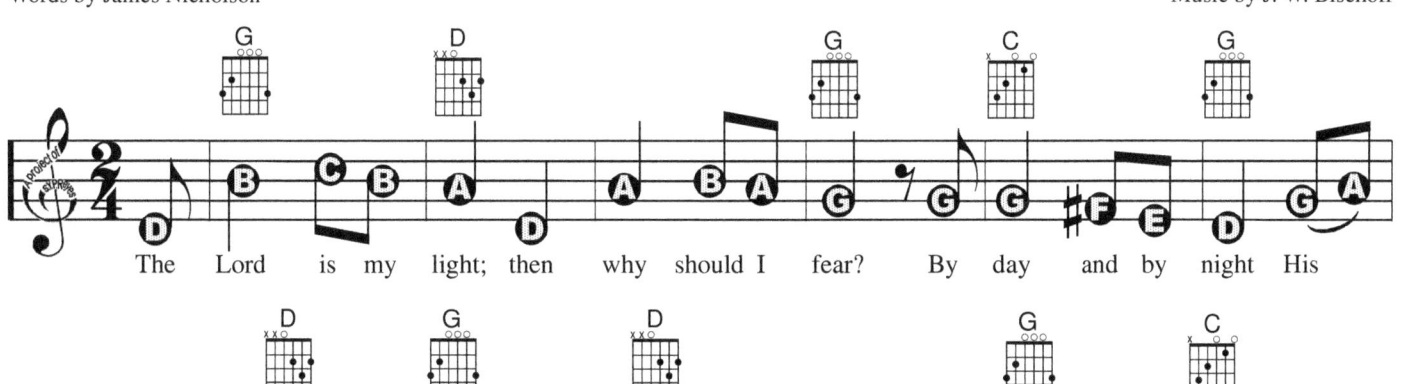
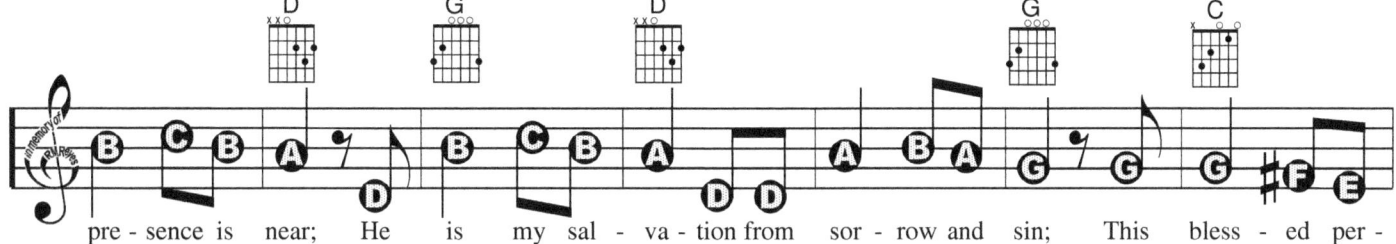
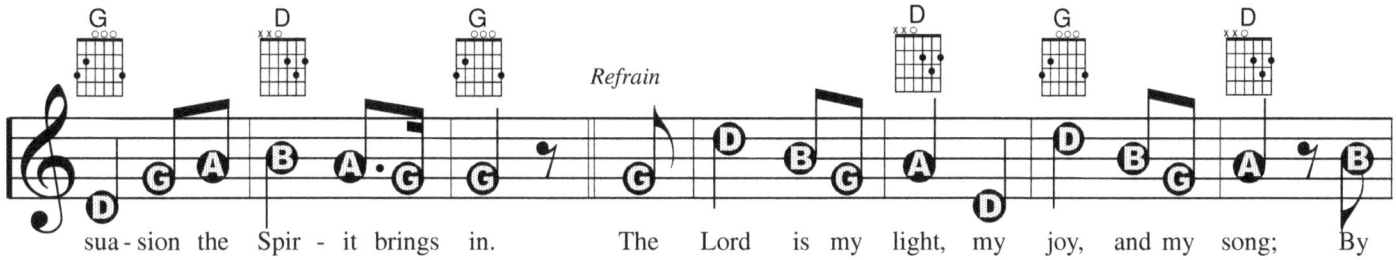
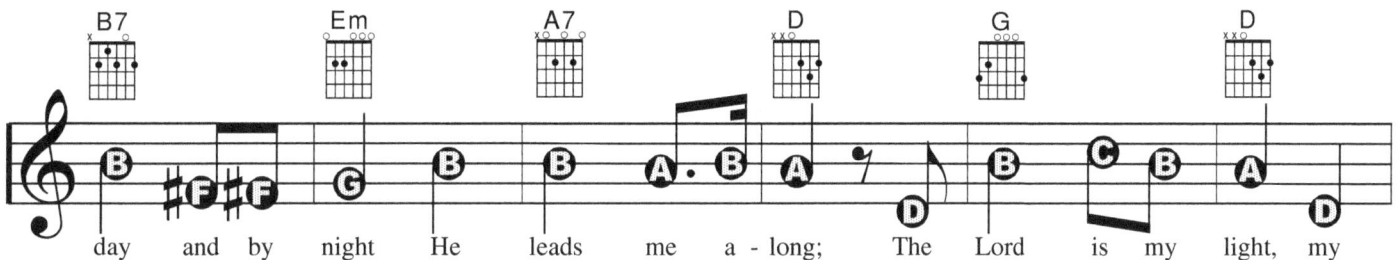
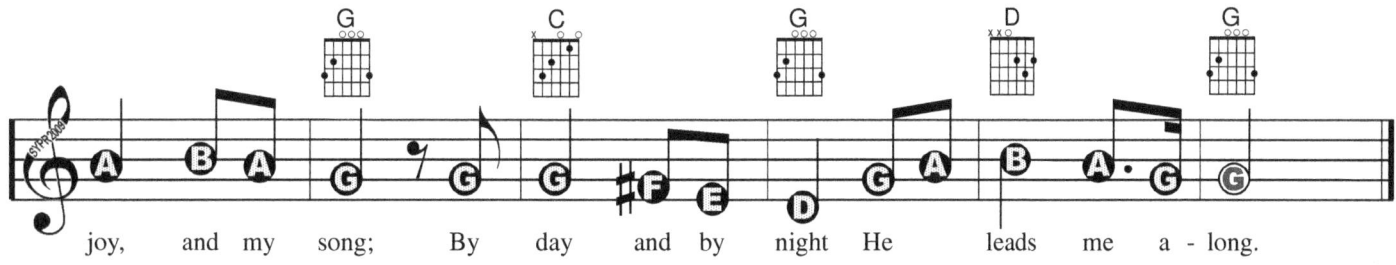

2. The Lord is my light; though clouds may arise,
   Faith, stronger than sight, looks up to the skies
   Where Jesus forever in glory doth reign:
   Then how can I ever in darkness remain?
   (Refrain)

3. The Lord is my light, the Lord is my strength;
   I know in His might I'll conquer at length;
   My weakness in mercy He covers with power,
   And walking by faith, He upholds me each hour.
   (Refrain)

4. The Lord is my light, my all and in all,
   There is in His sight no darkness at all;
   He is my Redeemer, my Saviour and King;
   With saints and with angels His praises I sing.
   (Refrain)

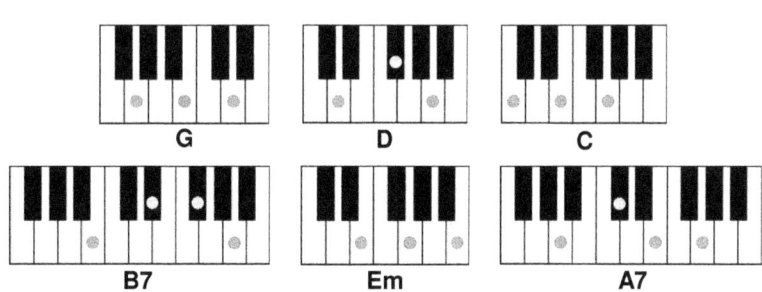

There Is a Fountain

Words by William Cowper
Early American melody

There is a fountain filled with blood Drawn from Immanuel's veins; And sinners, plunged beneath that flood, Lose all their guilty stains, Lose all their guilty stains, Lose all their guilty stains; And sinners, plunged beneath that flood, Lose all their guilty stains.

2. The dying thief rejoiced to see That fountain in his day;
   And there may I, though vile as he, Wash all my sins away;
   Wash all my sins away, Wash all my sins away,
   And there may I, though vile as he, Wash all my sins away.

3. Thou dying Lamb! Thy precious blood Shall never lose its pow'r,
   Till all the ransomed church of God Are saved, to sin no more,
   Are saved, to sin no more, Are saved, to sin no more,
   Till all the ransomed church of God Are saved, to sin no more.

4. E'er since by faith I saw the stream Thy flowing wounds supply,
   Redeeming love has been my theme, And shall be till I die,
   And shall be till I die, And shall be till I die,
   Redeeming love has been my theme, And shall be till I die.

5. Lord, I believe Thou hast prepared, Unworthy though I be,
   For me a blood-bought, free reward, A golden harp for me!
   A golden harp for me! A golden harp for me!
   For me a blood-bought, free reward, A golden harp for me!

6. There in a nobler, sweeter song, I'll sing Thy power to save,
   When this poor lisping, stammering tongue Is ransomed from the grave;
   Is ransomed from the grave, Is ransomed from the grave,
   When this poor lisping, stammering tongue Is ransomed from the grave.

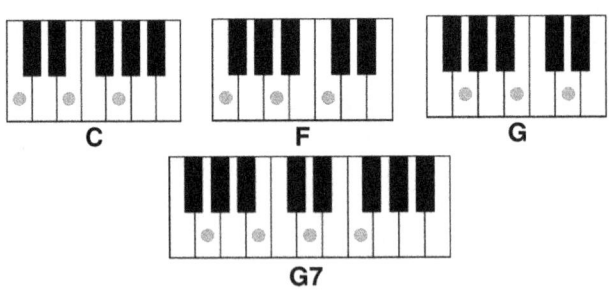

There's a Song in the Air

Words by Josiah Holland
Music by Karl Harrington

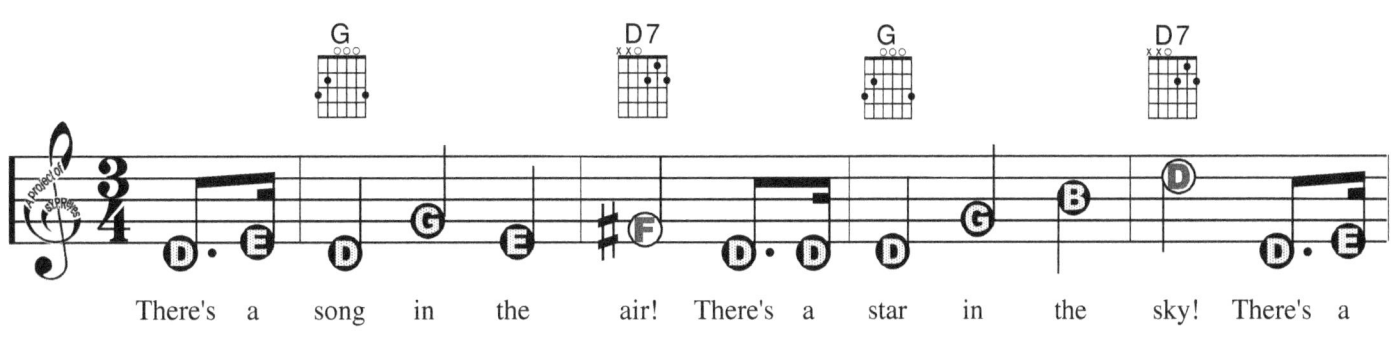

There's a song in the air! There's a star in the sky! There's a

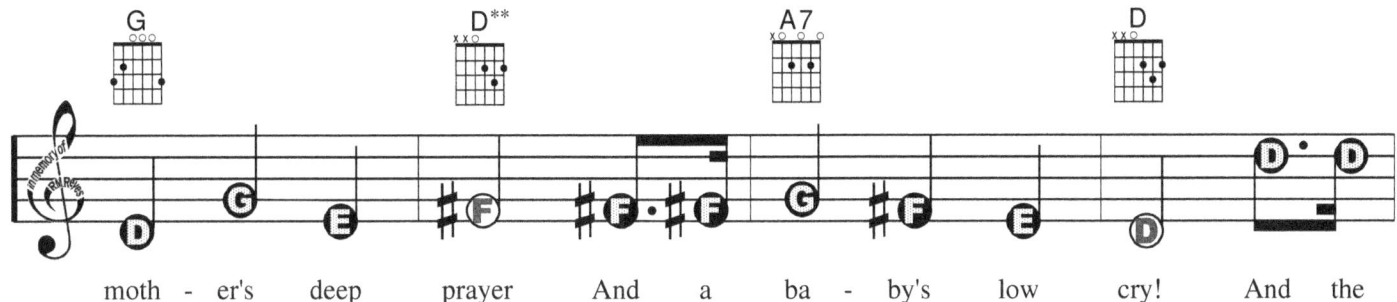

mother's deep prayer And a baby's low cry! And the

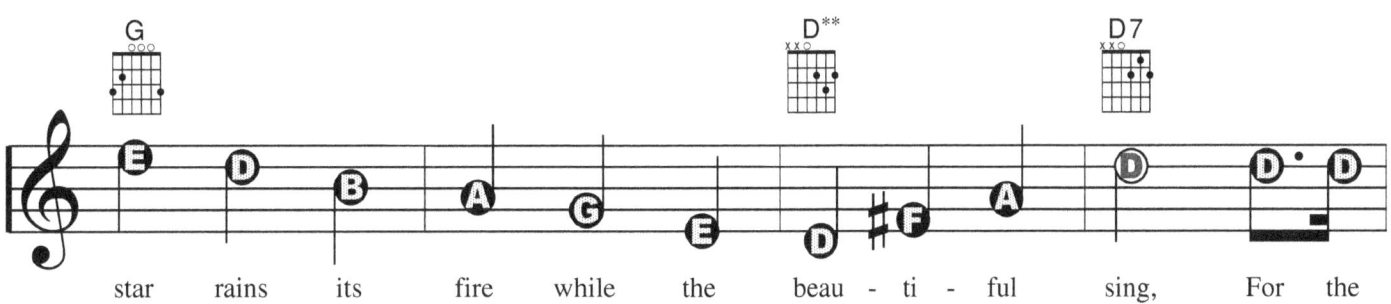

star rains its fire while the beautiful sing, For the

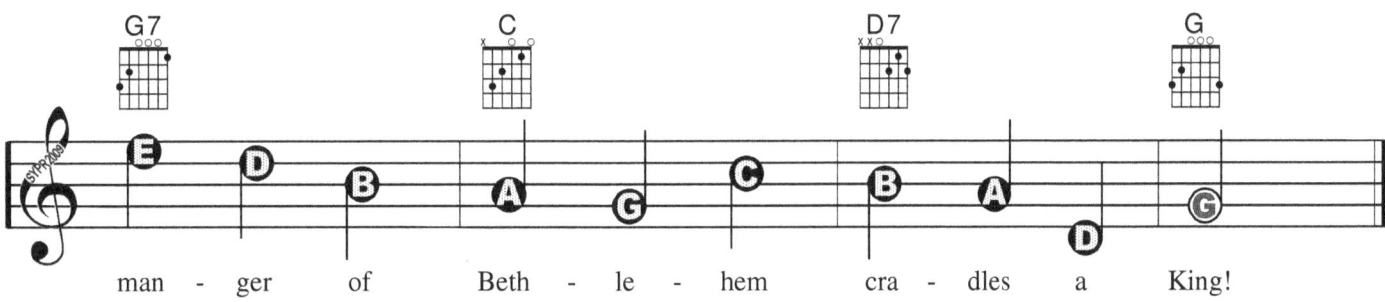

manger of Bethlehem cradles a King!

2. There's a tumult of joy O'er the wonderful birth,
   For the virgin's sweet boy Is the Lord of the earth.
   Aye! the star rains its fire while the beauitful sing,
   For the manger of Bethlehem cradles a King!

3. In the light of that star Lie the ages impearled;
   And that song from afar Has swept over the world.
   Every hearth is aflame, and the beautiful sing
   In the homes of the nations that Jesus is King!

4. We rejoice in the light, And we echo the song
   That comes down through the night From the heavenly throng.
   Aye! we shout to the lovely evangel they bring,
   And we greet in His cradle our Savior and King!

**On keyboard instrument, play second inversion

There's No Other Name Like Jesus

Words and music by F. E. Belden

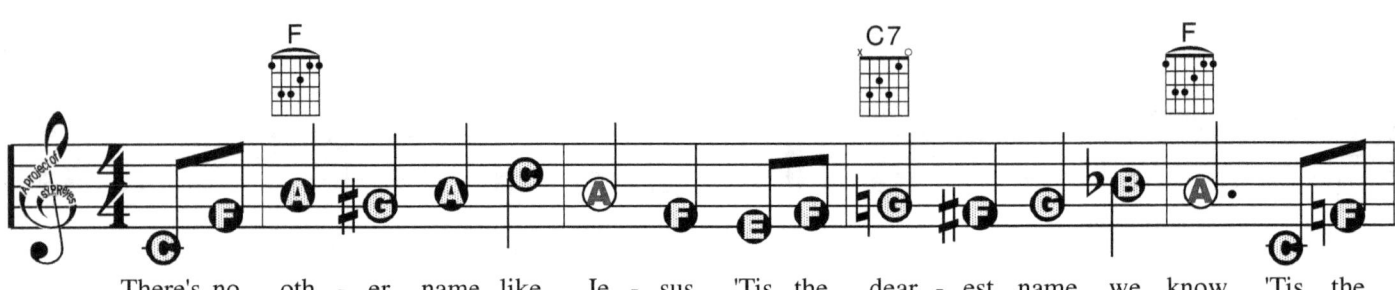

There's no oth-er name like Je-sus, 'Tis the dear-est name we know, 'Tis the

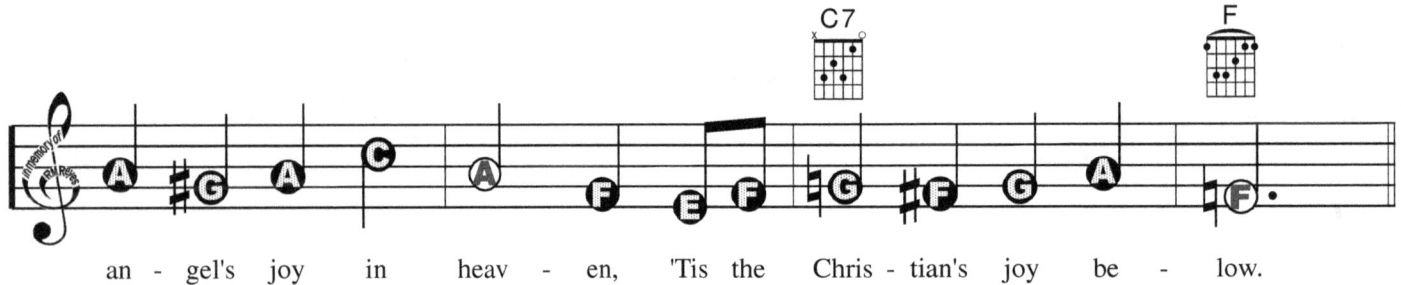

an-gel's joy in heav-en, 'Tis the Chris-tian's joy be-low.

Refrain

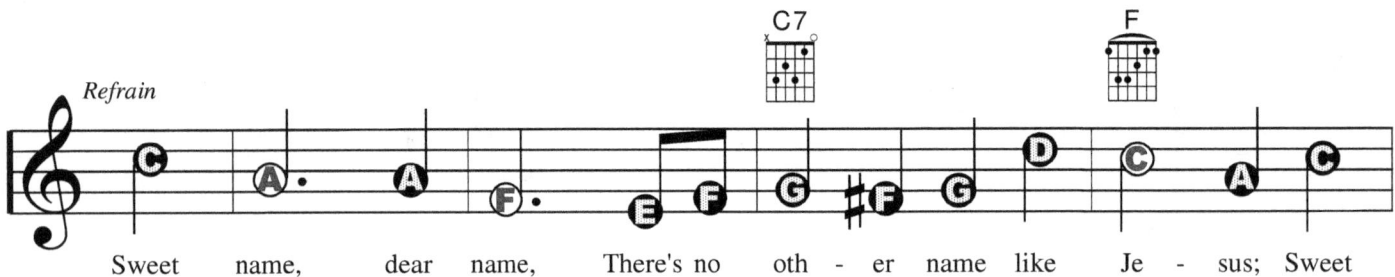

Sweet name, dear name, There's no oth-er name like Je-sus; Sweet

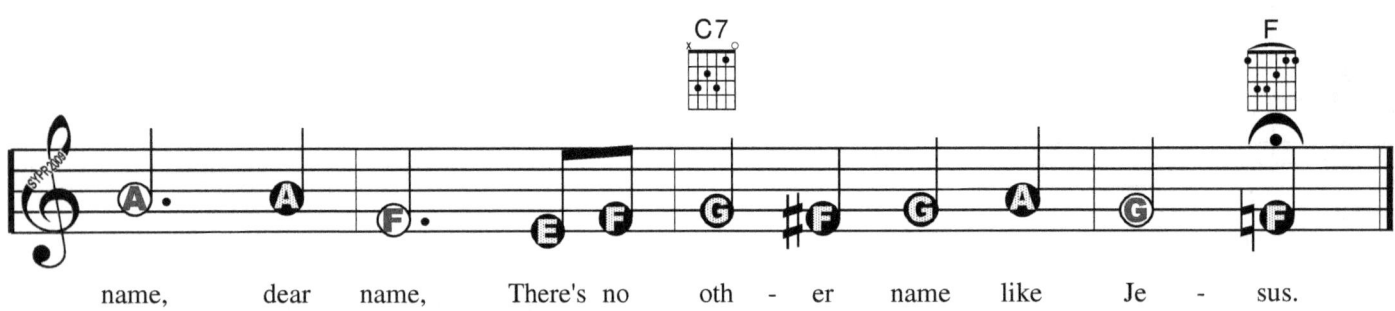

name, dear name, There's no oth-er name like Je-sus.

2. There's no other name like Jesus
   When the heart with grief is sad,
   There's no other name like Jesus
   When the heart is free and glad.
   (Refrain)

3. 'Tis the hope that I shall see Him
   When in glory He appears,
   'Tis the hope to hear His welcome
   That my fainting spirit cheers.
   (Refrain)

4. If He wills that I should labour
   In His vineyard day by day,
   Then 'tis well if only Jesus
   Blesses all I do or say.
   (Refrain)

5. If He wills that death's cold finger
   Touch my feeble, mortal clay,
   Then 'tis well if only Jesus
   Is my dying trust and stay.
   (Refrain)

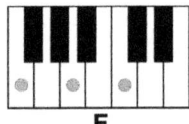
F

C7

There's Sunshine In My Soul Today

Words by Eliza Hewitt

Music by John Sweney

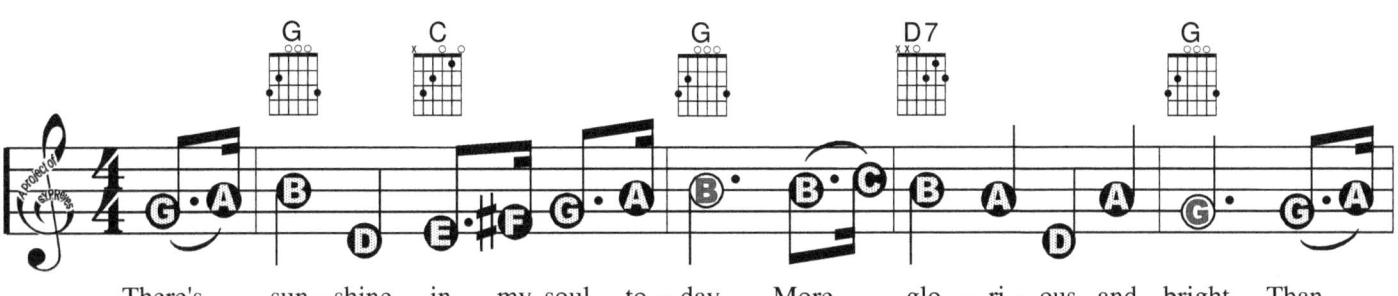

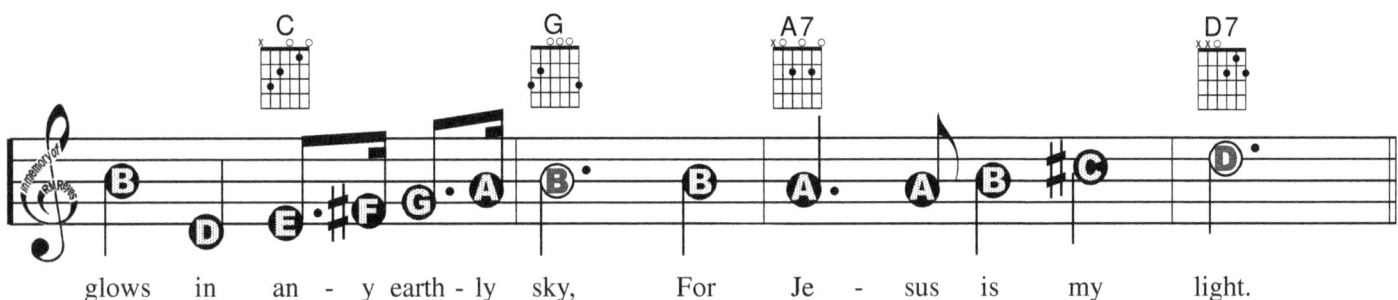

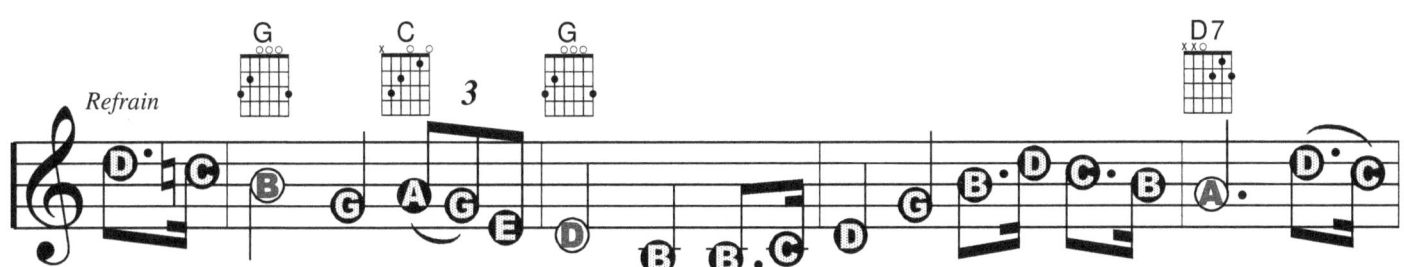

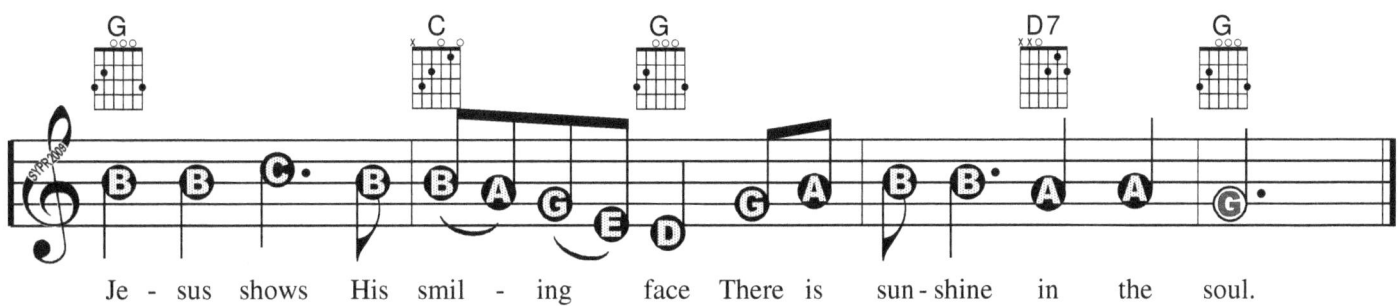

2. There's music in my soul today,
   A carol to my King,
   And Jesus, listening, can hear
   The songs I cannot sing.
   (Refrain)

3. There's springtime in my soul today
   For when the Lord is near,
   The dove of peace sings in my heart,
   The flowers of grace appear.
   (Refrain)

4. There's gladness in my soul today
   And hope, and praise, and love,
   For blessings which He gives me now,
   For joys "laid up" above.
   (Refrain)

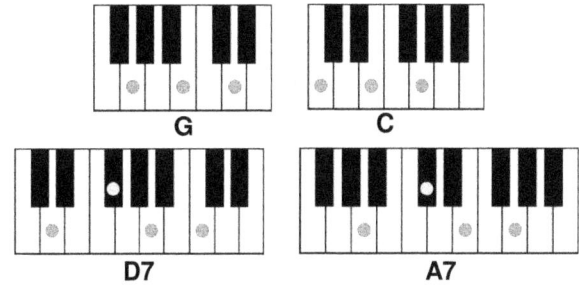

'Tis Almost Time for the Lord to Come

Words and music by G. W. Sederquist

2. The signs foretold in the sun and moon
   In earth and sea and sky,
   Aloud proclaim to all mankind,
   The coming of the Master draweth nigh.
   (Refrain)

3. It must be time for the waiting church
   To cast her pride away,
   With girded loins and burning lamps,
   To look for the breaking of the day.
   (Refrain)

4. Go quickly out in the streets and lanes
   And in the broad highway,
   And call the maimed, the halt, and blind,
   To be ready for the breaking of the day.
   (Refrain)

'Tis So Sweet to Trust in Jesus

Words by Louisa Stead   Music by William Kirkpatrick

'Tis so sweet to trust in Je - sus, Just to take Him at His word;

Just to rest up - on His prom - ise, Just to know, "Thus saith the Lord."

Refrain

Je - sus, Je - sus, how I trust Him; How I've proved Him o'er and o'er!

Je - sus, Je - sus, pre - cious Je - sus! O for grace to trust Him more!

2. O how sweet to trust in Jesus, Just to trust His cleansing blood;
   Just in simple faith to plunge me 'Neath the healing, cleansing flood.
   (Refrain)

3. Yes, 'tis sweet to trust in Jesus, Just from sin and self to cease;
   Just from Jesus simply taking Life, and rest, and joy and peace.
   (Refrain)

4. I'm so glad I learned to trust Thee, Precious Jesus, Savior, Friend;
   And I know that Thou art with me, Wilt be with me till the end.
   (Refrain)

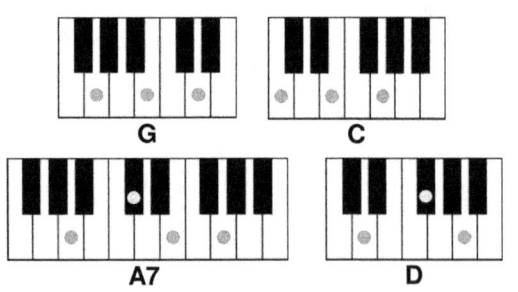

To God Be the Glory

Words by Fanny Crosby
Music by William Doane

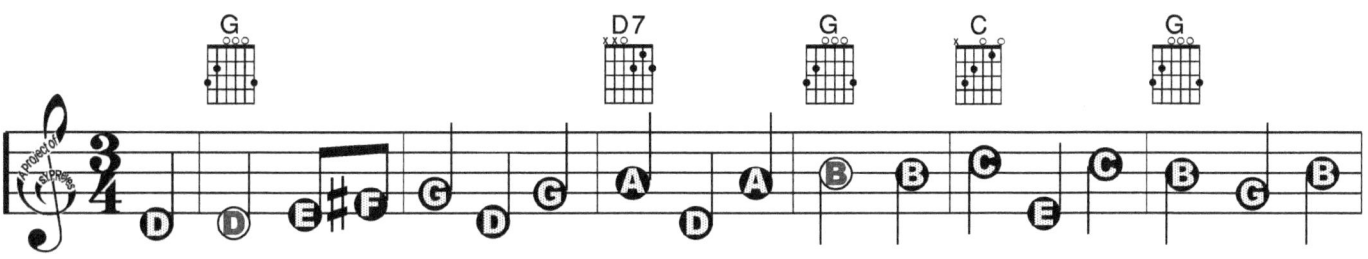
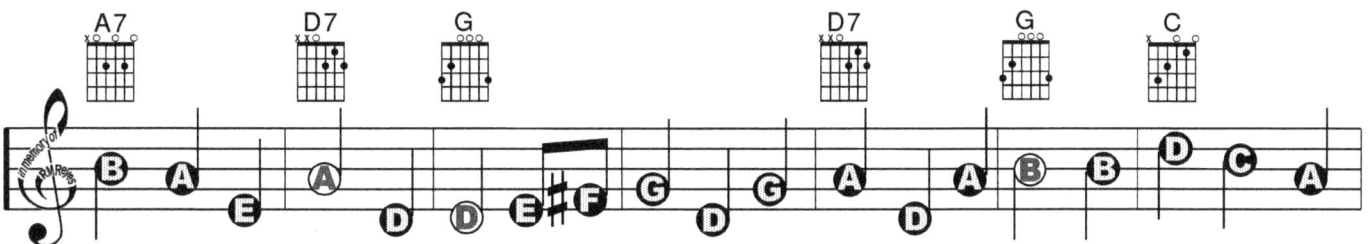
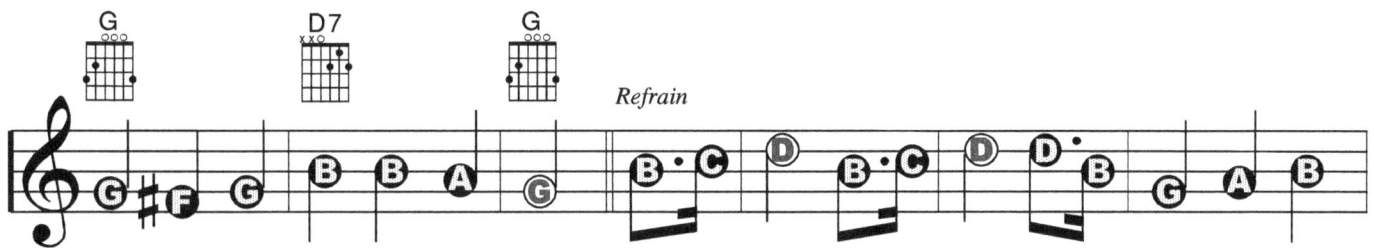
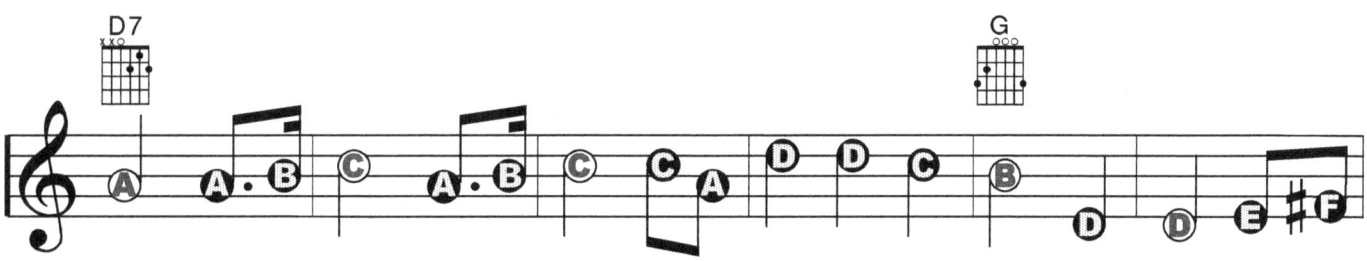
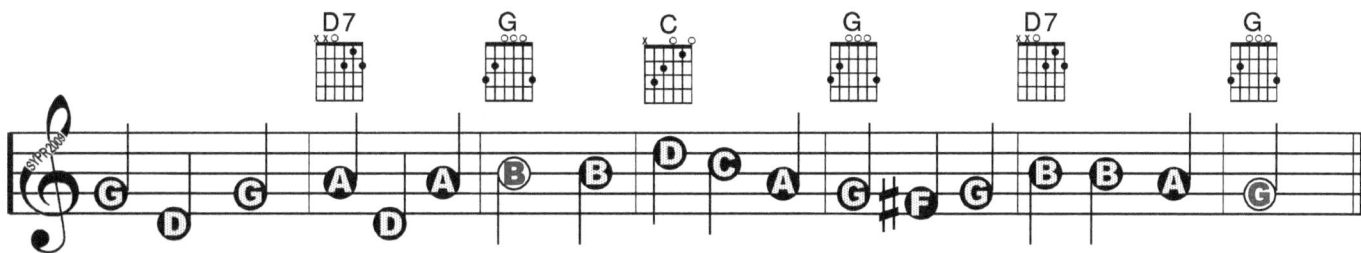

2. O perfect redemption, the purchase of blood,
   To every believer the promise of God;
   The vilest offender who truly believes,
   That moment from Jesus a pardon receives.
   (Refrain)

3. Great things He hath taught us, great things He hath done,
   And great our rejoicing through Jesus the Son;
   But purer, and higher, and greater will be
   Our wonder, our transport, when Jesus we see.
   (Refrain)

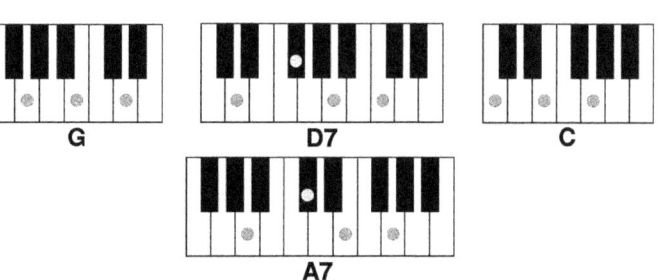

Trust and Obey

Words by J. H. Sammis
Music by Daniel Towner

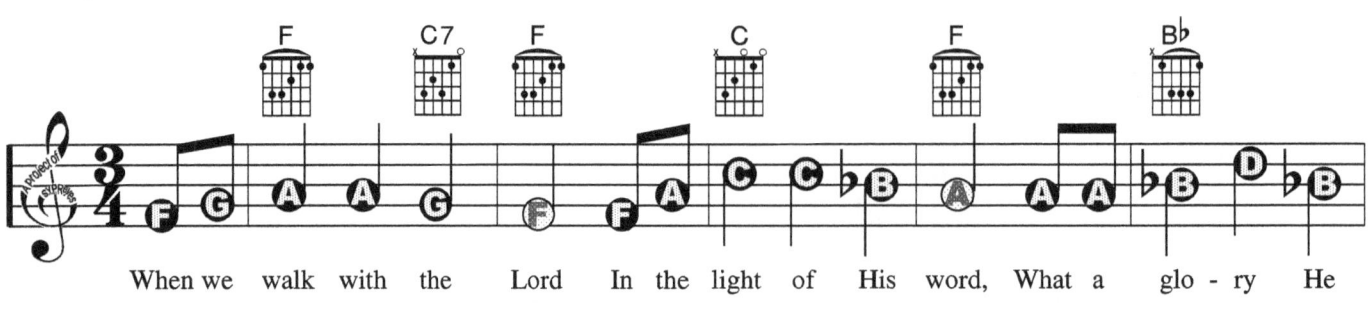
When we walk with the Lord In the light of His word, What a glo-ry He

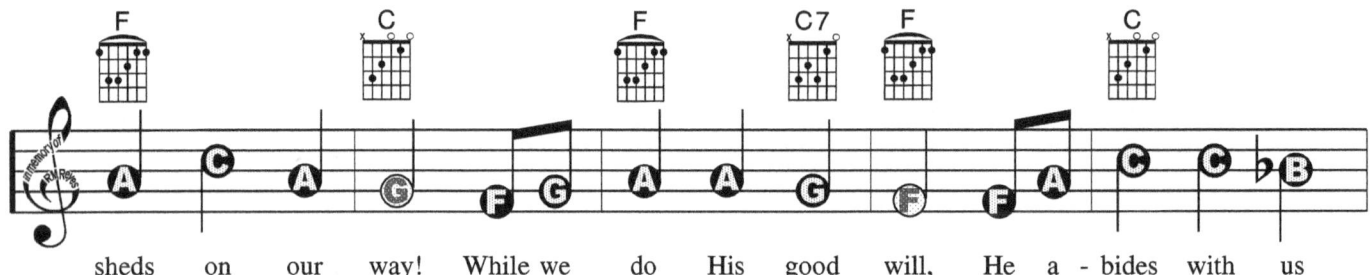
sheds on our way! While we do His good will, He a-bides with us

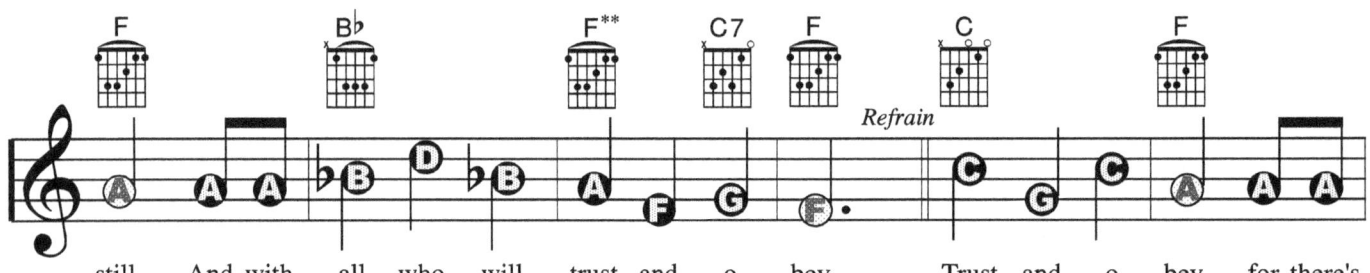
still, And with all who will trust and o-bey. Trust and o-bey, for there's

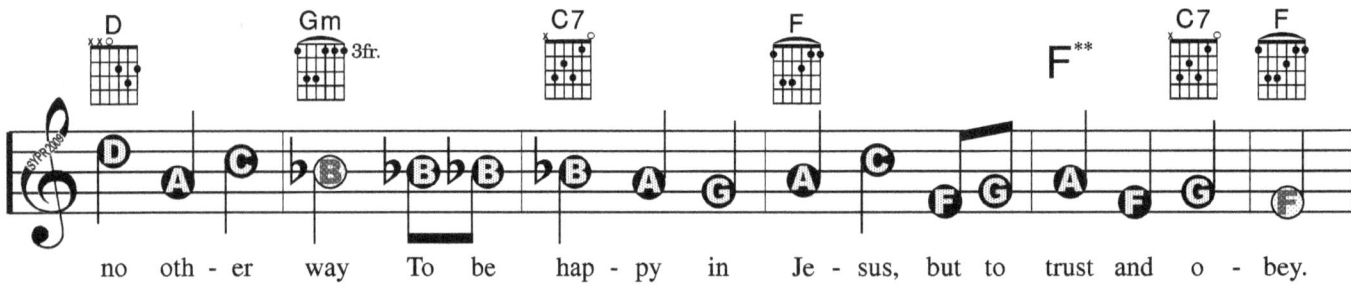
no oth-er way To be hap-py in Je-sus, but to trust and o-bey.

2. Not a shadow can rise, Not a cloud in the skies,
   But His smile quickly drives it away;
   Not a doubt nor a fear, Not a sigh nor a tear,
   Can abide while we trust and obey.
   (Refrain)

3. Not a burden we bear, Not a sorrow we share,
   But our toil He doth richly repay;
   Not a grief nor a loss, Not a frown nor a cross,
   But is blest if we trust and obey.
   (Refrain)

4. But we never can prove The delights of His love,
   Until all on the altar we lay,
   For the favor He shows, And the joy He bestows,
   Are for them who will trust and obey.
   (Refrain)

5. Then in fellowship sweet We will sit at His feet,
   Or we'll walk by His side in the way;
   What He says we will do, Where He sends we will go,
   Never fear, only trust and obey.
   (Refrain)

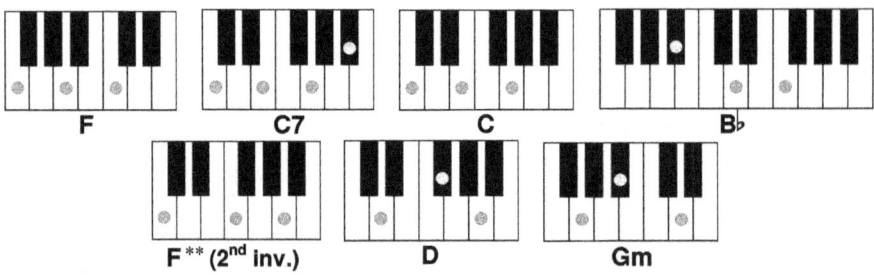

**On keyboard instrument, play second inversion*

Under His Wings

Words by W. O. Cushing
Music by Ira Sankey

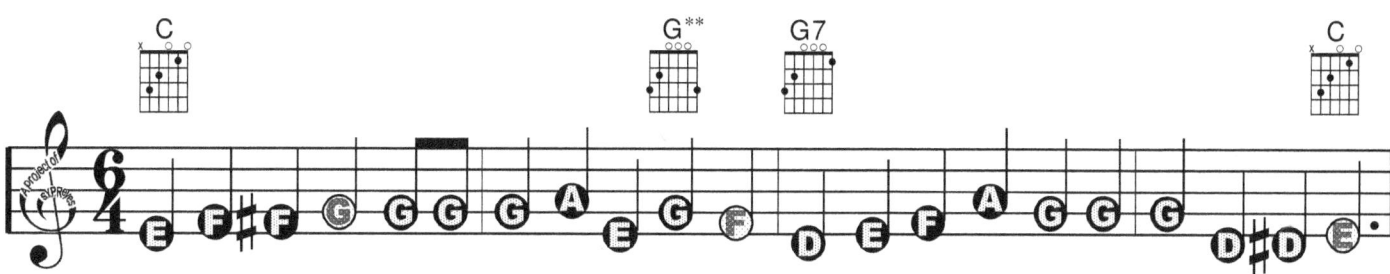

Un - der His wings I am safe - ly a - bid - ing; Though the night deep - ens and tem - pests are wild,

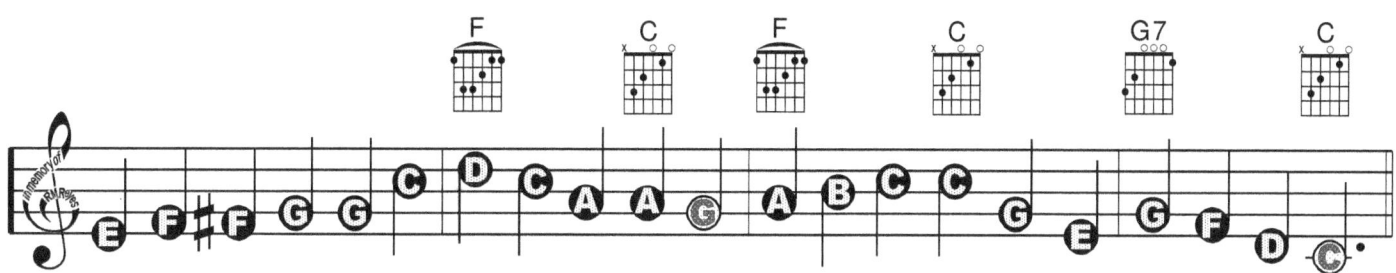

Still I can trust Him; I know He will keep me; He has re - deemed me, and I am His child.

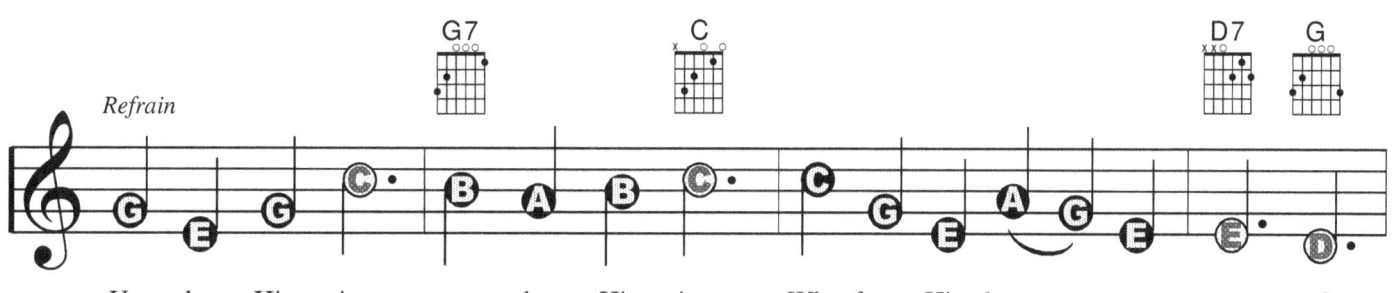

Refrain
Un - der His wings, un - der His wings, Who from His love can sev - er?

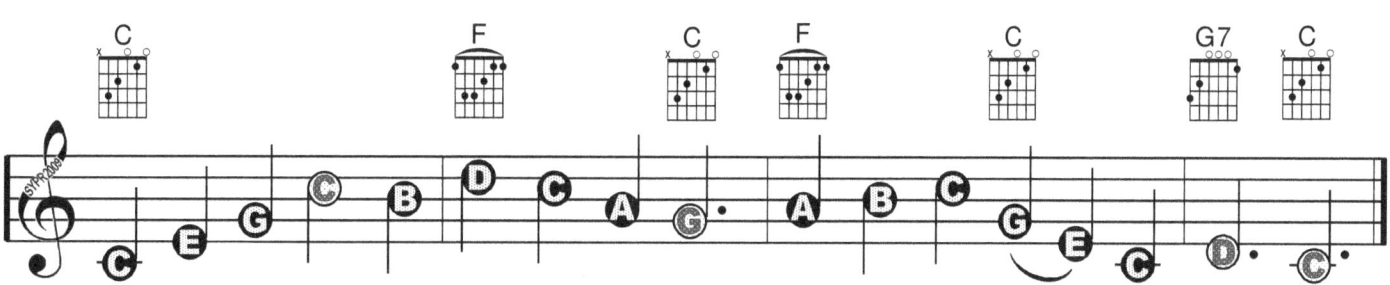

Un - der His wings my soul shall a - bide, Safe - ly a - bide for - ev - er.

2. Under His wings, what a refuge in sorrow!
   How the heart yearningly turns to its rest!
   Often when earth has no balm for my healing,
   There I find comfort, and there I am blest.
   (Refrain)

3. Under His wings, O what precious enjoyment!
   There will I hide till life's trials are o'er;
   Sheltered, protected, no evil can harm me;
   Resting in Jesus I'm safe evermore.
   (Refrain)

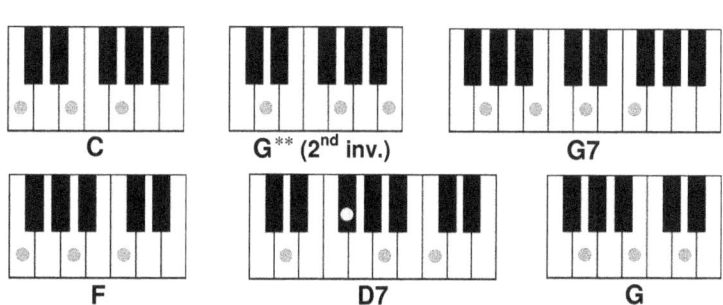

**On keyboard instrument, play second inversion

Watch, Ye Saints

Words by Phoebe Palmer
Music by William Kirkpatrick

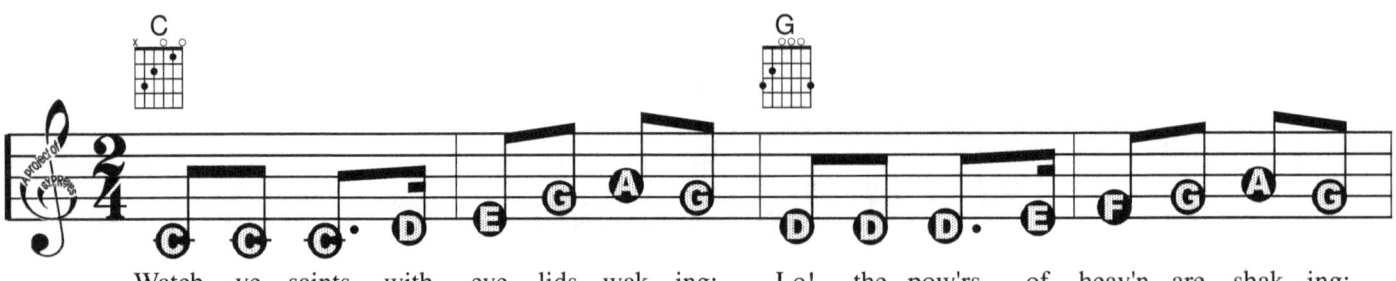

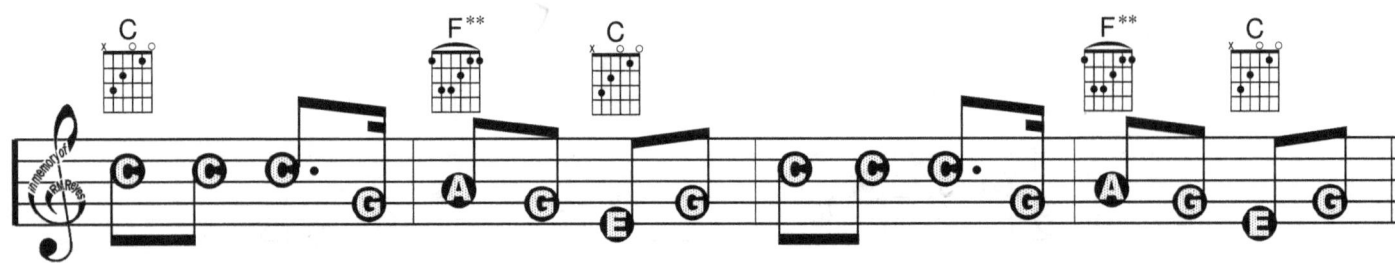

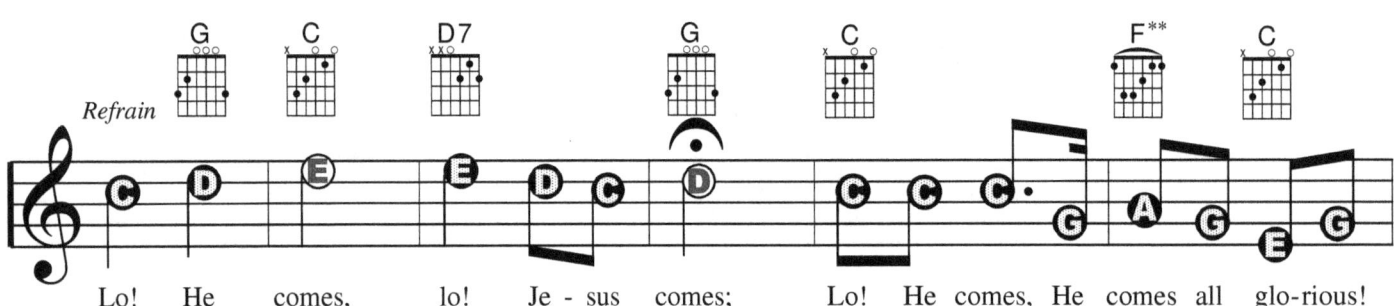

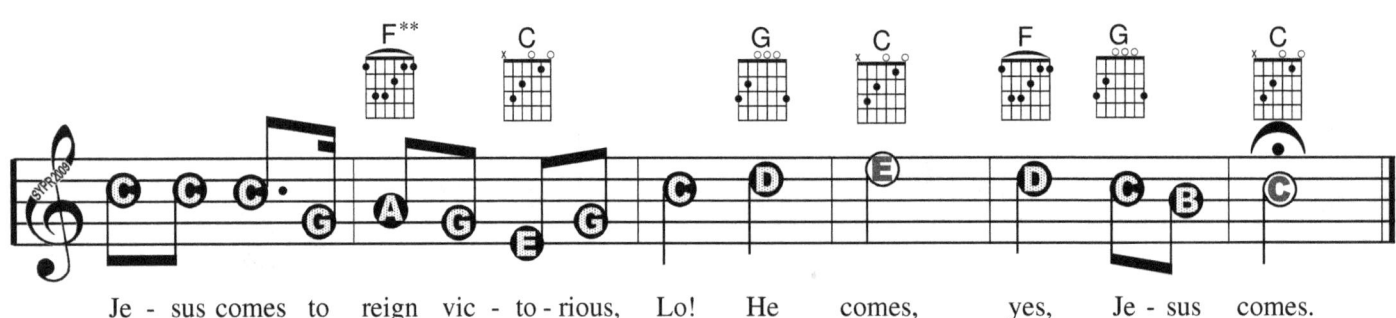

2. Lo! the promise of your Saviour,
   Pardoned sin and purchased favour,
   Blood-washed robes and crowns of glory;
   Haste to tell redemption's story.
   (Refrain)

3. Kingdoms at their base are crumbling,
   Hark! His chariot wheels are rumbling;
   Tell, O tell of grace abounding,
   While the seventh trump is sounding.
   (Refrain)

4. Nations wane, though proud and stately;
   Christ His kingdom hasteneth greatly;
   Earth her latest pangs is summing;
   Shout, ye saints, your Lord is coming.
   (Refrain)

5. Sinners, come, while Christ is pleading;
   Now for you He's interceding;
   Haste, ere grace and time diminished
   Shall proclaim the mystery finished.
   (Refrain)

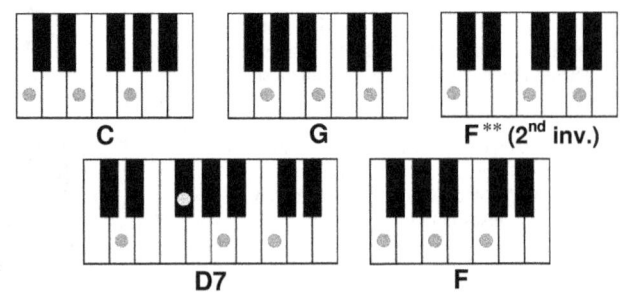

**On keyboard instrument, play second inversion

We Gather Together

English translation by Theodore Baker
Netherland Folk Tune

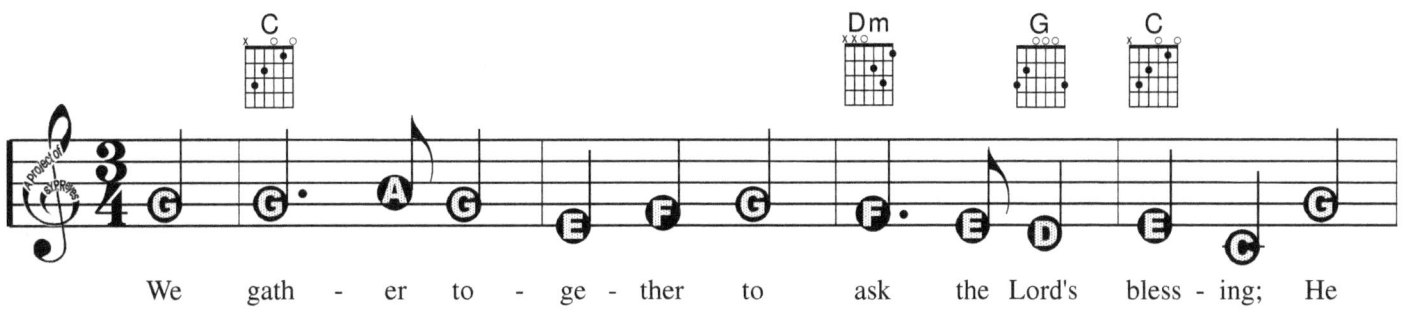
We gath-er to-ge-ther to ask the Lord's bless-ing; He

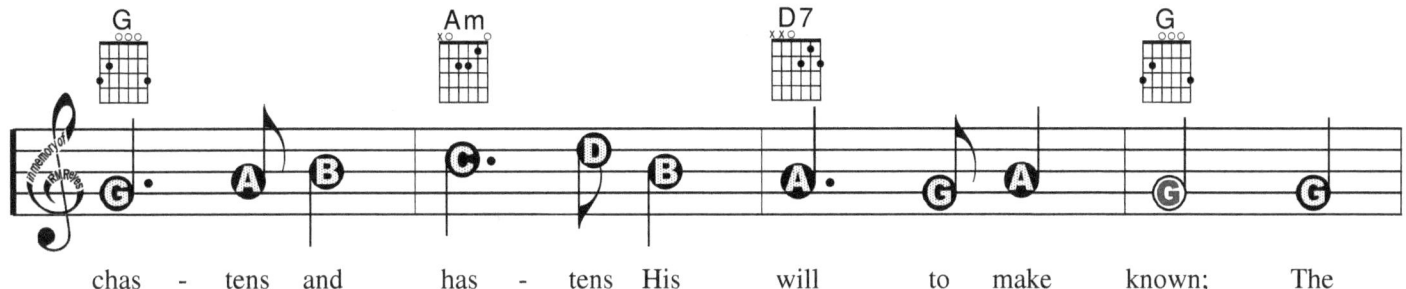
chas-tens and has-tens His will to make known; The

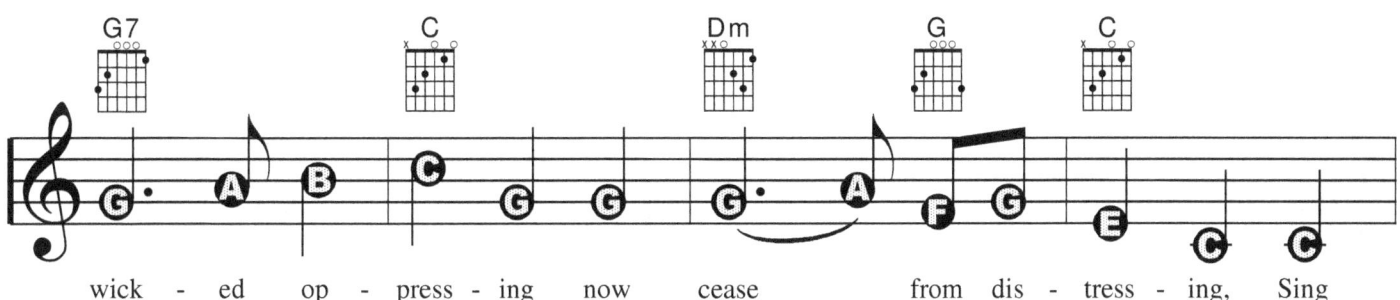
wick-ed op-press-ing now cease from dis-tress-ing, Sing

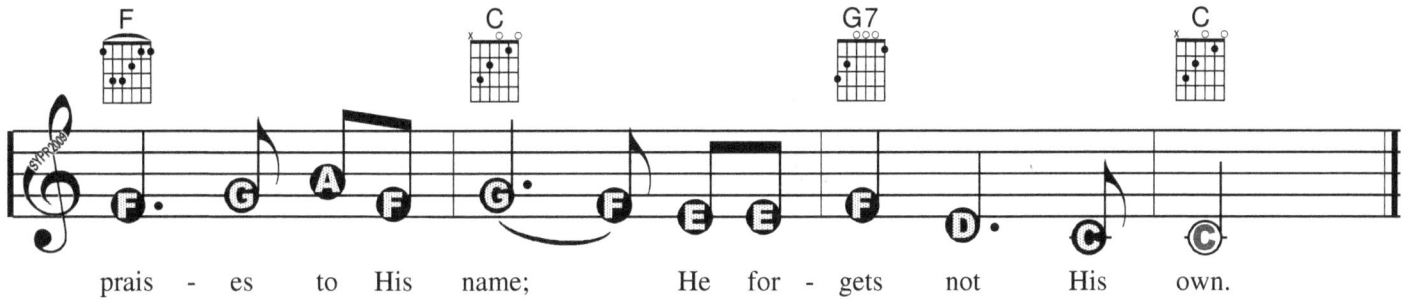
prais-es to His name; He for-gets not His own.

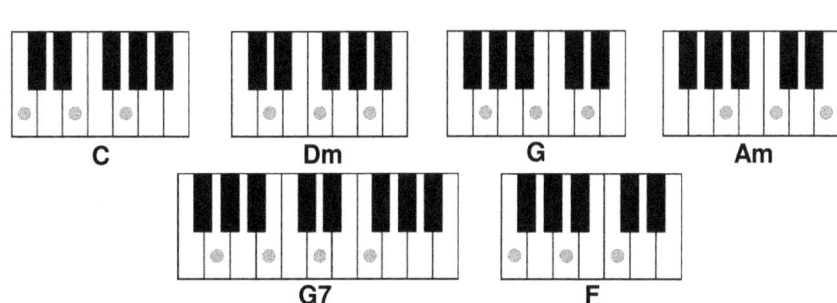

2. Beside us to guide us our God with us joining,
   Ordaining maintaining His kingdom divine;
   So from the beginning the fight we were winning;
   Thou, Lord, wast at our side; all glory be Thine!

3. We all do extol Thee Thou Leader triumphant,
   And pray that Thou still our Defender wilt be.
   Let Thy congregation escape tribulation;
   Thy name be ever praised! O Lord make us free!

We Know Not the Hour

Words and music by F. E. Belden

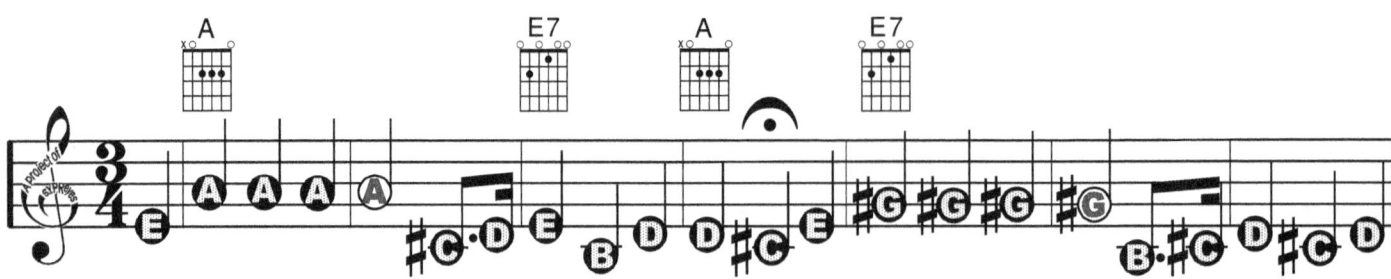

We know not the hour of the Master's ap-pear-ing; Yet signs all fore-tell that the mo-ment is

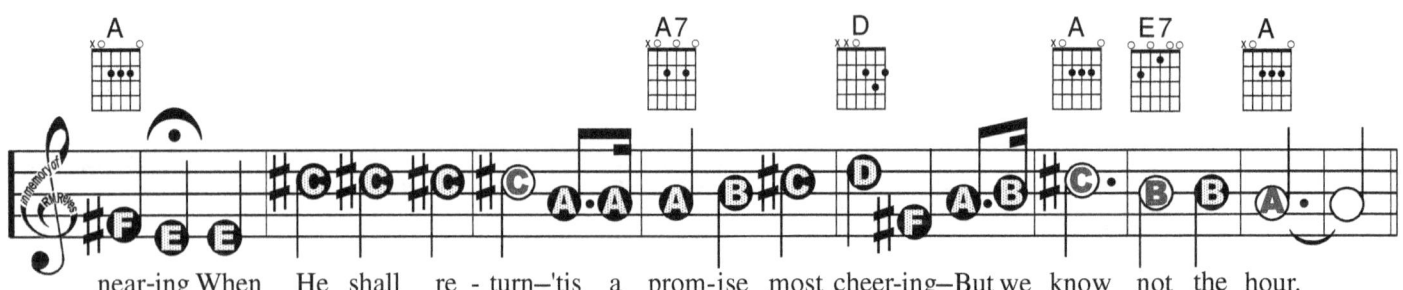

near-ing When He shall re-turn—'tis a prom-ise most cheer-ing—But we know not the hour.

Refrain

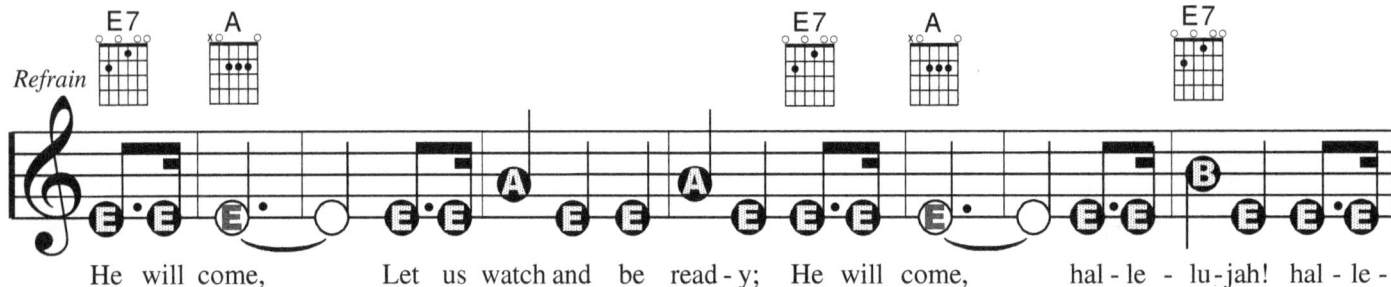

He will come, Let us watch and be read-y; He will come, hal-le-lu-jah! hal-le-

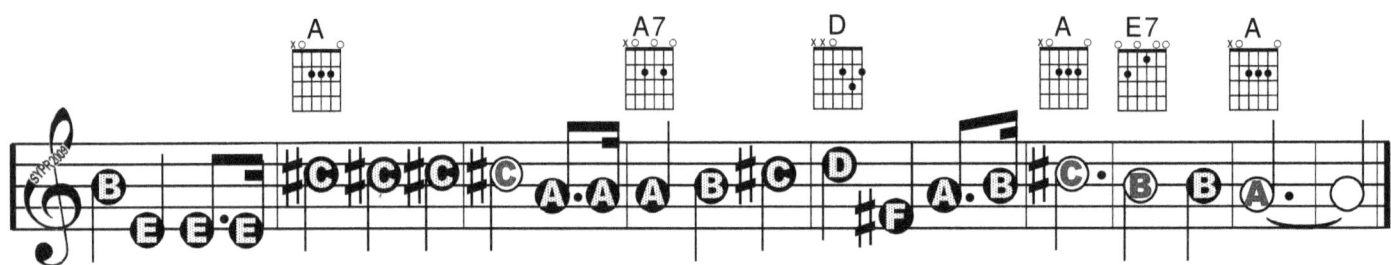

lu-jah! He will come in the clouds of His Fa-ther's bright glo-ry—But we know not the hour.

2. There's light for the wise who are seeking salvation;
   There's truth in the book of the Lord's revelation;
   Each prophecy points to the great consummation--
   But we know not the hour.
   (Refrain)

3. We'll watch and we'll pray, with our lamps trimmed and burning;
   We'll work and we'll wait till the Master's returning;
   We'll sing and rejoice, every omen discerning--
   But we know not the hour.
   (Refrain)

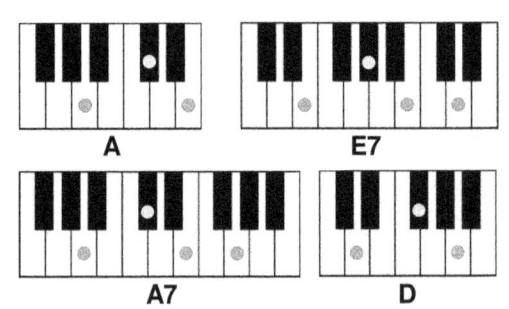

We Three Kings

Words and music by John Hopkins

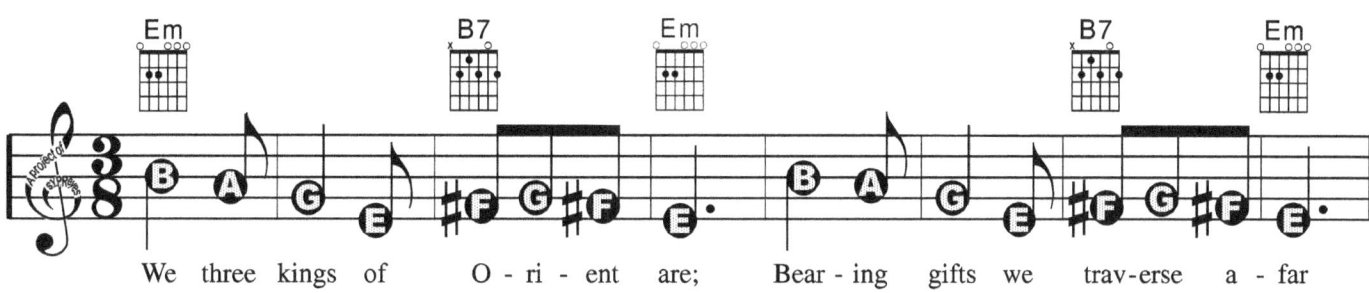

We three kings of O - ri - ent are; Bear - ing gifts we trav - erse a - far

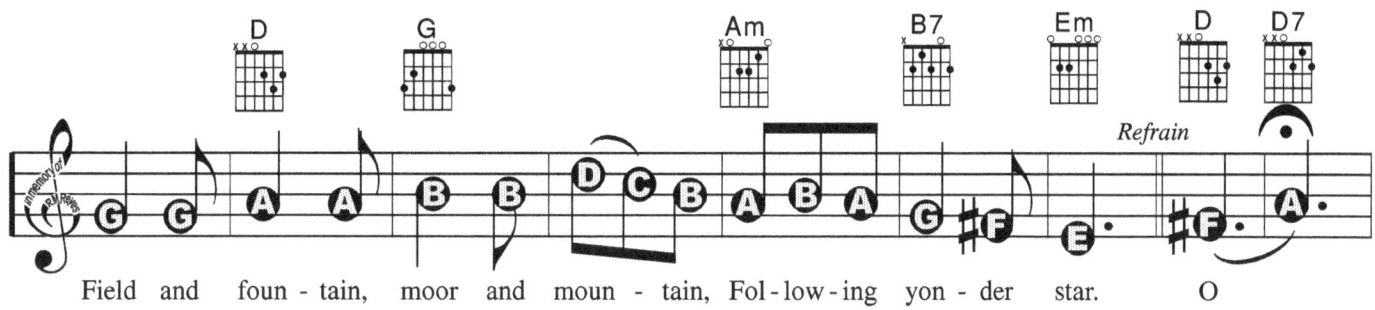

Field and foun - tain, moor and moun - tain, Fol - low - ing yon - der star. O

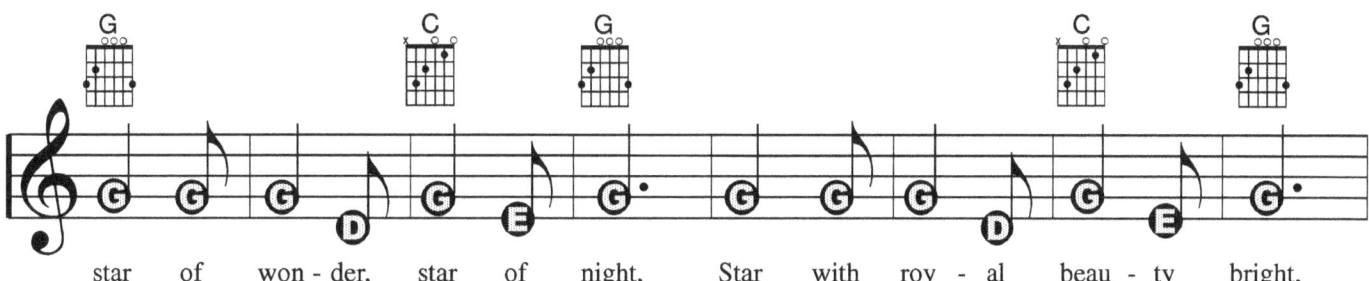

star of won - der, star of night, Star with roy - al beau - ty bright,

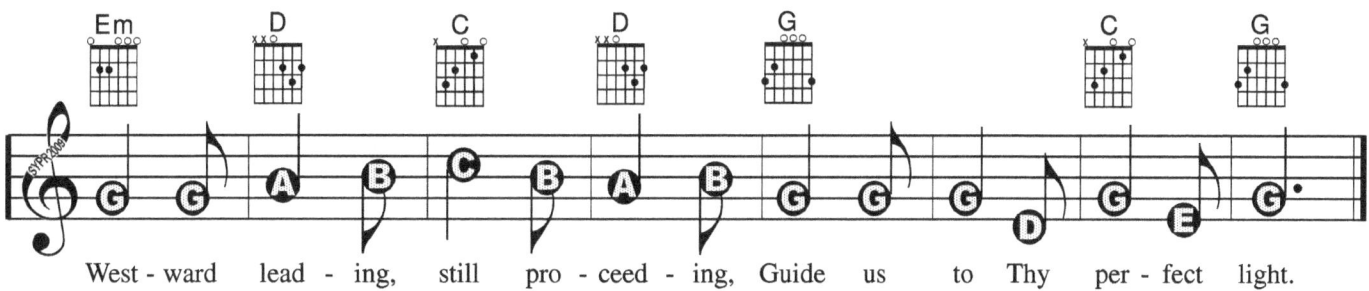

West - ward lead - ing, still pro - ceed - ing, Guide us to Thy per - fect light.

2. Born a King on Bethlehem's plain,
Gold I bring to crown Him again,
King forever, ceasing never
Over us all to reign.
(Refrain)

3. Frankincense to offer have I;
Incense owns a Deity nigh;
Prayer and praising all men raising,
Worship Him, God on high.
(Refrain)

4. Myrrh is mine; its bitter perfume
Breathes a life of gathering gloom:
Sorrowing, sighing, bleeding, dying,
Sealed in the stone-cold tomb.
(Refrain)

5. Glorious now behold Him arise,
King and God and sacrifice;
Alleluia, Alleluia!
Sounds through the earth and skies.
(Refrain)

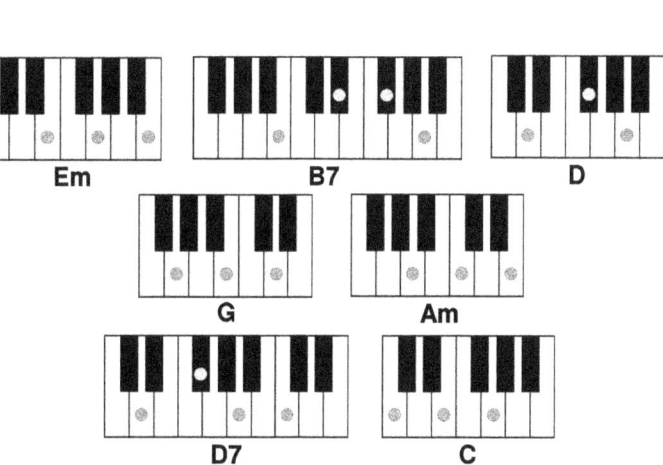

What a Friend We Have in Jesus

Words by Joseph Scriven
Music by Charles Converse

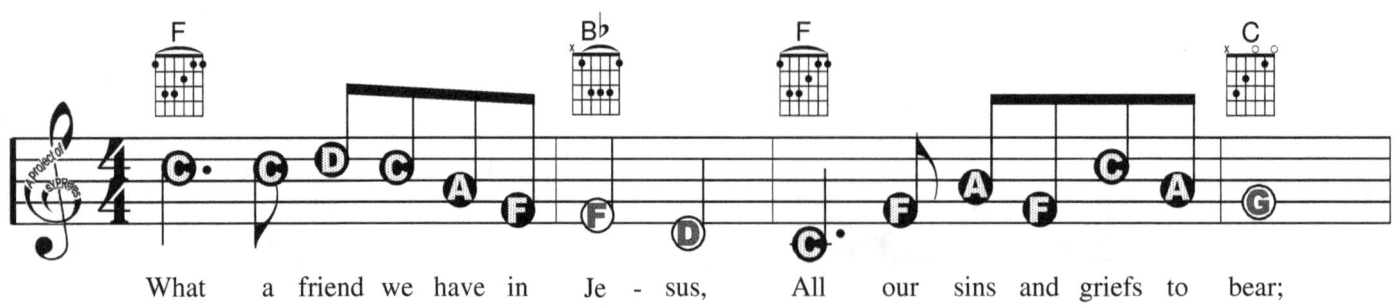

What a friend we have in Je - sus, All our sins and griefs to bear;

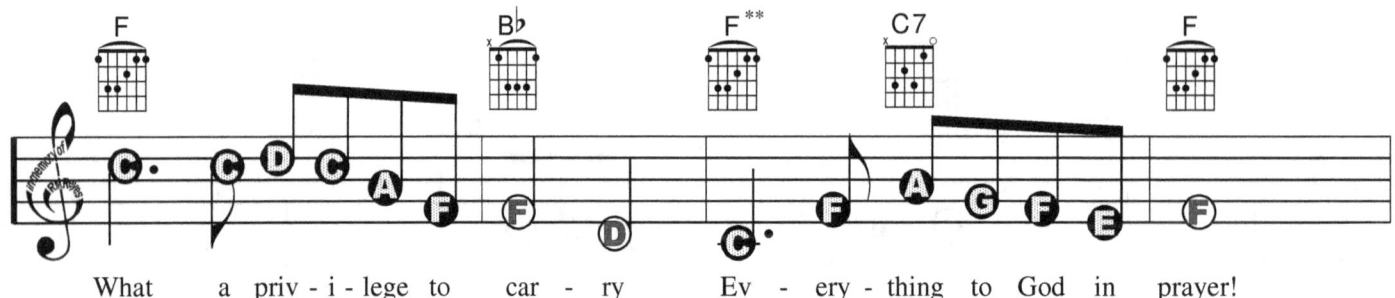

What a priv - i - lege to car - ry Ev - ery - thing to God in prayer!

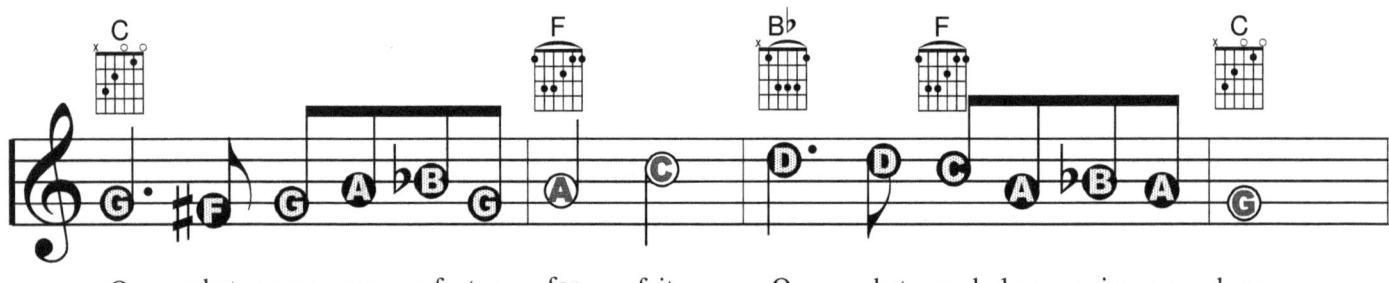

O what peace we of - ten for - feit, O what need - less pain we bear,

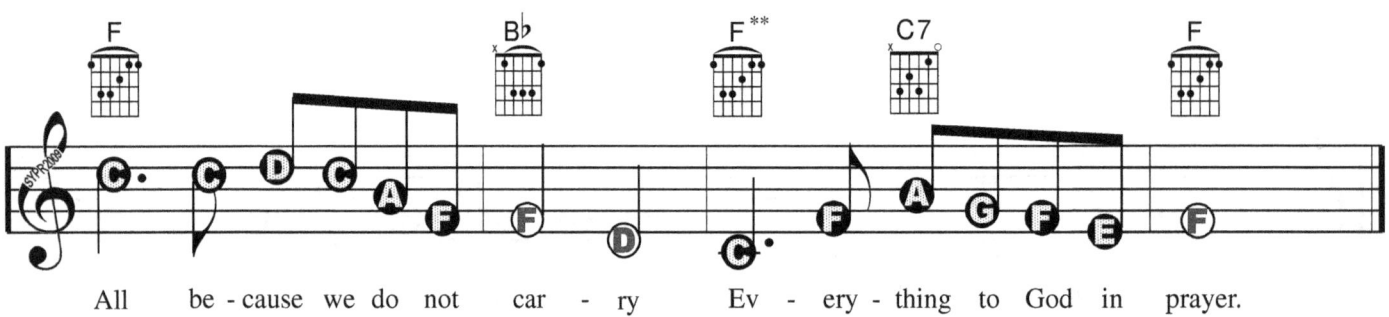

All be - cause we do not car - ry Ev - ery - thing to God in prayer.

2. Have we trials and temptations? Is there trouble anywhere?
We should never be discouraged; Take it to the Lord in prayer!
Can we find a friend so faithful, Who will all our sorrows share?
Jesus knows our every weakness; Take it to the Lord in prayer!

3. Are we weak and heavy laden, Cumbered with a load of care?
Precious Savior, still our refuge, Take it to the Lord in prayer!
Do thy friends despise, forsake thee? Take it to the Lord in prayer!
In His arms He'll take and shield thee, Thou wilt find a solace there.

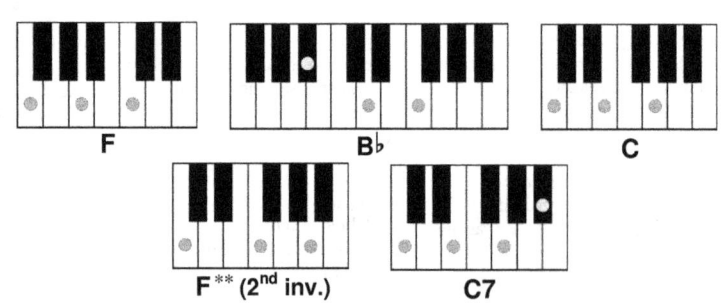

**On keyboard instrument, play second inversion*

What a Wonderful Savior

Words and music by Elisha Hoffman

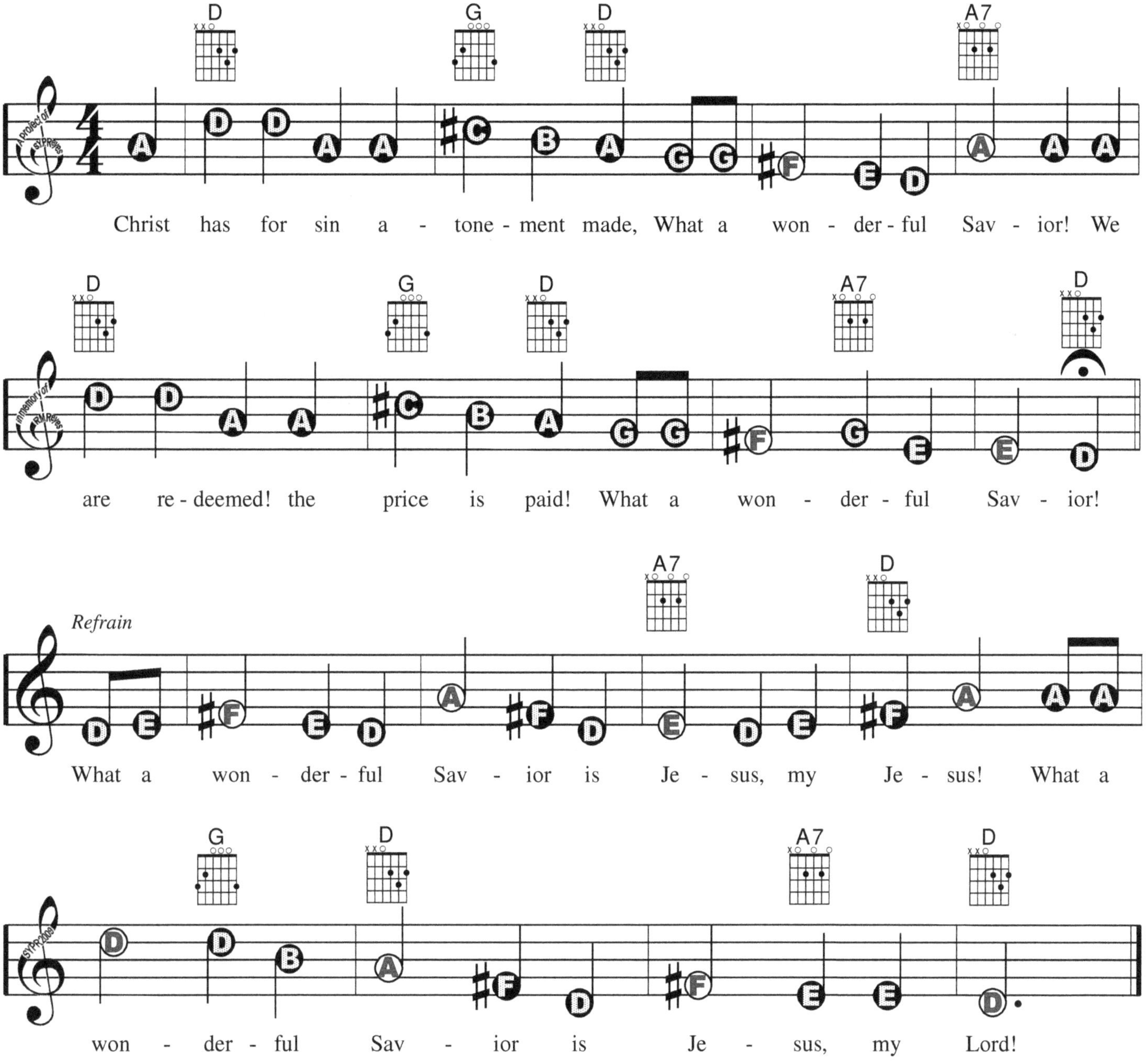

D G D A7
Christ has for sin a - tone - ment made, What a won - der - ful Sav - ior! We
D G D A7 D
are re - deemed! the price is paid! What a won - der - ful Sav - ior!
Refrain
A7 D
What a won - der - ful Sav - ior is Je - sus, my Je - sus! What a
G D A7 D
won - der - ful Sav - ior is Je - sus, my Lord!

2. I praise Him for the cleansing blood, What a wonderful Saviour!
   That reconciled my soul to God What a wonderful Saviour!
   (Refrain)

3. He walks beside me all the way What a wonderful Saviour!
   And keeps me faithful day by day What a wonderful Saviour!
   (Refrain)

4. He gives me overcoming power, What a wonderful Saviour!
   And triumph in each trying hour; What a wonderful Saviour!
   (Refrain)

D
G
A7

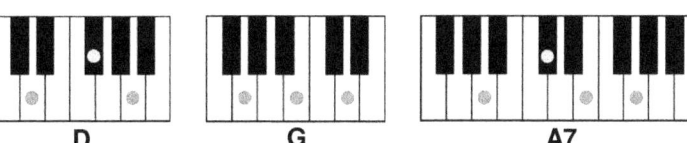

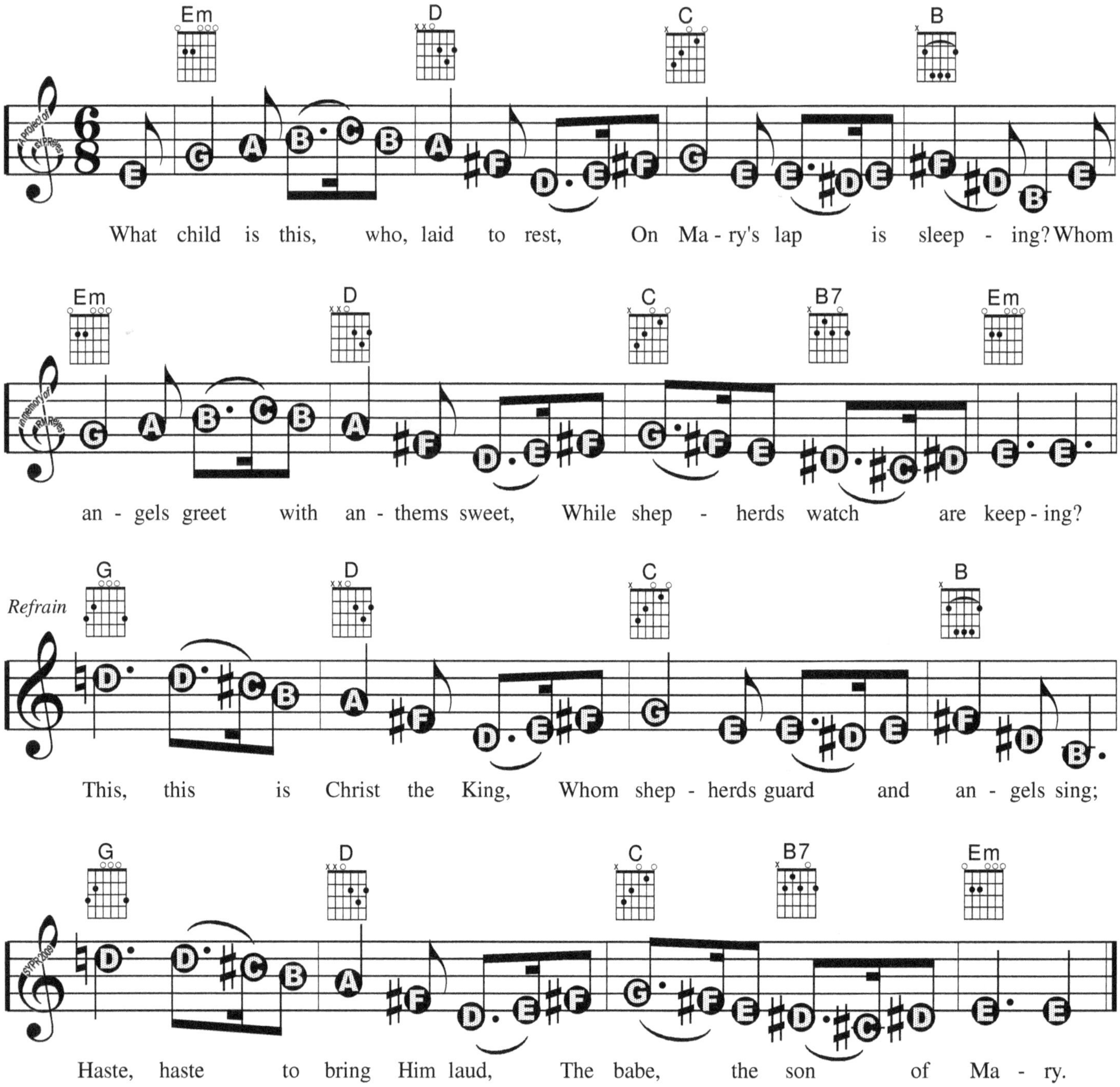

What Child Is This?

Words by William Dix

English Folk Melody

Em D C B
What child is this, who, laid to rest, On Ma - ry's lap is sleep - ing? Whom
Em D C B7 Em
an - gels greet with an - thems sweet, While shep - herds watch are keep - ing?
Refrain
G D C B
This, this is Christ the King, Whom shep - herds guard and an - gels sing;
G D C B7 Em
Haste, haste to bring Him laud, The babe, the son of Ma - ry.

2. Why lies He in such mean estate
   Where ox and ass are feeding?
   Good Christian, fear: for sinners here
   The silent Word is pleading.
   (Refrain)

3. So bring Him incense, gold, and myrrh,
   Come, peasant, king, to own Him,
   The King of kings salvation brings,
   Let loving hearts enthrone Him.
   (Refrain)

Em
D
C
B
B7
G

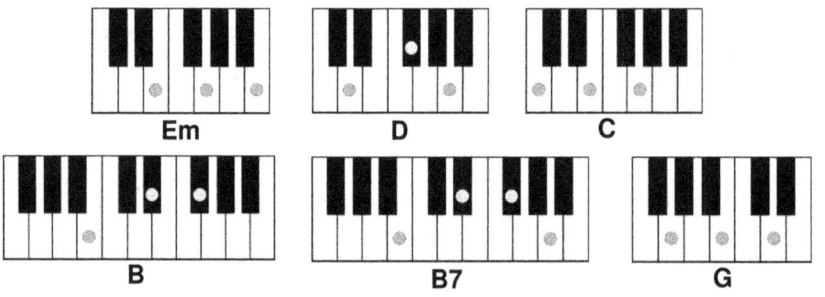

When He Cometh

Words by W. O. Cushing

Music by George Root

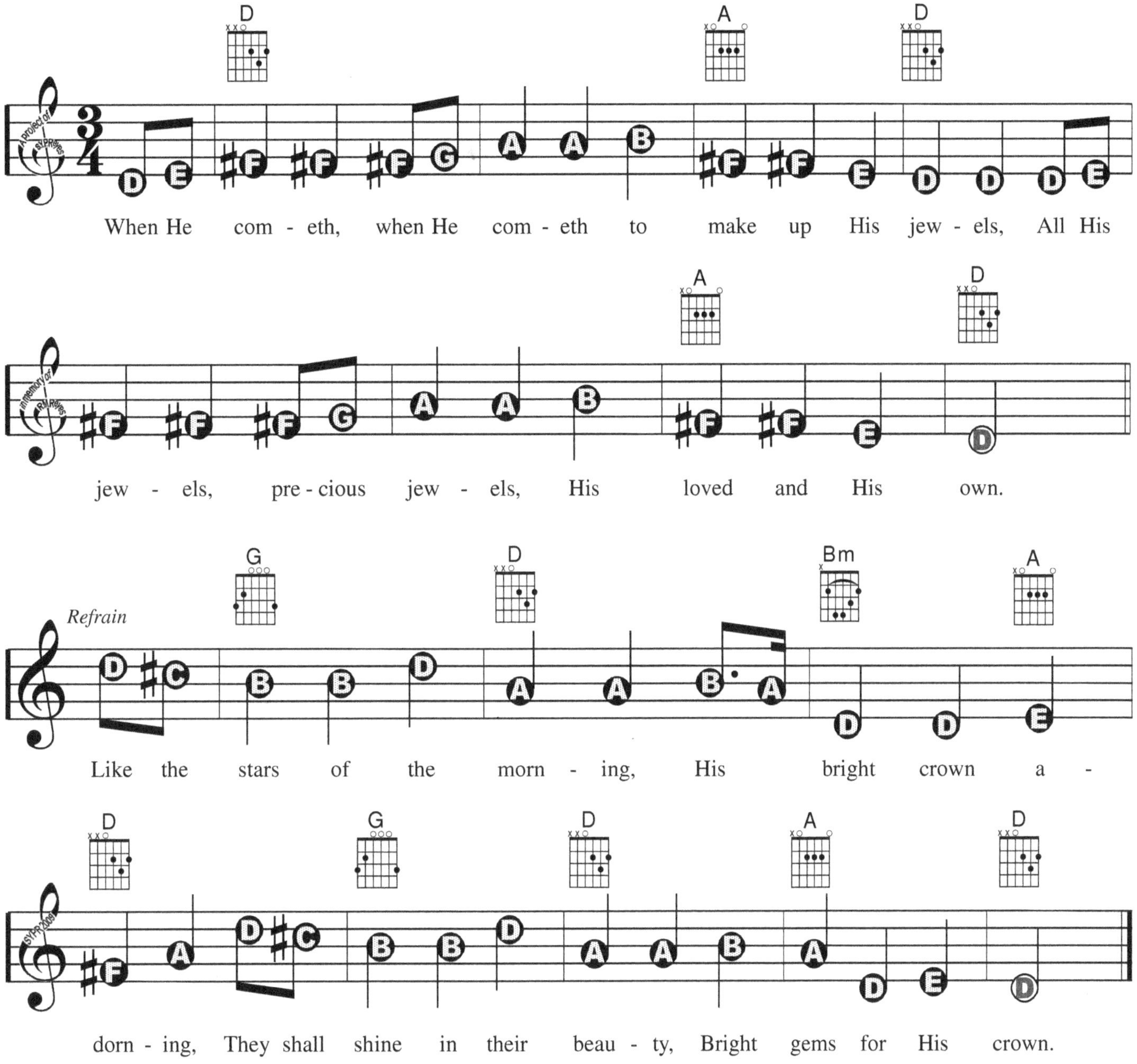

D A D
When He com - eth, when He com - eth to make up His jew - els, All His
A D
jew - els, pre - cious jew - els, His loved and His own.
Refrain
G D Bm A
Like the stars of the morn - ing, His bright crown a -
D G D A D
dorn - ing, They shall shine in their beau - ty, Bright gems for His crown.

2. He will gather, He will gather The gems for His kingdom,
All the pure ones, all the bright ones His loved and His own.
(Refrain)

3. Little children, little children Who love their Redeemer,
Are the jewels, precious jewels His loved and His own.
(Refrain)

D
A
G
Bm

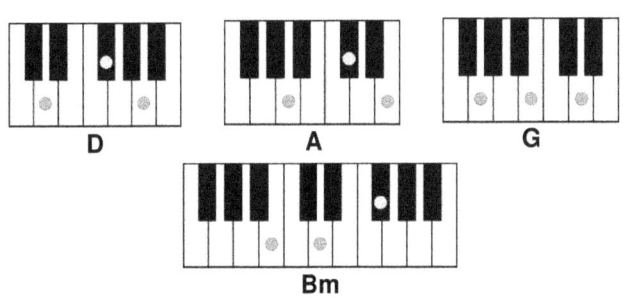

When the Roll Is Called Up Yonder

Words and music by J. M. Black

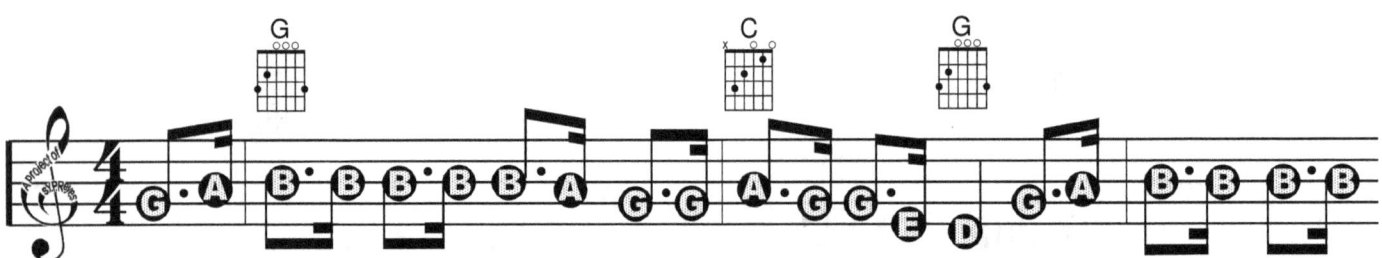

When the trum-pet of the Lord shall sound, and time shall be no more, And the morn-ing breaks, e-

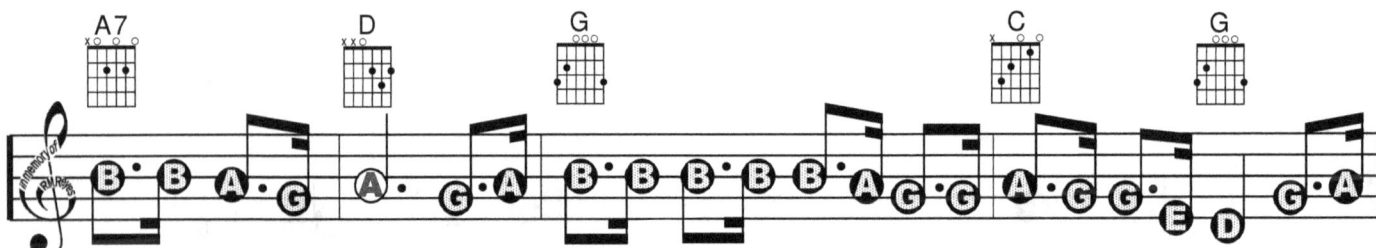

ter-nal, bright and fair; When the saved of earth shall gath-er o-ver on the oth-er shore, and the

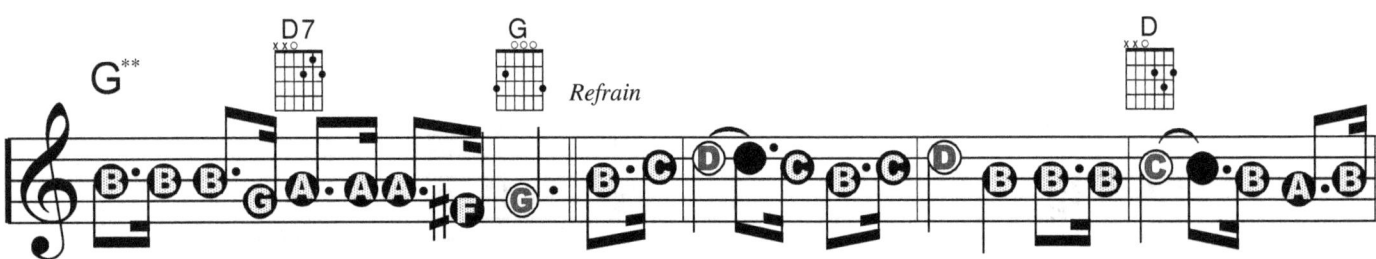

roll is called up yon-der, I'll be there. When the roll is called up yon-der, When the roll is called up

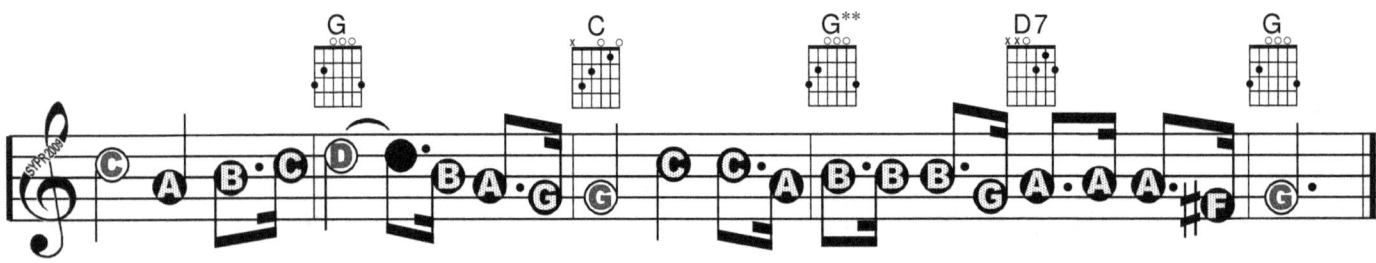

yon-der, When the roll is called up yon-der, When the roll is called up yon-der, I'll be there.

2. On that bright and cloudless morning, when the dead in Christ shall rise,
   And the glory of His resurrection share;
   When His chosen ones shall gather to their home beyond the skies,
   And the roll is called up yonder, I'll be there.
   (Refrain)

3. Let us labour for the Master from the dawn till setting sun,
   Let us talk of all His wondrous love and care,
   Then, when all of life is over, and our work on earth is done
   And the roll is called up yonder, I'll be there.
   (Refrain)

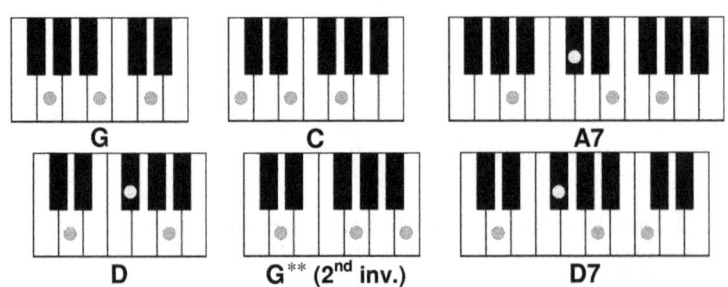

**On keyboard instrument, play second inversion

150

When We All Get to Heaven

Words by Eliza Hewitt

Music by Emily Wilson

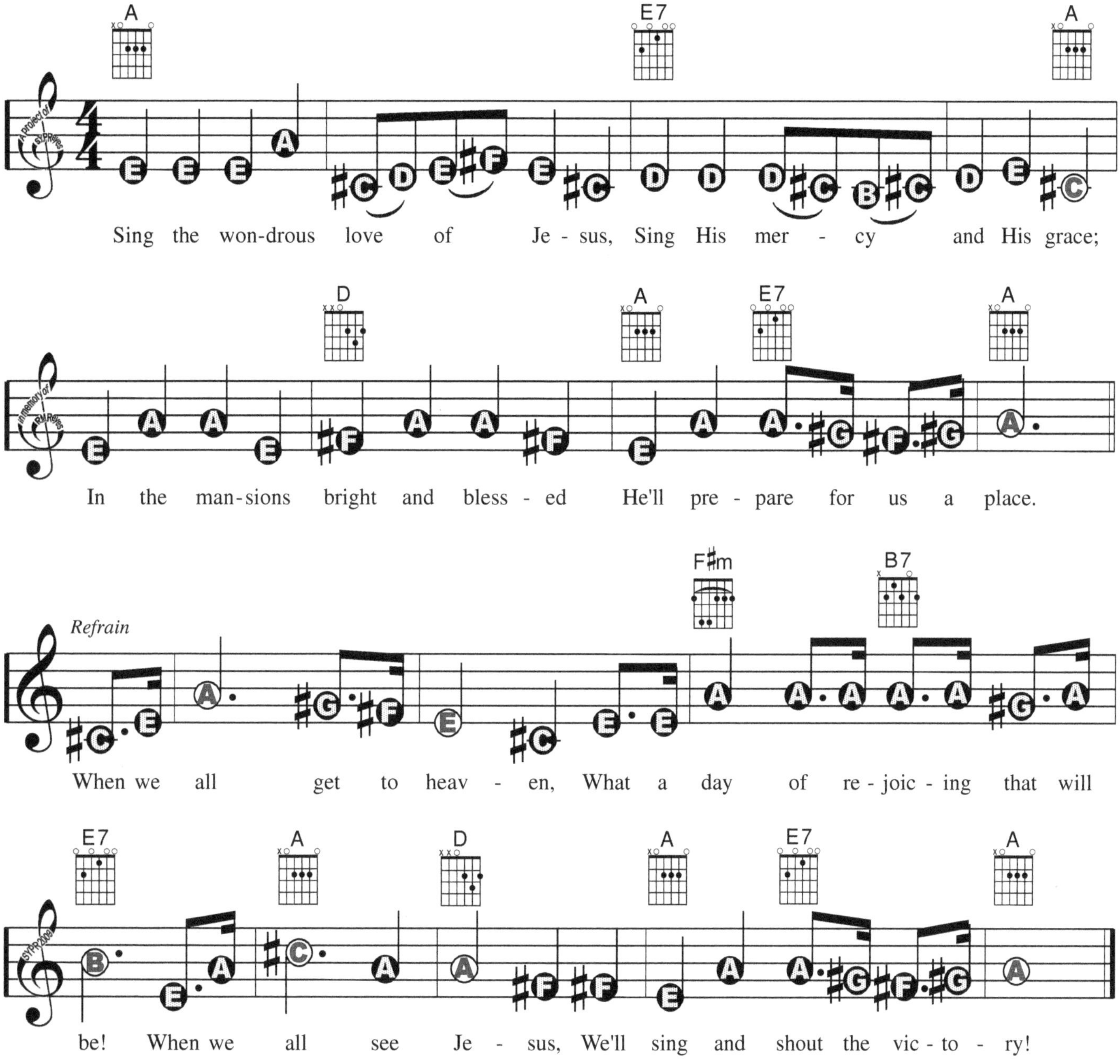

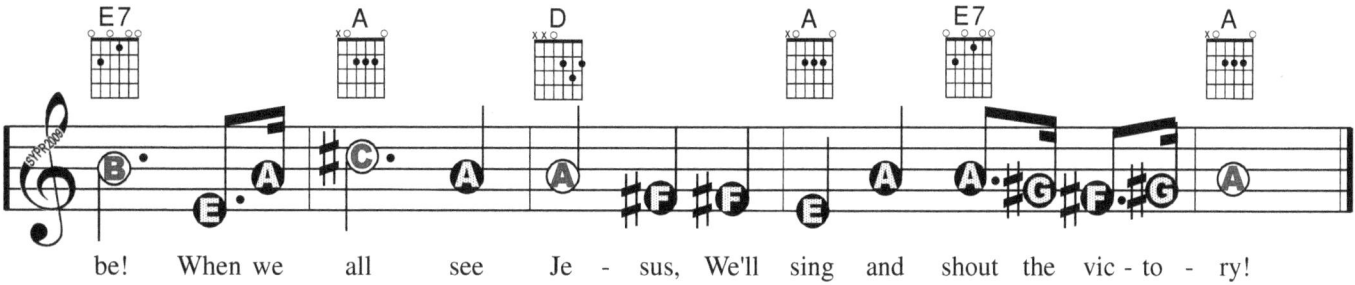

A E7 A
Sing the won-drous love of Je - sus, Sing His mer - cy and His grace;
D A E7 A
In the man-sions bright and bless - ed He'll pre - pare for us a place.
Refrain
F#m B7
When we all get to heav - en, What a day of re - joic - ing that will
E7 A D A E7 A
be! When we all see Je - sus, We'll sing and shout the vic - to - ry!

2. While we walk the pilgrim pathway Clouds will overspread the sky;
But when travelling days are over Not a shadow, not a sigh.
(Refrain)

3. Let us then be true and faithful, Trusting, serving every day;
Just one glimpse of Him in glory Will the toils of life repay.
(Refrain)

4. Onward to the prize before us! Soon His beauty we'll behold;
Soon the pearly gates will open--We shall tread the streets of gold.
(Refrain)

A
E7
D
F#m
B7

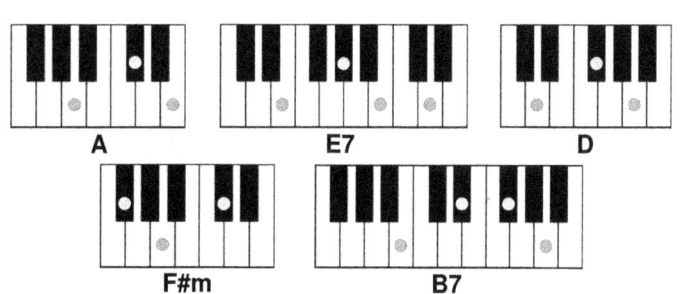

Whiter Than Snow

Words by James Nicholson
Music by William Fischer

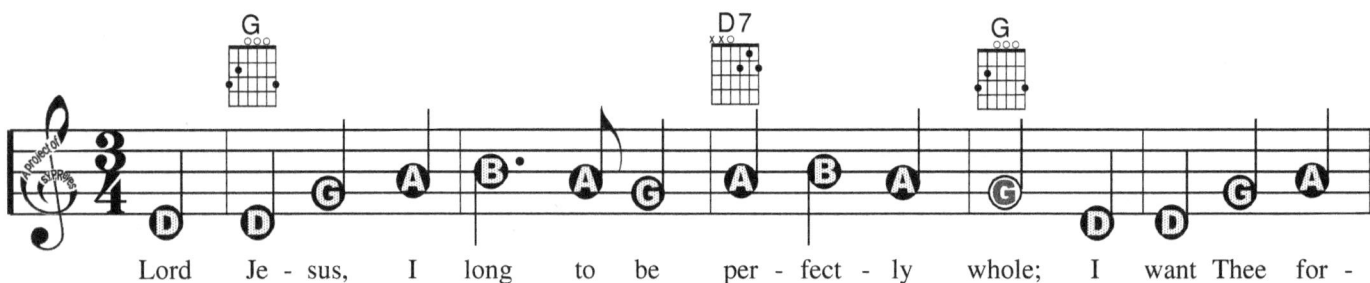
Lord Je-sus, I long to be per-fect-ly whole; I want Thee for-

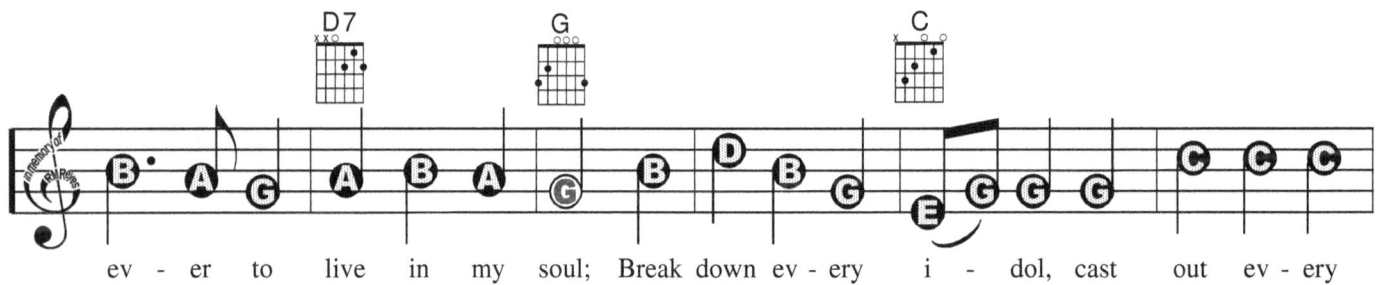
ev-er to live in my soul; Break down ev-ery i-dol, cast out ev-ery

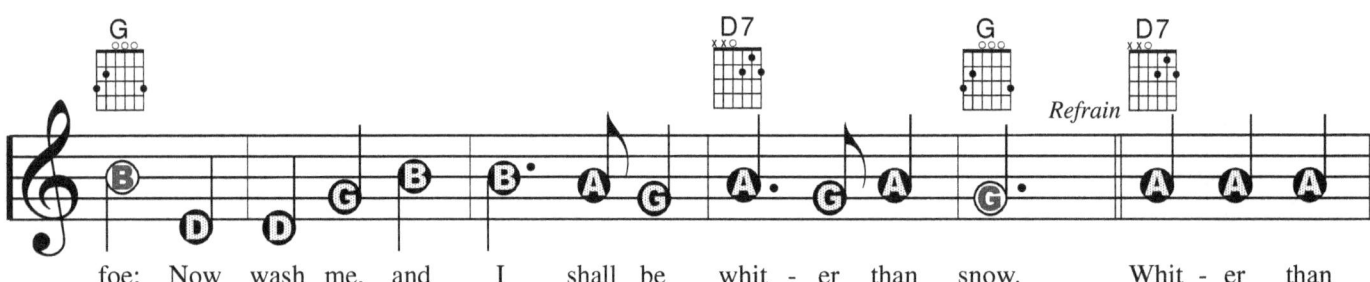
foe; Now wash me, and I shall be whit-er than snow. Whit-er than

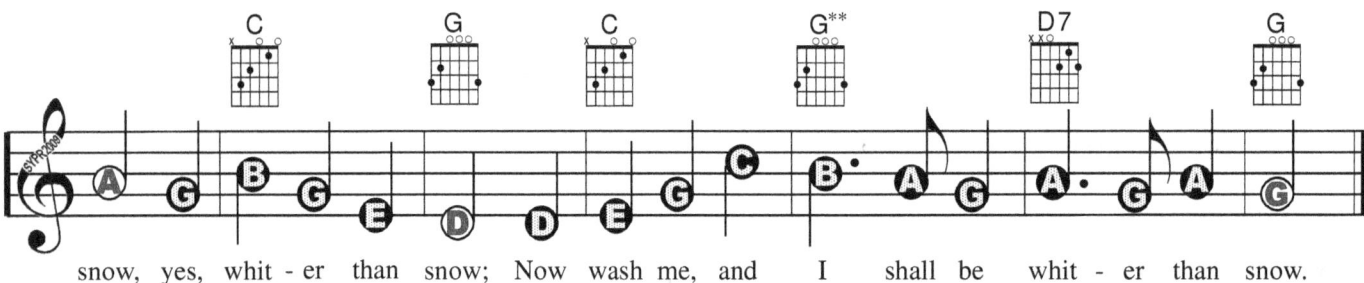
snow, yes, whit-er than snow; Now wash me, and I shall be whit-er than snow.

2. Lord Jesus, look down from Thy throne in the skies,
   And help me to make a complete sacrifice;
   I give up myself, and whatever I know;
   Now wash me, and I shall be whiter than snow.
   (Refrain)

3. Lord Jesus, for this I most humbly entreat;
   I wait, blessed Lord, at Thy crucified feet,
   By faith, for my cleansing; I see Thy blood flow;
   Now wash me, and I shall be whiter than snow.
   (Refrain)

4. Lord Jesus, Thou seest I patiently wait;
   Come now, and within me a new heart create;
   To those who have sought Thee, Thou never said'st No;
   Now wash me, and I shall be whiter than snow.
   (Refrain)

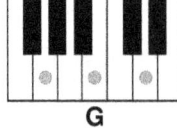
G

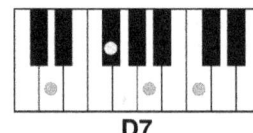
D7

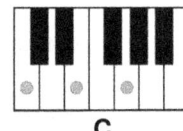
C

G** (2nd inv.)

**On keyboard instrument, play second inversion

152

Wholly Thine

Words and music by F. E. Belden

I would be, dear Savior, wholly Thine; Teach me how, teach me how; I would do Thy will, O Lord, not mine; Help me, help me now.

Refrain
Wholly Thine, wholly Thine, Wholly Thine, this is my vow; Wholly Thine, wholly Thine, Wholly Thine, O Lord, just now.

2. What is worldly pleasure, wealth, or fame,
   Without Thee, without Thee?
   I will leave them all for Thy dear name,
   This my wealth shall be.
   (Refrain)

3. As I cast earth's transient joys behind,
   Come Thou near, come Thou near;
   In Thy presence all in all I find,
   'Tis my comfort here.
   (Refrain)

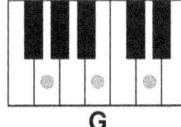

153

Will Your Anchor Hold?

Words by Priscilla Owens
Music by William Kirkpatrick

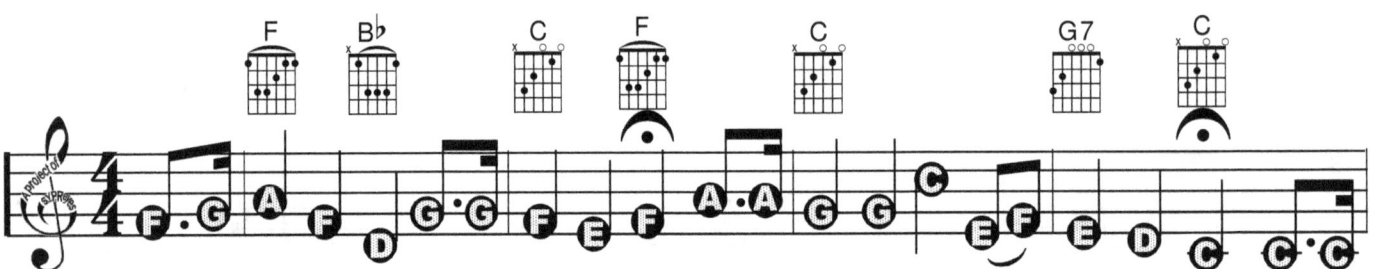

Will your an-chor hold in the storm of life, When the clouds un-fold their wings of strife? When the

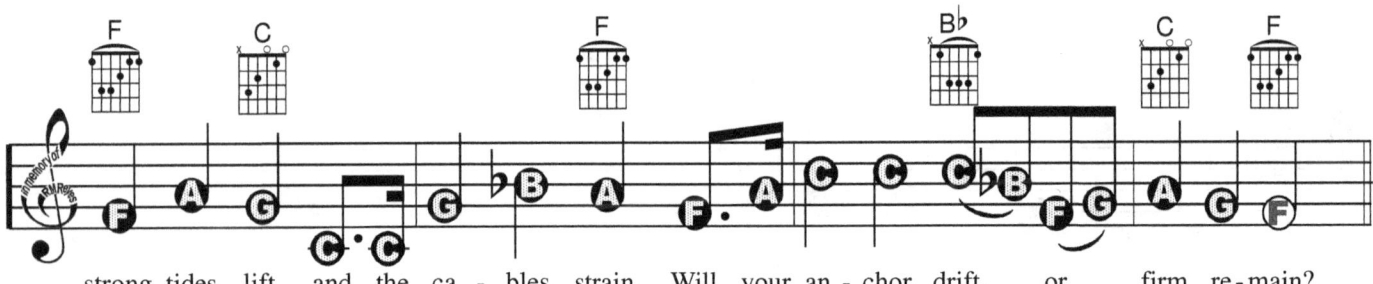

strong tides lift, and the ca-bles strain, Will your an-chor drift, or firm re-main?

Refrain

We have an an-chor that keeps the soul Stead-fast and sure while the bil-lows roll;

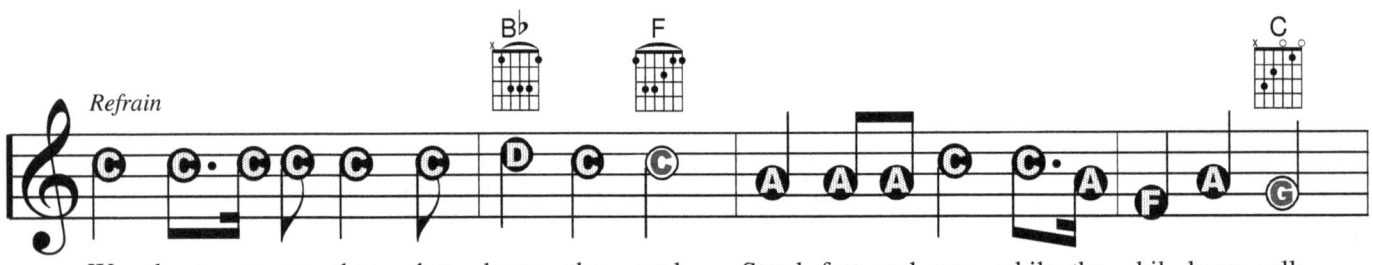

Fas-tened to the Rock which can-not move, Ground-ed firm and deep in the Sav-ior's love.

2. If 'tis safely moored, 'twill the storm withstand,
   For 'tis well secured by the Saviour's hand;
   And the cables, passed from His heart to thine,
   Can defy the blast, through strength divine.
   (Refrain)

3. It will firmly hold in the straits of Fear,
   When the breakers tell that the reef is near:
   Though the tempest rave and the wild winds blow,
   Not an angry wave shall our bark o'er flow.
   (Refrain)

4. It will surely hold in the floods of death,
   When the waters cold chill our latest breath;
   On the rising tide it can never fail,
   While our hopes abide within the veil.
   (Refrain)

5. When our eyes behold, in the dawning light,
   Shining gates of pearl, our harbor bright,
   We shall anchor fast to the heavenly shore,
   With the storms all past forevermore.
   (Refrain)

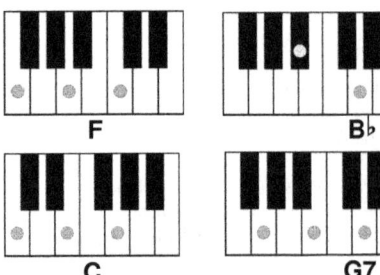

Worthy, Worthy Is the Lamb

Author and composer unknown

Wor - thy, wor - thy is the Lamb, Wor - thy, wor - thy is the Lamb;

Wor - thy, wor - thy is the Lamb, That was slain.

Refrain

Glo - ry, hal - le - lu - jah! Praise Him, hal - le - lu - jah!

Glo - ry, hal - le - lu - jah To the Lamb!

2. Saviour, let Thy kingdom come!
   Now the power of sin consume;
   Bring Thy blest millennium,
   Holy Lamb.
   (Refrain)

3. Thus may we each moment feel,
   Love Him, serve Him, praise Him still
   Till we all on Zion's hill
   See the Lamb.
   (Refrain)

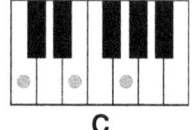
C

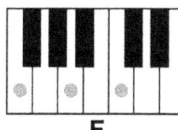
F

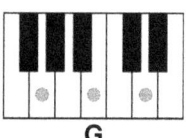
G

155

Appendix A: Exploring Some Variations in Playing Chords on the Piano

Broken Patterns

When instead of playing a chord as one "block" (with all three or four chord tones *blocked* together and played simultaneously) you break it up in parts, it is called a *broken* chord. Let's look at two common ways a chord can be played in broken style:

- **Play the lowest chord tone alone first, then the rest of the upper chord tones together.** It is best to play the lowest note firmly and decisively, and the upper notes somewhat more lightly. If the song is in triple meter (meaning you feel the beats in cycles of three), the cluster of upper chord tones may be played twice. This style is effective for rousing gospel songs. Shown below is how this pattern is applied to the three chords used in the opening measures of "Pow'r in the Blood". Notice how the notes to be played together at the same time are aligned vertically.

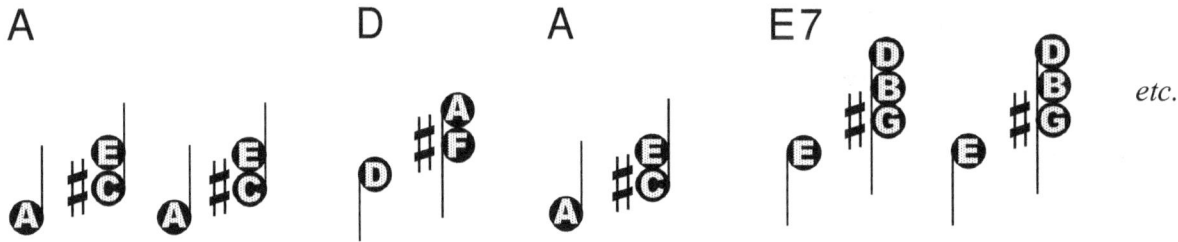

This second example is in triple meter. Try playing it for "Jesus Saves".

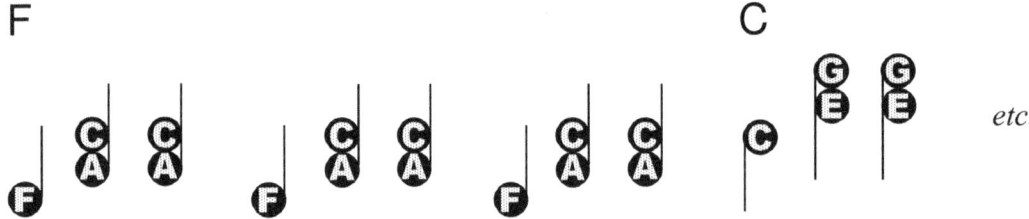

- **Play each chord tone one at a time starting from the lowest.** For seventh chords, either one of the middle chord tones may be omitted (e.g with the D7 chord, which is composed of the notes D-F#-A-C, omit either F# or A). This pattern works well with hymns that are more meditative and have a flowing triple meter. Play the following accompaniment for "Sweet Hour of Prayer":

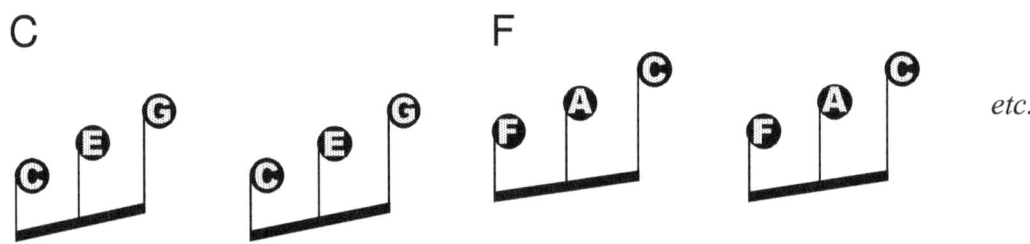

A slight variation of this *one-chord-tone-at-a-time* pattern consists of **playing the middle note again at the end of the pattern described above**. The additional note makes it fit nicely into duple meters (beats are in cycles of two). Try this one for "I Surrender All".

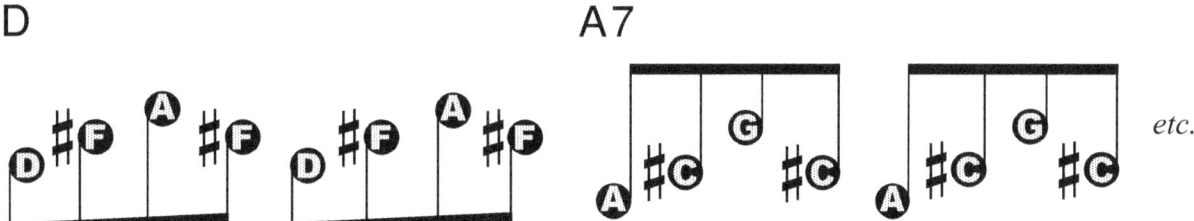

Chord Inversions

Chords are most often played in what is called their *root position*. A chord is said to be in its root position, if the lowest note you play is the root. The root of a chord is the note by which it is named. For example, the root of the G Major chord is **G**.

Inversions are chord positions other than the root position. If the lowest note you play is the next chord tone up from the root, the chord is said to be in its *first inversion*. Keep in mind that playing inversions does not involve a change in the notes that comprise the chord—only their arrangement is changed.

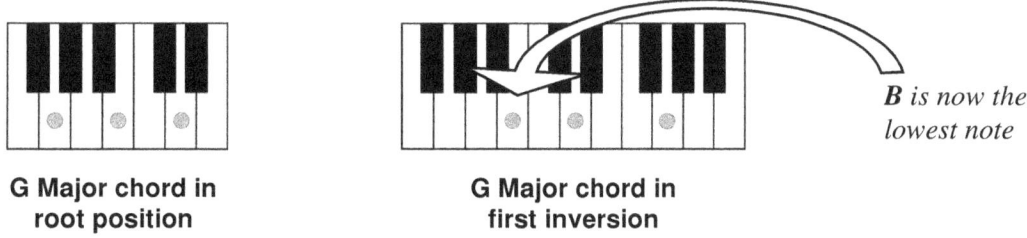

G Major chord in root position

G Major chord in first inversion

B is now the lowest note

The *second inversion* of a chord is formed by playing the *second next* chord tone up from the root as the lowest note.

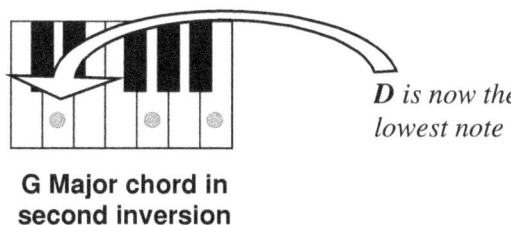

G Major chord in second inversion

D is now the lowest note

Mastering how to play a chord in its different positions is very helpful in trying out various other accompaniment patterns. Below is a recommended exercise.

 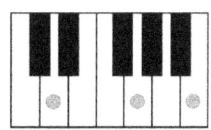 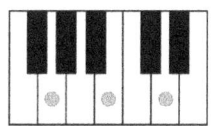

1. **Play the chord in root position**
2. **Move up and play the 1st inversion**
3. **Move up again and play the 2nd inversion**
4. **Move up again to play the chord in root position an octave higher than where you began**

157

Appendix B: Interpreting Guitar Chord Diagrams[1]

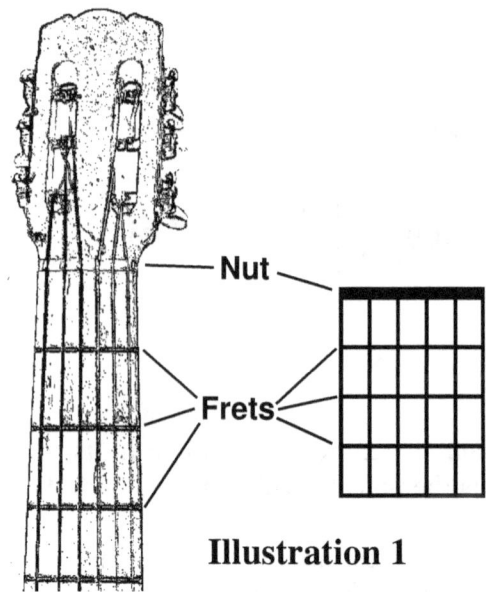

Illustration 1

A **guitar chord diagram**, also called a **chord chart**, is pretty simple to understand because it is but a drawing of the guitar fingerboard when the guitar is standing upright. The vertical lines represent the six strings of the guitar, the rightmost being the highest sounding string and the one that ends up in the bottom spot when the guitar is held in the playing position. The thick horizontal line on top represents the nut, and the rest of the horizontal lines represent the metal frets (Illustration 1). Sometimes, the nut is not shown and a note on the side specifies a particular fret number. (See Illustration 3.)

The black dots inside the grid indicate where to place the tips of the left hand fingers. The exact string number and fret number should be noted carefully in order for the chord to be played correctly. (See Illustration 2.)

In certain chords, you will see an arch connecting two black dots (Illustration 3). This calls for *barre* playing, which means that instead of pressing with just the fingertip, the forefinger presses flat against the fingerboard across two or more strings on the same fret.

An "x" above a string means not to play that string. A hollow circle (o) above a string, on the other hand, indicates it is an *open* string; it is played as is, without any of the left hand fingers pressing anywhere on it. (See Illustration 2.)

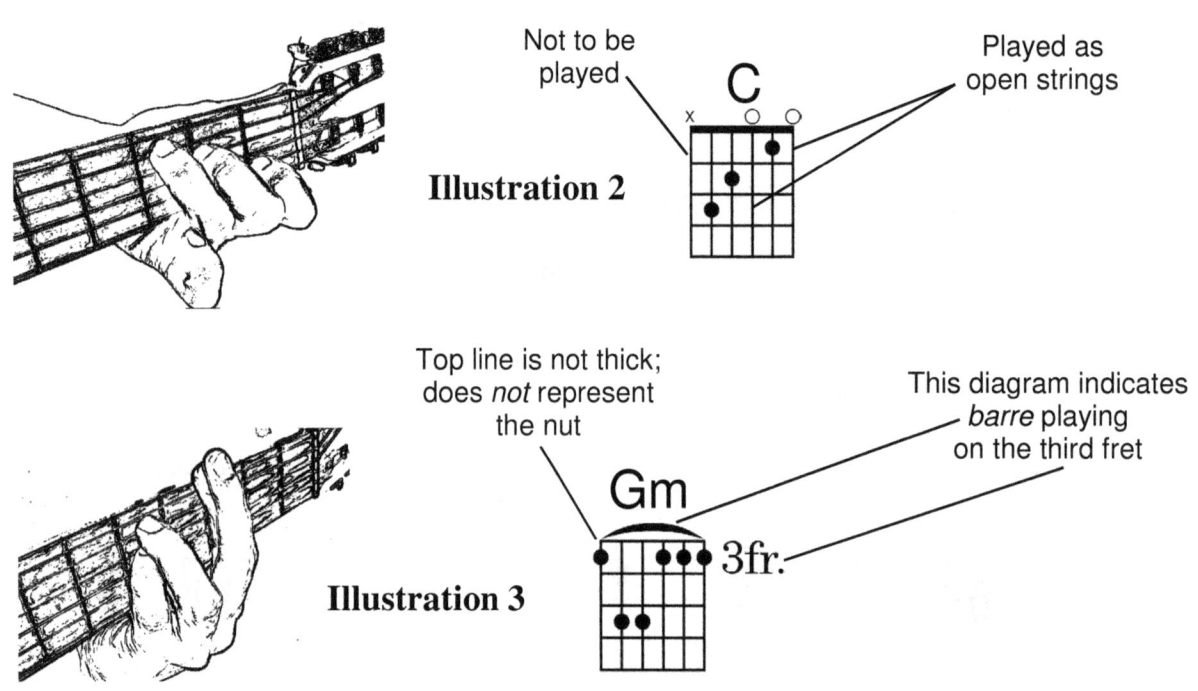

Illustration 2

Illustration 3

---

[1] Based on Foden-Roberts *Chords for Electric or Unamplified Guitar* (Deer Park, N.Y.: Wm. J. Smith Music Co., Inc., 1966).

Appendix C: Special Additional Songs

One important value of hymns is the capability to teach and reinforce doctrine. This is why singing has always been an integral part of the life of God's people. In this section, I have decided to include three songs not found in *The Seventh-day Adventist Hymnal,* which each focus on one of our distinctive doctrines as a church. (Assistance from someone music literate will be needed for correct rhythm since two of the melodies are unfamiliar.)

The first one printed below, is a song inspired by a hymn that our pioneers used to sing entitled "The Mercy Seat", written by Hugh Stowell. Though it appeared in earlier hymn collections under that title, when it got published in the 1941 *Church Hymnal* and the 1985 *Seventh-day Adventist Hymnal* it bore the title "From Every Stormy Wind" (the first line of the hymn's first stanza). Needing something new for our church to sing before the pastoral prayer, I gleaned some phrases from this beautiful song about Christ's ministry in the heavenly sanctuary, modified some of the words and set them to a tune that is more familiar. The music of "Sun of My Soul" (SDAH 502) proved a perfect fit.

"It's the Sabbath" is a gem shared by family friend Tita Rose Rada years ago when I was still teaching in the Music Department of Philippine Union College (now Adventist University of the Philippines). We used to sing it every Friday evening in our campus church as a sort of theme song for vespers.

Finally, "Soon, Jesus Will Return" by Heidi Cerna captures not just the buoyancy that cheers those who have the blessed hope, but the urgency of the times, as well, challenging the believer to faithfully carry out his mission while awaiting Christ's imminent appearing.

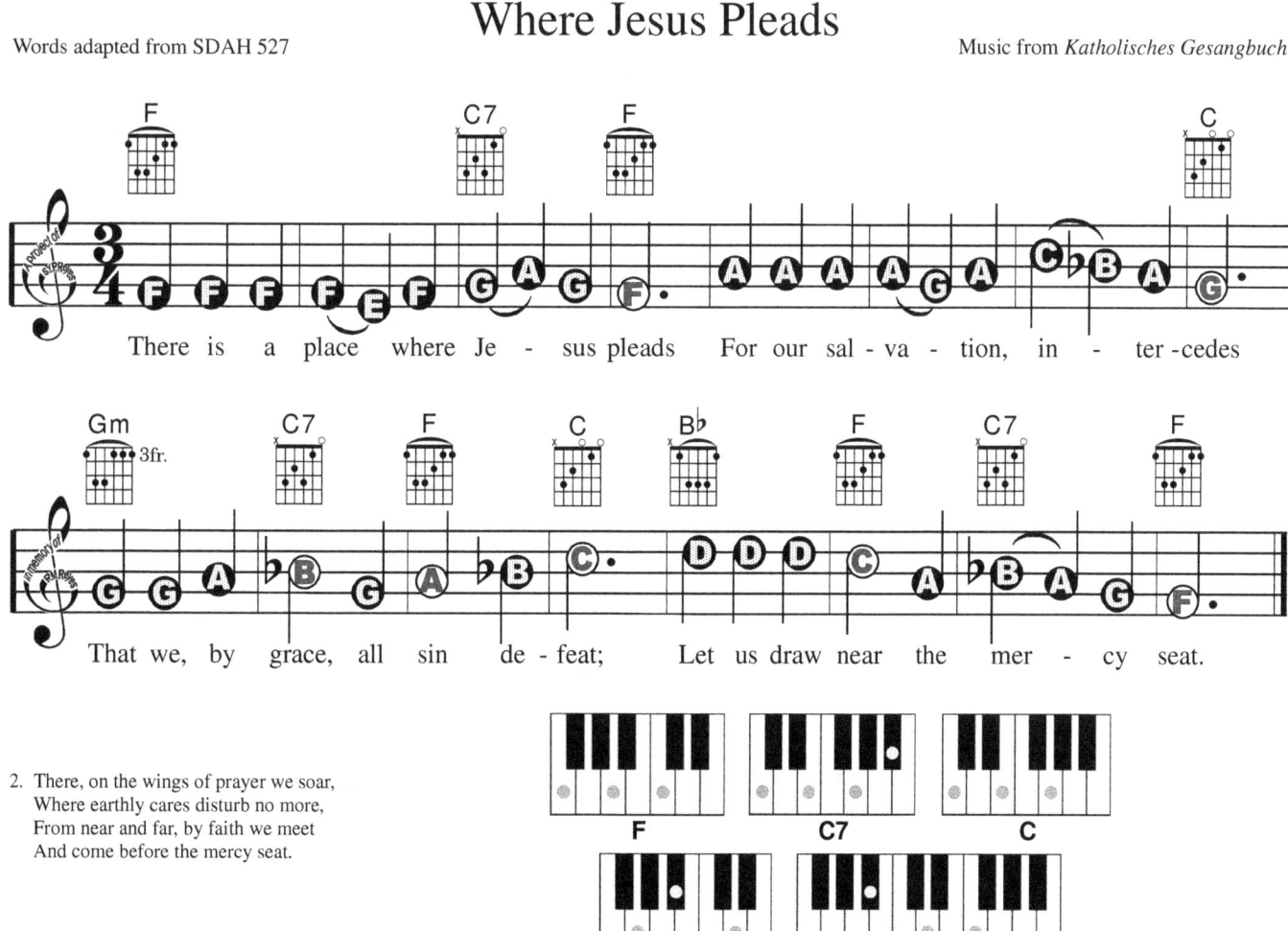

Where Jesus Pleads

Words adapted from SDAH 527

Music from *Katholisches Gesangbuch*

2. There, on the wings of prayer we soar,
   Where earthly cares disturb no more,
   From near and far, by faith we meet
   And come before the mercy seat.

It's the Sabbath

Words by Sam Leer and Rose Rada
Music by Sam Leer

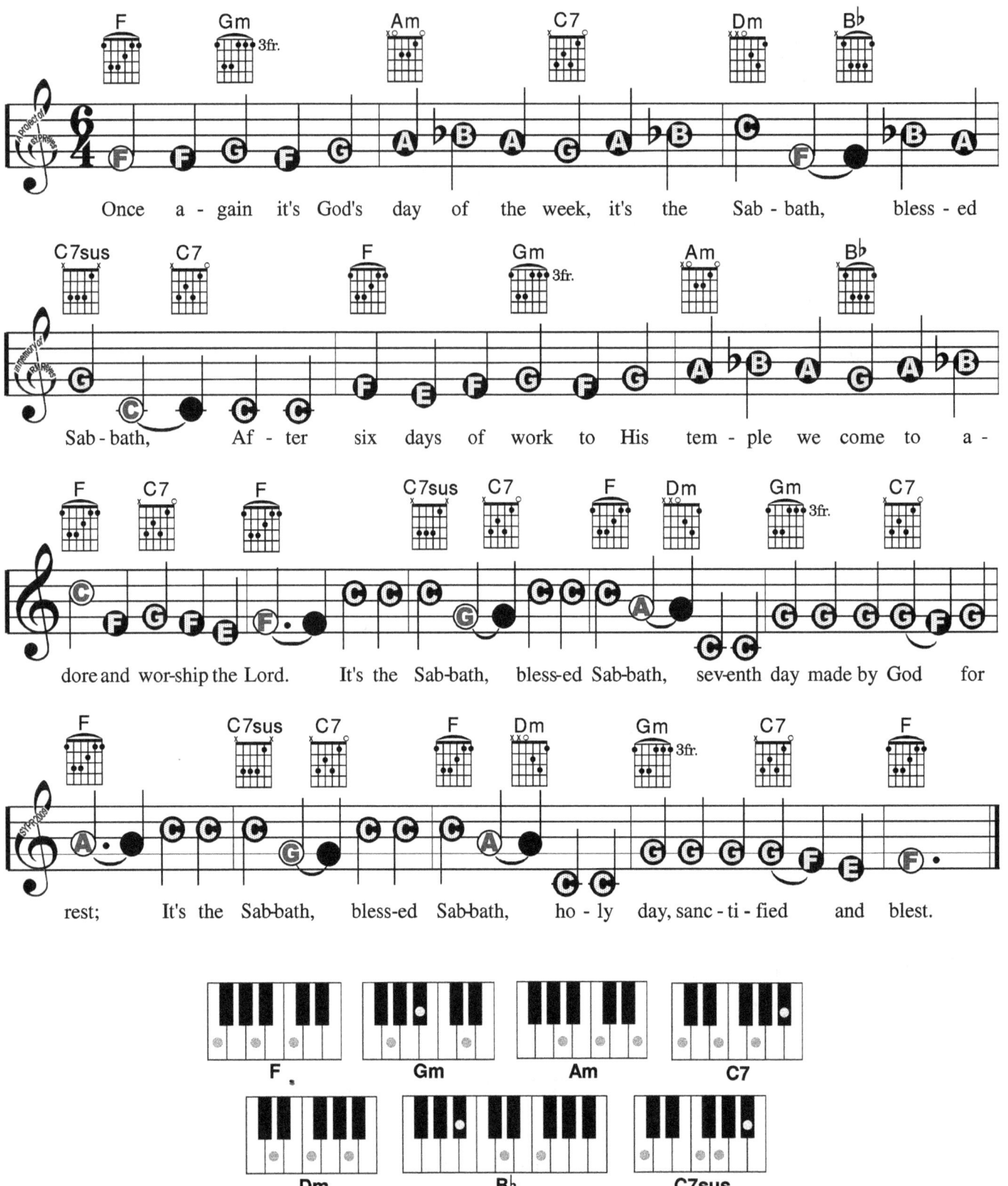

Soon, Jesus Will Return

Index of Hymns

A Mighty Fortress Is Our God 7	It Came Upon the Midnight Clear 58
A Shelter in the Time of Storm 8	It Is Well With My Soul 59
Abide With Me 9	It May Be at Morn 60
All Hail the Power of Jesus' Name 10	Jesus Is All the World to Me 61
All the Way 11	Jesus Is Coming Again 62
Amazing Grace 12	Jesus Paid It All 63
And Can It Be 13	Jesus Saves 64
Anywhere With Jesus 14	Jesus, Savior, Pilot Me 65
At the Cross 15	Jesus, the Very Thought of Thee 66
Away in a Manger 16	Joy to the World 67
Before Jehovah's Awful Throne 17	Just As I Am 68
Beneath the Cross of Jesus 18	Lead On, O King Eternal 69
Blessed Assurance 19	Leaning on the Everlasting Arms 70
Blest Be the Tie that Binds 20	Let All Mortal Flesh Keep Silence 71
Break Thou the Bread of Life 21	Lift Him Up 72
Come, Christians, Join to Sing 22	Live Out Thy Life Within Me 73
Come, Thou Almighty King 23	Lord, I'm Coming Home 74
Come, Thou Fount of Every Blessing 24	Love Divine 75
Cover With His Life 25	Marching to Zion 76
Crown Him With Many Crowns 26	More About Jesus 77
Does Jesus Care 27	More Love to Thee 78
Don't Forget the Sabbath 28	My Faith Looks Up to Thee 79
Draw Me Nearer 29	My Hope Is Built on Nothing Less 80
Face to Face 30	My Jesus, I Love Thee 81
Fairest Lord Jesus 31	My Maker and My King 82
Faith Is the Victory 32	Near the Cross 83
Faith of Our Fathers 33	Near to the Heart of God 84
Far From All Care 34	Nearer, My God, to Thee 85
For the Beauty of the Earth 35	Nearer, Still Nearer 86
Give Me the Bible 36	Nothing Between 87
God Be With You Till We Meet Again 37	O Brother, Be Faithful 88
God Will Take Care of You 38	O Come, All Ye Faithful 89
Hail Him the King of Glory 39	O Come, O Come, Immanuel 92
Happy the Home 66	O Day of Rest and Gladness 90
Hark! The Herald Angels Sing 40	O Day of Rest and Gladness (alternate tune) 91
Have Thine Own Way, Lord 41	O How I Love Jesus 93
He Hideth My Soul 42	O Jesus, I Have Promised 94
He Leadeth Me 43	O Let Me Walk With Thee 95
Hiding in Thee 44	O Little Town of Bethlehem 96
Higher Ground 45	O Worship the King 97
Hold Fast Till I Come 46	O Zion, Haste 98
Holy, Holy, Holy 47	Only Trust Him 99
How Sweet Are the Tidings 48	Onward, Christian Soldiers 100
I Hear Thy Welcome Voice 49	Pass Me Not, O Gentle Savior 101
I Know Whom I Have Believed 50	Power in the Blood 102
I Love to Tell the Story 51	Praise God, From Whom All Blessings 103
I Must Tell Jesus 52	Praise Him, Praise Him 104
I Need Thee Every Hour 53	Praise to the Lord 105
I Sing the Mighty Power of God 54	Redeemed, How I Love to Proclaim It 106
I Surrender All 55	Rejoice, the Lord Is King 107
I Will Follow Thee 56	Rejoice, Ye Pure in Heart 108
In a Little While We're Going Home 57	Rescue the Perishing 109

Rock of Ages 110	There's a Song in the Air 133
Safely Through Another Week 111	There's No Other Name Like Jesus 134
Savior, Like a Shepherd 112	There's Sunshine in My Soul Today 135
Shall We Gather at the River 113	This Is My Father's World 136
Showers of Blessing 114	'Tis Almost Time for the Lord to Come 137
Silent Night 115	'Tis So Sweet to Trust in Jesus 138
Softly and Tenderly 116	To God Be the Glory 139
Sound the Battle Cry 117	Trust and Obey 140
Stand Like the Brave 118	Under His Wings 141
Stand Up! Stand Up for Jesus 119	Watch, Ye Saints 142
Standing on the Promises 120	We Gather Together 143
Sweet By and By 121	We Know Not the Hour 144
Sweet Hour of Prayer 122	We Three Kings 145
Take My Life and Let It Be 123	What a Friend We Have in Jesus 146
Take the Name of Jesus With You 124	What a Wonderful Savior 147
Take the World, but Give Me Jesus 125	What Child Is This 148
Tell Me the Old, Old Story 126	When He Cometh 149
Tell Me the Story of Jesus 127	When the Roll Is Called Up Yonder 150
The First Noel 128	When We All Get to Heaven 151
The Lord in Zion Reigneth 129	Whiter Than Snow 152
The Lord Is in His Holy Temple 130	Wholly Thine 153
The Lord Is My Light 131	Will Your Anchor Hold 154
There Is a Fountain 132	Worthy, Worthy Is the Lamb 155

Special Additional Songs

It's the Sabbath 160
Soon, Jesus Will Return 161
Where Jesus Pleads 159

playhymns@gmail.com

A Final Word

If this songbook enriches that part of your being which instinctively finds fulfillment in making music, and if it enhances your moments of private communion with God through musical expressions of praise and adoration, in ways that previously seemed impossible for you, then my labors in putting it together will have been amply rewarded.

Let me hasten to add, however, that an even greater blessing awaits the one who, beyond relishing the pleasure of playing an instrument just for personal enjoyment, takes this newfound skill and uses it to minister to others. No matter how humble your hymn-playing ability may be at this point, you will find that if you so desire and ask the Lord, He can use your music to uplift souls in need. Take that guitar or portable keyboard and go visit a shut-in neighbor, a church member who is sick, or anyone you know needs encouragement in fighting life's battles. Your own faith will be invigorated!

And now let me address a special category of individuals whom we might call "reluctant church musicians". While many of us are privileged to belong to churches that are blessed with much musical talent, there are numerous smaller churches around that do not have the benefit of accompaniment for their congregational singing. Although this does not make their worship less acceptable to the Lord—we are told that the human voice surpasses all other instruments when the heart is filled with God's love[1]—it is also a fact that instrumental accompaniment adds to the liveliness of the song service[2]. Hence, I challenge those who are able to play the simplified hymns in this book to play for their church when no other instrumentalist is available to serve. You will discover that as you offer whatever little you have to the Giver of gifts, He blesses it mightily and it soon becomes much!

However small your talent, God has a place for it. That one talent, wisely used, will accomplish its appointed work. By faithfulness in little duties, we are to work on the plan of addition, and God will work for us on the plan of multiplication. These littles will become the most precious influences in His work.[3]

Finally, should you find doors open for you to advance in your music skills, I urge you to take these opportunities. Is there someone you know who is willing to teach you how to work with chords? Learn what you can from that person. Are music lessons being offered somewhere near you? Perhaps after playing from this book, learning to read notes will not be as difficult for you as you feared. Go forward in faith as the Lord leads you on to higher ground in your music-making experience, until that glorious day when He places in your hand a shining harp, and your fingers sweep its "strings with skillful touch, awaking sweet music in rich, melodious strains."[4]

"The ransomed of the Lord shall return, and come to Zion with songs
and everlasting joy upon their heads: they shall obtain joy and gladness,
and sorrow and sighing shall flee away" (Isa. 35:10).
"Joy and gladness shall be found therein, thanksgiving, and the voice of melody" (Isa. 51:3).
"As well the singers as the players on instruments shall be there" (Ps. 87:7).
"They shall lift up their voice, they shall sing for the majesty of the Lord" (Isa. 24:14).[5]

---

[1] See Ellen White, *Selected Messages,* bk. 3 (Washington D.C.: Review and Herald, 1980), p. 335.
[2] See Ellen White, *Evangelism* (Washington D.C.: Review and Herald, 1946), pp. 500 and 502.
[3] Ellen White, *Christ's Object Lessons* (Washington D.C.: Review and Herald, 1941), p. 360.
[4] Ellen White, *The Great Controversy Between Christ and Satan* (Boise: Pacific Press, 1911), p. 646.
[5] Ellen White, *The Story of Prophets and Kings* (Mountain View, Calif.: Pacific Press, 1943), p. 730. Emphasis supplied.

We invite you to view the complete
selection of titles we publish at:

www.TEACHServices.com

or write or email us your praises,
reactions, or thoughts about this
or any other book we publish at:

TEACH Services, Inc.
P U B L I S H I N G
www.TEACHServices.com
P.O. Box 954
Ringgold, GA 30736

info@TEACHServices.com

Finally, if you are interested in seeing
your own book in print, please contact us at

publishing@teachservices.com.

We would be happy to review your manuscript for free.

www.ingramcontent.com/pod-product-compliance
Lightning Source LLC
Chambersburg PA
CBHW081838170426
43199CB00017B/2774